SECULAR
UTILITARIANISM

SECULAR UTILITARIANISM

Social Science and the Critique of Religion in the Thought of Jeremy Bentham

JAMES E. CRIMMINS

CLARENDON PRESS · OXFORD
1990

Oxford University Press, Walton Street, Oxford OX2 6DP
Oxford New York Toronto
Delhi Bombay Calcutta Madras Karachi
Petaling Jaya Singapore Hong Kong Tokyo
Nairobi Dar es Salaam Cape Town
Melbourne Auckland
and associated companies in
Berlin Ibadan

Oxford is a trade mark of Oxford University Press

Published in the United States
by Oxford University Press, New York

British Library Cataloguing in Publication Data
Crimmins, James E.
Secular utilitarianism: social science and the critique of
religion in the thought of Jeremy Bentham.
1. English philosophy. Bentham, Jeremy, 1748–1832
I. Title
192
ISBN 0–19–827741–5

Library of Congress Cataloging in Publication Data
Crimmins, James E., 1953–
Secular utilitarianism: social science and the critique of
religion in the thought of Jeremy Bentham / James E. Crimmins.
p. cm.
Includes bibliographical references.
1. Bentham, Jeremy, 1748–1832—Religion. 2. Utilitarianism.
3. Social sciences—Religious aspects—History. 4. Social sciences—
Religious aspects—Christianity—History. 5. Great Britain—
Religion—18th century. 6. Great Britain—Religion—19th century.
I. Title.
B1574.B34C75 1990 171'.5—dc20 89–49126
ISBN 0–19–827741–5

Set by Hope Services (Abingdon) Ltd.
Printed in Great Britain by
Bookcraft (Bath) Ltd,
Midsomer Norton, Avon

Dedicated to my parents,
Mary Rose Crimmins and James Stephen Crimmins

Acknowledgements

In the preparation and writing of this book I have received assistance from many quarters. My largest debt is owed to Douglas G. Long, whose enthusiasm, encouragement, and guidance immeasurably assisted the project through all its stages. His painstaking scrutiny of an earlier draft of the entire work is especially appreciated. He will perhaps better understand the warmth with which I express my gratitude if I supplement it by raising a glass of Swn y Mor to his name. Dr Long, I feel sure, will also understand if in the same breath I pay tribute to Professor W. H. Greenleaf and to the late J. C. Rees, who together sparked my initial enthusiasm for political thought in lectures given at University College Swansea in the early 1970s. Indeed, it was under the direction of John Rees that I enquired of Dr Long in 1980 if he would supervise my attempt at a doctoral thesis on Jeremy Bentham.

Appreciation is due to the Social Sciences and Humanities Research Council of Canada for the ample financial support it extended to me in the form of a Postdoctoral Research Fellowship from September 1985 to September 1987. Without the support of the Council matters would have proceeded at a very much slower pace. I am also indebted to the Government of Ontario, to the University of Western Ontario, and to the Catherine and Lady Grace James Education Trust of Wales for a variety of scholarships and grants which enabled me to undertake the initial research and writing upon which this study is founded.

Dr J. R. Dinwiddy and Dr. F. Rosen, past and present general editors of *The Collected Works of Jeremy Bentham*, granted me access to the papers and manuscript transcriptions of the late James Steintrager and to the transcriptions, by many hands, of Bentham's unpublished correspondence. Professor Steintrager's many years of work on Bentham's manuscripts on religion made my own efforts many times easier than they would otherwise have been. For generously supplying transcriptions of Bentham's exceedingly important 'Preparatory Principles', intended for a volume of the *Collected Works*, I again acknowledge Douglas G. Long. I am grateful, too, to Charles Bahmueller who also contributed transcriptions , this time on Bentham's early work on 'indirect legislation'. Bob Fenn of the

University of Toronto kindly gave me a draft version of his edition of 'The Commonplace Books of James Mill' and other items of Milliana.

Parts of the manuscript were read and commented upon by several colleagues, including Richard Vernon of the University of Western Ontario, John McEvoy of the University of Cincinnati, and Gary Owens of Huron College. All are to be thanked for their suggestions for improvements. For the loan of books and stimulating informal discussions on various aspects of the European Enlightenment I am indebted to Roger Emerson, who had the goodness to suffer a fool (i.e. a political scientist) gladly and to provide sustenance in countless other ways. John McDougall was ever ready to discuss my work even though his own interests lay in areas further afield. I would also like to remember the friends on both sides of the Atlantic who provided the necessary convivial release from my endeavours, especially Terry in Cardiff, Greg in Hay-on-Wye, Steve and Ian in Swansea, and in London, Ontario, John, Patrick, Greg, Laurie, Joe, and Ruban—without all of whom this book would probably have been completed very much sooner!

Thanks are also due to the archivists and librarians at University College London, the D. B. Weldon Library at the University of Western Ontario, and Huron College Library. The editors of the *Journal of the History of Ideas*, the *British Journal for Eighteenth-Century Studies*, and the *Harvard Theological Review* granted me permission to make use of articles published under my name in these periodicals, the bibliographic details of which are given in full at the back of the present publication. To Henry Hardy and his staff at Oxford University Press I am obliged for their courtesy, understanding, and efficiency in dealing with my manuscript. Such inelegances and infelicities of style as are still to be found in the text cannot be laid to the account of the editors.

Finally, special thanks are due to Johanne for her counsel and comfort during the past few years. I confess the years were more than I originally promised, but without her they would have seemed much longer. I know she will approve if I dedicate this book to my parents, whose faith in me extends over a period of time far beyond that taken to research and write it.

Naturally, the usual disclaimers apply: all the above-mentioned are exonerated from association with any inaccuracies, errors, or shortcomings in what follows.

J.E.C.

Huron College, London, Ontario
1989

Contents

List of Abbreviations

For full details of Bentham's works see the Bibliography.

An.	*An Analysis of the Influence of Natural Religion on the Temporal Happiness of Mankind* (1822)
AI	*Auto-Icon: Or Farther Uses of the Dead to the Living, A Fragment* (printed 1842, but not published)
BL Add. MSS	British Library Series of Additional Manuscripts
CE	*Church-of-Englandism and its Catechism Examined* (1818)
Comm.	*A Comment on the Commentaries* [*CW*]
Corr. i–vi	*Correspondence of Jeremy Bentham* [*CW*]
CW	*The Collected Works of Jeremy Bentham* (1968–)
Deon.	*Deontology together with A Table of the Springs of Action and the Article on Utilitarianism* [*CW*]
DNB	*Dictionary of National Biography*
Fall.	*Bentham's Handbook of Political Fallacies* (1952; repr. 1971)
FG	*A Fragment on Government* [*CW*]
IPML	*An Introduction to the Principles of Morals and Legislation* [*CW*]
JB	Jeremy Bentham
LG	*Of Laws in General* [*CW*]
NP	*Not Paul, but Jesus* (1823)
UC	Bentham Manuscripts at UCL (UC box number/followed by MS folio or page denomination, e.g. UC 130/42)
UCL	University College London
Works, i–xi	*The Works of Jeremy Bentham, Published under the Superintendence of his Executor, John Bowring*, 11 vols. (1838–43)

Introduction

THAT Jeremy Bentham (1748–1832) was an ardent secularist convinced that society could be sustained without the support of religious institutions or religious beliefs, is a fact writ large in the books on religion he wrote and published during the last twenty-five years of his life. His earliest writings on the subject, however, date from the 1770s when as a young man he first embarked upon his calling as a legal theorist and social reformer. Indeed, religion was never far from the centre of his thoughts throughout his long and industrious intellectual career.

The present study has two objectives. First, to illustrate the extent, depth, and nature of Bentham's concern with religion, from his Oxford days of first doubts, to the middle years of quiet unbelief, and, finally, the zealous atheism and secularism of later life when he pondered the vision of a world without religion. Secondly, to provide an interpretation of his utilitarian philosophy in which his religious views are located as an integral concern: on the one hand, intimately associated with the metaphysical, epistemological, and psychological principles which gave shape to his system as a whole and, on the other hand, central to the development of his entirely secular view of society.

1. The writings on religion

To those unaware of the vast range of Bentham's writings it is probably not known that, with various kinds of assistance from willing hands, he produced three volumes on the subject of religion, copies of which are extremely rare today: *Church-of-Englandism and its Catechism Examined* (1818), *An Analysis of the Influence of Natural Religion on the Temporal Happiness of Mankind* (1822), and *Not Paul, but Jesus* (1823). To these we can add the pamphlet *Swear Not at All* (1817), primarily a legal tract, but the theme of which (the evil consequences of imposing compulsory oaths) has an obvious bearing on religious matters. This attack on the Church and its doctrines, though its historical genesis can be traced to the 1770s, was launched in earnest in 1809. When

Bentham catalogued the instruments of corruption for his work on 'Parliamentary Reform' in that year, he included social and psychological sources of influence, under which he listed religious faith and the operations of laws imposing religious tests. These tended to corrupt morals and create confusion among the people, which in turn augmented the ease with which secular government could impose its will (UC 130/102; 126/19–23, 48–50). This relationship between religion and political subjugation, though not a new discovery for Bentham, came to dominate his thoughts during the next decade. It was not long before he was busy sketching outlines and plans for voluminous works on the established Church and its central doctrines. In the end, after several false starts and pauses to rethink the direction of his writing, Bentham only published certain parts of his work on religion: those which appeared under the titles mentioned above.

Given the nature of these volumes there was every reason for restraint. The post-Napoleonic years proved to be a period of political and social unrest. It was a time when persons of position might be excused for thinking that the duty of all good citizens was to strengthen the established political and ecclesiastical structures to whose maintenance the dearest interests of civilization and national survival seemed to be bound. No doubt such thoughts occurred to many of those who had most to lose. Yet if one expected such intemperate and radical attacks on the Church and the teachings of Christianity as Bentham's to cause popular dissension from England's official religion, or if one expected the wrath of the authorities to fall upon the author's head, one would be disappointed. If ever four works of an author of reputation 'fell deadborn from the press', to borrow David Hume's famous phrase,[1] these were they. Only *Not Paul, but Jesus* attracted public attention at the time of publication, occasioning replies from several justifiably outraged pastors.[2] Even Bentham seems to have been entirely indifferent to their fate once they were published. In the correspondence of the time they are hardly mentioned—surprisingly, considering the time he expended on them.

No doubt the fear of prosecution for 'blasphemy' was a factor influencing Bentham's decision to employ pseudonyms on the title-

---

[1] D. Hume, 'My Own Life', in *An Inquiry Concerning Human Understanding*, ed. C. W. Hendel (New York, 1955), 4. This is an allusion to Pope's comment on truth in the *Epilogue to the Satires* (1738), Dialogue II, l. 226: 'All, all but Truth drops dead-born from the Press.'

[2] These are discussed below in ch. 8. *CE* received a cursory treatment by W. Gifford in the *Quarterly Review*, 21 (1819), 167–77.

pages of these volumes: the *Analysis* appeared under the name 'Philip Beauchamp', *Not Paul, but Jesus* bore the witty if irreverent *nom de plume* 'Gamaliel Smith', and *Church-of-Englandism*, the most overtly polemical of the three, was originally intended to be given to the world as the work of 'An Oxford Graduate'. Because of his usual 'scribbling ways'—his habit of leaving one topic unfinished to pursue another—and other projects that pressed upon his time Bentham also found it expedient to use editors. During his career he frequently had occasion to resort to editors to produce his work for the press. With his approval, and presumably with some supervision, Étienne Dumont, James and John Stuart Mill, Samuel Romilly, Edwin Chadwick, Peregrine Bingham, and others, laboured to collate manuscripts, polish texts, and publish the works that now bear Bentham's name. Occasionally he quarrelled with some of these and ungraciously accused them of misinterpreting him, but in the case of the editors of the works on religion there do not appear to have been any such disagreements. As a result Sir John Macdonell thought it unclear precisely what share Bentham actually took in the production of these books: 'Having not a particle of literary vanity, he put no restraint on the editors of his manuscripts, and they did not hesitate to use this liberty'.[3] But this is misleading. In the main the volumes on religion represent the views and are the work of Bentham in the mature phase of his thinking on religious matters. That the editors acted under his guidance there is little reason to doubt.[4] It must be admitted, however, that students of Bentham have rarely taken much interest in his writings on religion (his 'Juggical' works, he would say).[5] Where they illuminate particular themes in his moral or legal theory scholars have occasionally enlisted their support, but their concern can hardly be described as anything other than incidental. Bentham's views on religion have still to be presented in full. Nor have they yet received a comprehensive critical examination. There are several reasons for this neglect of what constitutes a formidable proportion of Bentham's considerable output.

Among the worst of the failings of John Bowring as Bentham's

---

[3] DNB ii. 273–4.

[4] For additional information see my 'Bentham's Religious Writings: A Bibliographic Chronology', *The Bentham Newsletter*, 9 (1985), 21–33.

[5] 'Jug', 'Juggical', and 'Juggernautical' are code words employed by Bentham and his brother Samuel to refer to the Established Church, though occasionally they were used to refer to Christianity or simply religion in general. It appears that Bentham derived these terms from the 'Car of Juggernaut' under which pious Hindu devotees were crushed to death and happiness.

editor-in-chief was his exclusion of the writings on religion (*Swear Not at All* excepted) from the posthumously published *Works*.[6] We can safely assume that they were among those writings Bowring deemed too 'bold and adventurous' for publication.[7] Nevertheless, this suppression of the published and unpublished material on religious subjects amounted to a complete disregard of Bentham's wishes that they should be included in a collection of his works, the financing of which he had provided for in his will (UC 155/23–35). Bowring's refusal to publish that which was already in a finished state and did not require the time of an editor is particularly reprehensible. J. S. Mill complained emphatically of these omissions from the *Works*, commenting that while they may appear of 'exceedingly small value' they are at least Bentham's 'and the world has a right to whatever light they throw upon the constitution of his mind'.[8]

It is true that Bentham had said on several occasions that it would be better if certain parts of his work (especially the essays on homosexuality) were not published during his lifetime, on the grounds that this would jeopardize the good that his other efforts might produce (cf. esp. UC 161a/4), but he also indicated that the unpublished writings on religion should appear at some future date (UC 161a/14–19). Why did Bowring ignore these wishes? The truth of the matter is that, though a radical in politics and a firm adherent of the utilitarian doctrine, he could not find it within himself to apply the test of utility to Christianity. He could countenance *Swear Not at All* as an attack on the discriminatory practice of imposing oaths, but the other writings on religion simply went too far down the road to infidelity. As a Unitarian, a founder member of the Non-Con Club (1817) and the Unitarian Association (1818)[9]—the one established to promote the principles of truth and liberty, the other to protect the civil rights of Unitarians—he

[6] Bowring's edition of the *Works* has attracted little but contempt. On its first appearance one reviewer described it as 'incomplete, incorrect and ill-arranged', William Empson, in *Edinburgh Review*, 78 (1843), 516. On the other hand, G. F. Bartle argues that Bowring had little direct responsibility for the individual texts published in the *Works* (or, it seems, for the detailed arrangement of the volumes which he left to the publisher William Tait), though he did determine what was to be included and what left out: 'Jeremy Bentham & John Bowring: A Study of the Relationship between Bentham and the Editor of his *Collected Works*', *Bulletin of the Institute of Historical Research London University*, 36: 93 (1963), 34–5.

[7] J. Bowring, *Autobiographical Recollections of Sir John Bowring* (London, 1877), 339.

[8] J. S. Mill, 'Bentham' (1838), in *The Collected Works of John Stuart Mill*, ed. J. M. Robson *et al.* (Toronto, 1969–), x (1969), 99.

[9] R. W. Davis, *Dissent in Politics 1780–1830: The Political Life of William Smith, M.P.* (London, 1971), 202–3.

could not possibly follow Bentham down this particularly blasphemous path. Sadly, there is no record in the 'Memoirs', compiled by Bowring (*Works*, x–xi), or in Bowring's disappointing autobiography, of any exchanges between the two on religious matters. Yet Bentham must have been aware of his young friend's beliefs. Sir Leslie Stephen is perhaps correct to say that Bowring 'judiciously agreed to avoid discussions upon religious topics with his master'.[10] Even so it seems extraordinary that while Bentham was planning to republish part of *Church-of-Englandism* in 1825 Bowring was putting the finishing touches to a volume of prayers and hymns.[11] Yet this man of religion, this writer of hymns and prayers, was the man to whom Bentham consigned writings which could not but be offensive to him. Just how offensive they indeed were, the neglect of the religious works during the past 150 years sufficiently demonstrates.

If Bowring is the principal culprit in the offence of neglect he does not stand alone in the dock. John Hill Burton, in the first collection of Bentham extracts to appear, also failed to include selections from the religious publications, and in our own century he has been emulated in turn by Charles Everett, Mary Mack, and Bhikhu Parekh.[12] Of late only James Steintrager, to a lesser degree Mack in her intellectual biography of Bentham, and L. J. Hume have considered Bentham's thoughts on religious matters. Mack found fragments from some of the early unpublished manuscripts useful for illuminating the psychology of Bentham's mind as it developed in his formative years, and Hume has mulled over the relationship between the published work on religion and Bentham's political writings in the period after his supposed conversion to the democratic programme in 1809.[13] In a way these aspects of the work of Mack and Hume nicely complement one another, but even taken cumulatively they leave much to be said.

Before his death in 1981 Professor James Steintrager was engaged in the daunting task of editing the published writings on religion and related unpublished manuscripts for the new definitive edition of *The*

[10] Sir L. Stephen, *The English Utilitarians*, 3 vols. (1900; repr. London, 1950), i. 225.
[11] *Mother Church Relieved by Bleeding: Or Vices and Remedies Extracted from Bentham's Church of, Etc., Examined* (1823; 2nd edn. London, 1825); J. Bowring, *Matins and Vespers: With Hymns and Occasional Devotional Pieces* (London, 1825).
[12] J. H. Burton, *Benthamiana: Or Select Extracts from the Works of Jeremy Bentham* (Edinburgh, 1843); C. W. Everett, *Jeremy Bentham* (London, 1966), pt. 2; *A Bentham Reader*, ed. M. Mack (New York, 1969); *Bentham's Political Thought*, ed. B. Parekh (New York, 1973).
[13] M. Mack, *Jeremy Bentham: An Odyssey of Ideas 1748–1799* (London, 1962), L. J. Hume, *Bentham and Bureaucracy* (Cambridge, 1981).

Collected Works of Jeremy Bentham, currently being produced under the direction of the Bentham Committee at University College London. The first two volumes, covering Bentham's views on the Established Church, were to include *Swear Not at All*, together with some previously unpublished manuscripts from the 1770s and 1813, and *Church-of-Englandism*, together with some other related but unpublished material dated 1816. In addition to the published text of *Not Paul, but Jesus*, the third volume was to include the remaining two parts of this work and various fragments on the topic of Christian asceticism and 'Sexual Nonconformity' from the 1770s, 1785, 1814, and 1816. The final volume was to contain the *Analysis* plus a large collection of related manuscripts, which Bentham had originally intended to publish collectively under the general title 'The Usefulness of Religion in the Present Life Examined'.[14] At the time of writing none of these projected volumes has been completed, hence we must still deal with the scarce original publications where they are to hand and with whatever manuscript material is accessible.[15] In the present study I have made liberal use of the unpublished material, but where it has been possible to refer the reader to published sources without distorting Bentham's true opinions I have done so. Appendix *A* provides a comprehensive listing of the manuscripts on religion in the possession of University College and the British Library.[16]

2. *Traditional and revisionist accounts*

The relative inaccessibility of Bentham's writings helps to explain, at least in part, the misconceptions that have long existed about his views on religion. For many years the standard view was that he came to

[14] For details see J. Steintrager, 'Report on the Problems of Editing Bentham's Writings on Religion', App. B to Report by the General Editor [J. H. Burns], 12 June 1967 (Bentham Committee at UCL, unpublished). Steingtrager also published 2 essays on Bentham's views on religion: 'Morality and Belief: The Origins and Purpose of Bentham's Writings on Religion', *The Mill News Letter*, 6: 2 (1971), 3–15; 'Language and Politics: Bentham on Religion', *The Bentham Newsletter*, 4 (1980), 4–20.

[15] The responsibility for editing *Church-of-Englandism* has fallen to the lot of the present author, and a speedy publication is hoped for.

[16] Study of the voluminous MSS on religion has been limited by considerations of time, and so in some cases my knowledge of their content is drawn from the catalogues compiled by A. T. Milne, *Catalogue of the Manuscripts of Jeremy Bentham in the Library of University College* (1937; 2nd edn. London, 1962); and D. G. Long, *The Manuscripts of Jeremy Bentham: A Chronological Index to the Collection in the Library of University College London*, printed by the Bentham Committee at UCL (1982).

adopt an extreme position *vis-à-vis* religious matters as a consequence of his increasing frustration, in the decades after the French Revolution, with the obstacles posed to legal and social reform by the Establishment, including the Anglican Church and its bishops. This frustration, together with the influence of James Mill, to whom he was introduced in 1808, eventually brought Bentham to expound a radical democratic programme and to advocate sweeping changes in both secular and ecclesiastical government.[17] He gave little thought to the subject, so the argument goes, until the battle over school reform—the Lancasterian Controversy—occurred in the second decade of the new century. Bentham's writings on religious subjects were largely the product of spleen vented against the Church of England because of its determined and continued opposition to his plans for reform. As Leslie Stephen put it, Bentham 'was in the main indifferent to the whole question till it encountered him in political matters'.[18] The bishops' attempt to prevent the establishment of non-denominational schools was the final straw precipitating his direct, enraged attacks on the Church and religion generally.

The chronology of Bentham's writings and related political events of the time, it must be said, fit this interpretation well. It was in 1809 that he began, and for the most part completed, his *Plan of Parliamentary Reform*, in which he set out the basic tenets of his democratic politics—annual parliaments, secret, and universal suffrage.[19] Just as it is possible to explain this conversion to political radicalism in terms of Bentham's frustrations with a political regime which consistently refused to adopt his various suggestions for legislative, economic, penal, and judicial reform, so the move to religious radicalism can be explained in terms of the role played by the Church hierarchy in combining with the political establishment in order to thwart his endeavours. The purpose of his attack on established religion, therefore, was the same as that of his campaign against secular government. And so it would seem from

---

[17] The timing of Bentham's supposed 'conversion' to democratic principles is a matter of some debate. See e.g. Mack, *Jeremy Bentham*, pp. 17, 416, 432–40; and J. R. Dinwiddy, 'Bentham's Transition to Political Radicalism, 1809–10', *Journal of the History of Ideas*, 36: 4 (1975), 683–700.

[18] Stephen, *The English Utilitarians*, i. 315, 375–6; and É. Halévy, *The Growth of Philosophic Radicalism* [*La Formation du radicalisme philosophique*, 1901–4], trans. M. Morris (1928; London, 1972), 290–1, 295.

[19] The material from 1809–10 is contained in UC 126/1–449; 127/20–215; 128/1–130; 129a/1–265; and 130/1–205. The *Plan of Parliamentary Reform, in the Form of a Catechism* was eventually published with corrections and additions in 1817 and is included in *Works*, iii. 433–557.

Bentham's own account of the matter. In the *Plan of Parliamentary Reform*, for instance, he says he gave a 'sketch' of the 'temporal' nature of the constitution; in *Church-of-Englandism* his aim is to give a 'portrait . . . of a larger size' of the 'spiritual' nature of that same constitution (*CE* Preface, p. xi). Just as the *Plan* was to provide a critique of—and suggestions for reforming—political institutions, so *Church-of-Englandism* was to take the religious establishment to task for failing to perform its social and spiritual duties. As Bentham wrote to John Koe, his secretary of the time, 'Church Cat.[echism] follows up the blow from Plan cat[echism]: it goes to the destroying the whole mass of the matter of corruption which while the Tories feed upon in possession, the Whigs feed upon while they are anything in expectancy.'[20] Later in life the old sage in conversation with Bowring reflected upon the naïvety of his middle years when he industriously worked up one proposal after another only to see them shunned and ignored: 'I was . . . a great reformist; but never suspected that the people in power were against reform. I supposed they only wanted to know what was good in order to embrace it' (*Works*, x. 66). Most difficult of all for Bentham to comprehend was the rejection of the scheme for prison reform to which he devoted the best part of twenty years of his life. That it was an issue that touched him profoundly there is no doubt, as his voluminous correspondence on the subject, relating his hopes, expectations, and frustrations, clearly shows (cf. *Corr.* v. *passim*). The role played by Dean Horsley, the Bishop of Rochester, in the failure to construct the Panopticon, a cost effective circular prison in which 'to grind rogues honest and idle men industrious' (*Works*, x. 226), was a conspicuous one, and not one that Bentham was likely to forget or forgive. But I spare the reader the details of Panopticon; they have been well enough documented by others.[21] Suffice it to say that William Wilberforce

---

[20] JB to John Koe (14 Jan. 1818), Koe MSS, from a transcription at the Bentham Project, UCL. Bentham was particularly frustrated with his friends among the Whigs at this time, especially Samuel Romilly and Francis Burdett, for their reluctance to pursue wholeheartedly 'the cause of the people'. See JB to Francis Place, 6 Feb. 1818, MS insert in the BL copy of *CE*, shelf-mark 4106.bb.6.

[21] Whatever the depth of Bentham's antipathy towards the clergy after his initial experience of the Church at Oxford, his antagonism was to be heightened as a result of the Panopticon affair. After drafting a complete scheme for penal reform with the Panopticon prisons as its centre-piece and Bentham himself as the gaoler-in-chief, he entered upon negotiations with the government for the scheme's implementation in the early 1790s. After 20 years of effort and frustration, including wrangles over government compensation for his financial outlay, the scheme was finally laid to rest in 1820. For a history of the Panopticon project see L. J. Hume, 'Bentham's Panopticon: An

(1759–1833), who had collaborated with Bentham in the cause of prison reform, believed that it was as a consequence of the prevarications of the Establishment, religious and secular, over Panopticon, that Bentham made his first move toward religous heresy.[22]

This in essence is the substance of the traditional interpretation of the stimulus behind Bentham's writings on religion. On this view the Lancasterian Controversy was the straw that broke the camel's back. According to Charles Atkinson, Bentham 'in no way concerned himself with questions of dogma, until in later years he was aroused to active hostility by the attitude of the clergy on educational issues'.[23] C. K. Ogden concurs in this interpretation: it was 'after the opposition of the Anglicans to the educational reforms of the Lancaster group (1811) and his own Chrestomathic system (1812–17) that he entered the lists against the clerics'.[24] Henceforth political and religious radicalism walked hand in hand, their joint aim being the complete overhaul of English political and social institutions.

This version of events has been questioned in recent years by Mary Mack and in more detail, but along similar lines, by James Steintrager. Their argument comes to this: Bentham did not undergo a transitional period in religious matters, a transition from indifference to radicalism; he was always irreligious, or at least was so from a very early age. Neither Mack nor Steintrager found it necessary to analyse Bentham's opinions on religion in order to substantiate their position.

Mack, drawing imaginatively, but perhaps with too much conviction, on such accounts as we have of Bentham's early experiences with religion and his recollections in old age of his boyhood fears regarding devils and other superstitions, argues that the origin of his ethics 'lay . . . in the religious training he suffered as a boy . . . His child's [*sic*] revulsion was at the bottom of his Utilitarianism, hedonism, and contempt for the principle of asceticism and the religious establishment.' The young Bentham 'was permanently scarred by a terrifying, authoritarian, and hypocritical religious education'.[25] That his early experiences with

Administrative History', *Historical Studies*, 15: 61 (1973), 703–21, and 16: 62 (1974), 36–54; and G. Himmelfarb, *Victorian Minds* (New York, 1968), ch. 2.

[22] R. I. Wilberforce and S. Wilberforce, *The Life of William Wilberforce*, 5 vols. (2nd edn. London, 1839), ii. 172. For Wilberforce's association with Bentham in the Panopticon business see J. Pollock, *Wilberforce* (London, 1977), esp. pp. 137–9. For Wilberforce's outburst concerning the callous attitude exhibited by the Bp. of Rochester see his letter to JB (21 Nov. 1796), *Corr.* v. 309.

[23] C. M. Atkinson, *Jeremy Bentham: His Life and Work* (London, 1905), 210.

[24] *The Theory of Legislation*, ed. C. K. Ogden (London, 1931), p. xlvii n.

[25] Mack, *Jeremy Bentham*, pp. 13, 299; see also pp. 35–6, 45, 49.

religion were a significant feature of Bentham's upbringing indelibly etched upon his memory, I do not wish to deny. Terrified in early life by ghosts and by the threat of eternal damnation, and reduced to scepticism at Oxford over Church dogma, he was brought face to face with his doubts when required to subscribe to the Thirty-nine Articles. Even though the oath violated his conscience he was compelled to swear—an apparently traumatic experience for a young and thoughtful boy at England's premier place of learning and school of divinity. Unquestionably it was this experience which first led him to drift away from the Church.

To these early experiences Steintrager adds evidence of a more substantial nature in the shape of a collection of manuscripts on subscriptions to articles of faith probably written in 1773, and the preface to Bentham's anonymously published translation of Voltaire's *Le Taureau blanc* (1774)—neither of which is included in Bowring's edition of the *Works*.[26] The occasion of Bentham's first confrontation with organized religion was, suitably enough, the controversy over oaths which began at Cambridge in 1766 and spread over the next six years to the press and the Houses of Parliament. His manuscripts examining the problem of the Church's demand for subscriptions, together with occasional reflections on the authority of the Church and the impact on law and morals of swearing oaths (UC 5/1–32; 96/263–341), reveal a remarkable consistency with the views on compulsory oaths expressed in *Swear Not at All* nearly forty years later. The preface to *The White Bull, An Oriental History*, to give Voltaire's little tract its English title, treats principally of legal and political matters and does so in typically Voltairean fashion. At the same time Bentham hints that his satire can equally be applied to certain aspects of official religion, and there is the suggestion of a sceptical attitude towards historical Christianity. His remarks, however, are cautiously couched and not of a specific nature. As Charles Everett so vividly put it, *Le Taureau blanc* 'gave the young reformer a chance to take a shot from ambush at the reactionary forces in church and state'.[27]

To this evidence we might add two other items not mentioned by Steintrager. First, in the year or so after Bentham's initial brush with official religion, he returned to consider, albeit briefly, the obstacles posed to utilitarian legislation by the professors of the established religion in manuscripts titled 'Obstacles. Divine' and 'Obstacles to a

[26] For the substance of this argument see Steintrager, 'Morality and Belief', *passim*.
[27] C. W. Everett, *The Education of Jeremy Bentham* (New York, 1931), 68.

perfect system of legislation' (UC 97/1–116). Secondly, around the same time, Christianity was charged by Bentham with being the enemy of human happiness, and hence of utilitarian morality, in another collection of manuscripts on 'Sexual Nonconformity' (UC 73/90–100; 74a/1–25). The themes broached in these manuscripts were subsequently developed in the later writings on religion and we shall come to each of them in due course in the chapters ahead. For the moment we may content ourselves with the observation that in later life Bentham's bitterness with the bishops took on a philosophical character when his objections focused on the implicit tendency of religion—all religion— to oppose reform: 'For whenever sentence is passed against any particular mode of amelioration, it is always by virtue of the standing enactment against all—that this is by accusations of contrariety to the laws of nature and the designs of the Deity' (*An.* 91). None the less, Steintrager is essentially correct; Bentham's opinion in the years 1773–5 was in substance the same as that which, according to Stephen and Ogden, had supposedly developed only after the battle over school reform.

Why then did Bentham not publish his opinions on religion until forty or more years later? According to this revised explanation of the development of his views on religion he refused to publish—or rather deemed it expedient not to publish—anything systematic or concrete on religion for tactical reasons. He did not want needlessly to offend a powerful section of the Establishment that might otherwise be of assistance to him in his reforming efforts. While he still thought that reason would overcome prejudice Bentham refrained, wisely he thought at the time, from publicly attacking the Church and its teachings. Everett suggests that it would have been 'dangerous' for him to avow such views, and Mary Mack that 'As long as the palest shadow of possibility lingered that government might apply his reforms, Bentham concentrated rather on practical reforms than polemics. He was anxious to antagonize as few legislators as possible.'[28]

Though the polemical aspects of Bentham's work on Sir William Blackstone's *Commentaries on the Laws of England* (1765) in the 1770s should not be overlooked, in essence Everett and Mack are correct. Bentham indicated on a few occasions in the early part of his career that he was aware of the dangers of publishing anti-religious strictures. He refrained from publishing his manuscripts on subscriptions in 1773

[28] Ibid. 197; Mack, *Jeremy Bentham*, p. 305.

because he thought his material 'a little out of season' (UC 96/266). In other manuscripts, probably written in 1774, he pointed to the disgust incurred by Helvétius and Voltaire for publishing unpopular views (UC 159/270). Even more pointedly in 1776, while discussing the religious sanction in relation to legislation, he reflected: 'I . . . hear obloquy with her hundred tongues ready to (open against me) break for[th] upon me. I see the arm of . . . vengeance calling itself the arm of Justice uplifted to beat me down' (UC 96/26). Finally, in a draft letter to d'Alembert (Spring 1778) he pondered the reaction which his analysis of 'the delicate subject of the Sanction which I call Religious' might receive (*Corr.* ii. 115–18).

There can be no doubt, then, that Bentham was aware of the adverse effects his irreligious views might have if made public, and he certainly did not want to alienate those who might otherwise be sympathetic to his proposals for secular reform. As he wrote to George Grote in 1821 regarding the *Analysis*, it was his intention to maximize converts but also to avoid 'suffrance at the hands of the political and popular or moral sanction and suppression of the work at the hands of the political'.[29]

Bentham's caution was surely justified. He could expect little public support in a battle with religion. What he saw as the paralysing effect of religion on the nation's rulers, particularly the manner in which the ecclesiastical establishment obstructed salutary reform,[30] was scarcely

[29] JB to George Grote (1821), BL Add. MSS 29807/147, cited by Steintrager, 'Report on the Problems of Editing Bentham's Writings on Religion', p. 3. Ten years later, still troubled by the possibility of persecution, he wrote to his atheist friend Francis Place (24 Apr. 1831) reporting his conversations with one Archibald Prentice (1792–1857), later to pen *Some Recollections of Jeremy Bentham* (Manchester, 1837): 'As to the point in question, I took care not to let him know how my opinion stood; the fat would have been all in the fire, unless I succeeded in converting him, for which there was no time; all I gave him to understand on the score of religion as to my own sentiments was, that I was for universal toleration; and on one or two other occasions I quoted Scripture', BL Add. MSS 35419/73–4, from a transcription at the Bentham Project, UCL; also quoted by Graham Wallas, *The Life of Francis Place 1771–1854* (1898; 4th edn. London, 1951), 82. Bentham could even be slightly paranoic about the intentions of his religiously inclined associates. While engaged with Wilberforce on the Panopticon he avoided discussions of a religious nature. On one occasion (15 Nov. 1796) he wrote to his brother Samuel that Wilberforce 'is laying plots for converting me—I was hard put to it this morning to parry him' (*Corr.* v. 301; see also ibid. 306).

[30] That Bentham was fully apprised of clerical opposition to reform from a very early date is revealed in a manuscript of 1773, in which he refers to Locke's description of divines as the 'hatchers of all mischief' and comments that now, having lost the power to perpetrate such mischief, they 'content themselves with opposing good' (UC 96/328); see J. Locke, *A Letter from a Person of Quality to his Friend in the Country* (1675), in *The Works of John Locke: A New Edition, Corrected*, 10 vols. (London, 1823), x. 200.

a fact appreciated by the educated élite let alone the ordinary public. Moreover, the religious reaction of the second half of the eighteenth century had taken root both within and without the episcopal hierarchy. The middle classes, rapidly rising into power and influence, were bringing their own narrow view of religion along with them. Dissent had become the ally of liberalism, but Dissenters were frequently no less bigoted than Churchmen. In such circumstances it was diplomatic to adopt the reticence of the Whigs without their hypocrisy—neither to attack nor to affect religion.

3. Secular utilitarianism

So far as it goes, this revised interpretation of the chronology of Bentham's views on religion and the manner in which they came to be published is undoubtedly convincing. But the genesis and development of these views are not entirely explained by expatiating upon their political function. On a different plane they must be seen as part of his overall strategy to apply systematically the standard of utility to all the principal institutions of society. It is here that I depart from the line of research followed by Mack and Steintrager to offer what I believe to be a more complete and correct view of the character of Bentham's writings on religion.

In a jotting of the early 1770s Bentham had written that as far as religious matters were concerned his 'sole object' was 'to state in as clear terms as I am master of what I apprehend to be for the temporal benefit of . . . my fellow-men' (UC 69/36). The conviction that disputes in theology are by and large morally irrelevant is given an impressive echo in the manuscripts on subscription written around the same time. Here he writes that where matters of virtue and vice are unimportant, questions of theology, in so far as the disputes they occasion do not affect morals, are akin to problems in mechanics. Which is to say that 'Vice gains nothing [and] Virtue loses nothing by a decision of the Question one way more than another' (UC 96/327). Bentham was sure even then that it is indifference to human happiness that 'suffers . . . a man to acquiesce in such principles unfavourable to it which have been inculcated into him under the name of Religion' (UC 96/289). Looking back over his long life from the vantage point of 1832 he would have been satisfied that he had consistently postulated this antithetical relationship between utility and religion, viewing the gain of the one as invariably the loss of the other. Religion, he would say, contributed to fear and so caused pain and suffering. As practised by the Anglican Church it was unnecessarily prudish with regard to sexual matters, keeping men and women from harmless pleasures, and encouraged the substitution of blind and enervating faith for rational demonstration. In *Swear Not at All* and *Church-of-Englandism* he sought to expose the fallacies and fictions by which organized religion per- petuated these evils; in the *Analysis* he examined the theological basis of the fear induced by the notion of punishment in the hereafter and sought to expose the pernicious dependence of contemporary Christi- anity upon this doctrine; and in *Not Paul, but Jesus* and its related manuscripts he focused on the debilitating consequences of religious asceticism and closely scrutinized the credibility of the revelation and miracles of St Paul. Seen in this light the intellectual context in which the works on religion were conceived must be far broader in scope than is conveyed by Bentham's specific concerns with political issues. The writings on religion cannot be seen simply as a feature of a general political attack on the establishment. Rather they were intended, as Bentham sufficiently testifies, as a thorough examination of the utility of religion in all its various doctrinal and institutional aspects. Contrary to what he once claimed (UC 69/36), when he turned his attentions to religious subjects he did not view matters solely from the perspective of the politician.

Nor did Bentham focus upon religion as the theologian or Church historian might conceive of it. In his investigations of the relations between religion and other aspects of thought and conduct, his central enquiry was not as to whether and in what fashion our conceptions of the cosmic universe and attendant religious beliefs influenced or shaped our actions and social relationships. Very early in life Bentham had learnt that the privileged classes have a vested interest in maintaining the existing practices of official religion. Moreover, the fear of a punishing God, traditionally invoked to quell rumblings of discontent amongst the lower orders, was part and parcel of the faith expounded and protected by the ecclesiastical establishment. It was on these grounds that the 'alliance' of Church and State was commonly justified— each needed the other in order to survive. But in viewing religion as an instrument used to subjugate the masses, and in sounding the depth of the reluctance of the secular and ecclesiastical establishments to con- sider innovations to improve the lot of the ordinary people, Bentham realized long before Max Weber that these were general characteristics of the relationship between religion and political life.[31] Hence he focused on religion as a social sanction—that is, as an agency of motivation—on what he perceived as the disutility of religious motives and inclinations and, true to his utilitarian view of the unity of theory and practice ('praxis'),[32] upon this basis he zealously sought to change the world. Where Weber's primary interest was in religion as a soure of the dynamics of social change, Bentham looked on it as a significant psychological impediment to social improvement. He aspired, therefore, not only to reduce the influence of organized religion but ultimately, like Proudhon, to eliminate the notion of religion itself from the mind. In order to release people from the shackles of superstition and dogma, he recognized that religion must be closely scrutinized by the best and most searching tools available, since only then could its dispensibility be revealed.

If Bentham's writings on religious subjects cannot be described as theology, neither do their principal ideas constitute a philosophy of religion. Bentham hardly touched the foundations of the religious experience in a deliberate manner, and seems to have been singularly incapable of proceeding further than to consider religion as a set of rituals or as a social sanction founded on fear of the supernatural. When he announced to his friend John Lind (5 Oct. 1774) that he could have written Locke's *Essay concerning Human Understanding* (1690) in 'half the compass' he meant, among other things, that he would expunge the references to the incorporeal aspect of the human frame and to the life hereafter which supposedly held out an appeal to this higher or more sublime nature (*Corr.* i. 205). This denial of the richness of human nature obviated the need to discover its complexity and thereby disqualified Bentham from writing a penetrating philosophical examination of his subject. But this is not to say that there is not a philosophical dimension to his critique.

At the heart of my account is the proposition that not only were Bentham's views on religion substantially indicated many years before publication, but that they were developed and worked up towards completion in an intimate relationship with his theory of knowledge. The theoretical principles that Bentham brought to the study of religious questions, as to all other areas of his thought, he had been exploring independently in the 1770s in a collection of manuscripts under the

---

[31] M. Weber, *The Sociology of Religion*, trans. E. Fischoff (1922; London, 1965), 136–7.

[32] The term is used by Bentham at *CE*, App. IV, p. 233 n.

title 'Preparatory Principles'. In later life they were to be presented in a more systematic and complete form in a series of essays on logic and language. The writing of these essays dates substantially from 1811–21, the same period during which he was so heavily engaged in the study of religious matters. During this decade the two bodies of work—the writings on logic and language and the writings on religion—came to exhibit a symbiotic relationship, but there is sufficient evidence to show that Bentham was already conscious of this relationship over forty years before. There is, I would argue, a more or less precise correlation between the emergence of Bentham's opinions on religion and the development of the principles of his social science. Nor are there signs that his views on knowledge and existence altered in any important respect during the sixty years after he first formulated them in the 1770s. Extraordinary as it may seem, there were to be no periods of doubt for Bentham. Tensions caused by reflections on either religious or metaphysical matters are not evident in his work; to his initial views on both he remained true throughout his life. This relationship between metaphysics and irreligion in Bentham's utilitarianism has largely escaped the notice of students of his thought. L. J. Hume is one Bentham scholar who has recognized that some connection exists between the two, but he did little to develop this theme. In *Bentham and Bureaucracy* he presents the writings of the period 1802–22 as parts of a single intellectual enterprise, the purpose of which was 'a campaign against "misrule" in all its forms'. He points to an 'inner logic' in Bentham's progression from one topic to another, and suggests that close connections exist between the writings on parliamentary reform, which in some respects were an outgrowth of Bentham's legal studies, on the one hand, and the work on religion, education, psychology, language, and other subjects, on the other. The latter, Hume argues, 'usually had more than one purpose, but one of these was in each case, to reinforce his attack on influence or to add some refinement to his earlier argument about it'.[33] There is much truth in what Hume says, and the argument that the works of the later period were related in certain significant ways is central to my own position. It is also undeniable that the concept of 'influence' came to play a key role in Bentham's political campaigns, particularly from 1809 onwards when he became an advocate of democratic reforms. However, there

---

[33] Hume, *Bentham and Bureaucracy*, pp. 160, 167, 186. Ch. 6 of this work provides a detailed exposition of the development of Bentham's thought during this period of his life.

would appear to be little point in trying to analyse the discussion of revelation and miracles in *Not Paul, but Jesus* or the notion of futurity in the *Analysis*, for example, simply in terms of instruments of control in the hands of the clergy. To do so would constitute a failure to grasp how Bentham came to study these subjects and where they fit into the wider scheme of his science of society. Not everything can be reduced to a product of simple political motives and thereby fruitfully or correctly explained. Indeed, far too much emphasis has been given in recent years to Bentham's supposed conversion to political radicalism and not enough to the intellectual constructs upon which his utilitarianism as a whole is founded. So far as his views on religious matters are concerned it is readily apparent that they were not ideas fleetingly considered or expressed as a peripheral concern. His irreligion was deep-seated and warmly held from an early age and requires, therefore, that our framework of understanding be of a suitable nature. A more sensitive handling of the material is called for and, in particular, a close reading of Bentham's philosophical writings is essential, if the complete matrix of factors which influenced the form and content of his views is to be brought to light. It is to this specific concern that I devote Chapter 1.

However, I do not mean to banish politics entirely from my discussion. In Chapter 2 I want to suggest that Bentham's radical critique of religion, far from emerging as a consequence of his frustrations with secular reform, in actual fact facilitated the development of his later extreme stand on political issues. My argument, in brief, is this: Bentham had early in life fathomed the corruption and the reactionary characteristics implicit in the relationship between the ecclesiastical and secular arms of government, and this served to ease the path to his agitation for a complete overhaul of the system. In this sense irreligion both chronologically and logically preceded political radicalism; it was central to his emerging vision of the secular Utilitarian society. Whatever censorial sentiments Bentham expressed in his early critique of Blackstone (I have in mind his discussions of the nature of civil society, government, laws, and the administration of punishment) they were not those of a committed democrat.[34] As we have seen, in the years

---

[34] J. C. Rees and J. Lively appear to give the correct view of Bentham's utilitarian reasons for adopting the democratic programme in 1809: 'Bentham became a democrat only when he was convinced that democracy was . . . the sole form of government in which rulers would be obliged to respect social utility (and thus embark on his programme of legal reform). Where utilitarians believed they could control government

following it was his cautious hope for reforms in several areas of the law and social life which determined the tactic of self-administered censorship. Once the dilemma over strategy was behind him his views on religion were systematically presented and a second front opened up from which to mount an attack on the Establishment. What Bentham had understood early on in his career was the illusory nature of religion; what he now came to see was that the abolition of illusion depended on a substantial alteration of the social environment upon which it thrived. Piecemeal utilitarian reform in jurisprudence, the penal code, or politics could never be successful while established ideas about the foundations of the social order remained intact. From 1809 on, therefore, Bentham was engaged in an attack on the ruling hierarchy in its entirety, on its institutions, and its governing beliefs. He recognized that its political and legal structures were bolstered by religion, and that in return ecclesiastical institutions and practices were fully supported by government. To leave religion untouched was thus to leave a powerful ally of the legal and political regime free to operate unchecked. Political and religious radicalism from this point went forward hand in hand. But the ease with which Bentham was able to mount and pursue this formidable campaign suggests something beyond a simple conversion to democracy. It seems more than an idle specula-tion to suggest that it was his early radical stand on religious matters that—not only permitted, but—served to draw him into a more extreme position on political questions. This interpretation can convincingly be established, I believe, by exploring Bentham's views on religion as they are presented in his work on ethics and legal theory of the 1770s and 1780s, for it is here that the foundations were laid for his radically secular view of society—a vision of a world without religion from which he never wavered and which was to be fleshed out in later life in works such as the *Chrestomathia*, the *Constitutional Code*, and even the curious *Auto-Icon: Or Farther Uses of the Dead to the Living*.

Bentham's utilitarianism, of course, is often acknowledged to be in some sense 'secular', but what is meant by this it is rarely thought necessary to say. In the course of the eighteenth century ethical and social thought had undergone a large measure of secularization. But the term, as Jacob Viner and others have noted, is liable to be mislead-ing; as it is commonly used it does not mean a complete break with

without representative institutions they were unsympathetic to them', *Utilitarian Logic and Politics* (Oxford, 1978), 9. See also Michael James's comment in 'Public Interest and Majority Rule in Bentham's Democratic Theory', *Political Theory*, 9: 1 (1981), 49.

religious ideas. In Viner's view it represents 'a lessening of the influence . . . of ecclesiastical authority and traditional church creeds, and a shifting of weight from dogma and revelation and otherworldliness to reason and sentiment and considerations of temporal welfare'.[35] On this view the issue of secularization is one of degree: how far were ethical and social thinkers prepared to go in their secularism? Bentham stands at one extreme pole of this secular spectrum. For, beyond the light they cast on his intellectual development and the impact they had on disciples such as Francis Place, George Grote, and the younger Mill, Bentham's writings on religion reveal the careful and calculating manner in which the most penetrating legal and constitutional theorist of the age sought to secularize society, and illuminate his hopes for a world without religion. It is not my intention to stake out any specific ground in the continuing debate over the problems of defining the 'secular' and what constitutes secularity. But if secularization refers, as Owen Chadwick suggests it does (invoking a deliberately broad meaning of the term), to the tendency to do without religion,[36] then Bentham's crusade against the Church and its doctrines and his attempt to convince others to follow his lead, deserve attention as an important manifestation of this tendency. Indeed, one might justifiably argue that a greater intellectual force for secularization than Bentham did not exist in early nineteenth-century England. The evidence upon which this claim is based will be examined in Chapters 3–9.

In Chapters 3 and 4 Bentham's thoughts on subscriptions to articles of faith and the use of compulsory oaths, on penal laws against Catholics and Dissenters, and on the Common Law crime of 'blasphemy' are

---

[35] J. Viner, *The Role of Providence in the Social Order: An Essay in Intellectual History* (Princeton, 1972), 55.

[36] O. Chadwick, *The Secularization of the European Mind in the Nineteenth Century* (Cambridge, 1975), 17. It should be said, however, that Chadwick and Viner are probably mistaken in their view of the secular. Secular trends in the 18th cent. are not reducible simply to the tendency to do without religion. For instance, the more worldly approach of religion itself can be seen as contributing to the secularization of society, as can the proliferation of sectarianism within Protestant Christianity, and the expanding role played by the laity in Church affairs (laicization). More especially, as we shall see in the concluding chapter, the advocacy of 'secular religion' by Saint-Simon, Auguste Comte, and others greatly complicates the issue by positing the transposition of religious sentiments to secular objects. That the terms 'secular' and 'secularization' have a wide range of meanings is amply illustrated in my edited collection of essays *Religion, Secularization and Political Thought: Thomas Hobbes to J. S. Mill* (London, 1990). On this topic see also D. Martin, *The Religious and the Secular: Studies in Secularization* (London, 1969), ch. 4, and, for a stimulating history-of-ideas approach to the problem, R. Vernon, 'The Secular Political Culture: Three Views', *The Review of Politics*, 37: 4 (1975), 490–512.

discussed under the general theme of 'religious liberty'. Chapters 5 and 6 deal with Bentham's critique of the 'alliance' between Church and State, including his discussion of the role played by the ecclesiastical establishment in the education of England's youthful poor, and his proposals for disestablishment. Chapters 7–9 focus on his analysis of natural and revealed religion. Here I examine Bentham's arguments against the doctrine of 'design', his attitude towards miracles, the Scriptures, and Christian doctrines generally, and his criticisms of the Church's position on 'Sexual Nonconformity'. Finally, in a concluding chapter, the peculiar character of Bentham's vision of the secular Utilitarian utopia is illustrated. Throughout the whole, however, it should be apparent that for Bentham secularism and scientism, meaning here a commitment to the principles of a social science in emulation of physical science, are integrally related. To a substantial degree his strictures on religion were a product of his profound conviction that the way to social progress is through adapting the principles of natural philosophy to social analysis. When these were applied in the rigid manner chosen by Bentham, however, the end result was bound to be atheism. Irreligion, therefore, was central both to the character of his utilitarianism and to the possibility of the realization of the kind of society he envisaged.

PART I

A Utilitarian Science of Society

THAT Bentham aspired to create a science of society in emulation of Newtonian physics is a commonplace of the literature on utilitarian thought.[1] It is an aspiration he shared with many others of the age from Hartley and Hume to the continental *philosophes* and Priestley. Its quintessential expression is found in Hume's famous edict that social inquiry should be based on the 'experimental Method of Reasoning'. What is rarely considered, however, is that in Bentham this Newtonian endeavour gave form and substance to a trenchant and uncompromising critique of religion. The vital relationship between Bentham's theory of knowledge and his opinions on theological and ecclesiastical matters has received scant attention by scholars in the past.

It was Bentham's adaptation of the techniques and principles of natural science to the study of the law which was to draw him to take a stand on other social issues. In the process of clarifying the presuppositions and tools of analysis which would enable him to develop a truly scientific approach to the law, he could not help but reflect that precisely the same techniques were applicable in all the various regions of social science. Indeed, Bentham never failed to associate legal questions with a whole range of other areas of social activity in which improvements could be made—from the penal code and prisons, education and economics, to politics and religion. In each case, abuses and defects were to be exposed by the application of the methodology of natural science (as Bentham understood it). To understand the underlying tenets and character of Bentham's legal philosophy, therefore, takes us a long way towards an understanding of his utilitarianism, including his approach to matters of religion.

Drawing upon various writings, published and unpublished, early and late, on logic, ontology, and language, it is my intention in Chapter 1 to elucidate the metaphysical framework of Bentham's utilitarianism and to identify the suppositions which shaped it.[2] In doing so I want to provide evidence for the view that throughout his long life the principles of his theory of knowledge and his critique of religion were intimate

---

[1] That Bentham aspired to be the Newton of the moral sciences has been acknowledged e.g. by Stephen, *The English Utilitarians*, i. 179; and by Halévy, *The Growth of Philosophic Radicalism*, p. 6.

[2] R. Harrison's *Bentham* (London, 1983) is one of the few works that has attempted to reveal the unity and overall coherence of Bentham's work, showing that the more frequently studied political, moral, and legal thought can only be fully appreciated if seen within the context of his metaphysics and theory of meaning. Bentham's theory of language is very much at the heart of my own account of his views on religion, but for a detailed examination of the metaphysical underpinnings of his science of society I refer the reader without hesitation to Harrison's text.

parts of a single system, that the nature—and especially the implicit atheism—of the latter cannot be comprehended without recourse to the former.

In Chapter 2 I have expanded this analysis of the foundations of Bentham's utilitarian science of society to include his thoughts on ethics and legislation as they developed in the 1770s and 1780s. Here I examine his critique of the role of religion in contemporary moral theory and the prominent role he gave to jurisprudence as the key to maximizing social happiness. My argument is that this initial attempt to develop a secular science of society provided Bentham with the impetus for his later exhaustive onslaught on the 'alliance' of Church and State.

I

Science and Religion

The present work as well as every other work of mine that has been or will be published on the subject of legislation or any other branch of moral science is an attempt to extend the experimental method of reasoning from the physical branch/department/world to the moral.

UC 32/158; draft preface to a projected work on 'civil' legislation,
1792

Unlike God man's knowledge is confined to experience, hence he has knowledge only of what has been and what is, and nothing of what will be.

UC 69/40

THE history of Bentham's disaffection, first with the Established Church at Oxford and later with religious doctrines and beliefs generally, has never been satisfactorily recorded.[1] What is clear, however, is that his battle with religion began very soon after, or at about the same time as, the rudiments of his system were formulated in the early 1770s. Bentham's manuscripts of 1773 on the subject of subscriptions to articles of faith and his preface to Voltaire's *Le Taureau blanc* both suggest a mind coming to terms with the implications of a radically secular philosophy. At the same time Bentham was hard at work formulating the principles of his legal philosophy, the principles by which he was to expose the faults of existing law and legal theory and upon which he would construct his own legislative system.

It is evident from Bentham's early writings that he was from the first an empiricist. He held that all knowledge is derived from sensation: the intellect has no material to work with apart from that obtained by the senses. In the seventeenth century empiricism, as a philosophical tool of acquiring knowledge, had been appropriated to serve the needs

---

[1] The picture drawn by Mack of the young Bentham 'terrified and repelled by religion', oppressed by 'morbid piety', who could not understand 'why it must be painful to be good', (*Jeremy Bentham*, p. 35), is an exaggeration largely based upon the recollections of an old man who, it must be said, frequently let his fancy get the better of his memory.

of physical science. Suitably impressed by the progress made in this department of knowledge, Bentham carried over from his own amateur researches and reading in various areas of natural philosophy the basic principle that people can only know, in any certain or scientific sense of that term, that which can be observed and verified. He was passionately fond of experimental science, especially chemistry, in which he found no small degree of enjoyment in his early life. In 1782 he assisted his good friend and fellow chemical enthusiast Dr Francois Xavier Schwediauer (1748–1824) in the translation of *An Essay on the Usefulness of Chemistry and its Applications to Various Occasions of Life* (1783) by Torbern Olof Bergman, one of the foremost scientists of the period.[2] Indeed, one suspects that it was their shared interest in chemistry, rather than their supposed philosophic similarities,[3] which so much endeared Bentham to the dissenting theologian Joseph Priestley (1733–1804). To the study of botany he was devoted all his life, and he was fond of using medical allusions and analogies to convey the purposes of his writings. Nor were his references to medicine merely a literary device. On many occasions Bentham claimed that the science of legislation ought to be built on the same immovable basis of sensation and experience as that of medicine: 'In short what the physician is to the natural body, the legislator is to the political: legislation is the art of medicine exercised upon a grand scale' (UC 32/168). The basis of both sciences is observation of the human frame.

This was the core of the scientific approach for Bentham—it was an approach implicitly associated in his mind with a materialist ontology and a nominalist theory of language. He rejected all forms of idealism in philosophy, and as an atheist he held that there were no rational grounds which compelled belief in a God, in a Being transcending or immanent in the world of material reality. He insisted that existence is a purely material phenomenon—things are what they are because they have the appropriate size and shape, are made of matter of a specific

[2] For a discussion see B. Linder and W. A. Smeaton, 'Schwediauer, Bentham and Beddoes: Translators of Bergman and Scheele', *Annals of Science*, 24:4 (1968), 259–73. See also *Corr.* ii–iii, *passim*. The MSS for Bentham's preface to the translation are at UC 156/1–42.

[3] Priestley, like Bentham, was an empiricist, a materialist, and a nominalist, though he was inconsistent in his nominalism and put all 3 doctrines to a radically different use than Bentham. See J. G. McEvoy and J. E. McGuire, 'God and Nature: Priestley's Way of Rational Dissent', in R. McCormmach (ed.), *Historical Studies in the Physical Sciences*, 6 (Princeton, 1975), 325–404; J. G. McEvoy, 'Enlightenment and Dissent in Science: Joseph Priestley and the Limits of Theoretical Reasoning', *Enlightenment and Dissent*, 2 (1983), 47–67.

density, and so forth. As such, all matter is quantifiable in mathematical terms, and this extends to the pleasures and pains that we experience. Pleasures and pains were the ultimate phenomena to which all social action and social concepts, such as rights, obligation, and duty, could be reduced.

The focus on human action and the pleasures and pains which motivate that action constitutes the psychological foundation of Bentham's utilitarianism. Questions of utility, he would say, lie at the heart of all that an individual does or seeks to do. Even logic was viewed by Bentham in terms of the consequentialist element in thought and action (*Works*, iii. 219). Bentham's is, in other words, a peculiarly utilitarian logic reminiscent of Hobbes's notion of 'deliberation' as the reckoning of consequences towards the end of felicity.[4] This view of logic and its purpose naturally brought Bentham to despise the common notion of 'metaphysics', understood as abstract thinking or the science of things transcending what is physical or natural. Even so, at least in his early years, he frequently employed the term as a shorthand method to refer to his own speculations in the field of language.[5] These early speculations and the nominalist understanding of the world they fostered were central to the development of Bentham's theory of knowledge. Together they constitute an account of language in which general terms have no corresponding reality: words, ideas, and propositions must represent or describe tangible, discrete physical entities or they are abstractions. It is the task of ontology to reduce these abstractions or 'fictions' to what Bentham called 'real entities', but where ontological analysis fails to establish physical referents for a fiction it can be assumed that it does not exist in a tangible form and thus cannot be known. As Newton—at least in the mind of the eighteenth century— had banished the vocabulary of mysticism and superstition from physical science, so it was Bentham's aim to rid the moral sciences of the verbal and philosophical superstitions that bedevilled our understanding of human experience. His unique utilitarian logic together with the presuppositions of his nominalist metaphysics, and the theory of language in which these elements were formalized, were the tools enlisted for the task. Logic and language in all significant respects should accurately reflect reality; nominalism required the separation of wholes into their component parts and the reduction of fictions to concrete things.

---

[4] T. Hobbes, *Leviathan* (1651; Harmondsworth, 1981), pt 1, chs. 5–6.

[5] Later on, conscious of the disrepute which the term 'metaphysics' had occasioned in philosophy, Bentham drew back from it (*Works*, viii. 220–1).

Bentham's theory of knowledge is thus presented as a blend of three philosophically distinct but intimately associated theses: (*a*) an empiricist epistemology; (*b*) a materialist metaphysics; and (*c*) a nominalist science of meaning.

For J. S. Mill this constituted Bentham's 'revolution in philosophy': it was not his opinions 'but his method, that constituted the novelty and value of what he did'. He introduced 'those habits of thought and modes of investigation which are essential to the idea of science'.[6] And Mill might have added that to this method Bentham remained true in all areas of social science—from logic, morals, and education to political economy and jurisprudence—for the rest of his days.

1. Philosophic progenitors

The influences which brought Bentham to this theory of knowledge and the general approach to social action it entailed are not difficult to discern. Contrary to common belief, Bentham generously praised the thinkers he recognized as his forerunners. Whether he agreed with them in whole or, as was more often the case, only in part, he rarely failed to acclaim those who inspired him and who supplied the raw materials of his system. From Bacon and Newton he drew its basic tenets and from Locke and the French *philosophes* he garnered the principal notions of how a science of society might be practically developed. The intellectual contributions of these several writers have been well documented—what is important here is the nature of their influence on Bentham as he assiduously worked to develop his science of society.

The *philosophes* were the acknowledged propagandists of the new 'age of reason' and its discoveries in natural philosophy, and Bentham consciously identified with them in their endeavour through science to free the human psyche from the prison of superstition. Among the apostles of intellectual enlightenment to which the *philosophes* claimed to be the intellectual heirs were Bacon, Newton, and Locke, and in

---

[6] Mill, 'Bentham', in *Collected Works*, x. 83. Even Michael Oakeshott, in his otherwise disparaging essay ironically titled 'The New Bentham', conceded that Bentham was 'a master of detailed analysis', *Scrutiny*, 1 (1932–3), 116. It is appropriate to mention at this juncture that Bentham, like others of his day, employed the term 'science' in a broad sense: science is systematized or ordered knowledge, not merely of the physical world but of all disciplines. In this respect, for instance, there is a science of painting and music just as much as of chemistry, and theology or divinity is the science of religion.

many respects Bentham's own debt to his English ancestors is one that he acquired from his acquaintance with the writings of his French contemporaries.[7]

Bentham thought of Bacon as 'that resplendent genius', and on another occasion described him as 'the brightest genius' God ever made (*Works*, viii. 99, 437). Toward the end of his life, writing in the third person in the 'Article on Utilitarianism', he recorded the specific nature of his debt to his distinguished countryman:

> On his [Bentham's] entrance into the moral, including the political, branch of art and science, he found it in much the same condition as that in which Lord Bacon found the physical. The matter of what was called 'the science' was composed of a more or less copious assemblage of words, and the instruction afforded, such as it was, consisted principally, if not exclusively, in conveying intimation of the relation borne by the import of one of those words to the import of another. *Fiat experimentum* was the aphorism of Lord Bacon: and by this one direction that philosopher was regarded, and with truth, as having done more towards the advancement of that branch of art and science than had been done by all that had gone before him. (*Deon.* 295)

Though he seems not to have considered that his own technique differed not one jot from that of his illustrious forebear, Bentham goes on to explain that *observatio* is a more appropriate word than *experimentum* when referring to the moral world, because here the subject-matter of study consists not of material entities *per se*, but pleasures and pains. Ill-fitting as subjects for experiment—'especially in the case where the institutor of the experiment is any other person than the Sovereign or a person or persons constituted for the purpose in authority under him'—they are properly the subject-matter of observation (*Deon.* 295). In other words, human activity is rarely subject to the same controls that an investigator can apply in physical or chemical research, but this does not rule out a systematic and rigorous approach in social inquiry: if *fiat experimentum* was Lord Bacon's aphorism in physical science, then *fiat observatio* was to be Bentham's guiding aphorism in moral science.

Bacon, then, was the original inspiration behind Bentham's efforts through observation to discover first principles and to classify the divisions of knowledge. Through this inductive science philosophers were to claim dominion over nature, a dominion long denied them

---

[7] The excitement of Voltaire and d'Alembert for things English is amply displayed in their works, especially the first's *Lettres philosophique* (1734) and the latter's *Discours préliminaire* (1751) to Diderot's *Encyclopédie*.

because of their failure to deal with the *substantia* of the universe. Moreover, in Bacon's naturalistic scheme there was no place for knowledge which had for its purpose mere contemplation, the activity assigned by Aristotle to the metaphysician. The aim or end of all knowledge is the production of works for the promotion of human happiness. Bentham resisted the urge publicly to distance himself from the theological framework in which his distinguished predecessor developed his philosophy. But he could not, like Bacon, place the principles of knowledge under the jurisdiction of natural religion, nor could he place the principles of ethics under the jurisdiction of revealed religion. However, in this Bacon could be quietly ignored. It was his naturalistic schema (suitably cleansed of its associations with theology) and his emphasis on the adaptation of discoveries in natural philosophy to the improvement of social conditions which so impressed Bentham.[8]

The nature of Newton's influence on Bentham has rarely been considered in detail, and it is not at all certain what is meant when Bentham's system is described as 'Newtonian'.[9] After all, moral philosophy had seen several accomplished and self-proclaimed Newtonians ply their craft in the eighteenth century—the theologians Samuel Clarke (1675–1729) and William Wollaston (1660–1724)[10] among them—none of whom could reasonably be coupled with Bentham as adherents of the same school of thought. Certainly, Bentham could not be supposed an adherent of that aspect of Newton's thought which enjoined reverence to God—the first cause of things—and obedience to his will. Even so, Bentham's ambition to be the Newton of the moral world was given colourful expression on several occasions in his writings. In 1792, for example, drafting one of his many prefaces to a proposed *magnum opus* on the law he dramatically announced: 'What Bacon was to the physical world, Helvétius was to the moral. The moral world has therefore had its Bacon, but its Newton is yet to come' (UC 157/32). Yet it is not always easy to say what is intended by such grandiose

---

[8] Bentham might have wished that should he ever find himself in political office he would 'bring in industrious observations, grounded conclusions, and profitable inventions and discoveries', as Bacon once wrote of his own intentions to his uncle, the favourite of Elizabeth, Lord Burghley in 1592, *The New Organum*, ed. F. H. Anderson (1620; Indianapolis, 1960), introd., p. xxvii.

[9] For a discussion of the variety of ways in which Newton was viewed by the 18th cent. see G. Buchdahl, *The Image of Newton and Locke in the Age of Reason* (London, 1961).

[10] S. Clarke, *Discourse Upon Natural Religion* (1706); W. Wollaston, *The Religion of Nature Delineated* (1722).

statements. What can concretely be said of Newton's importance for Bentham?

First, it is clear that for Bentham Newton had come not to provide a substitute schema for development but to fulfil the promise of Bacon. The strength of Bacon's intellectual influence turned on the fact that his programme was substantially outlined and able to be developed and extended without being supplanted. It enabled Newton to reach a level of achievement beyond Bacon's own limited scientific capabilities, yet still remain faithful to the Baconian legacy. The chief difference between the two is the premium Newton placed on mathematics—he combined Baconian experimentation with a mathematical and quantitative technique. In thus enlarging upon Bacon's pioneering efforts Newton did not depart from the inductive method nor from such ancillary Baconian principles as the importance of utilitarian applications of science. He also shared Bacon's scepticism *vis-à-vis* the so-called 'authorities' of the past. The resulting synthesis, so appealing to Bentham's frame of mind, combined the certainty of experiment with the rigour of mathematics.[11] Secondly, guided by Newton, Bentham, in social thought as in natural philosophy, tended to view the world and its material parts in separation, as particles or atoms, unique and independent. Hence he reduced the elements of the moral world to its individual components, each person separately motivated by particular sensations which can be detected, and measured or quantified. Finally, and above all, Newton was for Bentham an exemplar, a discoverer of manifestly true universal laws of motion. What Newton had done for physical science, Bentham would do for moral science.

What distinguishes Bentham's own efforts from Newton's, and what is worthy of special consideration, however, is the central role he gave to metaphysics—definition, clarification, classification. No doubt, to give an organized account of the universe, to connect, to fit together in logical relations, the concepts and statements embodying whatever knowledge has been acquired, was an ideal also cherished by Newton. But in placing metaphysics at the centre of his systematization of knowledge Bentham drew upon other sources of enlightenment: Locke and, most important of all, the French *philosophes*. In this respect he stands as the cumulative vessel of the efforts of an age to sharpen, clarify, and demystify the vocabulary of social disciplines and practices. Indeed, the grand preoccupation of the age with metaphysics is

---

[11] R. B. Schwartz, *Samuel Johnson and the New Science* (London, 1971), 61.

inexplicable when separated from the larger context of what it means to be scientific (that is, systematic) in the analysis of society.

The exact details of Locke's account of language are not pertinent to the present discussion; what does matter is the crucial general idea that he bequeathed to eighteenth-century social science: the understanding that ideas are clarified by being broken down or reduced to their constituent parts, which in turn can be explained in terms of their origin in sense perception. As Locke described them, ideas either exist in simple isolation or they are compounded to form complexes, rather as material objects are compounded out of molecules or atoms.[12] Thought, at least reflective thought, is a kind of inner eye corresponding to the outer physical eye which perceives the physical world. Hence when Locke defines knowledge as 'the perception of the connexion and agreement, or disagreement and repugnancy, of any of our ideas', here perception is viewed as something which surveys two ideas as if they were discrete particles.[13] The development of the relationship between material objects and ideas described by Locke runs as follows: particles of material objects are perceived by the human sense organs, setting up a chain of effects in the nervous system, which eventually produce an idea in the mind, an entity entirely different from the original particles perceived.[14] It is this dualism—between the 'real' entities of the material world, endowed with mathematically transcribable primary qualities, and ideas in minds—which leads, by stages, to the referential or representational theory of meaning.

Renaissance philosophers had thought of language as a system of signs enmeshed in the similitudes and relations between things. The external characteristics of matter were looked upon as signifying a hidden power which could only be understood through deciphering the grammar of natural signs. Under the influence of Locke, the Enlightenment mind severed this inherent link between words and things. Locke described his method of understanding nature in these terms:

Words are general, . . . when used for signs of general ideas, and so are applicable indifferently to many particular things; and ideas are general when they are set up as the representatives of many particular things; but universality belongs not to things themselves, which are all of them particular in their existence, even those words and ideas which in their signification are general. When, therefore, we quit particulars, the generals that rest [*sic*] are only

---

[12] Locke, *Essay concerning Human Understanding*, in *Works*, i, Bk. II, ch. 2.
[13] Ibid. ii, Bk. IV, ch. 1, sec. 2, p. 308.   [14] Ibid. i, Bk. II, ch. 8.

creatures of our own making, their general nature being nothing but the capacity they are put into by the understanding of signifying or representing many particulars; for the signification they have is nothing but a relation that by the mind is added to them.[15]

No longer was energy to be expended on interpreting the language of nature. Rather, nature should be represented in human language. Precision in language thus became identified with the analytical procedure whereby the data of sensory experience were reduced to their representational components. Individuals could still develop whatever complex ideas they wished and name them as they wished, but to be understood they had, to some degree, to make their ideas (and hence their language) conform to the things to which they referred. For if ideas indicated by names did not in some way reflect tangible reality then, says Locke, 'men's language [would] be like that of Babel'.[16]

Locke appeared to muddy the waters when he appealed to 'reflection' as an introspective source of ideas—different from 'sensation'—about the nature of mental processes, and by and large eighteenth-century philosophers rejected the distinction. But they were virtually unanimous in applauding his dismissal of the doctrine of innate ideas and were quick to seize on the notion that the concepts of the mind were to be explained by reducing them to the combinations and permutations of simple ideas originating in experience. It was on these grounds that Bentham declared Locke to be the inventor of 'modern Metaphysics' (UC 69/177).

Locke's basic idea became the underlying assumption for empiricists on both sides of the English Channel. For instance, in Hume's *Treatise on Human Nature* (1739–40), with which we know Bentham was familiar, we find not only the distinction between simple and complex ideas, but also the conception that no idea can be properly understood without being traced to its origin, the primary impression upon which it is based.[17] As is well known, Hume was also convinced that, like natural science, moral philosophy must begin with empirical observation, that the techniques of the one were equally applicable in the case of the

---

[15] Ibid. ii, Bk. III, ch. 3, sec. 11, p. 172.

[16] Ibid., ch. 6, sec. 28, p. 227. For a discussion of these developments in language and understanding see M. Foucault, *The Order of Things: An Archaeology of the Human Sciences* (London, 1970), 17–63; K. M. Baker, *Condorcet: From Natural Philosophy to Social Mathematics* (Chicago, 1975), 109–28; O. Hannaway, *The Chemists and the Word: The Didactic Origins Of Chemistry* (Baltimore, 1975), 62–72.

[17] D. Hume, *A Treatise on Human Nature* (1739; Bk. III 1740), ed. L. A. Selby-Bigge (1888; repr. Oxford, 1975), Bk. I, pt 1, sec. 1, and pt. 3, sec. 2.

other. The facts with which moral philosophers are to deal are those to be discovered by Lockian introspection—a kind of scientific psychology. Similarly, when Bentham insisted on the unity of science it was on the ground that the same method and principles that applied in one branch of it were applicable in the others, and when he set out the tenets of his moral theory his thoughts turned inward to the psychological makeup of the human frame (though his final picture, it must be said, remained a conspicuously external one). In these respects he went no further than the investigations already conducted and the techniques suggested by Bacon, Newton, and Locke, and heralded in Hume's *Treatise*.

Locke's theory of language was taken up and developed by other writers in England, most notably John Horne Tooke (1736–1812). Tooke made it his own personal discovery that, through the application of the principles of etymology, all words can be reduced to names of sensations, and on this basis he endeavoured to lay the groundwork for a universal grammar.[18] Tooke's philological system was eagerly applauded by Bentham, who expected great things from its application to the learning of foreign languages (*Works*, viii. 15, 188).[19] It was to be left to another age to ponder the obstacles posed by the consideration that cultures develop different modes of thought and principles of language. To an age impressed by the progress of physical science and consumed by the attempt to adapt its techniques to a study of the moral world, Hazlitt voiced the grounds for the appeal of Tooke's *Diversions of Purley* (1786, 1805). 'Mr. Tooke', he wrote,

treated words as the chemists do substances; he separated those which are compounded from those which are not decompoundable. He did not explain the obscure by the more obscure, but the difficult by the plain, the complex by the simple. This alone is proceeding upon the true principles of science: the

[18] James Mill had early become acquainted with Tooke's teachings and coupling these with Hartley's psychology he set about providing a scientific account of mind. His indebtedness to Tooke's *Diversions* is defined by the epigraph he placed at the head of his chapter on abstraction in the *Analysis of the Phenomena of the Human Mind*, 2 vols. (1828; repr. New York, 1967). The passage contained Tooke's basic belief that 'the perfections of Language, not properly understood, have been one of the chief causes of the imperfections of our knowledge', *The Diversions of Purley*, 2 vols. (1786, 1805; 2nd edn. London, 1798; repr. Menston, 1968), i. 37.

[19] For Bentham's references to Tooke see *Works*, viii. 120, 185–91; and also JB to S. Bentham (6 May 1777, and 27 Oct. 1778), *Corr.* ii 47–8, 181–4. Compared with Tooke, James 'Hermes' Harris (1709–80), despite some path-breaking speculations regarding the evolution of language, had barely scratched the surface of the possibilities for a universal grammar. For Bentham's references to Harris's *Hermes: Or a Philosophical Enquiry concerning Language and Universal Grammar* (1751; repr. Menston, 1968) see *Works*, viii. 85 n., 110 n., 112 n.

rest is pedantry . . . Our philosophical writer distinguished all words into *names* of *things*, and directions added for joining them together, or originally into *nouns* and *verbs*.[20]

In Tooke Bentham would also have found the view that the operations of the mind are really operations of language, that all the operations of thought rely absolutely on language. This is not an idea that can be traced to Locke, but it did not prevent Tooke from triumphantly assert-ing that 'perhaps it was for mankind a lucky mistake . . . which Mr. Locke made when he called his book, An Essay on Human *Understand-ing*. For some part of the inestimable value of that book has, merely on account of its title, reached to many thousands more than, I fear, it would have done, had he called it (what it is merely) A *Grammatical* Essay, or a Treatise on *Words*, or on *Language*.'[21]

The writings of Hume and, later on, Tooke stand as eloquent evid-ence of the impact of Locke on language studies in eighteenth-century Britain, and Bentham found much to praise in the work of both writers. Nevertheless, neither Hume nor Tooke had developed their thoughts far enough for Bentham's liking. Hume, especially, seemed to disappoint Bentham, both in his natural philosophy and (as I shall show in the next chapter) in his thinking on morals. True, Bentham's attitude to abstract reasoning was much like Hume's. His adoption of the prin-ciples of the new science, his broad sympathy with the Lockian epistemo-logy, and alignment with modernism and its rejection of the uncritical reliance on 'authorities', together with his impatience with all forms of superstition, are obvious similarities with Hume. In Bentham's first substantial publication, *A Fragment on Government* (1776), he described Hume as 'that penetrating and acute metaphysician whose works lie so much out of the beaten track of Academic reading' (*FG* 440 n.). But his praise is mixed. He 'would not wish' to 'send the Reader', he writes, to any volume of Hume's Treatise but the third. As to the two first, he is inclined 'to join with those who are of the opinion that they might, without any great loss to the science of Human Nature, be dispensed with'. Bentham even thought that the same could be said 'of a consider-able part' of volume three, but that 'after all retrenchments, there will still remain enough to have laid mankind under indelible obligations' (*FG* 440 n.).

[20] W. Hazlitt, 'The Late Mr. Horne Tooke', in *Spirit of the Age* (London, 1825), quoted by H. Aarsleff, *The Study of Language in England 1780–1860* (1967; repr. London, 1983), 71.

[21] Tooke, *Diversions*, i. 31.

However 'acute and penetrating' Hume's metaphysics and epistemology, they were ultimately unacceptable to Bentham. Whereas Hume, the sceptical metaphysician, was content to point out the problems to comprehension encountered by the human understanding, for Bentham the destruction of unsubstantiated systems of belief was only a prelude to the reconstruction of social and political institutions. In this he owed more to his acquaintance with the literature of the French Enlightenment than to the writings of his sceptical compatriot. It was the *philosophes*, rather than Hume, who did most to publicize the greatness of Bacon, Newton, and Locke in establishing the credentials of the empirical tradition.

Perhaps the most concrete realizations of the Baconian scheme for the study of natural philosophy are the *Encyclopédie* of Diderot and d'Alembert and the French institutes and academies of learning which promoted the co-operation of scholars and the propagation of knowledge. 'Newtonianism', as many have observed, was the creation of Voltaire, who popularized the Englishman's discoveries in his *English Letters* (1734) and his *Elements of the Newtonian Philosophy* (1738), gaining for them a continental audience they would not otherwise have reached. Finally, the school of Locke found a home in France which in many ways overshadowed the productions of his disciples in England. By the mid-century English empiricism had triumphed in France; given a distinctly French flavour, it became a systematic materialism ripe for a contest with the moral, political, and theological foundations of the established order. Bentham found the forthright simplicity of this mode of thought refreshing and he eagerly petitioned to join the *philosophes* in the effort to introduce into moral science, to borrow a phrase from Peter Gay, the precision of 'Newton's Physics without Newton's God'.[22]

Bentham had already paid tribute to Voltaire by translating *Le Taureau blanc* in 1774, and a year before that had expressed admiration for Voltaire in his unequal fight against the intolerance and tyranny of France's judicial system (*Works*, i. 448). Later he sought to emulate Diderot and Voltaire by placing himself at the disposal of Catherine the Great (thereby joining them in the illusion that great things could be accomplished by despots enlightened enough to listen to the wisdom

---

[22] P. Gay, *The Enlightenment: An Interpretation*, 2 vols. (1966; New York, 1977), ii, Bk. III, ch. 3, pt. 2, title. See JB to Voltaire (Nov. 1776[?], unsent), *Corr.* i. 367–8; JB to d'Alembert (Spring 1778), *Corr.* ii. 115–18, 121–2; JB to A. Morellet (Spring 1778), ibid. 118–20; and JB to F. J. de Chastellux (Spring 1778 and 4 Aug. 1778), ibid. 120–1, 143–52.

of philosophers).[23] In 1778 Voltaire threw himself ardently behind the Economical Society of Berne and its scheme to offer a prize for the best criminal code.[24] In response, Bentham considered submitting his *Plan of a Penal Code* for the prize (*Corr.* ii. 248–53).

D'Alembert, praised for his conscious endeavour to introduce mathematical rigour into the conduct of the social sciences and for his observations on the language of science, was the inspiration, along with Bacon, behind Bentham's various attempts to construct a comprehensive 'encyclopedic' map of knowledge. Indeed, he gratefully acknowledged that he was following in the path of august persons when he included in the second edition of the *Chrestomathia* (1817) his most complete example of such a map, 'for which', he said, 'Bacon had found materials and d'Alembert the graphical form' (*Works*, viii. 7). The encyclopedic treatment of knowledge and learning was a characteristic of the age. The original plan belonged to an earlier period, to the work of Bacon, but little had been done to realize the idea until the genius and the labours of Diderot and d'Alembert in the middle of the eighteenth century. Their aim was to carry out the plan, foreshadowed in Bacon's *Novum Organum* (1620), of collecting into one comprehensive whole all the cumulative knowledge acquired since scientific practice had been liberated from the fetters of theology. Diderot's 'Prospectus' to the *Encyclopédie* was published in 1750 and the first volume, with d'Alembert's celebrated *Discours préliminaire*, appeared in 1751. The principles which guided the editors and the object of the work are explained, with repeated references to Bacon, in these essays and in Diderot's article 'Encyclopédie' in the fifth volume (1755). The principal idea is that human knowledge constitutes an aggregative whole and that there is a fundamental unity of all thought and knowledge, with the implied suggestion that similar techniques are therefore required in all the various branches of physical and moral science. But it was the prominence they gave to language studies as the basis for developing and applying natural sciences which particularly caught Bentham's eye.

---

[23] Bentham wrote to Catherine *c.*1776 (*Corr.* i. 366–7), and in or about 1780 he composed further letters to the empress, as well as to other sovereigns and statesmen, intended to accompany presentation copies of *IPML*. See JB to S. Bentham (10 Apr. 1780), *Corr.* ii. 414–20. From Jan. 1786 to Nov. 1787 Bentham resided in Russia hoping to gain Catherine's attention, but had little success in furthering his ambitions.
[24] Voltaire gave a donation to augment the value of the prize and characteristically coaxed additional financial support from the Empress Catherine and Frederick the Great, H. Mason, *Voltaire: A Biography* (Baltimore, 1981), 138.

A major tenet of the philosophy of the *philosophes* was that reasoning on the objects of sensation could take place only after they had been given 'signs'. The process of reasoning was the development of a well-made language using these signs, and the principles of any system of science were precisely formed propositions in the language of that system. A science, therefore, consisted of a set of propositions about the real world and the whole of the science must be contained in these propositions. 'A well treated science', wrote Condillac, 'is a well-made language.'[25] Language, then, is the key to precise reasoning and it is understandable that the *philosophes* took such an interest in language reform. Ultimately, d'Alembert's interest in the reform of scientific terminology led him to plan a dictionary, with the professed intention of removing what he considered to be errors of logic in the vocabulary of science that kept it from becoming an infallible instrument of reason.[26] Condorcet expressed similar sentiments: he declared that the first object of philosophy was to form a precise and exact language for each science. This language should 'bring to all the objects embraced by the human intelligence a rigour and precision which renders the knowledge of truth easy and error almost impossible. Then the development of each science would have the sureness of mathematics and the propositions which form the system all the certitude of geometry.'[27]

To the illustrious names of Voltaire, d'Alembert, Condillac, and Condorcet we must also add that of Adrien Helvétius. In the following chapter consideration will be given to the Helvetian inspiration behind Bentham's utilitarian ethics. Here I want to draw attention to the fact that, perhaps more than anyone else, Helvétius taught the significance of clarity in the use of language. In declared imitation of Descartes and Locke, he illustrated in no uncertain terms the problems created by 'the abuse of words' in both metaphysics and morality, producing 'a

[25] É. B. de Condillac, *Essai sur l'origine des connaissances humaines* (1746), in *Œuvres philosophiques*, 33 vols., ed. G. Le Roy (Paris, 1947–51), i. 105, quoted by T. L. Hankins, *Jean D'Alembert: Science and the Enlightenment* (Oxford, 1970), 111. The *Essai* was translated by Thomas Nugent as *An Essay on the Origin of Human Knowledge* (1756) and advertised as being 'a supplement to Mr. Locke's Essay on Human Understanding'. The *Essai* did not appear under Condillac's name until the 1st edn. of the *Œuvres* in 1769, though its authorship was widely known many years earlier. Coincidentally, this was also the year in which Bentham read Hume, Helvétius, and Beccaria for the first time.

[26] Quoted Hankins, *Jean D'Alembert*, p. 112.

[27] Marquis de Condorcet, *Œuvres de Condorcet*, 12 vols., ed. A. C. O'Connor and M. F. Arrago (Paris, 1847–9), iv. 271–2, quoted by Hankins, *Jean D'Alembert*, p. 112.

labyrinth in which the greatest geniuses have lost themselves'.[28] Though Bentham initially praised Locke for the invention of 'modern Metaphysics', in a manuscript probably from 1775, he gave the credit to Helvétius and defined it as the science of the meaning of words (UC 27/1). For all his accomplishments, however, Helvétius had not said everything that needed to be said. Bentham greatly admired his work: he had laid the 'true foundations of moral science'. In particular he had given as strong a voice as anyone to the view that the demystification of the language of moral science was the essential prerequisite to the progress of that science. But there was more to be done to bring it to perfection: 'having done enough for one man and more than had been done by any other man, he stopt then, leaving the superstructure to be raised by other hands' (UC 32/158). Though none could compare with Helvétius in terms of the practical application of linguistic analysis, the concern with language was a characteristic of the scientific enterprise undertaken by the generality of *philosophes*—especially d'Alembert, Condillac, and Condorcet, with whose work Bentham was well acquainted.[29]

The sentiments of the French *philosophes* found in Bentham a responsive soul who dutifully extended their analysis in the attempt to show the full breadth of its implications for social science. For Bentham, communication through language was basic not only to the progress of science but to the progress of social organization. The problem of truth was, he believed, contained in the confusion of linguistic errors. This discovery brought with it the realization that a theory of signs and a theory of science were part and parcel of the same enterprise. Clear thought and speech, fundamental to scientific theory, was an essential prerequisite for the rational ordering of both private and public affairs. The irrational and the 'metaphysical' (in the pejorative sense meant by Bentham to refer to all spurious reasoning upon the principles of nature and thought) had to be expunged from discourse, and the means to this was through linguistic analysis.

It was in this intellectual atmosphere that Bentham conceived and developed the principles of his utilitarian philosophy. From Bacon, Newton, Locke, the *philosophes*, and others too numerous to mention, he learnt and borrowed. It could not be said that the work of any one

---

[28] C. A. Helvétius, *De l'esprit: Or Essays on the Mind and its Several Faculties* (1759; trans. 1810, repr. New York, 1970), 27.

[29] Bentham refers to Condillac's 'little work on *Logic*' and notes in critical fashion the worth of his use of the term 'analysis' at *Works*, viii. 123–5 and n.

philosopher was sufficient to shape his thoughts, though Helvétius perhaps had more influence than any other. Bentham's education was selective and his intellectual borrowings were conducted in a critical manner. For instance, he followed Bacon in making the watchwords of his science of society 'observation' and 'experiment'. But in placing absolute confidence in our ability to perceive and record the world about us, he ignored Bacon's warnings that human perception is fallible, that experiments need to be arranged, controlled, and directed in such a way that there will be compensation for the weakness of our senses. He also put to one side the theological framework in which Bacon, Newton, and Locke conceived their philosophies of nature, and he conveniently ignored Locke's (and Hume's) efforts to define the limitations of the knowledge available to us. Finally, Bentham thought the *philosophes*, including Helvétius, less than rigorous in their analysis of social phenomena. More especially, they were on occasion inclined to the very same kind of metaphysical speculations that he abhorred. Even Voltaire could not bring himself entirely to disavow a form of deistic belief in God. But the quibbles do not outweigh the benefits. It was with these practitioners of the new science that Bentham wished to stand in a united front against cant, superstition, myth, and verbal mysticism, and for a future when reason would govern our actions in both private and public life. In the 1770s Bentham entered the fray imbued with the scientific spirit of his intellectual progenitors.

2. *Preparing the ground for censorial jurisprudence*

Initially, it was in the field of jurisprudence that Bentham's awareness of the importance of metaphysics was to bear fruit. The project of criticizing archaic legal theories was greatly assisted by the quest for clarification. Subsequently, the science of the meaning of words lay at the root of Bentham's work in all the various compartments of knowledge, including his critique of religion.

Professors Burns and Hart have informed us that Bentham's major project in the 1770s 'was conceived originally as a treatise on the "Elements of Critical Jurisprudence" or the "Principles of Legal Policy" ' (*IPML*, p. ii). This work, 'probably begun in 1770', was 'interrupted' from autumn 1774 to autumn 1776 when Bentham worked on his critique of Blackstone, a section of which he published at that time as *A Fragment on Government*. By 1 October 1776, however, Bentham could write to his father that 'I am now at work upon my capital work: I mean the Critical Elements of Jurisprudence' (*Corr.* i. 358). In 1782 this 'capital work' was conceived as having forty chapters; seven years later much of the material appeared as *An Introduction to the Principles of Morals and Legislation*, but by this time the planned work had taken on a more truly encyclopedic character comprising ten volumes. Though the work was never completed, the manuscripts are a gold-mine of information for Bentham scholars.[30]

As this *magnum opus* on the law took shape in the 1770s, legislation became for Bentham the central element in the analysis of a whole social system of human actions. What he called 'direct' legislation, involving the penalties for actions deemed unacceptable, was to be supplemented by a more subtle and complex form of 'indirect' legislation, designed not only to tell people what they should not do, but also to provide them with the motives (pleasures and pains in prospect) sufficient to divert their desires into channels deemed appropriate by the utilitarian legislator.[31] The basic premiss of this approach is that, though individuals wish to maximize their happiness, they may be (and often are) mistaken as to the best way of doing this. It is assumed that government can educate its citizens to make more effective choices, or at least can direct them into more appropriate paths to achieve their goals. In other words, by means of manipulation, political or otherwise, conditions were to be fashioned in which individuals could more effectively maximize happiness than if left to their own unaided devices. Nor did Bentham think this a subversive notion: that the 'uncoerced and unenlightened propensities and power of individuals are not adequate to the end without the controul and guidance of the legislator is a matter of fact of which the evidence of history, the nature of man, and the existence of political society are so many proofs'.[32] On these

---

[30] According to one MS reference, 'Crit[ical] Jur[isprudence] Crim[inal]'—the focus of Bentham's attention in 1778—and the 'Principles of Legal Policy'—including what was to become *LG* (1970)—were parts of the same work (UC 140/14). For further information see JB to Lord Ashburton (3 June 1782), *Corr* iii. 123–30. Besides *IPML* and *LG*, we can shortly expect definitive editions of *An Essay on the Influence of Place and Time on Matters of Legislation* and *An Essay on Indirect Legislation* [*CW*], both of which are significant sources not only for Bentham's legal theory but also provide insight into what a society fashioned according to utilitarian principles might look like.

[31] For a discussion of this aspect of Bentham's work see D. G. Long, *Bentham on Liberty: Jeremy Bentham's Idea of Liberty in Relation to his Utilitarianism* (Toronto, 1977), 136 ff.

[32] *Jeremy Bentham's Economic Writings*, ed. W. Stark, 3 vols. (London, 1952–4), iii. 311.

terms, jurisprudence came to mean nothing less than a general science of society.

During the early stages of this 'capital work' Bentham repeatedly found himself frustrated by the inadequacies and peculiarities characteristic of current legal terminology. Sometime in 1776, presumably after completing *A Fragment*, he came to the conclusion that the *magnum opus* could not go forward until he had properly clarified the terms of his analysis. Only then, he was persuaded, could he proceed with his plan to assess critically the strengths and weaknesses of contemporary legal theory and practice, and to supply the defects according to clearly stated principles of improvement. The manuscripts (some 614 pages) in which Bentham first worked out the fundamental tenets of his approach are collectively titled 'Preparatory Principles' (i.e. of censorial jurisprudence). They have not been published but there can be no doubt that they were intended to be introductory to the real work of revising England's legal system:

The truth is the present is but a vestibule of the . . . building that is to follow, . . . An introduction of the work that is to come; . . . A work the business of which is the construction of a standard of right and wrong and the application of it to the several Laws that shall present themselves, and in consequence to the several modes of conduct that are the objects of them:

This was the end of all; this was that which presented itself to my mind, before the necessity of the present one was even so much as suspected. But I had not travelled far in this pursuit before I found that proceeding upon/with the common stock of words I was unable so much as to name that branch of the law or of man's conduct that was the subject of my disquisitions. Here then, I was obliged to make a pause: to undertake a new and difficult work, in order to put myself into a condition to undertake what then seemed to me . . . a work still more difficult, but which now I trust will be much less so . . . Before I enter'd upon the main work I had as it were my tools to make; I had my materials to parcel out and describe and find names for. (UC 140/21)

The science of jurisprudence (and the understanding of human conduct that this required), then, had to wait upon the fashioning of the appropriate 'tools', more specifically the analysis of terminology. Later in the manuscripts Bentham explicitly connected this introductory work with the problem of designating appropriate names: 'It is the knowledge of the true significance of words, says Helvétius after Hobbes, that distinguishes one man in point of understanding from another' (UC 69/195). Given the immense scope of the proposed *magnum opus* (a complete code or system of laws) the exposition of the 'fundamental terms of Universal Jurisprudence' (UC 159/269) became a pivotal process influencing the development of Bentham's science of society.[33]

The 'Preparatory Principles' manuscripts contain exactly what is implied by their title: a collection of definitions, distinctions, axioms, and aphorisms which together constitute the foundations of Bentham's thought. The aim was to supply the tools for clarifying or demystifying the 'fictions' of current legal practice and of Blackstonian legal theory as a prerequisite to elaborating certain propositions about the moral world. This is the domain which the social scientist must critically and comprehensively survey, since on this foundation the science of legislation is to be established.

The secret to the progress of both jurisprudence and moral science Bentham declares to be attention to words. 'A sober and accurate apprehension of the import of words' is recommended as the 'true key to Jurisprudence and the only effectual antidote against the fascinations of political enthusiasm' (UC 69/62). Foremost in his mind here is the vicarious claim to nonsensical 'natural rights' upon which the American constitution is, in his view, based. By comparison, he always believed that the reason why the principle of utility was not correctly understood was the rhetoric employed by its opponents. Thus in his constant battle to win minds over to utility he had frequent occasion to comment on the tactics of his adversaries. Jottings such as '*Per* Burke: "I hate metaphysics." *Per* J. B., because they substitute clear ideas in Psychology to the obscure ones in which he triumphed' (*Deon.* 50), are not uncommon in his writings. Metaphysics, as Bentham understood it, was the key to cutting through the philosophical and theological claptrap that dogged our understanding of the natural and the moral world. For this reason he referred to it as 'the most sublime and useful of all human sciences' (UC 69/155).

Bentham's materialist view of existence is the basic presupposition of his theory of knowledge and hence of his social science. In the 'Preparatory Principles'—against the marginal 'What Things Exist?'—

---

[33] The point is emphasized by Bentham's all-encompassing definition of a law as 'an assemblage of signs declarative of a volition conceived or adopted by the *sovereign* in a state, concerning the conduct to be observed in a certain *case* by a certain person or class of persons, who in the case in question are or are supposed to be subject to his power: such volition trusting for its accomplishment to the expectation of certain events which it is intended such declaration should upon occasion be a means of bringing to pass, and the prospect of which it is intended should act as a motive upon those whose conduct is in question' (*LG* 1).

he posits the primacy of the material world as the essence of an objective reality: 'I assume and take it for granted, that among the objects or supposed objects that offer or are supposed to offer themselves to our senses, are some that actually exist.' Since he cannot deny that it is he who is writing and that a table exists on which rests the paper containing his scrawl, he refused to consider opposing views of the matter, including Berkeley's view of immateriality.[34] Bentham simply accepted the existence of the material world 'without scruple notwithstanding [that] it has been the subject of so much controversy' (UC 69/1). Thus traditional metaphysical problems, such as the relation between our sensory perceptions and their supposed physical causes, are summarily dismissed as being of no practical importance. Bentham had no difficulty defining the doctrine of utility as a philosophy of experience, if by experience we understand him as meaning the perception of material reality. When clarifying what ought to be the connection between law and utility he indicates the bedrock of fact which experience provides:

When a man takes upon himself to *blame* or *approve* a mode of conduct, and can give a reason for it, his reason is always . . . an expression of a general matter of fact the truth of which rests upon experience. [For example,] When I say the custom in parents of providing sustenance for their children is an useful custom, when I blame the not observing it, and give the utility of it as a reason for observing it or what comes to the same thing, where I give the mischief of not observing it as a reason for blaming the non-observance of it, I allege a matter of fact . . . a set of facts and call in experience to witness. (UC 69/11–12)

Convinced that the reality of the world of appearances is straightforwardly a matter of experience, Bentham argued that when all the characteristics of the evidence we observe is noted, belief and disbelief are no longer at our discretion—one or the other is the necessary consequence of the preponderance of evidence on the one side or the other. The business of knowing is simply a matter of observation, inference, and verification. Knowledge in all the branches of art and science is gained in precisely the same manner.

Having established the essential unity of knowledge, Bentham next sought to locate all the various branches of art and science in an encyclopedic schema which would reveal their manifold interrelation-

---

[34] Bentham took issue with Berkeley's view of the relationship between sense perception and material reality on several occasions, employing on one such occasion an argument reminiscent of Johnson's famous refutation (*Works*, viii. 189 n.).

ships. Here the Baconian urge to classify and demarcate the various compartments of knowledge enhanced the importance of precision in language. Hençe, in discarded drafts of an introductory nature, probably from the 1770s, in which a preliminary attempt is made to set out the principles of a work on happiness, Bentham placed at the head of the list an 'Encyclopedical Sketch—Station of Jurisprudence in the Map of Knowledge'. The list then continues with headings under which the terms 'happiness' and 'unhappiness' can be analysed—those mentioned include 'Ingredients', 'Dimensions', 'Definitions' of related concepts, 'Axioms', and 'Comparative *values*' (UC 14/1). Such lists are not unusual in the early manuscripts and they clearly reflect Bentham's preoccupation with the presuppositions of his evolving science of society and particularly with its linguistic elements. But such schematic flourishes also reflect the experiential view of knowledge which informs his utilitarian system. In a jotting of 1773 he even proposed the establishment of academies of research and scholarship for every conceivable branch of human knowledge including 'English Language', the 'Moral Sciences', 'Political Ethics', and 'Religion'. The materialist underpinnings of this enterprise are soon revealed when, almost as an afterthought, Bentham dismisses the need for an Academy of Divinity: 'for the present exclude Religion because [it is] not safe to meddle with: and in future, because there will be found to be nothing in it to meddle with' (UC 96/111). In yet another 'Encyclopedical Sketch' two years later divinity is back in favour as one of the three 'master sciences', together with jurisprudence and ethics, though its content is left unexplained (UC 96/132). But this was the fancy of a moment. When Bentham put together his 'Encyclopedical Table, or Art and Science Table' for the 1817 edition of the *Chrestomathia*, and in contradistinction to the encyclopedical trees of Bacon and d'Alembert upon which it was modelled, all mention of divinity was omitted.[35] Whereas in d'Alembert's schema under the division of reason (including all divisions of a philosophical nature) we find the 'Science de Dieu' divided into 'Théologie Naturelle' and 'Science des Esprit [*sic*]', and this further subdivided into 'Religion' and 'Superstition', on the

---

[35] D'Alembert's tree was influenced by E. Chamber's *Cyclopedia: Or, A Universal Dictionary of Arts and Sciences*, 2 vols. (London, 1728). In the 'Article on Utilitarianism' Bentham informs us that he took the encyclopedical trees of Bacon and d'Alembert 'for his starting post in the career of improvement', and that the major source of their defects was the failure to take notice of happiness as the 'common bond of connection . . . for all the several branches of art and science' (*Deon.* 310–11). For a discussion of the faults of 'D'Alembert's Encyclopedical Map or Tabular Sketch' see *Works*, viii. 73–82.

one side, and 'Divination' and 'Magic Noire', on the other, Bentham's table excludes all such references. Nor does he, in the explanatory section of his text, discuss the reasons for omitting them (*Works*, viii. 82–95). He readily acknowledged that we possess an incorporeal nature, but what he meant by this is that we own an intellect which enables us to think and communicate; there is no suggestion that our incorporeal make-up extends beyond this. Clearly, by the time Bentham came to write the *Chrestomathia* he believed that the illusory character of religion had been conclusively established. The work of the Academy of Divinity, as I shall show in subsequent chapters, had been undertaken and completed by Bentham himself.

Presupposing that his theory of language was a neutral tool of clarification, Bentham always claimed to be operating in an objective manner when applying the techniques of natural science to the moral world. The 'Preparatory Principles' testify to this objective intention:

To be skilled in Metaphysics is neither to hold for Atheism nor for Theism. Metaphysics is neither infidelity nor credulity. It is not to know that there are neither God nor Angels. It is not to hold the soul to be mortal, nor to hold it to be immortal. But it is this: in talking whether of God or of Angels or of the immortality of the soul or of its mortality . . . to know and to be able to make others know what it is we mean. (UC 69/155)

In this regard metaphysics involved the synthesis of materialism and a theory of language which posited a straightforward correlation between things, on the one hand, and words, propositions, and ideas, on the other. The Lockian inspiration behind this is evident. Metaphysics, Bentham writes, is

that science which teacheth the signification of words, and the ideas which they signify: which it does . . . [by] shewing how all the ideas we have that are complex, arise from, and are made up of simple ones. Thus it is that . . . every science has its metaphysics: there is no science that has not a set of terms that are more particularly its own, standing for ideas that are more particularly its own. (UC 69/177)

A good neutral dictionary is essential to the possibility of a science of morals and legislation, just like any other science, and in religion, as elsewhere, Bentham professed to keep personal prejudices out of the matter.

If clarity in language was the key to the progress of science then it was incumbent upon Bentham to suggest ways in which its terminology might be improved. In the 'Preparatory Principles' Bentham developed two devices to aid in the demystification of language: definition and the theory of 'real' and 'fictitious' entities. It was in his reading of Locke and the French *philosophes* that he discovered these tools of analysis.

In the *Discours préliminaire* d'Alembert had written of the 'many questions' and the amount of trouble we might be spared 'if we finally determined the meaning of words in a clear and precise way'.[36] In words strikingly reminiscent of d'Alembert (though he may also have seen something similar in Hobbes's *Leviathan*) Bentham asserts in the 'Preparatory Principles' that 'the heights of science' are only to be scaled via an 'orderly, unbroken, well compacted chain of definitions' (UC 69/158).[37] In 1779 Bentham even employed a boy 'and set him to read Johnson's Dicty, for me to class the words by bidding him mark one with M. for Metaphysics, another E. for Ethics (etc.)', continuing the classification by numbering subsequent terms M1, M2, and so forth. In this manner he expected to deploy 'a compleat vocubulary for each science'.[38] If scientific method demanded definitions these Bentham was determined to provide. In a jotting of the previous year he enthusiastically proclaimed the lineage of his interest in definition:

Define your words says Locke: Define your words says Helvétius. Define your words says Voltaire: Define your words says every man who knows the value of them, who knows the use of them, who understands the things they are wanted to express: Define them for the rules of Physics: define them for the sake of Ethics; but above all define them for the sake of law. Philosophers I have obeyed you. I *have* defined my words: and with more especial care, where with venturous/presumptuous grasp I have taken in hand the sceptre of legislation. (UC 27/45)

Definition, central to any theory of language, was for Bentham the 'sole and sovereign specific against the maladies of confusion and debate' (UC 69/144). In the 'Preparatory Principles' he begins by analysing key terms in political and legal theory. Convinced that 'the import of . . . fundamental words, is the hinge on which the main body of the science [of Jurisprudence] turns' and that 'it is not uncommon for questions of the first practical importance to depend for their

---

[36] J. d'Alembert, *Preliminary Discourse to the Encyclopedia of Diderot*, trans. R. N. Schwab (1751; Indianapolis, 1963), 40.

[37] For the relationship between definition, reason, and science see Hobbes's *Leviathan*, pt. 5, ch. 5, and for the 'necessity of definitions' see ch. 4, pp. 105–6. However, though Bentham owned that so far as the importance of definitions to science were concerned 'the merit of invention belongs to others' (UC 27/3), he rarely mentioned Hobbes among their number.

[38] JB to S. Bentham (9 Nov. 1779), *Corr.* ii. 319–20.

decision upon questions concerning the import of these words' (UC 69/60), Bentham was vehement in his denunciation of ambiguities in legal terminology. Language which has no bearing on the facts of experience is irrelevant, useless, frequently pernicious and almost certainly opposed to truth. Armed with a set of properly defined fundamental terms the jurist would find himself 'rich in means for the solution of any problem in his science' (UC 69/161).

This view of definition is the basic element in Bentham's theory of language. The definitional procedure he developed in the 'Preparatory Principles' begins by determining the general category or classification of terms which includes the one to be defined, and then proceeds by distinguishing between it and all the rest (UC 69/144). How does this work in practice? The opening pages of *A Comment on the Commentaries*, largely completed in 1774, contain an early account of 'the office of definition' (*Comm.* 3). Here Bentham explains how definition by *genus* and *differentia* can make an idea determinate for someone if that person is already acquainted with examples of the *genus* and *differentia*. Predictable results follow when this procedure is applied to Blackstone's definition of law. For Blackstone 'A Law is a *rule of action* which is prescribed by some superior, and which the inferior is bound to obey.'[39] According to Bentham, there are three classes of substances: substances themselves, modes of substance, and qualities of substance. To what class of substances does the *genus* 'rule of action' belong? Bentham's comment is to the point:

As to myself I know that it is not from hearing pronounced the words 'rule of action', that I can obtain any conception of any class of objects at all, and it is then only that I begin to have some confused conception of such a class, when I understand that the term is applied to objects of that class which is signified by the term law. If this be the case with other people, so far then is the definition from contributing to render intelligible the word defined that it is to that word itself that it owes all the intelligibility it possesses. (*Comm.* 5–6)

This is the first shot in Bentham's long campaign against Blackstone. His aim, he says, is 'To purge the science [of jurisprudence] of the poison introduced into it by him and those who write as he does'. The purifying instrument is '*Definition*, perpetual and regular definition, the grand prescription of those great physicians of the mind, Helvétius and

---

[39] For Blackstone's precise definition see *Commentaries on the Laws of England*, 4 vols. (1765–9; repr. Chicago, 1979), i. 38, emphasis added. Contrast this with Bentham's very broad definition of what constitutes a law at *LG* 1 (see above n. 33).

before him Locke' (*Comm.* 346). 'Nothing', Bentham insists, 'can be done on the subject of law that deserves the name of Science, till that universal precept of Locke, enforced, exemplified and particularly applied to the moral branch by Helvétius, be steadily pursued, "Define your words" ' (*Comm.* 347). In his earliest writings and throughout his life Bentham practised the precept, digging 'deep into the mine of Definition . . . without which no materials can be obtained, fit to form the foundation of a science' (UC 27/2).

The theory of 'real' and 'fictitious' entities proved to be just as valuable an instrument of demystification for Bentham. Integral to his theory of definition is the implicit distinction it involves between words or propositions which represent tangible objects in the material world and those which refer to intangibles. 'The substances that are capable of being defined', he writes, 'are only [those that] are significant of themselves', and 'Substantives in general are such as denote substances' (UC 69/170). Naturally, not all terminology denotes a corresponding material substance; hence the employment of fictions, a class of substantives which aid discourse (words such as right, power, community, motion, gratitude). In each case, however, such fictions must be reducible to individual real entities, or they are intangibles in an absolute sense, indescribable and hence beyond definition. Moral terminology, for example, can usually be rendered meaningful in terms of the perceptible pleasures and pains which are experienced by specific individuals. Theological propositions about the nature of the universe, on the other hand, are in a different category. Having no correlation with material reality, Bentham's theory of definition has already prejudged them as irrelevant; they deal not with the facts of ordinary experience but with a reality which transcends the materialism of the physical world. Just as the language of opinion can have no place in the discourse of science, natural or moral, neither can the untestable, unverifiable propositions of theology. Bentham intended to ground his utilitarian philosophy 'on matters of fact', rather than on mere 'words', by making words and 'matters of fact' always interchangeable (UC 69/ 6–7). His aim was to construct for his own systematic use a vocabulary readily reducible to its component simple ideas, and in the process to scrutinize closely the potential enemies of such progress—complex, and particularly 'abstract' or 'fictitious', ideas.

Bentham was first introduced to legal fictions via the lectures of Blackstone which he attended at Oxford. His doubts about this mode of communicating ideas were later confirmed by his reading of the great man's *Commentaries on the Laws of England* (*Comm.* 45).[40] But it was d'Alembert who gave him the terminology he required: '*être fictif* is the expression employed by him for the designation of the sort of object for the designation of which the appellation *fictitious entity* has ever since been employed' (*Works*, iii. 286). Real entities, writes Bentham in the 'Preparatory Principles', are either 'substances' or 'perceptions'—his primary example of the latter being pleasures and pains (UC 69/62–3). Fictitious entities, or fictions, might be necessary or unnecessary, but in each case require demystification if they are to be correctly understood. In *Of Laws in General* he points out that though fictions are not real entities, they may in some cases be reduced to real entities and thereby defined and explained (*LG* 284). Moreover, some fictitious entities are essential to human discourse. Hence not all fictions were to be abolished. As a general rule, however, Bentham suggested the following strategy: 'avoid them or explain them by the relation they bear to the real ones and the law is clear' (*LG* 252). Accordingly, he was ever ready in his legal studies to dispel the confusion which fictions interposed between fact and understanding in order to obtain 'a clear perception of the state of things' (*LG* 251).

The instrument Bentham employed for demystifying fictions he called 'paraphrasis', and in *A Fragment* stipulated that its central aim was the reduction of fictions to their constituent real entities. By paraphrasis a fiction is explained by being employed in a sentence or proposition, which is then translated into another sentence the words of which 'are expressive of such ideas as are *simple*, or more immediately resolvable into simple ones than those of the former'. For Bentham this is 'the only method in which any abstract terms can, at the long run, be expounded to any constructive purpose: that is in terms calculated to raise *images* either of *substances* perceived, or of *emotions*;—sources, one or other of which every idea must be drawn from, to be a clear one' (*FG* 495 n.). Where this ontological procedure cannot be successfully conducted then the fiction is shown to be an abstraction having nothing to do with demonstrable reality.

Bentham elaborates his general point by drawing our attention to the word 'right' and prepares the ground for his later famous denunciation of rights as a 'nonsense' and natural inalienable rights as 'nonsense

---

[40] That Bentham's early experience with ghosts, no less than his familiarity with legal fictions, 'can be shown to have played their part in determining the intensity and pertinacity of his researches', is the argument of a substantial part of C. K. Ogden's introduction to *Bentham's Theory of Fictions* (London, 1932).

upon stilts' (*Works*, ii. 501). 'The word right', he explains, 'though a substantive is not significant of itself any more than a proposition is significant of itself. The word right is not significant of itself any more than the word "for" is significant of itself . . . Who will undertake to define "For"? No man. As little is it possible to define a right' (UC 69/ 170). Grammatically, the word 'right' is a substantive, but it is 'not significant of itself', meaning that it does not represent an object or body or collection of bodies in the real world. This analysis was extended in the *Introduction* to encompass a number of other ethical catchwords and phrases, such as Moral Sense, Common Sense, Rule of Right, Fitness of Things, Law of Reason, Natural Justice, Natural Equity, Good Order. All are dismissed on the grounds that they are merely empty phrases expressive of the sentiments of the persons advocating them (*IPML*, ch. 2). Not representing material reality, they could not be considered useful. Indeed, they were surely pernicious, serving as a 'pretence, and aliment, to despotism; if not . . . in practice, a despotism however in disposition' (*IPML* 28 n.). It was for precisely the same reasons that the fictions of the religionists, amply dissected in the *Introduction*, were also taken to task in the 'Preparatory Principles'. The idea of God, it seems, is no better a guide than Natural Reason or Natural Law in indicating proper rules of conduct (UC 69/132–3):

To maintain that there is a command from God to such an [*sic*] such an effect, and at the same time to allow that no signs of it can be produced, is . . . to make no differences between expression and non-expression, between signs and no signs, between speaking and non-speaking, between writing and non-writing. (UC 69/139)

On this interpretation it is impossible that theology can throw any light on morality or jurisprudence. Bentham's utilitarianism entails an unamibiguously secular and empiricist conception of the world as one of substance and materiality.

For the rest of his life Bentham was to denounce from this platform the abstractions of philosophy, politics, and law. If the works of Plato were 'the grand original mint of moral unintelligibles' (UC 69/102), radicals like Tom Paine were the purveyors of political fictions, and Blackstone was foremost amongst the 'dealers of fiction' in the field of law (*Comm.* 45). But if the irrational and the 'metaphysical' had to be expunged from moral and legal discourse, then the writing was clearly on the wall for theology also, and with equally drastic results. Ultimately, given the nature of Bentham's theory of language, this was bound to mean the imposition on religious thought and writing of an alien human-centred conception of language (and, indeed, of existence), an imposition which effectively stripped religion of its trans-physical content. Indeed, there is a manuscript fragment from the year 1773 which speaks characteristically of Bentham's aspiration to follow in the footsteps of Newton and Locke, but which is also indicative of the subsequent direction of his views on religion. In the process of eulogizing the achievements of these 'heroes of the intellectual world', Bentham pauses to reflect that both men were religious heretics: 'fire is not more at variance with water, than was Locke with orthodoxy . . . Newton was an [*sic*] Heretic: the few lost hours which that great man stole from the region of certainty to waste upon the region of unintelligibles led him into Heresy' (UC 5/23). Locke and Newton are not to be lauded for their religious opinions, heretical or otherwise, since they held these despite their great knowledge of the workings of human nature and of the general laws of the universe. It was in this respect that they left 'the region of certainty' to inhabit 'the region of unintelligibles'. From the beginning, then, science (as Bentham understood it) was deemed to be antithetical to religion, and the manner in which he rigidly applied scientific principles to the examination of religious beliefs and the doctrines of the Established Church speaks volumes for his approach to moral science in general. Moreover, and more especially, it provides us with a lucid and compelling testimony to his atheism and to his desire to free society from all considerations of a religious nature.

3. The unfinished 'Book on Logic' and the 'fictions' of religion

The culmination of Bentham's thoughts on metaphysics was reached in the second decade of the new century. The 'Book on Logic', on which he worked at intervals between 1811 and 1821 (and to which he returned from time to time during his final years), was intended to give a full description of his method. The work was never completed. Much of the material for it, however, reappears in several fragments in Bowring's edition of the *Works*. The essay on 'Nomography' with an appendix on 'Logical Arrangements, or Instruments of Invention and Discovery employed by Jeremy Bentham' appears in the third volume, and included in the eighth volume are the 'Essay on Logic', 'A Fragment on Ontology', the 'Essay on Language', and the 'Fragments on

Universal Grammar'. To these we must add the *Chrestomathia*, including Appendix IV—an 'Essay on Nomenclature and Classification'—in which Bentham offers a revision of d'Alembert's classification of the sciences in the form of a remodelled encyclopedical tree. At first look its subject-matter does not appear to fit a treatise on education, but Bentham's aim was to survey the whole field of knowledge and to assist educators by indicating those subjects which offered the greatest utility. Divinity, as I have already said, is conspicuous by its absence. We need not explore this appendix or the other essays in detail.[41] For the most part they contain elaborations of the principles set forth in the 'Preparatory Principles'. But there are a few passages pertinent to Bentham's thoughts on religion to which attention must be given. In these later writings the ramifications of his theory of language for religion were explictly stated.

Bentham was particularly concerned in these essays to explore the implications of the dichotomy between 'real' and 'fictitious' entities (cf. *Works*, vii. 196–8, 262). Confusion, he points out, is often the consequence of taking a fictitious entity to have a real existence, and all too often the creation and employment of fictions afford opportunities for deception to those who would employ such means to further their own ends. Inspired by 'mischievous immorality in the shape of mischievous ambition' the clergy and the legal profession are, as ever, foremost in Bentham's mind as the perpetrators of such frauds (*Works*, viii. 199). Fraud and professional chicanery are camouflaged by a screen of obscure and complex language which the lay person cannot hope to penetrate. Some fictions, of course, are harmless, and the validity of particular fictions (where convenience is not obviously the reason for their employment) must be judged by their utility. Political and legal fictions such as 'obligation', 'right', 'power', 'privilege', words to which we fail to assign fixed ideas, are to be explained 'by showing how they are constituted by the expectation of eventual good and evil, *i.e.* of pleasures and pains, or both as the case may be' (*Works*, viii. 293). The coupling of consequentialism to materialism in this fashion constitutes Bentham's real advance from the philological work of the *philosophes*. Bentham's reductionist logic is most obviously understood when considering the psychical fictitious entities of ethics, where terms such as 'appetite', 'desire', 'motive', and 'interest' have to be redefined

---

[41] Once again, Harrison has already supplied us with a superb analysis of their essential arguments in his already mentioned work on *Bentham*. I cannot do more than refer the reader to this.

in terms of pleasures and pains 'in the several shapes of which they are susceptible' (*Works*, viii. 290). Whatever of truth there is in a fictitious entity, therefore, belongs to it only in so far as the proposition has for its subject some real entity (*Works*, viii. 246). Paraphrasis will reveal that fictions, such as a right or an obligation, have for 'their real *source*' sensation, that is to say, 'perception considered as productive of pain alone, of pleasure alone, or of both' (*Works*, viii. 247).[42] The materiality of the external world thus had its counterpart in Bentham's system in the materiality of the psychic functions we possess.

The imagined infallibility of this approach was to make it more than merely a useful propaganda weapon in Bentham's campaign against the clerics. Indeed, even when his original hostility could be traced to some other source—an experience or event in his early life—he later enlisted metaphysics to provide the essential supporting arguments his analysis required. The case of the term 'Church' is a good example. Disaffected with the overbearing authority of organized religion while still a youth at Oxford, Bentham's animosity increased throughout his middle years as the bishops in the House of Lords vetoed one progressive reform after another (or so it seemed to Bentham), until in later life he became openly and vehemently hostile to the political influence of the Church of England. His original distaste for established religion, therefore, could not be said to derive from the presuppositions of his social science. In the 'Essay on Logic', however, Bentham presents us with a calm but pointed conjectural history of the term 'Church' and its signification, applying in masterful fashion the linguistic principles of his social science. The hyperbole and vitriolic language which all too frequently mar his writings on religion of the same period are not to be found here. Instead his exposition is both instructive and thoughtfully crafted as befits a work on logic.

In several respects Bentham's exposition follows that given by Hobbes in *Leviathan*. Hobbes distinguished several meanings of 'Church': it signifies an edifice distinctive from the temples of pagan religions; as a translation of the Greek *ecclesia* it signifies 'a Congregation, or an Assembly of Citizens, called forth, to hear the Magistrate speak unto them'; and it is a descriptive term used to set the followers of Christ

---

[42] It never seemed to occur to Bentham that the terms 'pleasure' and 'pain' were themselves abstractions which also require explanation. Just as he proposed the utility principle as the foundation of his social science, not demanding any further proof of its validity, so pleasures and pains were likewise viewed as the ultimate matter to which all social constructs could be reduced and thereby explained.

apart from those of other religions. But its most important sense for Hobbes is that in which it can be personified in the person of its sovereign. Without this transference of authority from the Christian congregation to a sovereign there can be no Church in this last sense: 'A company of men professing Christian Religion, united in the person of one Sovereign; at whose command they ought to assemble, and without whose authority they ought not to assemble.'[43] Similar semantic probems of definition lie at the heart of Bentham's analysis. But whereas Hobbes is concerned to describe the nature of a Christian commonwealth and to reveal the basis for obligation to authority within it, Bentham's aim is far different—it is to expose the fraud that language can be misused to cover. It is worth following his exposition at length.

The development of the term 'Church' from its Greek form *ecclesia*, which signifies an assembly of persons for any purpose, to the early Christian usage, where it signifies an assembly of those of a particular faith, was accompanied, says Bentham, by the evolution of the role of the instructor or teacher of the faith. The English word 'minister' came to be substituted for the Latin word signifying 'servant' to designate these instructors, and later on the English word 'bishop' was substituted for the Latin *episcopi* signifying 'overseers of the behaviour of the faithful'. In the process of this transformation those who were originally servants of the assembly now became its rulers. At the same time the word 'Church' came to signify different things to different people: 'vis. 1. The whole body of the persons thus governed; 2. The whole body of the persons thus employed in the government of the rest; and, 3. The all comprehensive body, or grand total, composed of governed and governors taken together' (*Works*, viii. 249). Added to this, a fourth meaning soon evolved and was used to designate the place of assembly itself; as a result God, 'although present at all times in all places, was regarded as being in a more particular manner present at and in all places of this sort' (*Works*, viii. 250). Not long thereafter these places became objects of veneration to the members of the assembly—in one word, they became 'holy'. An 'insensible transition' then took place by which the terror and respect that the members held for their 'holy' place of worship 'came to extend itself to, upon, and to the benefit of, the class of persons in whose hands was reposed the management of whatsoever was done in these holy places: holy functions,

---

[43] Hobbes, *Leviathan*, pt. 2, ch. 29.

made holy places, holy places and holy functions made holy persons' (*Works*, viii. 250). Bentham's anticlericalism is introduced with a certain amount of irony: 'Upon contemplating themselves altogether in the mirror of rhetoric, it was found that all these males put together . . . composed one beautiful female, the worthy object of the associated affections of admiration, love, and respect—the Holy Mother Church' (*Works*, viii. 250). This institution took on a holiness which far out-stripped 'the aggregate mass of holiness' of the several parts ('holy males') of which it was composed. The consequence was the elevation of the Church to infallibility even though its holy men remained fallible: 'Her title to implicit confidence, and . . . implicit obedience, became at once placed upon the firmest ground, and raised to the highest pitch' (*Works*, viii. 250). The authority of the Church could not suffer disobedience lightly and the punishment of offenders was now demanded, for it was thought that a Church capable of being disobeyed was capable of being violated and its existence jeopardized. The members (now the real servants) of the Church universally condoned the infliction of punishment on recalcitrant members, and hence served to further secure the position and advantage of their rulers (*Works*, viii. 250–1).

One assumes at this point that Bentham has brought the history of the 'Church' up to its present condition. What are his conclusions? He refrains from any overt political statement, leaving this to *Church-of-Englandism*, but it is clear that a linguistic analysis based on the potted history he presents here will throw up problems of an insuperable nature. For it is obvious that an attempt to define 'Church' categorically is doomed to fail; no one exposition, complete and correct, can be given of it. For the same reason that he denied a real existence to groups or collectivities beyond the existence of their individual parts, and a real existence to universals or abstract terms, Bentham's favourite analytical tool was the decomposition or breaking-up of the complex into the simple.[44] Definitional analysis requires that we classify phenomena by a 'dichotomous' or 'bypartite' division of generic terms. By repeating the operation indefinitely the analyst aims to ensure that each class is genuinely exclusive and that nothing is left out of the account or ever counted twice. 'God', of course, is uniquely resistant to such analysis, but 'Church' provided Bentham with a suitable subject. In the attempt to define 'Church' he had recourse to logical or bypartite division as

---

[44] Bentham records a debt to d'Alembert for this mode of analysis (*Works*, viii. 63 ff., 266–70).

the necessary preliminary or accompaniment to definition, but this division made any further exposition in the shape of definition redundant (*Works*, viii. 251). Linguistic analysis shows that the several senses of 'Church' are easily mistaken for each other, such that the term invariably produces confusion. 'In all matters relative to the Church', writes Bentham,

in so far as concerns the interests of the members of the Church, the good of the Church ought to be the object pursued in preference to any other. By any of two [*sic*] persons this proposition may, with perfect sincerity, have been subscribed. But according as to the word Church, the one or other of two very different, and in respect of practical consequences, opposite imports, has been annexed, their conduct may, on every occasion, be with perfect consistency exactly opposite; one meaning by the word church *the subject many*,—the other, by the sameword, *the ruling few*. (*Works*, viii. 251)

The snipe at the clerics is again barely disguised, but the linguistic analysis can hardly be faulted. What is meant by 'Church' by one person may not be what is meant by another, and if there is nothing more to 'Church' than the sum of its individual parts, then what is meant by 'the good of the Church' becomes highly problematic. The consequence is confusion. But it is also Bentham's point that the confused mind is easily deceived and manipulated, and that ambiguous terms are very often employed to serve precisely this purpose. 'By the priest and the lawyer', he writes, 'in whatsoever shape fiction has been employed, it has had for its object or effect, or both, to deceive, and, by deception, to govern, and, by governing, to promote the interest, real or supposed, of the party addressing, at the expense of the party addressed' (*Works*, viii. 199). In *Church-of-Englandism* the manner of such deception is not left for the reader to infer, but is plainly stated. However, to read this work without the benefit of Bentham's logic and an understanding of his theory of language is to view it in an incomplete fashion. Often what looks to be petty carping and trivial criticism (though Bentham was prone to this too) in *Church-of-Englandism* and the other writings on religion, is really the consequence of a detailed analysis which does not appear in these texts.

Critical in this respect are Bentham's discussions of the nature of the soul and of the supposed existence of God. True, his writings on religion provide ample evidence of his views on these matters, but it is to 'A Fragment on Ontology' that we must look for the definitive statement of his position.

For the orthodox Christian it was important that there be two substances, one material, the other immaterial. The immateriality of the soul was a necessary condition for immortality. Any suggestion that the two substances be reduced to one—to material substance—effectively eliminated the soul. The belief in the soul's immortal nature and in the existence of an all-powerful and omnipresent God are fundamental to Christian doctrine; they must have appeared to Bentham as obvious and attractive subjects for linguistic analysis.

Some kind of distinction between a physical body and an immaterial soul is probably as old as human culture. But it was Plato who systematically developed the body–mind dichotomy and first attempted to prove the immortality of the soul. Bentham's disdain for the idealism of Plato (*Works*, viii. 120) is matched by his dismissal of the Christian view of the soul as a receptacle of grace—not surprisingly, neither of these views of our incorporeal essence can be located in material reality (save in the reductionist sense explained above), and hence knowledge of the soul is beyond our ken. Bentham's conclusion was that the soul could not be classified as anything other than an inferential entity (*Works*, viii. 196). Lest there be any doubt as to his meaning, he adds in a footnote that those who do not believe in the reality of the soul as an independently existing phenomenon must conclude that it is a fictitious entity, in which case it might be considered as 'that whole, of which so many other psychical entities, none of which have ever been considered any otherwise than fictitious, such as the understanding, and the will, the perceptive faculty, the memory, and the imagination, are so many parts' (*Works*, viii. 196 n.). Stripped of all mysticism and superstition, this is Bentham's conception of the soul. With reference to the existence of God his position is no less clear:

Should there be a person who, incapable of drawing those inferences by which the Creator and Preserver of all other entities, is referred to the class of real ones, . . . the class to which such person would find himself in a manner, compelled to refer that invisible and mysterious being would be, not as in the case of the human soul to that of fictitious entities, but that of non-entities. (*Works*, viii. 196 n.)[45]

[45] Though he had employed the term 'non-entity' in earlier writings (*Comm.* 14, 20) Bentham may also have seen it used in a religious context in the writings of Joseph Priestley who, in the absence of scriptural evidence to support the idea of a separate immaterial soul, declared: 'It is no article in his [the Christian's] faith I am oppugning [*sic*], but really an *upstart thing*, and a *nonentity*', *Disquisitions Relating to Matter and Spirit*

The thrust of what Bentham says here could hardly be plainer.[46] According to the referential theory of language a true verbal structure is one that is *like* what it describes. Reality is first 'known' and then represented by language. There is no reality beyond sense experience and therefore no reality beyond the language that describes this reality. Northrop Frye, who has brought his own unique learning to a study of the nature of language and theories of language, explains the dire consequences for the belief in a Divine Being and for religion generally of a language characterized by the descriptive function:

In a conception of language where no premises are beyond scrutiny, there is nothing to stop anyone from returning to square one and the question: Is there a God? What is significant about this is that the answer . . . can only be no, because any question beginning with 'is there' is, so to speak, already a godless question, and 'a god' is for all practical purposes no God.[47]

Not amenable to sense perception and therefore unknowable, 'God' is linguistically unfunctional, except when employed in a historic sense or when used to describe other, presumably pre-scientific, belief systems. By extension, when the method is rigidly adhered to, all questions of a spiritual or transcendental nature are unmeaning within this theory of language: for all useful purposes God, the soul, grace, and the like, are illusions. This is how matters stood for Bentham. He hedged somewhat later on in 'A Fragment on Ontology' when he spoke of God both as an 'inferential Being' and as the name of a 'real' entity. Yet even here he is clear that the notion of the act or will of God is a fiction (*Works*, viii. 208). Oddly enough, at another point Bentham acknowledged that describing 'God' in terms of a 'non-entity' involved him in a simple contradiction (*Works*, viii. 198).[48] On the other hand, in the 'Essay on Logic'—though disingenuously suggesting that his explanation might be applicable to 'Gods of different dynasties' and other

---

and *The Doctrine of Philosophical Necessity Illustrated* (1777; repr. New York, 1976), 176–7. Priestley did not apply the term to the idea of God, the essence of which, he argued, is simply unknown to us (ibid. 152).

[46] See also *A Table of the Springs of Action* (1815) where Bentham states plainly that 'a proposition which has for its subject no other than a fictitious entity has neither truth nor meaning: it is no better than a heap of nonsense' (*Deon.* 74).

[47] N. Frye, *The Great Code: The Bible and Literature* (Toronto, 1982), 16.

[48] See also *Works*, x. 523, where, at the head of a letter to the radical reformer Major Cartwright, Bentham writes: 'My Dear Friend—I am a non-entity. A non-entity is nothing, and can do nothing. Why will you persist in regarding me as an existing being?' These remarks refer to Bentham's position in 'the kingdom of reform', in which, he maintains, he is 'not worthy to set a foot'.

mythical subjects—he indicated that such entities might be better termed 'fabulous' in order to distinguish them from fictitious entities. Whether persons or things, however, it seems that 'fabulous entities' are 'supposed material objects, of which the separate existence is capable of becoming a subject of belief, and of which accordingly, the same sort of picture is capable of being drawn in and preserved in the mind, as of any really existing object' (*Works*, viii. 262).

God, for Bentham, then, as for twentieth-century positivists like A. J. Ayer, is the name of a fictitious but believed-in reality, appeals to which disguise certain other realities.[49] For Bentham, as for Ayer, metaphysical assertions more generally and religious assertions in particular, while they purport to give information about a transcendent reality, actually do no more than express the feelings and attitudes of those who utter them. This means that it is only possible to provide a sociological explanation for the prevalence of these illusions; a rational or scientific explanation is out of the question. Hence, whereas Bentham can envisage that the soul may exist as the sum of the elements of the human psyche, the sum of all psychical functions, he cannot transform the notion of God into anything reminiscent of the common usage of the term 'God'. The only conclusion available to him, therefore, is that it refers to a 'non-entity'. The mysticism that he has stripped from the idea of the soul cannot be stripped from the idea of God to leave anything remotely acceptable in its place.[50]

4. Certainty and the critical mind

That the notion of God is a source of fictions and that God is a non-entity are conclusions to which Bentham felt inevitably drawn by his ontology, and it was these principal ideas which lay at the heart of all his thoughts on religious beliefs. If you do not have good, that is to say scientific, grounds to suppose or infer the existence of God, what is there left to say about a religion which merely assumes his reality? Theology or the science of divinity, it seems, has no place in a serious discussion of ontology, save as a rich source of illustrative examples.

---

[49] For the classic statement of Logical Positivism see A. J. Ayer, *Language, Truth, and Logic* (1936; 2nd edn. London, 1946).

[50] If any stronger indication of Bentham's attitude towards these beliefs be needed, it can be found in his rejection of the need to discuss the nature of 'mysterious' entities: they may, he writes, 'without much detriment . . . to any useful art, or any other useful science, be left in the places in which they are found' (*Works*, viii. 196).

Over forty years before he wrote down his thoughts on the soul and the nature of God Bentham had intimated that the science of divinity might be a barren field of inquiry: 'Either Divinity is an important science', he wrote in the 'Subscription' manuscripts of the 1770s, 'or it is important to know that it is not: It is of importance, and of the last importance to know whether any of it is of importance, and how much and what, if any' (UC 5/18). This, then, is the extent of Bentham's ontological interest in the matter. Nor is there anything further on the subject in the extant manuscripts upon which the 'Essay on Ontology' is based (UC 102/1–79). The fruit of the ontological investigations he began in the early 1770s and continued into his final years was to show that divinity (as a science) served the entirely negative function of revealing the absurdities fostered by the superstitions which have their source in religious beliefs. Bentham's perception of the relation between human error and religion, and of the solvent provided by the methodology of physical science, was given remarkable expression in the pages of the *Chrestomathia*:

In knowledge in general, and in knowledge belonging to the physical department in particular, will the vast mass of mischief, of which perverted religion is the source, find its preventive remedy. It is from physical science alone that a man is capable of deriving that mental strength and that well-grounded confidence which renders him proof against so many groundless terrors flowing from that prolific source, which, by enabling him to see how prone to error the mind is on this ground, and thence how free such error is from all moral blame, disposes him to that forbearance towards supposed error, which men are so ready to preach and reluctant to practise. (*Works*, viii. 13)

The reference to 'perverted' religion is a sop to the more sensitive of Bentham's readers. Nevertheless, the bottom line is clear: the remedy for all the mischiefs perpetrated by religion was to be found in physical science. Though prone to error, we need not accept anything that cannot be supported by experiment and observation. For Bentham 'blind faith' could never provide an adequate substitute for hard empirical facts. Far from being the sceptic who holds that we must tolerate because we can never be certain of anything, his position in politics, philosophy, jurisprudence, and theology alike was that whatsoever is known must be based on reasoned argument from a solid scientific foundation of acceptable evidence. Hence, if Bentham was an advocate of the voice of reason, it was only in so far as this meant faith in the authority of science.

It is readily apparent, however, that Bentham's approach entails a bias against the claims of religion. The only objects which have any real existence are those which are corporeal, single, and entire of themselves; the business of knowing is simply a matter of observation, inference, and verification. In the 'Essay on Logic' he put it thus: 'Experience, Observation, Experiment, Reflection, or the results of each and all together; these are the means, these are the instruments by which knowledge—such as is within the power of man—is picked up, put together, and treasured' (*Works*, viii. 238). It is evident that on these terms the belief in a transcendent order is an illusion, and religious beliefs cannot be anything other than the consequence of our appalling ignorance of the world we inhabit, of its matter and its principles of motion.

Implicit in this argument is the potential for certainty we possess. This is made explicit by Bentham in the 'Fragments on Universal Grammar': 'Take any conceivable state of things at pleasure—either it exists or it does not exist, between its existence and non-existence there is no medium; suppose it to exist, all uncertainty is out of the question, suppose it not to exist, all uncertainty is equally out of the question' (*Works*, viii. 348–9 n.). Bentham could not accept Locke's distinction between certainty, on the one hand, and truths not founded upon certain knowledge, on the other,[51] and neither could he associate the 'experimental method' with the epistemological scepticism of Hume. In Bentham's metaphysical schema, things—perceived and verifiable —and words—properly constituted—come together in a simultaneous act of seeing and naming. Classification in this manner precludes all uncertainty. Hence, if Locke and Hume, albeit in their different ways, recognized the limitations of their epistemology, Bentham followed the inexorable logic of the premises of his own system through to its inevitable and entirely predictable conclusions.

Reason, ably supported by the techniques of the new science, was the essential means for distinguishing the believable from the incredible. The act of delegating to someone else decisions as to what is true or false Bentham likened to a 'species of idolatry'—'the worshipping of dead men's bones' (*Fall*. 26). There are no prior commitments for the critical mind; holy books stand with the books of dead philosophers—neither are to be given priority in veracity or authority over any other source of knowledge. The only commitment is

---

[51] Locke, *Essay concerning Human Understanding*, in *Works*, iii, Bk. IV, ch. 15.

to the method of inquiry itself. For the critical mind the source of religious knowledge is identical to the source of knowledge of every other kind, to which is added the proviso that all the hard data of experience must be tested and verified.[52] No claims to 'sacredness' could exempt something from the ordinary processes of historical and analytical examination. That a person should claim a 'sacred authority' was cause for even greater scepticism. The critical mind does not allow the privileged few to decide what the many may or may not hear, what is within their comprehension, or what might be offensive to them. The critical mind, it is said, is not anti any religion or any doctrines a priori, but it is anti any teaching that has to be accepted, like the revelations of Judaism, Christianity, and Islam, on the mere authority of an institution that declares them to be true. Bentham does not simply announce in *Not Paul, but Jesus* that all revelation is false, but argues that any claim of the truth of revelation must meet the same standard for acceptance as those by which we judge every other claim. This, naturally, is to 'load the dice', since Bentham's rationalism consists in his assimilation of religious beliefs to every other kind of belief, in the demand that they should be true in the sense of corresponding to an objective reality existing outside ourselves, and that they should be experientially perceptible to us.

The corollary of this methodological principle is that we are all ultimately responsible for the opinions or beliefs we hold. In the technical sense we can let the Church or State make our decisions for us, but this is only to make decisions at one remove, since we must still take responsibility for the initial decision to delegate (*Works*, viii. 321). By accepting the opinions of authority or complying with customary or habitual procedures, whether in religion or elsewhere, we do not escape responsibility for our speaking or acting in accordance with those opinions or procedures. It is incumbent upon us that we review these and if we find them unsatisfactory we must reject them; uncritical acceptance of an opinion is our own responsibility and, if it be false, is just as blameworthy as if we adopted it merely to serve some ulterior purpose. Bentham, of course, thought the outcome of such an examination to be a foregone conclusion. He knew very well that freedom of inquiry in religious matters tended to undermine the

---

[52] For an examination of the 'critical' tradition in theological thought see D. Howlett, *The Critical Way in Religion: Testing and Questing* (New York, 1980). In Howlett's book Hume and the French *philosophes* are considered significant contributors to the critical tradition as it developed in the 18th cent., but Bentham is omitted.

foundations of belief, and argued (*c.*1795) that the more absurd the religion the sooner its adherents 'are obliged to come to the principle of non-examination and explicit faith'. 'But if once they examine', he cautioned, 'all is over' (UC 99/121). The same liberty of discussion which nourished the early Church and fuelled the Reformation 'would now infallibly prove mortal to it in its maturity' (UC 87/25, 58).[53]

Bentham was equally certain of the consequences if his contemporaries ignored reason and continued to place their trust in the institutions and doctrines of religion. If science was the antithesis of religion it could also be said that religion was the foe of science—it has distinguished itself in history by opposing the growth of knowledge. Bentham points to several examples in the early manuscripts: the 'punishment of Gassendi for maintaining the true system'; 'Aristotle's philosophy forbidden by parliament of Paris on pain of death'; and 'Locke expelled from Oxford, and his philosophy always discountenanced' (UC 6/35). And again, this time in the *Analysis*, he writes of the 'immaterial Autocrat' and his 'sacerdotal class' of priests who have always had 'a deadly interest against the advance of knowledge' (*An.* 124). A jotting from Bentham's 'Commonplace Book' of the years 1781–5 underscores this theme and the implicit connection between belief in religious doctrines and subservience to the authority of the Church:

> When a man has once got into the way of making Revelation serve him instead of Reason, and the opinions which men in authority hold instead of Revelation, and the opinions which men in authority avow instead of what they hold, he is prepared for the embracement of every absurd and mischievous error, and for the rejection of every salutary truth. (*Works*, x. 144)

The result of this psychological process is to undermine the ability of people to reason for themselves and to improve their stock of happiness. With their minds 'enfeebled', the only support they can find for such a system is 'blind credulity', and they will resist all objections and defend that system not because it is true, but simply because they have resolved to defend it (*Works*, x. 144). The patent fact of human fallibility was unambiguously stated by Hume, who declared with seeming finality that there is nothing of which we can really be sure. Bentham would not go as far as this, but in religion he sought to explode once and for all the myth of authority which he had first hounded in his early writings on jurisprudence. Because we are fallible

---

[53] The last 2 quotations are taken from Long, *Bentham on Liberty*, p. 138.

and prone to errors how can we accept that any one person or group of persons can ever be right by virtue of their office? And, if we do place our trust in such persons, how can we be sure that we are not being deceived by them? It is such questions as these which make sense of Bentham's boundless passion for criticism. With Voltaire and Hume, Bentham was for J. S. Mill 'the great questioner of things established, . . . the great *subversive*, . . . the great *critical* thinker of his age and country'. Great, Mill explained, because under his influence 'the yoke of authority has been broken, and innumerable opinions, formerly received on tradition as incontestable, are put upon their defense and required to give an account of themselves.'[54] It is, of course, in the fields of ethics and legislation that Bentham's approach to social analysis has had its most impact, and it is to this that we must now turn.

[54] Mill, 'Bentham', in *Collected Works*, x. 78–9.

2

Ethics and the Science of Legislation

> Weak reasoners in morals, by a kind of instinct, take shelter
> behind the altar. Yet not even this shall save [them]. Mankind is
> too deeply interested in the display of those truths which [they]
> would keep concealed . . ., to make it pardonable to desist from
> the pursuit. The Sanctuary is in its own nature common ground,
> unless where fenced about by Intolerance which it can never be
> but by the help of Usurpation . . . No foreign arguments are
> needed to set against [their] doctrines: to expound is to expose
> them: to *confront* them is *to confute*.
>
> 'Preparatory Principles', headed 'Divine Law', UC 69/107

BENTHAM'S religious radicalism was not confined to the pages of
unread manuscripts for over forty years, only to surface as an ingredient
in the radical political attack of the second decade of the nineteenth
century. A careful reading of the early celebrated writings on ethics
and legislation (notably the *Introduction*, i.e. *IPML*) reveals in no uncertain terms the nature of Bentham's secularizing intentions. The
Introduction, it should be said, was published long before his association
with Bowring began in 1820; hence it was impossible for the latter to
expunge its offending statements (a tactic employed with disastrous
results in Bowring's 1834 edited version of the *Deontology*).[1] Bentham's
animosity toward fundamental articles of Christian belief was clearly
indicated here and in other writings of the period. Indeed, the critique
of religion he supplied in the early works on ethics and legislation was
typically of a radical nature and there is no question that he was there
mapping out an entirely secular science of society.

Bentham set out to establish that as an agent of moral welfare
religion is inadequate, not to say pernicious, and that we should look to
legislation to replace it as the principal means of harmonizing interests
in society in order to produce the greatest happiness. In the process he
consciously contrasted his rational legislative version of the utilitarian
doctrine with the religious brand of utilitarian thought that dominated
English ethics at that time. It will assist our understanding of the

---

[1] See the editorial introduction to *Deon.*, p. xxxii.

relationship between religion, ethics, and legislation in Bentham's thought, therefore, if we know precisely what it was that he rejected. The intellectual context of his thought is incomplete if we fail to take notice of the writings of the eighteenth century 'theological' exponents of utility,[2] for the moral theory to which they gave voice was integral to the social and political fabric of the age against which secularists, like Bentham, rebelled.

1. The religious tradition of utilitarian ethics

Bentham's attentions were focused on religious affairs primarily in two periods or phases of his life—from 1773 to 1782, and from 1809 to 1823. In the early period he wrote *A Comment on the Commentaries* (largely completed 1774–5, with additions 1776–7, but not published until 1928),[3] *A Fragment on Government* (1776), and the *Introduction* (printed 1780, published 1789).[4] In these works and in other manuscripts which date from this time, especially those headed 'Crit[ical] Jur[isprudence] Crim[inal]'—part of the proposed *magnum opus*—Bentham struggled to confine his thoughts on religion to a critical, but generally restrained (when compared with the later works) appraisal of the traditional relationships between religion, ethics, and legislation. For the most part religion is here viewed apart from ecclesiastical establishments, though there is some trace of the anticlericalism which pervades the later religious publications. With the notable exception of

---

[2] The term 'theological utilitarianism' was coined by W. H. Lecky and later used by Ernest Albee to describe the moral thought of those 18th-cent. moralists who, while giving prominence to the principle of utility as the standard for assessing the worth of an action, found in the Christian religion the essential motive to virtue. Neither Lecky nor Albee, however, saw any need to present these moralists as exponents of a distinctive doctrine. They appear to have assumed that before Bentham utilitarianism as a school of thought in England was a loose and somewhat diffuse one, encompassing writers of different temperaments and purposes. Theological utilitarianism, though significant, represented merely a transitory stage prior to the final, secularized, maturity of utilitarian moral theory. See W. E. H. Lecky, *History of European Morals from Augustine to Charlemagne*, 2 vols. (London, 1869); E. Albee, *A History of English Utilitarianism* (London, 1901); and for a discussion see my 'John Brown and the Theological Tradition of Utilitarian Ethics', *History of Political Thought*, 4:3 (1983), 523–50.

[3] J. Bentham, *A Comment on the Commentaries*, ed. C. W. Everett (1928; repr. Darmstadt, 1976).

[4] *LG* also belongs to this early period: a continuation of *IPML* substantially completed by 1782, the manuscripts were discovered at University College Library by C. W. Everett in 1939 and subsequently edited and published by him as *The Limits of Jurisprudence Defined* (New York, 1945).

his preface to *Le Taureau blanc* and the unpublished fragments on subscription, Bentham at this time refrained from overt criticism of the Established Church. Even so, his basic denial of the truth of religion is evident from the beginning, and it is this which lies at the heart of his religious radicalism.

The second and later phase is the period in which Bentham's views on the Church and on the nature of religion generally reached a final form and were published at great, not to say excruciating, length. In these works Bentham launched a massive strike at all the various manifestations of Church influence, both spiritual and temporal. No longer content to confine himself to the particular theoretical deficiencies of religion as an agency of moral welfare, his critique now encompassed Church institutions and practices as well as fundamental Christian beliefs. The test of utility was applied to both and the results were overwhelmingly negative.

What this pattern of development in Bentham's thoughts on religion indicates is the striking transformation that 'utilitarianism' as a social philosophy underwent in his hands. For it has rarely been acknowledged that, in the age before he wrote, the doctrine of utility was nurtured at the breast of the same Church that he came so much to revile.

A few years before Bentham published his now famous *Introduction* another advocate of utility had made a reputation in the field of ethics in England. In 1785 the Revd William Paley (1743–1805) published his *Principles of Moral and Political Philosophy*.[5] His account of a utilitarian God promoting the happiness of his basically self-interested human creatures was similar to that expounded by his near contemporary and admirer Edmund Law, Bishop of Carlisle (1703–87); had been set out a generation before by the Revd John Brown (1715–66) and Abraham Tucker (1705–74); and, a generation before these, though in much less detail, by the Revd John Gay (1699–1745), while a little earlier than Gay one can find similar ideas set out in unsystematic form in the work of George Berkeley, Bishop of Cloyne (1685–1753).[6] *Contra* Hume, throughout the century these Church

    [5] *IPML* had been completed and printed as early as 1780 but not published until 1789. George Wilson wrote to Bentham (24 Sept. 1786) during his sojourn in Russia informing him of Paley's success, in reply to which (19–30 Dec. 1786) Bentham affected indifference (*Corr.* iii. 490–1 and 513–14).

    [6] G. Berkeley, 'Passive Obedience' (1712) and 'An Essay towards preventing the ruin of Great Britain' (1721), in *The Works of George Berkeley Bishop of Cloyne*, ed. A. A. Luce and T. E. Jessop, 9 vols. (London, 1948–57), vi; J. Gay, 'Preliminary Dissertation concerning the Fundamental Principle of Virtue or Morality', prefixed to W. King, *Essay*

moralists expounded a doctrine of utility which depended as much on orthodox Christian teaching as Bentham was to depend on empiricism, reason, and an abhorrence for traditional metaphysics. The religious tenets of their ethics demanded belief in a benevolent God whose will is to be obeyed, in the immortal nature of the soul, and in a future day of reckoning when virtue will be rewarded and evil punished. But the persuasive power of the theory had its source not in these beliefs alone, but in their succinct combination with a hedonistic psychology as a prerequisite to understanding and directing human nature. Preaching spiritual perfection and happiness as the indispensible criteria of the good life, both in this world and in the world to come, the principle of utility nestled comfortably in the proselytizing arms of the Church, and added substance to the claim that for the sake of the well-being of the community the privileged position of the clergy as the guardian of the nation's morals should be protected by the state.

All these religious moralists employed the utilitarian language of happiness and its component parts. From Locke they learnt that it is considerations of pleasure and pain that supply individuals with the impulse to action, and to this they added that the criterion of virtue is the standard of universal happiness.[7] But what specifically distinguishes them is the endeavour to reintroduce, against the current trend, religion into ethics. The problem they addressed was to what extent the obligation to pursue personal happiness could in practical terms influence individuals to pursue the great end of virtue, the maximization of the happiness of all. The solution lay not in postulating a 'moral sense', in unsupported reason, or in the mere observance of human laws, but in the adherence to the will of God and in the Christian belief that at some time after death he will dispense to each his just deserts.[8]

---

on the Origin of Evil (London, 1732); [A. Tucker], *The Light of Nature Pursued* by 'Edward Search', 7 vols. (London, 1768–78); J. Brown, *Essays on the Characteristics of the Earl of Shaftesbury* (1751; 3rd edn. London, 1752); E. Law, 'On Morality and Religion' and 'The Nature of Obligation of Man, as a sensible and rational Being', in W. King, *Essay on the Origin of Evil*, trans. E. Law (1732; 5th edn. London, 1781).

[7] See A. P. Brogan, 'John Locke and Utilitarianism', *Ethics*, 69:2 (1959), where he argues that Locke formulated the basic theses of 18th-cent. utilitarianism. Brogan, however, seems to assume that utilitarian ethics in the century after Locke was all of a kind, and that John Gay and others simply 'took Locke's theses and organized them into a systematic presentation'.

[8] It is true that the rudiments of a similar view of the motivation supplied by the afterlife are to be found in Locke, but it is hardly developed by him. See *Essay concerning Human Understanding*, in *Works*, ii, Bk. II, ch. 21, secs. 38, 70. For Locke, Christian ethics are 'natural': the reason for doing what Christ said is not simply that Christ had said it, but that in conforming to his will one promotes one's own happiness, and to this

John Brown (who was to earn high praise from no less than J. S. Mill for the ability with which he set out the doctrine of utility),[9] reasoned that legislation was inadequate to the task of motivating individuals to practise virtue, that is, to the pursuit of general happiness. He did not say that laws were entirely ineffectual, but pointed out their limitations as the foundation for a progressive system of ethics. In the *Essays on the Characteristics of the Earl of Shaftesbury* (1751) Brown recognized that laws endeavour 'by the infliction of Punishment on Offenders, to establish the general happiness of Society, by making the *acknowledged Interest* of every *Individual* to coincide and unite with the *public* Welfare'.[10] Nevertheless, laws, by their very nature, are fundamentally limited in what they can effect in the way of motivation. They can only govern external actions, invariably leaving inner thoughts untouched. As the impetus for benevolence must come from within, so virtue cannot depend on laws alone; a 'natural' or 'internal' motive is required, and this only religion can supply. Religion, the law of God, and not human law, therefore, is the chief and essential support of morality; it supplies universally the ethical imperative to be good which legislation provides imperfectly. People can only be uniformly convinced of their duty to pursue universal happiness by 'the lively and active Belief of an all-seeing and all-powerful God, who will hereafter make them happy or miserable, according as they designedly promote or violate the Happiness of their Fellow Creatures'.[11] The harmony between the private interests of the individual and those of the public at large is here firmly based on the necessity that each person, according to the teachings of Christ, take into account in all their thoughts and deeds their own eternal happiness. As William Paley was to remark:

A man who is in earnest in his endeavours after the happiness of a future state, has in this respect, an advantage over all the world: for, he has constantly before his eyes an object of supreme importance, productive of perpetual

---

end all men are impelled by their natural self-love. Even so, it is a fact of some interest that Locke ultimately failed to live up to the promise of his maxim that 'reason must be our last judge in everything' (ibid., Bk. IV, ch. 19, sec. 14) and instead recommended a morality based on faith and revelation.

[9] 'We never saw an abler defence of utility than in a book written in refutation of Shaftesbury, and now little read—Brown's "Essays on the Characteristics"' (Mill, 'Bentham', in *Collected Works*, x. 86–7).

[10] Brown, *Essays on the Characteristics*, p. 209.

[11] Ibid. 210.

engagement and activity, and of which the pursuit (which can be said of no pursuit besides) lasts him to his life's end.[12]

The communal rewards of this doctrine are manifest. Each individual is responsible not only for his own spiritual well-being, but (towards this end) for the temporal well-being of everyone else with whom he has an association. To 'be good' means that we actively pursue the happiness of others whenever it is within our power, for only by so doing can we secure our own happiness in the most encompassing sense of this term—eternal happiness.

To divorce morality from religion, therefore, was a sophistication (if that it be) which it did not occur to the religious utilitarians to entertain. On the contrary, the threats posed to religion by, on the one hand, the theological divisions of the day, and on the other, the apparent indifference of the laity to (and even disdain for) its established norms and practices, made the defence of Christian beliefs of paramount interest to moralists, like Brown and Paley, who found in religion the means by which the desired end of morality could be achieved. Mounting public enthusiasm for a more worldly approach to ethics not only lent a sense of urgency to this defence, but also required that it take a practical as well as a theoretical form.

When Ernest Albee came to trace the history of utilitarianism at the beginning of the twentieth century he represented its secular and theological exponents as each in turn contributing to the stockpile of utilitarian thought as it expanded and was handed down from one generation of moralists to the next. If John Gay influenced Brown and Paley, so this argument goes, then indirectly he also influenced Bentham.[13] But did Gay really have an influence on Bentham? Gay's 'Dissertation' is indeed a seminal work and shares certain features with Bentham's *Introduction*. We should not, however, read too much into this. For example, it suits Albee's argument to draw our attention to the similarity between the list of sanctions that each set out—physical (or natural), moral (or virtuous), political (or civil), and religious[14]— but the supposed connection may well be spurious since it is likely that both were borrowing from Locke.[15] A more telling point of comparison

---

[12] W. Paley, *Principles of Moral and Political Philosophy*, Bk. I, ch. 6, in *The Complete Works of William Paley*, 4 vols. (London, 1825), i. 34.

[13] See Albee, *A History of English Utilitarianism*, ch. 9.

[14] See ibid. 182; L. A. Selby-Bigge (ed.), *British Moralists: Being Selections from Writers Principally of the Eighteenth Century*, 2 vols. (Oxford, 1897), ii, sec. 863; *IPML* 34.

[15] Locke, *Essay concerning Human Understanding*, in *Works*, ii, Bk. II, ch. 28, sec. 7.

(though one less supportive of Albee's thesis) centres upon the degree of importance each attributed to the authority or will of God. As we have seen, as a source of pleasures and pains Bentham thought this a 'fiction'. Nowhere did he acknowledge any necessity for the intercession of religion in the practical moral life. 'The principle of utility', he wrote, 'neither requires nor admits of any other regulator than itself' (*IPML* 33).[16] Gay, on the other hand, reduced all forms of obligation to the religious—'the will of God is the immediate criterion of Virtue, and the happiness of mankind the criterion of the will of God'.[17] The language of happiness is common to both, but the spiritual part of human nature, fundamental to the thought of the religious exponents of utility, is not considered a factor by Bentham.

Indeed, it was principally as a consequence of the efforts of Bentham that utility came to be identified with a social philosophy opposed to the teachings of Christianity. A feature of this development, closely connected in the mind of Bentham with the application of the methods of natural science to social analysis, is the substitution of legislation for religion as the paramount agency for resolving conflict between the personal interests of private individuals and the general needs of society. This feature is central to my analysis of the relationship between religion, ethics, and legislation in utilitarian thought.

Bentham described the difference between the object of his own ethical system and that of the 'religionists' in his Commonplace Book of the years 1781–5: 'The laws of perfection derived from religion, have more for their object the goodness of the man who observes them, than that of the society in which they are observed. Civil laws on the contrary have more for their object the moral goodness of men in general than that of individuals' (*Works*, x. 143). There is a curious tension here between Bentham's nominalism with its regard for discrete entities and the emphasis he places on the abstract and collective, but the shift in focus indicated clearly distinguishes the central aim of his work from that of his Christian precursors. Moreover, it heralded the approaching demise of the religious version of the doctrine of utility as

---

The 3 sanctions set out by Bentham in *FG* correspond precisely to those of Locke (both omit the physical; added by Bentham in *IPML*).

[16] In the earlier *Comm.* Bentham put it thus: 'The principle of utility once adopted as the governing principle, admits of no rival, admits not even of an associate' (*Comm.* 27). Another variation occurs in the marginals for the *Table of the Spring of Action*: 'Principle of Utility allows no rival. Whatever is not under is opposite to it' (*Deon.* 31).

[17] Selby-Bigge, *British Moralists*, ii, sec. 864.

the basis of a persuasive theory of morals.[18] For in the course of the attempt to prove the worth to society of a rational system of jurisprudence, founded on empiricism and nominalist logic, Bentham took great pains to discredit religion as a necessary motivational factor in effecting the occurrence of actions conducive to general happiness. In later life he articulated the essence of this intellectual appraisal of the role of religion in society thus: 'How did I improve and fortify my mind? I got hold of the greatest happiness principle: I asked myself how this or that institution contributed to the greatest happiness— *Did* it contribute?—If not, what institution *would* contribute to it?' (*Works*, x. 581). The probing of the deficiencies of religion as an agency of social welfare in the work on ethics and legislation was eventually to be complemented by the explicit political attack on the Church in the later works, but the connection between the interests of society and the legislative means to advancing these was present and prevalent from the first.[19]

2. Secular influences

Bentham's disdain for religion and emphasis on legislation had its source not only in his scientific method but also in two distinct areas of his early life: his personal experiences with religion and the influence of writers to whose thought he found himself most receptive. As noted above, Mary Mack has claimed that Bentham's early brushes with religion at Oxford lay at the bottom of his utilitarianism, and Bentham himself late in life lent this view some credence (*CE*, pp. xiii–xxvii). As an explanatory factor, however, it is limited. While it indicates his early

[18] It does not alter this assessment that John Austin set out a version of the religious doctrine of utility in the lectures he gave at UCL, published under the title *The Province of Jurisprudence Determined* (1832; London, 1971). It was Bentham's secular version of the doctrine that came to dominate in 19th-cent. England.

[19] Yet it was well into the 19th-cent. before the radical nature of Bentham's utilitarianism was appreciated outside the band of philosophical radicals that gathered about him. As J. B. Schneewind has so rightly said, it was only from the middle of the 1830s that Paley was no longer considered the central figure in philosophical discussions of utilitarianism, *Sidgwick's Ethics and Victorian Moral Philosophy* (Oxford, 1977), 151. It should also be noted that though Dr Southwood Smith, W. J. Fox, and John Bowring were closely associated in practical affairs with Bentham, other Unitarian philosophers saw Paley as the fountain-head of the utilitarian doctrine. For instance Bentham is mentioned only in passing by T. Belsham in *Elements of Philosophy of the Human Mind and of Moral Philosophy* (London, 1801); and by W. Jevons in *Systematic Morality*, 2 vols. (London, 1827).

disaffection with religion, it does not sufficiently explain the peculiar scientific nature of his utilitarianism with its all-pervasive emphasis on the role of legislation. Attention is better directed to the intellectual influences and exemplars to which he was exposed as a youth, for it was these who gave form and direction to his immature thoughts and grievances.

Throughout his life Bentham claimed that in developing the key practical ideas of his moral and legal philosophy he was indebted above all others to Helvétius and Beccaria—that is, to theorists sympathetic to utility but of a very different cast of mind from the religious exponents of the doctrine. In the previous chapter I tried to show that it was in the work of these continental *philosophes*, among others, that he found principles of natural science employed as the foundation of social philosophy. Here I am more particularly concerned with the priority they gave to legislation as the principal means to achieving social felicity at the expense of the claims of theology. Before discussing the nature of these influences on the moral and legal thought of the young Bentham, however, we should perhaps say something of David Hume, whose major works Bentham had read and who was an undeniable presence in the history of secular thought during this period.[20] Bentham could not help but note Hume's deliberate and concerted efforts to introduce the 'experimental method' into moral reasoning. None the less, there is an understandable ambivalence in his references to Hume's moral thought which, since Hume is frequently cited as of integral significance in the development of eighteenth-century utilitarian thought, deserve our attention.

It was in Hume's *Treatise*—which declared that all social inquiry should be based on the 'experimental Method of Reasoning'—that Bentham tells us he found virtue equated with utility:

That the foundations of all *virtue* are laid in *utility*, is there demonstrated, after a few exceptions made, with the strongest force of evidence: . . .

For my own part, I well remember, no sooner had I read that part of the work which touches on this subject, than I felt as if scales had fallen from my eyes. I then, for the first time, learnt to call the cause of the people the cause of Virtue. (*FG* 440 n.).[21]

----

[20] For the influence of Hume, Helvétius, and Beccaria on Bentham see Mack, *Jeremy Bentham*, ch. 3; N. Rosenblum, *Bentham's Theory of the Modern State* (Cambridge, Mass., 1978), ch. 2; H. L. A. Hart, 'Bentham and Beccaria', in *Essays on Bentham: Studies on Jurisprudence and Political Theory* (Oxford, 1982); Harrison, *Bentham*, esp. ch. 5.

[21] It is likely that Bentham was mistaken and that he had in mind Hume's *Enquiry Concerning the Principles of Morals* (1751), in *Enquiries concerning Human Understanding*

Bentham goes on to say that he could not see any more than Helvétius the reason for Hume's exceptions to this rule, but this is understandable when Bentham's dogmatic utilitarianism is compared with the more sensitive handling of the logic of moral judgement set out by Hume. The 'exceptions' are indicative of Hume's commitment to a 'moral sense' account of obligations. Later on Bentham's disappointment with Hume became explicit. 'Added Observations' on the *Table of the Springs of Action* include the following remarks:

611. Of ERROR, inconsistency is a natural accompaniment—not so of TRUTH.
612. Hume acknowledges the dominion of utility, but so he does of the moral sense: . . .
614. Here then is a compromise of incompatible contradictions—necessary result inconsistency (*Deon.* 57).

The 'inconsistency' consists in the exempting of some cases from the governance of utility—some actions can be assumed to be self-interested, but not all; social analysis is based on the calculation of consequences, but this is not always the case. Such disregard for uniformity in first principles seemed guaranteed to undermine the effort to place ethics upon a scientific footing. On another occasion, reflecting on his intellectual influences in the 'Article on Utilitarianism', Bentham states that the idea attached to utility by Hume was 'altogether vague' and consequently of little practical use (*Deon.* 290).[22] Fully cognizant of the differences between his own speculations in the realm of morals and those of the Scotsman, in later life Bentham even went so far as to state that he gained little from his reading of Hume. Having forgotten, it seems, his generous if qualified praise of the *Treatise* in *A Fragment on Government*, in the *Chrestomathia* he was only prepared to single out the lesson taught by Hume's distinction between 'is' and 'ought' (*Works*, viii. 128 n.). As important a discovery as this was to the young Bentham in his subsequent career as critic and inventor, it is difficult to believe that Hume's influence can be reduced

and concerning the Principles of Morals, ed. L. A. Selby-Bigge (3rd edn. rev. P. H. Hidditch, 1748, 1751; Oxford, 1975), sec. 5, 'Why utility pleases'.

[22] There is little to substantiate and, if this were the place, much to say against the claim of John Plamenatz that Hume 'is rightly regarded as the founder of utilitarianism'. Plamenatz appears to base this on the fact that Hume provided his successors with the concept of 'utility'. Hume's employment of the term and his tendency to equate it with 'virtue' are not in question, but his connection with the 'moral sense' school of moral thought is no less important. With this in mind Plamenatz's statement that Hume 'is a utilitarian but . . . not a complete one' does not do justice to the richness of Hume's ethics; J. Plamenatz, *The English Utilitarians* (Oxford, 1958), 22, 28.

to this. Even if only in terms of a general awareness of Hume's reputation as a critic of things established and as an unbeliever—and this is the very least one can surmise since Bentham had read the *Treatise* and, by his own admission, profited from it—we can assume an influence greater than Bentham was willing to allow in later life.

It was disingenuous of Hume to suggest that his essay 'On Miracles' alone was, of all his writings, offensive to Christians.[23] Not only had he produced other writings critical of Christianity, but the omission of the essays 'Of Suicide' and 'Of the Immortality of the Soul' (under threat of a law suit) from the *Dissertations* (1757) is an indication that he knew that he had.[24] Equally likely to give the impression that Hume was an unbeliever are such writings as the *Natural History of Religion* (1757), the essays 'Of Superstition' and 'Of Enthusiasm', the posthumously published *Dialogues concerning Natural Religion* (1779), those parts of the *Enquiries* where religion is indicated as the corrupter of true philosophy, and occasional passages in *The History of England* (1754–62), at least parts of which Bentham had read.[25] It is possible that Hume was not an atheist in the modern sense (that is, one who is certain that God does not exist), but he openly if cautiously undertook to show that belief in the existence of God could not be based on empirical grounds. He was an equally open and scathing critic of organized religion, entirely happy to trace the origins of religion to natural causes, to reduce the allegedly supernatural to the natural.

Admittedly, there is no evidence that Bentham had absorbed Hume's far-reaching philosophical critique of the basic tenets of Christianity contained in these various works. But, at the same time, the secular direction of Hume's thought could not be missed by so perceptive a mind as the young Bentham possessed—he could not help, for example, but be impressed that in the *Treatise* Hume ignored God and religion altogether. The first assumption of Hume's science of politics is that human nature is uniform; everyone is governed in the public realm, whether acting alone or in combination, by self-interest. It is, he claimed, 'a just *political* maxim, *that every man must be supposed a*

---

[23] Hume to Hugh Blair (1761), *The Letters of David Hume*, ed. J. Y. T. Greig, 2 vols. (Oxford, 1932), i. 351.

[24] E. C. Mossner, *The Life of David Hume* (Edinburgh, 1954), 319–35.

[25] For these references and an analysis of Hume's religious scepticism in the *Enquiry concerning Human Understanding* I am indebted to D. F. Norton, *David Hume: Commonsense Moralist, Sceptical Metaphysician* (Princeton, 1982), 279–90.

knave'.[26] Given this assumption of motivation, it is the task of the legislator to draw up plans to balance the interests that are advanced among the nation's citizens for the general good of the community. This being the case the nation's capacity to survive in an orderly and virtuous condition depends upon its institutions. Just as the 'tumultuous governments' of classical Athens were due to 'defects in the original constitution', so the stability of modern Venice is firmly grounded on the orderly form of its government.[27] Constitutions, government institutions, and legislation are for Hume the primary determining factors of the moral and political welfare of the State. It is these structural arrangements which give it order and upon which the comfort and well-being of its citizens depend. Religion, therefore, will only be of incidental interest for the inquirer anxious to provide a scientific study of political life. What the legislator will learn from this science is that, on the basis that there exists a certain regularity between causes and effects, 'wise regulations in any commonwealth, are the most valuable legacy that can be left to future ages'.[28]

The 'science of man', then, for Hume underlay all moral reasoning. Theology was no longer to be enlisted to explain natural phenomena where common sense could supply cogent explanations based on other principles, and the criterion for assessing the moral worth of actions was to be not God's will but the happiness of people and usefulness to the community. Critical judgement based on observation and experience was to be substituted for blind faith and superstitious fancies. The rewards and punishments of futurity play no part in Hume's scheme of ethics; social morality is utilitarian and secular.

Helvétius wrote in the same spirit of secularized positivism. In his Commonplace Book of the 1770s Bentham noted that 'From Locke [the law] must receive the ruling principles of its form—from Helvétius of its matter' (*Works*, x. 71), and there are many other references to Helvétius in the manuscript material of this period. After reading Helvétius's *De l'esprit* (1758) in 1769 Bentham was inspired to ask himself 'Have I a *genius* for anything?' and more specifically, since Helvétius had pointed to legislation as the most important of earthly pursuits, 'have I indeed a genius for legislation?'. To which he replied

---

[26] D. Hume, 'Of the Independency of Parliament', in *Essays Literary, Moral, and Political* (London, n.d. [1870?]), 29.

[27] Hume, 'That Politics may be reduced to a Science', ibid. 19. See also Hume, *An Enquiry concerning Human Understanding* (1748), in *Enquiries*, sec. 8, pt. 1, p. 90.

[28] Hume, 'That Politics may be reduced to a Science', in *Essays Literary, Moral, and Political*, p. 19. See also the essay 'Of National Characters' in the same volume.

'fearfully and tremblingly—Yes?!' (*Works*, x. 27).[29] There can be no doubt that the influence of *De l'esprit* upon Bentham was considerable. If he vacillated in the case of Hume, his praise for *De l'esprit* was rarely qualified. In an 'Article on Utilitarianism', written in later life, he maintained the same enthusiasm he had for the work sixty years before:

Important is the service for which morals and legislation stand indebted to this work: . . . The light it spreads, on the field of this branch of art and science, is to that steady light which would be diffused over it by a regular institute or say didactic treatise, like what the meridian sun sheds over a place when bursting forth one moment from behind a cloud it hides itself the next moment behind another, is to that comparatively pale but regular and steady system of illumination afforded to a street by two constantly lighted rows of lamps. (*Deon.* 325)

It was not merely for the idea of the relationship between genius and legislation that Bentham was grateful to Helvétius. In a manner infinitely more determinate than that shown by Hume, Helvétius gave form to the project of maximizing public utility. In *De l'esprit*, announced Bentham, 'a commencement was made of the application of the principle of utility to practical uses' (*Deon.* 290). Helvétius's contribution in this respect was twofold. First, he established the connection 'between the idea attached to the word "happiness", and the ideas respectively attached to the words "pleasure" and "pain" . . . [A]ttached to the words "utility" and "principle of utility" were now ideas in abundance, ideas which could not be but continually present and familiar to the most inattentive, unobservant and scantily-instructed minds' (*Deon.* 290). Secondly, he suggested the implicit relationship that *ought* to exist between the principle of utility and legislation. Near the beginning of *De l'esprit* Helvétius announced that it was upon the Newtonian principle of physical motion that he sought to found moral science: 'If the physical universe be subject to the laws of motion, the moral universe is equally so to those of interest.' Interest is 'the mighty magician' of action and a principle 'so agreeable to experience' that it is, therefore, 'the only and universal estimator of the merit of human actions'.[30] Just as gravitation is the great causal principle which explains

---

[29]　There are several sections of *De l'esprit* devoted to a discussion of 'genius', by which Helvétius meant the ability of men to discover or invent objects of importance to the well-being of mankind. In this respect Helvétius mentions the effect on human progress of the work of a wide variety of literary and philosophical figures including, naturally, Newton and Locke. For Helvétius's discussion of 'genius' see esp. *De l'esprit*, Essay III, ch. 1.

[30]　Ibid., Essay II, ch. 2, pp. 42–3.

the behaviour of the heavenly bodies, so interest or personal happiness is the causal principle which explains human behaviour. Utility, therefore, understood as general happiness, 'ought to inspire the legislator with the resolution to force the people to submit to his laws; to this principle, in short, he ought to sacrifice all his sentiments, and even those of humanity itself'.[31] The combination of these two features of Helvétius's thought gave Bentham the rough outline of his legislative project to fashion a society based on utilitarian principles. Helvétius had written that 'morality is evidently no more than a frivolous science, unless blended with policy and legislation . . . .; if philosophers would be of use to the world, they should survey objects from the same point of view as the legislator.'[32] It was from this that Bentham took his lead: utility can only be maximized by designing a system in which each person by following his own interest will contribute to the general happiness. It is the task of the legislator so to arrange matters, employing coercion where necessary, so that self-interest and general interest coincide. As Helvétius put it: 'All the art therefore of the legislator consists in forcing [us] by self-love to be always just to each other.'[33]

Bentham was always loud in his praise of Helvétius's refusal to compromise his scientific principles by making concessions to theology. 'What Bacon was to the physical world, Helvétius was to the moral', is a typical pronouncement from the enthusiastic Bentham (UC 32/158). But if Bacon was a philosopher dedicated to understanding the intricacies of a world divinely ordered by the hand of God, Helvétius was just as keen to keep theological considerations out of the matter. He not only dispensed with religion but condemned it bitterly. Even in the face of Jesuitical persecution, he was virulently critical of the role hitherto played by religion in moral life.[34] Those 'of more piety than knowledge', he declared in the later *De l'homme* (1777), who argue that the virtue of a nation, its humanity, and refinement of manners depend on the purity of its religious worship are 'hypocrites', and sadly 'the common part of mankind' have believed them 'without examination'. All experience and history show that the prosperity and virtue of a nation depends on the excellence of its legislation and little else. Religion is not merely ineffectual in the pursuit of happiness, it is an

---

[31] Ibid., ch. 6, p. 63. [32] Ibid., ch. 15, pp. 124–5.
[33] Ibid., ch. 24, p. 185.
[34] That the Jesuits posed a formidable personal threat to Helvétius after the publication of *De l'esprit* in 1758 is part of the story of D. W. Smith's *Helvétius: A Study in Persecution* (Oxford, 1965).

obstacle to it. 'What does the history of religions teach us? That they have every where lighted up the torch of intolerance, strewed the plains with carcasses, embued the fields with blood, burned cities, and laid waste empires; but they have never made men better.' The 'true doctors of morality' are not the priests but the magistrates, since only 'sagacious laws' can produce 'universal felicity'.[35]

If in Helvétius Bentham found the essential connections between the idea of happiness and the ideas of pleasure and pain and between these and the role of legislation, to Cesare Beccaria he gave the laurel for inspiring him to introduce 'the precision and clearness and incontestableness of mathematical calculation' into the field of jurisprudence (*Works*, iii. 286). This was Beccaria's unique addition to the project initiated by Helvétius. With the idea that it was possible for legislators to calculate the precise amounts of punishment required to deter persons from criminal acts, in *Dei delitti e delle pene* (1764) Beccaria wrote that 'If geometry were applicable to the infinite and obscure combinations of human actions, there ought to be a corresponding scale of punishments, decending from the greatest to the least.'[36] By thus measuring utility, with 'geometrical precision', appropriate punishments could be devised in order to effect deterrence. The end in view is to harmonize self-interest with social well-being by constructing a system of laws and punishments 'upon the foundation of self-love', making 'the general interest . . . the result of the interests of each'.[37]

In the pantheon of the young Bentham's exemplars Beccaria stands as 'the father of *Censorial Jurisprudence*' (*FG* 403), a philosopher not afraid to tackle the established legal systems of the day. Bentham was later moved to address the following eulogy to the Italian *philosophe*: 'Oh, my master, the first evangelist of Reason . . . you who have made so many useful excursions into the path of utility, what is there left for us to do?—Never to turn aside from that path.'[38] Concerned in the first place to offer a critical challenge to the legal systems of the age, but perhaps mindful too of the persecution that was the reward of

[35] C. A. Helvétius, *A Treatise on Man: His Intellectual Faculties and his Education* [*De l'homme*, 1777], trans. W. Hooper, 2 vols. (London, 1810), i. 144, 148, 196.

[36] C. Beccaria, *An Essay on Crimes and Punishments* [*Dei delitti e delle pene*, 1764; first Eng. trans. 1767], trans. H. Paolucci (Indianapolis, 1975), ch. 3, p. 64.

[37] Ibid. 10, 59.

[38] UC 32, a fragment headed 'Introduction, Principes Projet Matiere', (*c.*1785–90), trans. from Bentham's French by Halévy, *The Growth of Philosophic Radicalism*, p. 21. The reference to the evangelical nature of Beccaria's work is consistent with Bentham's habit of borrowing the terminology of religion to dramatize the efforts of the secularists, including his own. This is discussed below in the Conclusion.

unbelievers who dared to publish their heresy, Beccaria cautiously refrained from considering religion. He mentioned it in passing as one of the three sources, together with 'natural law' and the 'established conventions of society', of the moral and political principles that govern our lives.[39] However, by concentrating upon the 'established conventions' Beccara's aim was to apply systematically the principles enunciated by Helvétius, specifically those regarding the nature of motivation and the role of legislation. In the course of doing so he made much of, and expressed almost word for word, the utilitarian formula 'the greatest happiness of the greatest number', later popularized by Bentham, as the criterion for evaluating the measures of the legislator.[40] Beccaria, more than anyone else of the day, made jurisprudence a secular science.

It was in 1769 that the works of Hume, Helvétius, and Beccaria had first come to Bentham's attention. The next few years were spent elucidating the insights they provided principally within the context of his study of the law. From the first, however, criticisms of religion were intimately connected in his mind with the belief that the role of the legislator should be paramount in all matters of social felicity. By the early 1770s, as he himself testified in the early correspondence and in the later memoirs, Bentham had before him the basic principles of his system.[41] In an unpublished manuscript of this time he writes that the fewer the principles to which a science can be reduced the nearer it is to perfection, and that before Helvétius and Beccaria the principles of morality and censorial jurisprudence were many:

Happily this is the case no longer. Beccaria has with an applause that in this country seems to be universal, Beccaria has established . . . for . . . censorial Jurisprudence, as Helvétius for morality in general as an all commanding principle the principle of utility. To this then all other . . . principles that . . . can be proposed, if legitimate . . . stand in subordination: . . . any one . . . which cannot is to be . . . cast out as spurious. (UC 69/17)

---

[39] Beccaria, *An Essay on Crimes and Punishments*, p. 5.

[40] How this formula travelled from Francis Hutcheson via several hands to Beccaria, later to be taken up by Bentham, is the subject of Robert Shackleton's informative essay 'The Greatest Happiness of the Greatest Number: The History of Bentham's Phrase', *Studies on Voltaire and the Eighteenth Century*, 90 (1972), 1461–82.

[41] See *Corr.* i, Letter 192; ii, Letters 248, 250, and 251; and *Works*, x. 70, 79, 142. Bentham was always happy to indicate his pleasure whenever he found these basic principles enunciated. Hence, despite the concessions to Christianity it contained, he could still commend the Marquis de Chastellux's *An Essay on Public Happiness* [*De la félicité publique, ou considérations sur le sort des hommes dans les différentes époques de l'histoire*, 1772], 2 vols. (London, 1774; repr. New York, 1969). See UC 142/211–13.

And cast out as spurious religion was to be. Drawing freely upon the work of Helvétius and Beccaria, Bentham began to map out the details of his secular view of social life and in the process trained a critical eye upon the claims of religion.

In the manuscript pages of 'Crit[ical] Jur[isprudence] Crim[inal]'— a surprising number of which are devoted to an analysis of the religious sanction, he intimated distaste for the practice of mixing religion with law. 'Religion', he writes, 'is a source from whence the Legisl'or hitherto at least has drawn & continues to draw more mischief than he . . . has benefit.' To the objection that divine justice serves a higher end than human justice he replies that 'The only merit of Human Justice is its subserviency to Human Happiness. If Divine Justice has not that merit, what *has* it?' (UC 69/13). And again, this time concerning the uncertainty of the supposed rewards and punishments of the afterlife, he remarks:

I protest against the embarrassing this or any other political question with theological considerations. I . . . lay myself at the feet of one of the most illustrious fathers of our Church [William Warburton], for I aver with him that the happiness of this life is the only proper object of the Legislator . . . Unlike God man's knowledge is confined to experience, hence he has knowledge only of what has been and what is, and nothing of what will be. (UC 69/140)

Another reason why religion should not be mixed with jurisprudence was because it lent the latter a sanctimonious air which frequently posed an obstacle to its reform. Bentham took up this theme in his work on Blackstone's *Commentaries*: 'nurtured in the Sanctuary of religion [Oxford]', Blackstone could not see his way to criticizing the legal system he purported to analyse; he saw only what is and nothing of what might or should be. The *Commentaries* was a work of exposition merely and, therefore, unavoidably fraught with the fictions and fallacies that attend its subject-matter (*Comm.*, ch. 1, sec. 3). For example, according to Blackstone the Law of Revelation is included in the general concept of the law of nature, and 'no human laws are of any validity, if contrary to this; and such of them as are valid derive all their force, and all their authority, mediately or immediately, from this original'.[42] The law of nature is the will of God, and we are to discover this law by virtue of our reason. But if this is so, quips Bentham, 'it is in the regions of non-entity [reason] is to discover them' (*Comm.* 14). Such philosophizing is a confusion of discredited theories. To say that

[42] Blackstone, *Commentaries*, i. 41.

human laws which conflict with Divine Law are not binding, that is to say, are not laws, is to talk nonsense, and the concept of Natural Law is itself 'nothing but a phrase', a 'formidable non-entity' (*Comm.* 20). Nor could Revelation be of service in solving these apparent contradictions, for it is a thousand times easier to say even what the Common Law might be than it is to determine Divine Law from the Scriptures. Blackstone's propositions are repugnant to 'real fact'. Anyone 'who had been at all accustomed to examine into the import of words' could have seen this. 'The wonder is the greater', writes Bentham, 'as the fictitiousness of the "precept", the "command" in one case, and the reality of it in the other, is all that he could have, according to the amount he gives us of the Law of Revelation, to distinguish that from this' (*Comm.* 13 n.). In a manuscript of *c.*1773 Bentham's position is clearly conveyed by the margin heading 'The Idea of God useless in Jurisprudence' (UC 96/139).

3. *Secular* versus *religious utilitarianism*

By the time Bentham printed the *Introduction* in 1780 his views on the obstacles posed by religion to a rational system of jurisprudence were complete in all important details, and they stayed with him for the rest of his days. True to the spirit of Helvétius and Beccaria, he announced that the principle of utility is the foundation of his system. Its object 'is to rear the fabric of felicity by the hands of reason and law' (*IPML* 11), and the principal means to achieve this is through government, whose business it is 'to promote the happiness of the society by punishing and rewarding' (*IPML* 74). As nearly as legislation conforms to the calculations demanded by utility 'so near will such process approach the character of an exact one' (*IPML* 40).

On these terms the science of legislation is viewed as a means to a practical end, that is, to the beneficial reform of society. As surely as the prevailing legal system favoured special privileges for the few at the expense of the happiness of the many, by changing the laws the evils of social life can be alleviated. The science of legislation must, therefore, be a study both of what the law is and of what the law ought to be. The first Bentham called 'expositional jurisprudence'; the second he referred to as 'censorial jurisprudence'. The 'expositor' is principally occupied in stating or in enquiring after facts; the 'censor' in discussing reasons: 'To the *Expositor* it belongs to shew what the

Legislator and his underworkman the *Judge* have done *already*: to the *Censor* it belongs to suggest what the *Legislator ought* to do *in future*' (*FG* 397–8). To augment knowledge is the function of the 'expositor'; refining knowledge is the task of the 'censor'.

These two aspects of the science of legislation, however, are not clearly distinct: the process of enlightenment began for Bentham with the criticism of established ideas but, as Douglas Long has pointed out, the Censor in defending his own censorial stance becomes his own Expositor. Hence Bentham's endeavour to perfect knowledge was to be achieved by a synthesis of the expository and censorial functions.[43] It is the special aim of the latter to provide an objective standard capable of evaluating the law as it is and spelling out what the law ought to be in order to conform to human nature. Accordingly, in the *Introduction* Bentham recognized that religion was of some influence in the field of morals, but there can be little doubt that he believed that its influence should be entirely obliterated. In the relative safety of the unpublished 'Crit[ical] Jur[isprudence] Crim[inal]' he had already stated as much:

A great source and subject of diversity, will be those whimsies, or those weaknesses or those prejudices, or those oppressions, or those impostures, which under the several national establishments come under the title Religion. With this title I shall have . . . no other concern else than to shew that reason which every lover of . . . mankind has to wish . . . to see it . . . greatly narrow'd at least if not . . . totally expunged. (UC 69/14)

In the rational society, a society organized and governed according to the dictates of utility, religion is superfluous to ethics and need not be a consideration for the legislator. But Bentham does not confuse the censorial and expositional functions of his study; in the knowledge that conditions are not yet ripe for its eradication he includes religion in his list of sanctions (together with the physical, moral, and legal) at the disposal of the legislator (*IPML* 37). While it exists and has influence, while it is yet a factor in moral motivation, the legislator can and should make use of it. Where social evils are beyond the curative power of other sanctions the legislator might on occasion have recourse to the religious sanction. Such occasions are those of drunkenness (not then restricted by legislation), and any evil act where there are not witnesses, such as smuggling. Here supernatural fears and threats might be of some use. Like the moral sanction the religious sanction

---

[43] Long, *Bentham on Liberty*, p. 13.

can be considered an 'auxiliary' sanction which the legislator can employ to supplement the work of the legal or political sanction (*LG* 196). The pleasures and pains of piety, those 'that accompany the belief of man's being in the . . . possession of the good-will or favour of the Supreme Being' (*IPML* 44), or his 'being obnoxious to the displeasure of the Supreme Being', are useful weapons in the legislator's armoury (*IPML* 48). If only as a game of bluff, then, religion has its uses. But Bentham is not concerned for its supposed impact in the afterlife, since 'this is a matter which comes not within the cognizance of the legislator' (*IPML* 202 n.). In this respect the religious sanction is an empty formula. Unlike the other sanctions which operate immediately in this world, the religious sanction holds out only an uncertain threat. The pleasures and pains of futurity are not intelligible to us. Not being experienced in this life they cannot be observed, and as they are not observable it cannot be said that we can truly know any thing of them (*IPML* 36).[44]

Bentham well understood that the clergy employ the religious sanction to some effect. No doubt the inculcation of the belief in the power of a supreme invisible being is useful in that it supplies the deficiencies in point of efficacy of the religious powers of this world, who cannot see all the acts which require punishment, nor be sure that the punishment they administer will always reach an offender (*IPML* 201). But where the motives supplied by religion are efficacious they are at best 'semi-social' in the sense that their consequences reach only to the sect or society governed by the particular religion from which they emanate. On the whole, however, religion ranks last in the list of sources of efficacious motives because it is the least likely to coincide with utility. Despite the ingenuity of the attempt, William Warburton (1698–1779), the erstwhile Bishop of Gloucester, had failed to substantiate the claim of the first book of the *Divine Legation of Moses* (1738), that the religious sanction has always been inculcated by legislators because of its utility. And, unless it can be shown that the actions enjoined or condemned by that sanction are useful to society, the mere inculcation of the belief in the afterlife is useless and may even be pernicious (UC 140/2). Only if God were universally supposed

---

[44] Elsewhere Bentham was not so circumspect: 'under the guidance of religion men have made to themselves an almighty being, whose delight is in human misery, and who, to prevent a man's escaping from whatsoever misery he may be threatened with in the present life, has without having denounced it formed a determination, in the event of any such escape, to plunge him into infinitely greater misery in a life to come' (*Deon.* 131).

to be as benevolent as he is wise and powerful would the dictates of religion coincide in all cases with those of utility (*IPML* 119). In plain terms, and quite apart from his epistemological difficuties regarding the existence of God, Bentham's position was that unless God aimed at increasing wordly happiness he could not be described as benevolent. In a manuscript of the period he notes: 'God is not good, if he prohibits our possessing the least atom of clear happiness which he has given us the physical capacity of attaining' (UC 70a/25). In other words, if God does not support utility this proves not that utility is not good, but that God is not good. Too often, it is God's malevolence that is brought to view by the teachers of Christianity:

> They call him benevolent in words, but they do not mean that he is so in reality. . . . For if they did, they would recognise that the dictates of religion could be neither more nor less than the dictates of utility: not a tittle different: not a tittle less or more. But the case is, that on a thousand occasions, they turn their backs on the principle of utility. (*IPML* 120)

Acts induced by the religious sanction which do not tend to the advantage of society are to be restricted by law, for religion itself is only a good in so far as it is the auxiliary of virtue. In short, its tendency ought to be in conformity with the plan of utility. Though he was ready to make use of religion in the existing social system, then, Bentham's reasons were not of a spiritual nature.

What of acts offensive to religion which are not prevented by human laws? Bentham derisively suggests that such actions do not need the punishment of mere mortals, because God will punish all sinfulness by his wrath—only the impious claim the right of punishment in such instances. The misery occasioned by penal laws meant to maintain the religious beliefs of official or established religion for ever raised his ire. 'When, when, alas!', he asks in the manuscript pages of 'Crit[ical] Jur[isprudence] Crim[inal]', 'will men cure themselves of the fond pretension of assisting the all-wise with their counsel, the almighty with their power?' Is it not written 'Vengeance is mine, saith the Lord'? (UC 140/13).

As an admirer of Voltaire, Bentham would not tolerate the clergy playing the role of 'middleman' in order to reveal God's will. Religious texts require interpretation, no doubt, but we are all fallible. In a more critical vein, Bentham charged that the clergy could not be trusted to live up to the otherwise meritorious features of their faith. Too often they have applied the title 'Divine Justice' to dictates 'which could have no other origin than the worst sort of human caprice' (*IPML* 110 n.). Too often they invoke the name of God to achieve ends wholly contrary to his supposed benevolent will and pernicious to society. In language reminiscent of Helvétius, Bentham chides the zealous advocates of Christianity with causing the 'sufferings of uncalled martyrs, the calamities of holy wars and religious persecutions, the mischiefs of intolerant laws' (*IPML* 121).

As a principle of ethics in the hands of its official professors, then, religion is found to be vague, theoretically deficient, and open to manipulation. In a direct attack on the religious exponents of utility, Bentham even argues that to unite this principle with religion is to apply it in a 'perverse' manner—in two respects. It is perverse in the first place because it lends credence to religious asceticism as a bona fide moral life. In a sense, asceticism can be said to have been a target for Bentham from the beginning, and in religion he found its primary vehicle. Having briefly touched on the subject in 1774 in connection with 'Sexual Nonconformity' (UC 73/90–100; 74a/1–25) he returned to it in the *Introduction* to give it a definitely religious context. His exhaustive analysis of the role of the religious sanction in morals and legislation during the 1770s brought him to this stand against religious asceticism, and he once again pondered the subject in 1780 in connection with his writings on 'indirect legislation' (UC 87/17–41). Religious asceticism repressed the quest for pleasure on the premiss that the pleasures and pains of this life are nothing in comparison with those of the future state (UC 69/12). 'The greater the . . . pleasures of a future life, the less ratio do the greatest possible pleasures or . . . pains of the present bear to them' (UC 140/2). Motivated by the prospect of pain which is 'the offspring of superstitious fancy', the religious ascetic is led by fear to approve of actions which diminish happiness and to disapprove of those that tend to augment it (*IPML* 17–18). Where the ascetic is not a 'fanatic' attempting to influence the happiness of others, religious asceticism is strictly a principle of private ethics and not therefore a subject for legislation (*IPML* 19). But if this principle should ever become general, were the world peopled by religious ascetics, they would turn it into a temporal hell (*IPML* 20). For the motive supplied by religion produces worse secondary mischief than even the worst in Bentham's category of motives—ill-will. Because it is a more constant motive than ill-will (vengeance and antipathy) it is all the more dangerous. Wherever it gives birth to mischievous acts and becomes fanaticism, it will normally be more pernicious than even the most dissocial of motives (*IPML* 156). Moreover, religious asceticism seems to be accompanied by a special intellectual blindness. The religious fanatic is not able to see that he is fighting against adversaries who 'think, or perhaps only speak, differently upon a subject which neither party understands' (*IPML* 156 n.); he does not realize that there would be even more heretics if there were more thinkers (*IPML* 133). Fanaticism, particularly religious fanaticism, 'never sleeps: it is never glutted: it is never stopped by philanthropy: it is never stopped by conscience: for it has pressed conscience into its service. Avarice, lust, and vengeance, have piety, benevolence, honour: fanaticism has nothing to oppose it' (*IPML* 156 n.).

Secondly, the union of utility and religion is perverse because it deflects the science of morals from its true focus of study—the observation and calculation of pleasures and pains. In the preface to the *Introduction* Bentham writes that, 'There is, or rather there ought to be, a *logic* of the *will*, as well as of the understanding' (*IPML* 8). Philosophers from Aristotle down have neglected the former and directed their attentions to the study of the latter. Yet the science of law is absolutely dependent upon a logic of the will. As John Hill Burton observed, for Bentham sanctions are 'the chains . . . which bind a man from following his own wild will'.[45] The science of legislation is, therefore, founded on this logic, on the study of the connection between pleasures and pains and actions. In essence this constitutes Bentham's advance from the work of Helvétius. As Long again has observed, 'his "logic of the will" was meant to be the social and moral equivalent of Newton's physical laws of motion: the core of a science of human nature upon which an entire catalogue of social sciences might be based'.[46]

For the 'theological' exponents of utility, the operations of the will were not understood in the way just outlined. It is not how wisely legislation binds the will to its purpose, but how nearly the will conforms to God's laws that is important. In the truly Christian commonwealth the will would be neither wild nor aimless, but would naturally be directed to the fulfillment of God's purpose. In short, the human will would become one with the Divine will. In the less perfect commonwealth the moral and legal sanctions serve their purpose, but

[45] Burton, *Benthamiana*, p. 358.
[46] D. G. Long, 'Physical Sciences and Social Sciences: The Case of Jeremy Bentham' (unpublished), *Proceedings of the Canadian Political Science Association Annual Convention 1975*, 3.

more weight attaches to the wrath of God, which is reserved for those who openly and deliberately flaunt his laws. For these laws, unlike those of society, are perfect, eternal, and immutably directed to the enduring happiness of all. Hence, the religious exponents of utility reduced all forms of obligation to the religious. As John Gay expressed it, 'the will of God is the immediate criterion of Virtue and the happiness of mankind the criterion of the will of God'.[47]

John Brown's explanation of the dimensions of the motivation supplied by religion was perhaps the subtlest of those set out by the religious utilitarians. What Brown, in language peculiar to the day, termed 'the religious principle', has two branches, the first of which is fear. His defence of religion in terms of this is of little interest. Fear, and specifically the fear of divine punishment, being a passion which we all have the capacity to feel, constitutes the lowest base from which we could become virtuous. Even so, says Brown, there is nothing slavish in this; rather it 'implies a lively and habitual Belief, that we shall be hereafter miserable, if we disobey [God's] Laws', and this does no more than induce 'a *rational Sense*' of evil and the determination to avoid it.[48] Of more interest is Brown's elucidation of the second branch of the religious principle, since it is here that the positive character of the motive to virtuous action which Christianity supplies is to be found. This branch of the principle is 'the Hope and Prospect of higher Degrees of future Happiness and perfection'.[49] To understand fully what Brown meant by this his theological position as a defender of orthodox beliefs must be borne in mind. Among the faithful of the day the spiritual dimension of the perfection of the soul was commonly held to be integral to the idea of personal happiness in its most encompassing sense. In Brown's Christian version of the doctrine of utility it could be no less so: here temporal happiness joins hands with the eternal happiness of the soul in pursuit of the ideal, the perfect harmony of virtue and happiness. For Brown,

'Man is never so sincerely or heartily *benevolent*, as when he is truly *happy* in himself'. Thus the high Consciousness of his being numbered among the Children of GOD, and that his Lot is among the Saints; that he is destined to an endless Progression of Happiness, and to rise from high to higher Degrees of Perfection, must needs inspire him with that Tranquility and Joy, which will

[47] Gay, 'Preliminary Dissertation concerning the Fundamental Principle of Virtue or Morality', in Selby-Bigge, *British Moralists*, ii, sec. 864.
[48] Brown, *Essays on the Characteristics*, p. 214.
[49] Ibid. 215.

naturally diffuse itself in Acts of sincere Benevolence to all his Fellow-Creatures.[50]

Only when a man 'is truly *happy* in himself' can he be expected to progress in ever greater degrees towards perfection, and it is religious consciousness which provides this happy disposition, making his own perfection and his contribution to human happiness possible. Neither happiness nor perfection on this view can be said to be the primary consideration for the true Christian, but each is essential for the possibility of the other. As Brown put it elsewhere,

> the whole *Weight* and *Energy* of the *Gospel* is employed in enforcing the Idea of *moral Perfection*, of our *nobler* SELF, of Self-Interest in the *higher* Sense, of the Necessity of extirpating every meaner Passion, and cherishing the great one of *unbounded Love*, as the necessary and only Discipline that can qualify us for future Happiness.[51]

Hence it is not that religion merely promises an extension or rectification of human justice, nor that the rewards and punishments of futurity are simply an addition to the imperfect rewards and punishments established by civil society. There is a specific aspect of religion which cannot be accounted for in such terms, something over and above the religious sanction which imparts to the doctrines of Christianity an undeniable efficacy. it is a spiritual quality which has nothing to do with visions or ecstasies, but everything to do with the will to be and to do good. This will is most appropriately characterized as love, and it is a love which causes each person to be loved in return, such that ever increasing numbers open their souls to benevolence. The notion of posthumous rewards and punishments provides an aid to this moral endeavour, but it is in religion in its positive role—that which prompts individuals not merely to refrain from evil but actually to do good, to love their friends and neighbours and thus progress on the path to perfection—that the Christian finds himself most fully in accord with God's benevolent will.

It was on these grounds that the religious exponents of utility held that the religious principle gave the fullest scope to human development. Its reality does not rest on simple *post facto* evidence, but is derived from the theological consideration that human nature has a spiritual as well as a physiological side. Despite their emphasis on the importance of the appeal to the concern for future happiness, Paley, Brown, and

---

[50] Brown, *Essays on the Characteristics*, p. 221.   [51] Ibid. 329.

the others recognized that the moral efficacy of religion is not constituted by this alone. Virtuous effort demands that we form an ideal of the highest good towards which this effort tends. That ideal is the harmony of virtue and happiness according to the laws and purpose of God, a harmony which is approachable in the present life but which is only truly realizable in the life to come. The virtuous person constantly reaches forth in a seemingly endless effort to reach perfection, but such endeavour, though fundamentally spiritual, is of great temporal significance in ordinary social and political life. It manifests itself in love, the love of God, and through him the love of all with whom one comes into contact; its consequence is a peaceful and ordered society and, in the best of all possible worlds, extensive benevolence leading to universal happiness.

Bentham's argument against this form of reasoning is founded upon his metaphysics and reveals how little he could empathize with or enter into the language of religion. The will of God, having no existence in reality that can be observed, is a fictitious entity. As he wrote in 1816, that 'such or such a thing is a cause of pain or pleasure is a matter of fact and experience: that the use of it has been prohibited by the Deity, is a matter of inference and conjecture' (UC 58/210).[52] In the *Introduction* he was equally clear that when moralists refer us to the 'will of God' their meaning is frequently confused, and this is not only a source of error but of positive evil. The revealed will of the Scriptures is too vague and subject to too great a range of interpretation to provide a general standard of ethics. What moralists usually settle for is 'the *presumptive* will: (that is to say, that which is presumably to be his will on account of the conformity of its dictates to those of some other principle' (*IPML* 31). But if this principle is not general happiness in this life then it is nothing more than either the principle of 'sympathy' or 'antipathy' in some other shape (*IPML* 31). The potential for evil lies in the fact that these principles—sympathy and antipathy—approve and disapprove of actions, not on account of their augmenting or diminishing happiness, 'but merely because a man finds himself disposed to approve or disapprove of them'. They provide no external criterion or 'extrinsic ground' for judgement; therefore, all is uncertain and unpredictable (*IPML* 25).

---

[52] Among MSS used by Bowring for the 1st vol. of *Deon.* published in 1834. Written in the hand of Bowring, it is likely that this is a rephrasing by him of Bentham's original, probably dating from 1816.

Bentham was later to expose this evil in terms of the influence on the will of the citizen exerted by illegitimate, as opposed to legitimate, sources of authority in society. The influence of a Church, which relies on interpretations of the 'will of God' and not on utility to determine what is or is not admissable, is just such an illegitimate use of authority, and where an ecclesiastical establishment has an influence in government the dangers to the comfort and well-being of the citizen are multiplied. However, Bentham's arguments concerning the redundancies of religious doctrines and their pernicious consequences when propagated by an unscrupulous clergy were clearly stated in his writings on ethics and jurisprudence during the early period of his career. Entirely cynical concerning the value of religion to society he demanded that it be replaced as the central agency of moral control and social regulation. Hence, we find that his critique of religion is closely associated with his emphasis on legislation and the logic of the will as the only sure means for promoting human happiness. At the heart of this vision of a secular society stands the principle of utility, and Bentham never doubted that it was an appropriate standard by which to measure the worth of religion. In the manuscript pages of 'Crit[itical] Jur[isprudence] Crim[inal]' he commended those writers who had gone before him in this:

A numerous tribe of anonymous writers in whom the acrimony they have shown in their attacks against religion in general, has been more conspicuous than any strength or regularity which they have display'd in the manner of conducting them, have mostly however had this merit in common, that they have professed to take this principle (utility) for their standard. (UC 159/270)

To advocate the principle of utility as the ultimate standard of all policies is to advocate the eradication of the influence of religion over the mind and the demotion of official religion from its privileged position as the protected ally of government. Legislation is to hold centre stage. Its aim is to achieve the greatest happiness by bringing about the concurrence of private and public interests. Government must induce individuals to follow the optimal path by holding out the prospect of rewards and punishments for the adherence to, or infringement of, laws prescribed in order to create the conditions in which the greatest happiness can be achieved.

4. *Secular utilitarianism and religious radicalism*

This is how Bentham's social science would have looked to any one thoroughly acquainted with it in 1780. With its peculiar metaphysics, emphasis on the science of legislation, and rejection of religion as an agency of moral welfare, it remained unchanging in all essential details to the end of his days. This understood, the chronological and logical development of his thoughts on religion can now be viewed in their correct light. Religious radicalism, heretofore thought to have been the product of Bentham's move to political radicalism in later life, was in fact there from the first and, therefore, precedes the period of his so-called conversion to democratic ideals by roughly forty years. In the unpublished work on subscriptions of 1773 he attacked the Established Church for perpetuating pernicious exclusionary practices, and in the preface to *Le Taureau blanc* he took the opportunity to strike a few more blows at organized religion. More significantly, in the 1775 manuscripts for 'Crit[itical] Jur[isprudence] Crim[inal]' and in the work for the *Introduction* in 1778–80, Bentham analysed in some detail the role of religion in ethics and jurisprudence and laid the groundwork for his entirely secular vision of a Utilitarian society. When he returned to the subject of religion in 1809 his stance had undergone a tactical modification. Now, in tandem with his advocacy of democratic reforms, he embarked on a wholesale attack on the Anglican religious establishment and its teachings, and this in a fashion he had once deliberately avoided. Always aware of the deficiencies of religion as an agency of moral welfare and of the guilt of the clergy in perpetuating practices detrimental to the end of human happiness, he now came to accept the logical outcome of his own arguments and to avow openly that no significant constitutional or practical reforms could be achieved without the destruction of religion, both as a dangerous form of history and as a powerful social institution. More particularly, Bentham viewed the Established Church as a 'state engine' legitimating the depredation, corruption, oppression, and hypocrisy of the age, and resolute in its resistance to improvement.

In taking this stand Bentham set himself in direct opposition to the social philosophy which had its source in the theological version of the doctrine of utility, and which had held sway in England for much of the previous century. For the regard for religious principles shown by the theological exponents of utility in their defence of the established faith required of them that they seek not only the maintenance of the Church, but also the stability of the political establishment of which it formed a part. Each needed the other in order to survive: if religion was an essential ingredient in the formation of that public spirit upon which the well-being of the State depended, the Church without the support of the State was an institution in much danger. This union between religion and political life was nothing new to the English political tradition; in the eighteenth century it manifested itself in the defence of the 'Warburtonian alliance' of Church and State which it became Bentham's dearest wish to sever.[53]

To those Churchmen convinced of his orthodoxy Warburton remained an inspiration throughout the century. Though later Anglican theologues could not always follow the Bishop of Gloucester down his frustratingly eccentric paths to orthodoxy,[54] they looked to the religion of the Established Church and its doctrine of futurity to halt the appalling degeneracy of the age.[55] It was thought that the design of those who, like Mandeville and Hume, divorced morality from religion was to overthrow religion itself, and that this could lead to the destruction of the very fabric of social and political life. Hence it was a matter of some urgency that a system of ethics better suited to a Christian people and more conducive to an ordered political society should be given fuller and more detailed expression than it had hitherto received. It was this that the religious exponents of utility set out to supply. To the regulating agencies of providence without Church and legislation without divinity, they opposed a philosophy based on Christian beliefs and a recognition of the importance of the Established Church for the teaching of those beliefs. But defending the Church and its role in civil society involved them in the defence of the established political order of which it formed an integral and

---

[53] Warburton pictured the 'alliance' as a divinely sanctioned compact between 2 sovereign and independent powers based upon a sense of the support which each 'society' afforded the other. W. Warburton, *The Alliance between Church and State* (1736), in *The Works of the Right Reverend William Warburton*, 12 vols. (London, 1811), vii, Bk. II, ch. 1.

[54] e.g. in a controversial set of passages Warburton attempts to found morality on an amalgam of principles drawn from reason, sentiment, and religion. See *The Divine Legation of Moses* (1738; rev. edn. 1754), in *Works*, i, Bk. I, sec. 6.

[55] The decay of religion was commonly connected by moralists of the age with the growth of luxury and of an ignoble and materialistic spirit. But for a more balanced view see C. J. Abbey, *The English Church and its Bishops 1700–1800*, 2 vols. (London, 1887), ii, ch. 6; N. Sykes, *Edmund Gibson, Bishop of London, 1669–1748: A Study in Politics and Religion in the Eighteenth Century* (Oxford, 1926), chs. 6–7.

indispensable part. Hence the connection between their theology and their social and political philosophy was unequivocal.

Paley, in pàrticular, in sermons, in pamphlets, and in his major work, the *Principles of Moral and Political Philosophy*, defended a host of practices and institutions on the grounds of utility. In 'A Distinction of Orders in the Church, Defended upon Principles of Public Utility' (1783) he defended the English ecclesiastical establishment and particularly the role of the clergy.[56] In the *Principles* he defended the rights of property and contract as then stipulated by law; the right of bishops to sit in the House of Lords; the need for oaths of allegiance and for subscription to the Thirty-nine Articles; and the need to reinforce the duty of submission to civil government (invoking Scripture here to support his arguments from utility).[57] Finally, in a short pamphlet, entitled *Reasons for Contentment* (1792), Paley warned England's labouring masses against revolutionary activities on the grounds that radical reform 'is not only to venture out to sea in a storm, but to venture for nothing'.[58] The poor have much to be thankful for, and should count their blessings. The only change to be desired is gradual change—'that progressive improvement of our circumstances, which is the natural fruit of successful industry; . . . This may be looked forward to, and is practicable, by great numbers in a state of public order and quiet; it is absolutely impossible in any other.'[59]

Paley, then, was no radical reformer. Nor, like the Bentham of the 1770s and 1780s, was he a democrat. He held that political innovation brought with it many unforeseen evils. Of course, there was always room for improvement, but in general terms the existing institutions of government and established electoral arrangements provided all the security society required.[60] Utility is the key to Paley's analysis, and it

---

[56] Paley, 'A Distinction of Orders in the Church, Defended upon Principles of Public Utility' (1783), a sermon, preached in the Castle Chapel, Dublin, at the consecration of John Law DD, Lord Bishop of Clonfert and Kilmacduagh, 21 Sept. 1782, in *Complete Works*, iv. 283–94.

[57] Paley, *Principles*, Bk. II, pt. 1, and Bk. VI, *passim*.

[58] Paley, *Reasons for Contentment Addressed to the Labouring Part of the British Public*, in *Complete Works*, i. 438. D. L. LeMahieu, *The Mind of William Paley: A Philosopher and his Age* (London, 1976), is incorrect in styling this work as a reply to Thomas Paine's *Rights of Man* (1791, 1792), since it was originally given as a sermon at Paley's Cumberland parish in 1790. However, it is possible that the appearance of Paine's work influenced Paley's decision to publish this sermon.

[59] Paley, *Reasons for Contentment*, in *Complete Works*, i. 437.

[60] In an ingenuous, but hardly persuasive, dig at the advocates of universal suffrage Paley writes that the right to vote, if it be a natural right as it is claimed, 'no doubt it must be equal; and the right . . . of one sex, as well as of the other'. Every plan of

was no less influential on his view of the role of religion. That his conclusions differed substantially from Bentham's only goes to prove the malleability of the principle of utility when moulded by different hands. The authority of the Established Church, he proclaimed, is 'founded in its utility': in its usefulness in inculcating the principles of Christianity, and in the support it gives to secular government. To this end Paley advocated, in their mutual interest, a strengthening of the ties between Church and State.[61]

Bentham's opposition in early life to the religious trappings of the moral thought expounded by the theological exponents of utility was complemented by his later explicit opposition to the conservative political philosophy it nourished. To appeal, as Paley did, to a questionable revelation weakened the utilitarian system. But worst of all, the use he made of his philosophy to justify current rules of conduct, rather than to press for improvement, made his aberration doubly reprehensible. In *A Fragment, A Comment*, and in the *Introduction* Bentham had shown every inclination towards a philosophy of radical secularization. In the last twenty years of his long life, his radical views on the relationship between religion, ethics, and legislation, and his scattered thoughts on religious establishments, were brought together and systematically presented. Taken together the religious publications constituted the second front of Bentham's onslaught on 'establishments' during this period.[62] In these works the Church is portrayed as the vicious enemy of human happiness, and its doctrines are shown to be miserably deficient when tested against the standard of utility. Organized religion, political power, and legal institutions were now seen to be all part of the same system standing together both as objects for radical reform and as supreme obstacles to it. The whole was to be irreparably fractured by undermining, ridiculing, and disproving Christian history, and by revealing the sinister interests which were the chief supports of ecclesiastical institutions.[63]

As hostile to religion as the early critique of legal theory and practice

representation, however, 'begins by excluding the votes of women; thus cutting off, at a single stroke, one half of the public from a right which is asserted to be inherent in all' (*Principles*, Bk. VI, ch. 7, p. 340 n.).

[61] Ibid., ch. 10, p. 412.

[62] This is how Bentham portrayed his intentions in a letter to John Koe (14 Jan. 1818)], Koe MSS, from a transcription at the Bentham Project, UCL.

[63] Bentham's *Fall.*, published in 1824, best reveals the extent of the connections perceived by him during this period between government, the legal system, and the Church and their common foundation on sinister interest.

may have been, it can hardly be compared with the harshness of the later religious publications. However, the move to overt radicalism did not involve a major shift or change in basic ideas. *Swear Not at All*, the first published work with a religious theme, for example, shows similarities to the unpublished material on subscriptions of 1773. Of more significance, however, is the consideration that the political stance of the Church, which Bentham now made no secret of his intention to overcome, can be shown to have its source in the doctrine of the alliance of Church and State justified on the premiss of the supposed utility of religion, which he had sought to expose as a fraud from the very beginning of his censorial work on jurisprudence. It became necessary for him to attack the Church publicly, since it was for this institution of reaction that the religious exponents of utility had provided a seemingly rational base. By 1809 or thereabouts, Bentham's disappointment with the Panopticon venture and other schemes for improvement had taught him that moderation and the apparent reasonableness of the reforms he proposed were not persuasive to those who held positions of authority in Church and State. In politics the radical remedy was in the first place to remove the distinction between rulers and ruled by investing sovereignty in the people. The ultimate success of this remedy in advancing the creation of a rational Utilitarian society, however, demanded another antidote to oppression, and that a prior one. It required the obliteration of the control exercised over the minds of the masses by the doctrines and institutions of religion.

That Bentham had made the first substantial steps towards this conclusion at a very early stage in his career has been the argument of the last two chapters, which together represented the kernel of my interpretation of the significance of Bentham's thoughts on religion within the formation and development of his social science. I have argued, in the first place, that the most important factor in any explanation of the genesis and character of his thoughts on religion must be that his adherence to, and interpretation of, the principles and techniques of natural science very early on led him to dismiss divinity as a science on the grounds that its subject-matter was impenetrable and ultimately unknowable. Secondly, I have suggested that Bentham sought to supply the deficiencies of a philosophy of society based on religion by means of an entirely secular morality which looked to legislation as the central agency of social harmony, and that this was a necessary prerequisite to the emergence of his radically secular view of the State. Finally, I have argued that Bentham's utilitarianism developed in part as a reaction to the kind of religious thinking on morals which prevailed in the England of his day. His secular version of the doctrine was very different from that of his Anglican precursors and not surprisingly led to very different social and political consequences. It has often been said that the doctrine of utility in different hands could take on a liberal or a radical character, but it seems to have escaped notice that for much of the eighteenth century it had been employed as a plank in the conservative platform.[64] Brown and Paley (among others) following Warburton, attempted to show that the worth of the Church, and of the political constitution of which it formed an integral part, could be established on the grounds of utility. Bentham, on the other hand, sought to establish the perniciousness of the Church and the doctrines it preached by his own secular version of this standard. Where religion was opposed to utility it was pernicious; where it agreed with it, it was entirely superfluous. Or as Bentham was flatly to state the equation: 'Morality may well say of religion—whenever it is not for me, it is against me' (*Works*, x. 70).[65]

---

[64] In the case of Paley matters were never quite that straightforward, as I have tried to show in my 'Religion, Utility and Politics: Bentham *versus* Paley', in Crimmins (ed.), *Religion, Secularization and Political Thought*, pp. 130–52. See also T. P. Schofield, 'A Comparison of the Moral Theories of William Paley and Jeremy Bentham', *The Bentham Newsletter*, 11 (1987), 4–22.

[65] Perhaps an allusion to Matt. 13: 30, where Christ rebukes the Pharisees thus: 'He that is not with me is against me.'

PART II
Church-of-Englandism

BENTHAM's writings in the last three decades of the eighteenth and first three decades of the nineteenth centuries on jurisprudence, ethics, penal laws, the poor law, and education, and his advocacy of democratic institutions, were a reflection in large measure of the transitional character of the period in which he lived. The post-Napoleonic years in particular saw rising agitation for political reform, the foundation of the great education movements, the repeal of the Combination Laws (1824) and of the Test and Corporation Acts (1828), the passage of Catholic Emancipation (1829), and the Great Reform Act (1832). In religion, as much as in any other area of social life, it was a period of change, a time which witnessed attacks on the Church from moderate Whig liberals and Dissenters as well as from the ranks of more recalcitrant radical unbelievers. The breakdown of traditional beliefs and the declining prestige of both the aristocracy and the clergy which accompanied this mood of dissatisfaction tended to throw individuals back upon themselves. They came to realize that they were living in a period of significant social change, a time when what had once been deemed permanent no longer looked quite so immutable. Bentham not only reflected this mood but encouraged it. In all that he wrote, in his writings on religion as much as in any others, his aim was to free the world of mysticism, superstition, falsehood, and confusions, of everything that prevented social improvement. He opposed the Established Church because he believed that it was an agency of misrule and served to prevent the adoption of much needed reforms.

Efforts for the diffusion of education, the more equal distribution of wealth, the mitigation of disease, the humanization of penal laws, and the protection of the helpless received little encouragement from 'holy Mother Church'. Comprehensive schemes of reform, it was claimed, were not only a drain on energies that would be better spent on devotional exercises or missions to convert heretics, but appeared in many cases to be designed to supersede the providence of God himself. To Bentham this was all so much empty clerical claptrap. The simple fact of the matter was that the Church stood in the way of improvement and, like England's legal and political structures, needed immediate and extensive reform. No one would claim that Bentham's publications on religious matters were among the most influential that he produced, but in this fundamental aspect they were surely in tune with the needs of his time. They stand as a formidable testimony to— descending at times to the level of a caricature of—the growing dissatisfaction of the age with organized religion.

This disgruntlement with the Established Church came after a long period of relative quiet on the ecclesiastical front. The second half of the eighteenth century had been for the most part orthodox, occasionally to the point of persecution (as in the case of the Gordon Riots of 1780), without being deeply theological. Doctrinal problems were largely ignored by the Church, and in clerical circles it was the era of the Church apologists, of Bishop Law and William Paley. Religion to these Christian moralists meant obedience to the will of God as revealed by the Scriptures and as interpreted and taught by the clergy of the Established Church. The speculative part of religion was generally accepted by the Anglican congregation because it was assumed to have a hard core of truth at its centre. Paley aside, few attempted elaborate demonstrations of the essential truths of their faith. This state of affairs was to be quickly shattered by the nineteenth-century inquiry into religion. The transition from an age when religion stood at the centre and pervaded every corner of social life to a time when the fragmentation of the Church became institutionalized was a dramatic one.

To understand this movement towards the secularization of life and thought one is irresistibly drawn to cast an eye over the condition of religion in the previous century. During this time, to borrow a phrase from that arch-traditionalist Edmund Burke, the Church and State were frequently considered to be 'one and the same thing, being different integral parts of the same whole'.[1] Having survived the theological squabbles of the seventeenth and early eighteenth centuries, religion remained an integral feature of social and political life.[2] Nevertheless, it was an age of declining popular influence for the official religion of England, particularly from the midpoint of the century onwards. There are several reasons why this should have been so.

In the first place, the intensity of the theological exchanges of the late seventeenth and the first half of the eighteenth centuries not only propagated the notion (born of the scientific achievements of the age) that individuals possessed the ability to reason for themselves, without

---

[1] E. Burke, 'Speech on a Motion made in the House of Commons by the Right Hon. C. J. Fox, May 11, 1792, for Leave to Bring in a Bill to Repeal and Alter Certain Acts Respecting Religious Opinions, upon Occasion of a Petition of the Unitarian Society', *The Works of the Right Honourable Edmund Burke*, 12 vols. (London, 1887), vii. 43.

[2] This is a central theme of J. C. D. Clarke's stimulating study *English Society 1688–1832: Ideology, Social Structure and Political Practice During the Ancien Regime* (Cambridge, 1985).

the aid of Scripture and Church authorities, about the nature of their world and their place in it, but also wearied them of theological controversy. Doctrinal differences between the orthodox and Arians (who denied the existence of the Trinity) and the Unitarians (who denied the divinity of Christ), between the Calvinists and Arminians over predestination and free will, between Deists (who denied the status of revelation) and those who argued that the doctrines of Christianity could not be established by intellect alone, were frequently conducted in a bitter manner and were often frustratingly tedious in form. Controversies which range abroad into fields where few have competence will soon fade in interest. And so it was in England around the mid-century. To be sure the Church rallied its wandering flock around the standard of orthodoxy, but increasingly the call most often heard was from those voices raised to damn religion altogether, and only materialists, atheists, or sceptics like David Hume, found any philosophical consolation in this.

Secondly, the age witnessed an increasing absorption in business matters and the material side of life. Here the concept of the alliance of Church and State served to conceal a profound dichotomy of interests. The State, in its new Walpolian guise, emerged as the engine for the development of the economic mind. The expansion of trade, the birth of joint stock companies, and the growth of industrial enterprises were all encouraged by the State. Yet these were distractions from the performance of religious duties. Some, like the Revd John Brown, who had considerable success with his critical *An Estimate of the Manners and Principles of the Times* (1757–8), clamoured against these developments, but generally religion turned a blind eye to some of the more dubious aspects of the commercial world. It found commerce to be based on selfish interests, but this was thought to be sinful only when practised in excess. Luxury and effeminacy, not wealth and enterprise, it was thought, were the enemies which turned people away from religion. In such a manner did Churchmen establish a compromise and at the same time justify their own, in some cases considerable, possessions of land and wealth.

Thirdly, and related to the foregoing, a more worldly approach to morality and politics was ushered on to the eighteenth-century stage. Religion was no longer uniformly viewed as the arbiter in all matters of public or social significance. Sensitive to its diminishing role in the world the Church expounded a more worldly religion which reflected not only this secular tendency, but also the economic facts of a prosperous and complacent age. The reduction of religion to little more than the conduct of prudence was soon enough accompanied by its demise as an independent force in public life. Sporadic attempts were made to halt the decline in the spiritual influence of religion, but coming from within the Established Church they all too frequently failed to distinguish between the need for a defence of fundamental Christian beliefs and an apology for the Church itself. Of course, there were sound tactical reasons why the two should go hand in hand, but the age demanded a more urgent and thoughtful defence of religion than the Church was likely to raise. More often than not Church and faith were presented as inextricably bound. In the work of William Warburton, the brilliant Bishop of Gloucester, and of later Anglican apologists like Brown, Law, and Paley, this invariably appeared to be the case. They defended religion in moral thought on the grounds of practical utility and the role of the Church in temporal matters for the same reason. A temporary success was all they could achieve. What they could not prevent, and what was probably the greatest threat to Christianity, was the general and growing inability of Christians to accept the central idea of their faith, that they were weak and sinful creatures visited by evil in this life, who could be assured of better in the world to come only on the condition of industry and humility.[3]

At the same time the pretence of ascendancy in spiritual matters was kept up within the Church by the maintenance of its privileged position as the ally of the State. This was achieved by a combination of, on the one hand, penal laws and the enforcement of oaths and subscription to articles of faith as indispensable requirements for admittance to public life—not only to ecclesiastical office, but to all manner of secular positions as well—and, on the other hand, by the studious cultivation of Crown patronage. Only those who publicly avowed their faith in Church doctrines were allowed officially to take university degrees, to occupy positions either in the Church or government, or be admitted to any office under the Crown. However, while restrictions on Catholics and Dissenters were harsh in theory, particularly for the former, penal laws for religious beliefs were far from strictly enforced. Though this was not an ideal state of affairs, as long as Roman Catholics stayed out of the public eye they were rarely molested, and Dissenters holding public office had gained relief for their consciences from 1727 onwards by virtue of an annually passed Indemnity Act.

[3] See R. N. Stromberg, *Religious Liberalism in Eighteenth Century England* (Oxford, 1954), 120.

Later in the century the attitude towards dissent became more liberal and in 1778 the disabilities that were imposed on Catholics by the 'Act for the further preventing the growth of Popery', passed in 1700, were removed. In the following year dissenting teachers were relieved from subscribing to certain of the Thirty-nine Articles.[4] These, however, were measures which received only a grudging acceptance by an ecclesiastical establishment committed to the maintenance of its political ascendancy over all other religions. The Test and Corporation Acts remained in place, interfering both with religious liberty and civil liberty, the most humiliating of the badges worn by those who differed from the established faith.

Whilst it dissipated its spiritual credibility in this manner the Church became more fully integrated into public life due to its ties of patronage with the State. Government control of the vast mass of Church benefices, the practices of preferment and pluralism (the holding of more than one benefice), and the high value of bishoprics together constituted the great engine of influence operated by successive ministries in the eighteenth century. Quite simply, ecclesiastical preferment depended on politics. Edmund Gibson, the Bishop of London, described his own policy thus: 'the persons whom I recommended to the favour of the Court, were such, as besides their known affection to the established Church, were also known to be well affected toward the administration in the State.'[5] Those who were useful to the administration travelled quickly up the ladder of preferment. The clergy in their turn could render valuable service to the party that sponsored them. The votes of the bishops and their proxies were often vital in the House of Lords. Outside parliament the literary talents of the clergy were exploited by both Court and Country parties, and each bishop controlled a network of interests in his diocese which were of great importance at election time. In short, the procedure of preferment, as described by Gibson in the early part of the century, brought 'the body of the clergy and the two Universities, at least to be easy under a Whig administration'.[6] But while this system worked to reduce the temperature of religious animosity, it naturally failed to act as a tonic for the general health of the Church. 'In spite of occasional outbursts of popular fanaticism, a religious languor fell over

---

[4] For extracts from these documents see E. N. Williams, *The Eighteenth-Century Constitution 1688–1815: Documents and Commentary* (Cambridge, 1970), ch. 5.

[5] Quoted by Sykes, *Edmund Gibson*, p. 408.

[6] Ibid.

England', is the estimate of the historian William Lecky.[7] This situation gave an impetus to all the vices associated with patronage and political influence (pluralities, sinecures, non-residence), and stocked the clerical ranks with many who were ill-suited for that profession. That it may also have served to enhance the cause of toleration in England is an accident of ecclesiastical history in this period for which the Anglican Church deserves little credit. It is against this background that Bentham's writings on 'religious liberty' and on the 'alliance' between Church and State should be read.

---

[7] W. E. H. Lecky, *History of England in the Eighteenth Century*, 8 vols. (1878–90; repr. London, 1907), i. 336.

Religious Liberty

> Whether your opinions be true or false, the dissemination of
> them beneficial or pernicious, I regard the cause for which you
> suffer as being the cause of whatever is good in religion or
> government: the cause of free enquiry, on which all truth, and
> consequently all useful truth, depends.
>
> JB to Richard Carlile (10 Apr. 1820), UC 10/18

THE history of Bentham's advocacy of a greater degree of freedom to
express religious opinions (and opinions *on* religion) without penalty
begins much earlier than the publication of *Swear Not at All*, the tract
in which he first publicly gave vent to his distaste for the exclusionary
practices of official religion. In essence it was present from the time
when he first speculated on religious matters. Nor is it surprising that
Bentham's first thoughts on religion should have focused on the issue
of toleration. The eighteenth century was an age which wrestled long
and hard with the question of toleration. Ever since Locke wrote the
Epistola de Tolerantia Englishmen had been consumed by the problem
of delineating the precise degree of toleration of nonconforming sects
that a state religion should allow. The official view was that toleration
of dissenting religions was an integral element of the constitution, but
it was consistently denied that toleration implied any rights to political
power. The State might choose to tolerate opinions which differed
from those of the Established Church, but it could not admit
Dissenters to full citizenship without irrevocably destroying the theory
that the two institutions, Established Church and State, were
coextensive. The Church of England clergy certainly gave voice to the
ideal of toleration, but they also sought to curtail in practice what they
upheld in principle. The defeat inflicted on Fox's motion of 2 March
1790 for repeal of the Test Act was decisive enough (294 votes to 105)
to banish the question from parliament for many a long year.[1]

The *Epistola* foreshadowed the main arguments employed by
protagonists in the debate. Locke begins by making a clear distinction
between the functions of State and Church: the one is concerned with
property and general well-being, the other with the salvation of the

---

[1] S. Maccoby, *English Radicalism 1786–1832* (London, 1935), 444.

soul. This differentiation of functions limits the rights that Church and State possess *vis-à-vis* the citizen: the State has no right to impose a religious faith; the Church may not persecute rival sects. In this way Locke believed he had established the theoretical, as well as the practical, foundations of tolerance. However, Locke also argued that toleration could not be boundless. In fact he stipulated four categories of persons who were to be excluded from its terms: (*a*) those who profess a creed 'incompatible with human society and contrary to the good morals which are necessary for the preservation of civil society'; (*b*) those who 'arrogate to themselves, and to those of their own sect, some peculiar prerogative, contrary to civil right', whereby they claim the right of being intolerant towards those who do not share their faith (Locke gives the example of those who preach that heretics should not be trusted); (*c*) Roman Catholics—those belonging to a Church 'which is so constituted that all who enter it *ipso facto* pass into the allegiance and service of another prince'; and (*d*) those 'who deny the existence of the Deity' are not be tolerated under any circumstances.[2]

The objection to atheists rested partly on political grounds—the belief in God is necessary for the existence of moral conduct, for oaths and promises could mean nothing to an unbeliever. Hence it was claimed that atheism undermines the very basis of human society. But the objection was also partly theological or philosophical: 'the taking away of God', Locke wrote, 'even in thought, dissolves all.'[3] Though he was prepared to plead for a complete liberty of all 'purely speculative' opinions, he held that the belief in a Deity is not to be reckoned of this sort. A zealous atheist, such as Bentham, could not have been tolerated by the Lockian magistrate: 'a man who by his atheism undermines and destroys all religion cannot in the name of religion claim the privilege of toleration for himself.'[4] The position of Catholics was somewhat different; their exclusion from the terms of toleration was entirely political and understandable given the age in which Locke wrote. Individuals were to be left free to 'breed their children or dispose of their estates as they please', or to 'work or rest when they think fit', to practise polygamy or divorce, to eat or abstain from flesh or fish at certain seasons, and so on. These and similar 'indifferent' opinions and 'the actions following from them' deserve

---

[2] J. Locke, *Epistola de Tolerantia: A Letter on Toleration*, ed. R. Klibansky and J. W. Gough (Oxford, 1968), 131–5.

[3] Ibid. 135.

[4] Quoted by Klibansky and Gough from an earlier draft of the essay, ibid. 34.

toleration according to Locke. Unless they tend to be or are 'destructive to human society', the magistrate should not interfere in them unnecessarily; but when individuals 'mix with their religious worship and speculative opinions other doctrines absolutely destructive to the society wherein they live' the magistrate can no longer stand aside.[5]

The *Epistola* and Locke's other writings on toleration were reprinted periodically throughout the following century, in English and in French translations. The most notable French edition of the *Epistola* appeared in 1764, when it was coupled with Voltaire's treatise on toleration, under the title *Traité sur la tolérance, augmenté d'une lettre de Jean Locke sur le même* [sic] *sujet*.[6] In England, Locke's mantle was carried forth by several notable writers, but perhaps none more influential than William Paley. In the *Principles* he omitted to discuss the position of atheists, but in doing so he was far in advance of the teaching of the Church. So far as Catholics were concerned, he simply reiterated Locke's position that complete toleration was not yet possible while they still owed an allegiance outside the realm.[7]

Bentham broke from this tradition of writing about toleration. Very simply, he could accept no limits on toleration. The true doctrine of toleration, he noted in the *Analysis,* is 'that of leaving every man to recommend himself to God by the methods which he himself prefers, so long as he abstains from injuring others' (*An.* 40). There should be no exceptions. Though he admired Locke's work in metaphysics, in politics and religion they differed greatly. According to Bentham, if you allow the Church the luxury of intolerant laws you admit an engine of suffering and encourage an attitude ready to use it. He explained the growth of oppression from its roots in illusion in *Church-of-Englandism* thus:

From *imaginary* grace, imaginary *mystery*, imaginary *sacrament*, come imaginary *blasphemy*, imaginary *sin*; from imaginary sin, comes *real antipathy*; and from men, in ruling and otherwise influential situations, *real oppression* and *real persecution*, on that one part; *real suffering* on the other:—for, by the imaginary sin, is produced, in the ruling breast, along with the antipathy, a preference for gratifying it. (*CE* 85)[8]

[5] From an earlier draft, ibid. 17.

[6] This was published when Voltaire's campaign denouncing the execution of the Huguenot Jean Calas was at its height, and it is likely that Voltaire himself penned 'the masterly, searing preface' to Locke's essay, and that he deliberately chose to reaffirm the tradition of Locke's *Epistola* in his battle against the Jesuitical intolerance which dominated the French judicial system (ibid., preface, pp. xxix–xxx).

[7] Paley, *Principles*, in *Complete Works*, ii. 412.

[8] The psychology of intolerance is explored by Bentham at *An.* 76–83.

The only effective means to stifle the progression from such beliefs to human pain is to allow a complete toleration of all religious beliefs. Indeed, on one occasion Bentham voiced an objection to the very idea of toleration itself, since it implied that the Established Church was right in its beliefs, though magnanimous enough to allow a muted expression of contrary opinions. 'The word *toleration* [is] objectionable', he wrote. 'It is a legitimation of tyranny—It supposes a just cause of destruction and forbearance arising from want of inclination' (UC 5/149). For this reason Bentham occasionally employed the alternative terminology of 'religious liberty'. Nor was this a mere semantical difference.

The term 'tolerance' is correctly defined as an attitude or state of mind leading to 'toleration' as a policy or practice. The terms were used interchangeably in Locke's time and throughout the age following. Essentially, they were used to refer to a situation in which there existed an established or orthodox religion or Church, though dissent from it was permitted under certain conditions. Bentham's use of the terms 'religious liberty' was premeditated and intended to suggest something qualitatively different from the Lockian meaning of toleration. In its broadest meaning he used the phrase to refer to a situation in which every one is free to believe or disbelieve what he chooses and to form or join a Church or to refrain from doing so, without interference by the State and without the State giving any preference to one Church or form of religion rather than another. This formulation, unlike Locke's view of the matter, divests the Established Church of its privileged position and, more especially, includes under its rubric atheists as well as dissenting sects. Religious liberty, if it is to mean anything at all then, means liberty for all religions, and even the liberty not to be religious—like interest and love, Bentham held that religion should be free (*Corr.* iii. 518).[9]

The political implications of this position are readily apparent: on Bentham's view the freedom to disbelieve without penalty will bear witness to the extent of liberty enjoyed in a society. The problem of atheism and nonconformity is simply a question of oppression, of the unreasonable denial by government of civil and political liberties. Legislation using religion as the criterion of exclusion was established

---

[9] On another occasion Bentham wrote: 'As for trade, so for religion, . . . the best thing that a government could *now* do, would be not to meddle with it always excepted the purifying it from whatsoever portions of the *matter of wealth*, *power*, or *dignity*, in the shape of the *matter of corruption*, superstition have ever daubed it with' (*CE* 149).

and enforced in England solely to serve the interests of the few at the expense of the interests of the many. This was a long-standing grievance held by Bentham. In his Commonplace Book of the years 1781–5 he wrote: 'Offering rewards for faith, and punishments for the want of it, is . . . like offering rewards for, and punishing the want of, prejudice and partiality in a judge. To say, believe this proposition rather than its contrary, is to say do all that is in your power to believe it' (*Works*, x. 146). In some fragments on juries from *c.*1791 he specifically pointed to laws that enhanced religious preference and intolerance as in need of urgent attention (UC 35/11–12). Bentham was always struck by the absurdity of such laws and the religious tests that accompanied them.[10] However, it was in the manuscripts (1782–9) later used by Étienne Dumont for the *Traités de législation* (1802) that Bentham mounted the most concerted attack of his early career against the absurdities of penal laws against religious nonconformity. He begins in his usual exhaustive manner, dividing the persons whom the legislator wishes to influence by interfering in religious affairs into three categories: 'those who are already of the same opinion with the legislator; those who reject that opinion; those who neither adopt nor reject it'.[11] Penal laws aimed at the regulation of religious beliefs will be effective only in the case of the last mentioned category of persons, since these are people who may be influenced by the security offered by compliance with the legislative will. For those who conform voluntarily a coercive law is not needed, and for sincere nonconformists it is useless, as is proved by the fact of their nonconformity. When a person has formed an opinion punishments will not change it; if anything they will serve to confirm the person in that opinion. This is likely, says Bentham, for two reasons: 'partly because the employment of constraint is a tacit avowal that arguments are wanting; partly because recourse to violent means produces an aversion to opinions so sustained'. In short, punishment 'never can oblige a man to believe, but only to pretend that he believes'.[12]

The attempt to regulate religious beliefs through coercion is pernicious on other grounds: penal legislation employed to augment

[10] Bentham made a few jottings *c.*1778 under the title 'Toleration—Emp. Russia' (UC 96/282), and he later considered writing an essay 'On Toleration' in reply to an article in the *Public Advertiser* of 12 May 1789 concerning the penal laws against nonconformists (UC 169/152).

[11] Bentham, *The Theory of Legislation*, p. 435.

[12] Ibid. UC 87/20–6 contains some of the material concerning religion and penal legislation used by Dumont.

the power of the established religion 'acts as an indirect means against that essential part of morals, which consists in respect for truth, and respect for public opinion'.[13] It becomes necessary that one section of the people accustom themselves to parroting the opinions of another part in order to maintain peace and security. In this hypocrisy, though 'innocent falsehoods' are distinguished from 'criminal falsehoods', a class of privileged lies are allowed as a defence against tyranny. 'In the midst of these subtilties [*sic*]', writes Bentham,

respect for truth disappears; the limits of good and evil are confounded; a train of less pardonable falsehoods is introduced under cover of those already described; the tribunal of opinion is divided; the judges who compose it do not follow the same law; they do not clearly know what degree of dissimulation they ought to condemn or what they ought to excuse. The votes are scattered and contradictory, and the moral sanction, having no longer, a uniform regulator, grows weak and loses its influence. Thus, the legislator who imposes religious tests becomes the corrupter of the nation.[14]

For Bentham, naturally, it was the clergy of the Anglican Church who lay behind the preservation of such discriminatory legislation. Their aim was to limit liberty in religion as a prerequisite to staving off any attempt at revisionism in doctrine or reform of the institutions of the Church. 'Examination and discussion', Bentham explained, 'are dreaded by men who feel the ground shaking under their feet. It will not do to allow any alterations in a building which lacks a foundation . . . In one word, according to this system, it is necessary to put a bandage about the eyes, lest we be wounded by the light of day.'[15]

It was *not despite*, then, but *because of* his criticisms and reservations about the efficacy of religion, that Bentham argued that its practice should be allowed unfettered by legislation. For only then could one expect any salutary effects in the field of public morals and, more particularly, reforms in the institutions and doctrines of the Established Church. The end in view, however, should not be construed simply in terms of the adaptation by government of policies of toleration. These would, of course, be welcomed, but Bentham had something more in mind than merely this: opposition to Anglican dominance meant also a repudiation of that political and social framework by which the religious establishment was maintained. Conceived at the earliest period of his philosophical career, his aim was to remove toleration

---

[13] Bentham, *The Theory of Legislation*, p. 437.
[14] Ibid. 436.   [15] Ibid. 437.

from the realm of State policy. Bentham reduced the problem to a simple formula: to sever Church from State is to divest government of any need to impose limitations on religious beliefs and practices. For where there exists no such relationship there exists no need for policies of toleration since all religions are tolerated.

This was not an ideal readily embraced by the supporters of the status quo. As Robert Paul Wolff has pointed out, 'a grudging acceptance of the *de facto* heterodoxy and not . . . Protestant devotion to the freedom of individual conscience' was the principle source of the Anglo-American tradition of religious liberty.[16] Eventually, it was the high social cost of suppression that caused the State to tolerate divergent religions. Even so, the theoretical arguments for religious liberty had been persuasively set forth by Bentham a long time before they became a commonplace of English social and political life.[17]

The theme of 'religious liberty' provides a thread by which we can weave together a variety of issues addressed by Bentham in his battle with the English theocracy—from his early denunciation of subscription to articles of faith, the problems of oaths generally, and his lifelong struggle against restrictions limiting freedom of expression, to the political problems of the Irish Catholics.[18] The writings I shall be using, however, are of a highly fragmentary nature. I cannot pretend to do more than to piece together the thoughts of a man who began writing on such matters in the early 1770s and who remained involved with them into the final years of his life sixty years later.

---

[16] R. P. Wolff, 'Beyond Tolerance', in R. P. Wolff *et al.*, *A Critique of Pure Tolerance* (Boston, 1970), 15.

[17] Not surprisingly there are several striking similarities between the views of Bentham and the younger Mill on the question of religious liberty, but I certainly do not wish to claim that all legislation in 19th-cent. England relieving Dissenters of penalties for their beliefs or the long series of Oath's Acts, can be traced to the influence of Bentham and his disciples. This would appear to be the implausible position taken by A. V. Dicey, *Lectures on the Relation between Law and Public Opinion in England during the Nineteenth Century* (1905; 2nd edn. London, 1962), 204.

[18] Bentham's discussion of the more peculiar plight of homosexuals in England I consider below in ch. 9.

3

The Subscription Controversy

IN 1773 or early 1774 Bentham gave serious consideration to the notion of publishing an attack on the practice in the universities of imposing on students subscription to articles of faith.[1] The manuscripts he prepared for this work have never been published; for over one hundred years they have rested undisturbed in the vaults of the library at University College London (UC 5/1–32; 96/263–341). Before turning to look at the content of these manuscripts, however, it will be useful to review briefly as much of Bentham's personal history as is germane to his interest in subscription and also provide something of the historical context in which his writing on this subject occurred.

1. Oxford, Cambridge, and the 'Feathers Tavern Petition'

It is to Bentham's stay at Oxford (1760–4), which he entered as a precocious youth of not quite thirteen years and left a young man of sixteen, that we must look for concrete evidence of his early disaffection with the Church. When he entered The Queen's College, to which he had been sent by a father ambitious for his son's future career in the law, several of the more than fifty volumes he took with him were of a religious nature, most notably Buchanan's *Psalms*, the *Rational Catechism*, the *English Common Prayer Book*, and Milton's *Paradise Lost* and *Paradise Regained*.[2] There is nothing to suggest that Bentham was not sincerely religious at this time. It is doubtful whether John Bowring is correct in saying that the fact that he did not have to take the university oaths on account of his tender age 'relieved his mind from a state of very painful doubt' (*Works*, x. 36). Only a short time before this he had subscribed to the statutes of the university

---

[1] A reference to a letter in a journal of the day which appeared 'between the 30 July and the 5th August 1773' (UC 5/28) suggests that Bentham began this work soon after, i.e. late 1773 or early 1774.

[2] Everett, *The Education of Jeremy Bentham*, p. 24, and *Jeremy Bentham*, p. 15. For a complete listing see *Works*, x. 36 n.

without murmur.[3] But his objections to the swearing of oaths began to dawn upon him soon after, for graduation from Oxford at that time required subscription to the Thirty-nine Articles of the Anglican Church.[4] Being properly raised in religious matters one would expect Bentham, like the rest of his university contemporaries, to take the Articles on trust and to subscribe without question. But Bentham was not like his contemporaries; being the enquiring young genius he was, he set out to examine that which he would be asked to profess to believe. 'The examination', he recalled in later life, 'was unfortunate' (*Works*, x. 93). At the head of the Articles he found a statement of Charles I's declaring that they were to be understood literally. His distress upon reading them was predictable: 'In some of them no meaning at all could I find; in others no meaning but one which, in my eyes, was but too plainly irreconciliable [*sic*] either to reason or to scripture.' The master responsible for clearing up such doubts in the minds of students was of little assistance. Bentham was told that it was presumptuous for one so young to question that which had been framed 'by some of the holiest as well as the best and wisest men that ever lived' (*Works*, x. 93). He signed but there is no question that the experience left an indelible mark upon him, and the requiring of oaths was a subject to which he was to return again and again. The beginning of his disaffection with official or organized religion dates from this time. As he was to say on many future occasions, by imposing the practice of subscription to articles of belief, stated as they were in vague and ambiguous language, the Church made perjurers of its congregation. Moreover, this initial experience with oaths at Oxford soon brought him to the political significance of the charade: oaths and the like are demanded because the State requires them to be performed in order to further its own interests; the hypocrisy is masked by outward reverence and the fulfilment of formalities which themselves hardly constitute a sacrifice.

---

[3] Bentham subscribed to the Statutes of the University of Oxford on 28 June 1760 and took up residence at The Queen's College the following Oct. (Everett, *The Education of Jeremy Bentham*, p. 23).

[4] Archbishop Cranmer's Forty-two Articles of 1553 were revised in 1558 and again in 1563. When all hope of reconciliation with Rome was destroyed in 1571, Art. 29 was restored (omitted in 1558 because of its offensiveness to Catholics), and with a few other minor changes the Articles were approved by Convocation and clerical subscription henceforth required by law. Save for a Puritan-sponsored amendment to Art. 16 in 1643, these are the Articles which have come down to us today. For a brief historical discussion see E. J. Bicknell, *A Theological Introduction to the Thirty-Nine Articles of the Church of England* (1919; 3rd edn. rev. H. J. Carpenter London, 1955), 7–21.

Bentham's second brush with the intolerance of official religion occurred only six months later. In a letter to his father (4 Mar. 1761) he mentions a number of his friends at Queen's who had been converted to 'the Methodistical doctrine' and describes them as 'such Fanaticks that they are much more Enthusiastical than the Methodists at London' (*Corr.* i. 36). The Methodists were not an organized religion separate from the Church of England at this time, but their tendency to hold private meetings of small numbers and their enthusiasm for prayer and hymn singing rankled with the official clergy.[5] The suppression of the Methodists by the university authorities was immediate and final. Charged and convicted of heresy they were 'sent down', and Bentham was left to reflect that religious sentiment and the Church did not always see eye to eye. Later on in the preface to *Church-of-Englandism* he went so far as to claim that this incident was the occasion of his first doubts concerning the Church: 'by the sentence which those readers of the Bible were thus expelled from the University, that affection which at its entrance had glared with so sincere a fervor [*sic*]—my reverence for the Church of England—her doctrine, her discipline, her Universities, her ordinances—was expelled from my youthful breast' (*CE*, p. xix).

These two incidents, the subscription experience and the suppression of the Methodists, both occurring within his first year at Queen's, began a train of thought in his mind that remained unbroken throughout his life. Both the Church and the universities, for Cambridge was similarly characterized by ecclesiastical dominance, were henceforth inextricably linked in his mind with the perpetration of hypocrisy. Oxford was the training school of theology, the sanctuary of religion, the jealous guardian of the Church tenets in their pure form. These tenets were found by Bentham to be unmeaning in several crucial instances, and the university, by imposing subscriptions, forced perjury upon its pupils. Moreover, Bentham was soon to be made aware that, while genuine religious zeal was suppressed at Oxford, at the same time it housed the infamous Hell Fire Club, 'a club of Unbelievers, Atheists, and Deists', all the members of which would have had to subscribe to the Thirty-nine Articles of the Established Church (*Works*, x. 39). All

---

[5] That Bentham should consider joining his companions (*Works*, x. 93) is perhaps proof that he had not yet lost all religious belief, and undermines Mack's view that 'his religious convictions had been fixed by the oath-taking ordeal he underwent at Oxford' (*Jeremy Bentham*, p. 49). Yet neither could it be said, as John Hill Burton suggests, that Bentham entered adult life as a 'zealous supporter' of the Church (*Benthamiana*, p. xiii).

his life he viewed with horror the compulsion to adhere outwardly to what one did not inwardly accept. He found little of Christian morality among either the pupils or the masters at Oxford and to the end of his days spoke of his time there with acrimony.

Not that Bentham's disgruntlement with Oxford was confined to religious matters. In his intended preface to Bergman's *Essay on the Usefulness of Chemistry* he vilified its professors 'who deem it if not more useful at least more ornamental to know what the ancients have dreamt than what the moderns have observed' (UC 156/6). His despair at the neglect of the sciences at Oxford was particularly notable, as was his frustration with a theology he described as 'that scourge and reproach to human kind'.[6] Mystery is the key to 'the Oxford Theology', he recalled in the *Deontology*. At Oxford, mystery— 'that appetite which . . . keeps itself in the hunt for absurdity and nonsense'—is ever present and 'the more mystery the more merit' (*Deon.* 159). The superiority in learning of the Scottish universities he put down to the fact that they do not demand subscription from their students (*Deon.* 55).

Over the next few years, as we have seen, Bentham read widely and slowly garnered the knowledge that gave form to his secular version of the doctrine of utility. It was to be almost ten years after he graduated from Oxford, however, before he first wrote upon religious matters. When he did it was fitting that his subject should be subscription to articles of faith. Some time in 1773 or early 1774 he broke off from his work on Blackstone's *Commentaries* to jot down his thoughts on the matter. It seems likely that it was the 'Subscription Controversy', which began among the dissatisfied masters of Cambridge in 1766 and over the next eight years engaged the pens of several eminent clergymen, that reminded Bentham of his own unhappy experience at Oxford. According to the *Gentlemen's Magazine* (June 1772) between 1766 and 1772 the issue was debated in over forty pamphlets.[7] The

---

[6] The latter phrase appears in isolation on the same page as a paragraph in which Bentham complained that he learnt nothing about the physical world while at Oxford: 'This complaint would not long subsist if but half of the time were given there to the study of chemistry that is consumed for example in the study of the Greek Testament: a curious study indeed but which certainly is not necessary to salvation, since the poor to whom the kingdom of heaven belongs by excellence, are necessarily debarred from it: and which if it is not necessary to salvation is certainly not necessary for any else.' For this and other quotations from the Bergman MSS lamenting the dearth of natural philosophy taught at Oxford see Linder and Smeaton, 'Schwediauer, Bentham and Beddoes', pp. 268–9.

[7] For a discussion of the controversy see D. A. Winstanley, *Unreformed Cambridge: A*

controversy heightened in 1771 when Francis Blackburne, the Rector of Richmond in Yorkshire, drew up proposals for a petition for relief of Dissenters to be presented to parliament. In essence, it was a plea for a relaxation of the terms of subscription to the Thirty-nine Articles. This became known as the 'Feathers Tavern Petition'. Of the 250 subscribers to the petition who met under Blackburne's leadership at London's Feathers Tavern only a few were laymen; the overwhelming majority were beneficed clergymen and Fellows of the University of Cambridge.[8] In February of the following year the House of Commons rejected the petition by a vote of 271 to 71.[9] The failure of the petition, however, did not signal the end of the affair, and for another two years a gentlemanly but vigorous debate ensued at the universities. Bentham was almost certainly aware of these exchanges and may have been tempted to enter the fray with an offering of his own. The issue was a delicate one and he perhaps showed good sense in withholding his efforts; they were unlikely to win him friends and were sure to turn many against him.

Edmund Law was at the forefront of the debate. A subscriber to Blackburne's petition, he remained on the side of reform and in 1774 published his *Considerations on the Propriety of Requiring Subscription to Articles of Faith*. He was answered by Thomas Randolph, President of Corpus Christi, Oxford, in a tract bearing the title *The Reasonableness of Subscription to Articles of Religion* (1774). William Paley, who had inexplicably refused to sign the petition, now entered the debate on the side of the reformers and published anonymously his *Defence of the Considerations* (1774). The arguments contained in this pamphlet stand as a summary of the position of the reformers, and were repeated later by Paley in a brief chapter on subscription included in the *Principles*.[10] It was this part of that 'capital book' that George Wilson singled out for

Study of Certain Aspects of the University in the Eighteenth Century (Cambridge, 1935), 301–16; C. Robbins, *The Eighteenth-Century Commonwealthmen* (Cambridge, Mass., 1961), 324–35; M. L. Clarke, *Paley: Evidences for the Man* (Toronto, 1974), 17–23; LeMahieu, *The Mind of William Paley*, pp. 16–19.

[8] Abbey, *The English Church and its Bishops*, ii. 124.

[9] Even so there shortly followed at Cambridge (23 June 1772) the substitution of a declaration of bona fide Church membership for subscription to the 3 articles of the 36th Canon (Dicey, *Lectures on the Relation between Law and Public Opinion*, App. Note III, 479). Bentham noted this fact at UC 96/272.

[10] Here, and in his *Defence of the Considerations*, Paley adopted the same line as he had previously argued in his Cambridge lectures. This is clear from his extant lectures notes (BL Add. MSS 12079/113–14, cited Clarke, *Paley*, p. 21).

criticism in his letter to Bentham informing him of Paley's success in giving currency to the doctrine of utility (*Corr.* iii. 490).

The primary concern in subscription, Paley argued, is the intention of the imposer. In the case of the Thirty-nine Articles the imposer was the legislature of 1571. It is this intention which has to be understood and satisfied by the subscriber:

> They who contend, that nothing less can justify subscription to the Thirty-nine Articles, than the actual belief of each and every separate proposition contained in them, must suppose, that the legislature expected the consent of ten thousand men, and that in perpetual succession, not to one controverted proposition, but to many hundreds. It is difficult to conceive how this could be expected by any, who observed the incurable diversity of human opinion upon all subjects short of demonstration.[11]

What the authors of the law intended, according to Paley, was to exclude from office, in Church and State, Catholics and other non-conformists who were hostile to an episcopal constitution. Anybody who fell under this category ought not to subscribe, nor should anyone else 'who is not first convinced that he is truly and substantially satisfying the intention of the legislature'.[12] The conclusion Paley drew is that it is legitimate for all others to subscribe, regardless of individual doubts pertaining to separate articles of faith.[13] The argument for the exclusion of certain religions on political grounds is reiterated later in the *Principles* in the chapter on religious establishments and toleration:

> The State undoubtedly has a right to refuse its power and its confidence to those who seek its destruction. Wherefore, if the generality of a religious sect entertain dispositions hostile to the constitution, and if government have no other way of knowing its enemies than by the religion which they profess, the professors of that religion may justly be excluded from offices of trust and authority.[14]

The argument is reminiscent of that given by Locke in the *Epistola*. Despite his liberal interpretation of what it means to subscribe to the Thirty-nine Articles, Paley thought subscription and other methods of

---

[11] Paley, *Principles*, in *Complete Works*, ii, Bk. III, pt. 1, ch. 22, p. 135.

[12] Ibid.

[13] The latitude in interpretation demanded by Paley and others was to be officially granted in 1865, when Convocation revised the oath of subscription so that belief was professed to the effect that 'the doctrine of the Church of England therein set forth [is] . . . agreeable to the Word of God' (Bicknell, *A Theological Introduction to the Thirty-Nine Articles*, p. 21).

[14] Paley, *Principles*, in *Complete Works*, ii, Bk. IV, ch. 10, p. 410.

exclusion enforced by the State to be necessary to preserve the constitution, and thus to protect the privileged position of the Church.

2. Unpublished manuscripts on subscription

Bentham's attack on the ecclesiastical establishment in later life showed full awareness of the connection between the policies of exclusion and the nature of the alliance between Church and State. But it is also the case that in the early unpublished manuscripts on subscription his arguments, though fragmentary, were no less clear about the significance of this relationship. Intolerance, he writes, is the inevitable product of the existence of an established religion:

> We see in this country where it is established, disputes rising upon disputes, precisely . . . because it is established: We see in other countries where it is not established, where the opinions it is designed to suppress are suffer'd to be expressed, and all sorts of other opinions which it is never expected [?] to suppress, men living without dispute. (UC 5/5)

The political consequences of tolerance cannot be ignored. If the State does not protect those who differ from it on the score of religion then what allegiance do Dissenters owe to government? Intolerance is a threat to the security of the society; it is the road to civil unrest (UC 5/4). But tolerant attitudes are not enshrined solely in government policies. In anticipation of John Stuart Mill, Bentham saw that the disapprobation of the people at large towards so-called heretical opinions can be more tyrannical even than official oppressive measures and its consequences just as threatening (UC 5/2). The malice of our fellow men, he says, is typically the result of a rigid adherence to superstitious dogmas, dogmas from which, he (with tongue in cheek) thanks God, he has long since freed himself (UC 5/8).

Though there are a few occasional asides dealing with specific Church doctrines, in these early manuscripts Bentham was primarily concerned with the problems posed by religion as it was established in England. He freely admitted that the penal laws for religious non-conformity were rarely enacted, and that those in existence commonly lay dormant upon the statute books. The reason for this, he suggests, is the Englishman's 'general aversion to intolerance'. 'The sense of the whole nation', he continues, is 'manifested by the uninterrupted sleep in which these laws have hitherto been continued' (UC 96/325; cf.

also 96/330–5). What then is the reason for their continuance? Would repeal really pose a threat to the security of England? Bentham points to the United States, as he was to do so many times again in the future, to prove otherwise; there, at least, the lack of religious penal laws has not occasioned any threat to the security of the State. Witness 'the code of legislation in the Carolinas', he demands (UC 96/325). Nor has the Empress of Russia 'been brought even by the experience of riots and insurrections on religious accounts to withdraw her Law of universal toleration'. Why not? Because, 'that wise and magnanimous Princess knows, that knowledge is the only antidote to these disorders, together with that freedom of examination which produces and disperses it' (UC 96/282).

Bentham's focus in these manuscripts, however, is on the compulsory subscription to articles of faith imposed by the ecclesiastical government of the Anglican Church. Subscription appears to be the most innocent form of public profession of one's faith, but in reality, says Bentham, it is one of the most perfidious of methods employed by the Church to protect its privileges and interests. Leaving us in no doubt as to his position on this matter, the title he suggests for his proposed work based on these manuscripts is 'Subscription a State-poison' (UC 5/13). As a consequence of his own experiences at Oxford he was certain that subscription entailed a perversion of the moral understanding and the intellect. Subscriptions are poisonous because they lead us to mistrust our own reason, and to assert belief in that which we plainly cannot comprehend and even that which under other circumstances we would deny outright (UC 5/5). Added to this, the confusions caused by the linguistic vagaries in which religious beliefs are couched by the Church inculcate an obsequiousness to authority, secular as well as ecclesiastical, which has always constituted an impediment to improvement (UC 97/48; cf. also 5/6). Those of more scrupulous conscience pay the penalty for their honesty in refusing to subscribe to articles of faith they find abhorrent to their conscience; they are condemned as atheists, while those 'who sign any thing are the Godly, the Salt of the Earth' (UC 96/275). Bentham proposed a new form of subscription which he deemed a more honest avowal than the formularies of the Church of England:

I A.B. do sincerely promise and swear that I will not look for the truth—that if I meet it by accident in the way, I will turn aside from it. That my word shall be at perpetual variance with my thought, or else that I will not think at all. That I will hear only the arguments on one side—or if I hear the other, which shall only be in the view to answer them I will keep my temper worked up to a fit of spleen against them all the while—I renounce impartiality as the arbiter of falsehood—I embrace prejudice, as the safeguard of all truth. (UC 5/10)

In writing these manuscripts Bentham almost certainly had the contemporary controversy over subscription at the universities in mind, but his analysis was of far greater breadth and the stance he adopted much more extreme than that of the clerical combatants in the contest. Subscription was not merely an outdated practice or merely too strictly enforced; for Bentham it was a recipe for stagnation, a positive counter to efforts at reform both eccesiastical and political. Foreshadowing his later much voiced grievances against the Church as an obstacle to reform, in these early manuscripts he laid bare what he saw as the real crux of the matter. Under the heading 'Obstacles to Improvement', he writes:

That state of prepared imbecility which is necessary to a mind for the tranquil reception of one parcel of Nonsense, fits it for another . . . A man who after reading the scriptures can bring himself to fancy the doctrines of the Athanasian Creed . . . his mind if not already blotted over with hieroglyphical chimeras is a sheet of blank paper, on which any one who will press hard enough may write what scrawls he pleases. (UC 97/48; cf. also 5/6)

The Athanasian Creed is a formulary at the core of Anglicanism: here it is denounced as, 'That compound of everything that is either odious or contemptible in language . . ., doctrines without sense, and curses without mercy' (UC 5/28). The linguistic referent is a testimony to Bentham's developing interest in the malleability of language, but the political point is that the practice of subscription made it easy for unscrupulous clergymen, many of them ill-educated for their posts, to corrupt the young by inculcating in their minds whatever fears and fancies might be conducive to ecclesiastical authority. Such a clergyman 'stamps the figure upon the infant mind of his [own] mutilated and stunted intellect' (UC 97/48). This process of 'prepared imbecility' leads to the docile acceptance of authority and ultimately to the refusal in later life to consider measures of reform. If good legislation presupposes a psychological insight into human behaviour, the clergyman's bad education keeps him blind to the real needs of his congregation and, therefore, makes him a bad legislator. Nor could his pupils, raised according to the same system and the tenets of the same tradition, be expected to fare any better. The process is a self-perpetuating one.

There is little doubt, too, that in these early manuscripts Bentham drew upon his recollections of Oxford, where he found evidence neither of Paley's convenient understanding of legislatorial intent nor of the latitude of interpretation that the Tractarians were later to profess *vis-à-vis* the Thirty-nine Articles. Bentham could never forget that the heresy for which his Methodist friends were expelled from the University was the different interpretation they held of certain of the articles (*CE* 15). Under the heading 'Ironical Proposal' he suggests that a court of divines be established to adjudicate once and for all on controversial articles of faith, publish its decisions, and then call on the members of each university to subscribe sincerely to its findings (UC 96/268). Bentham hints that this practice might usefully be adopted in every other science. But he did not intend the suggestion, that only if the subject-matter of subscriptions were fixed would they do no harm, to be taken seriously (UC 96/273). He never deviated from the belief that insincerity is bound to be the price of subscription. A man might attempt some form of reconciliation between his oath and his beliefs, or he might try to live with the knowledge of their incompatibility, but more often than not 'he resolves to forget his declaration as fast as possible, and think nothing about the matter' (UC 96/270). On these terms a 'subscribing University' is 'an institution for the retardment [*sic*] of political & moral . . . knowledge, much more certainly, than for the advancement of any other' (UC 96/269). Here the college tutor is ever ready 'to make an apology of his own tranquility by defending the necessity and proclaiming the lightness of those fetters, under which his more scrupulous brethren groan in vain'. All enquiries that threaten this tranquility are to be stifled; the vigour of youthful minds is to be cut short (UC 96/270). 'Hence that foul mixture of Servility and Tyranny: Servility, in bearing the yoke themselves; Tyranny in imposing it on others: Servility presumptive & probable: Tyranny demonstrated and certain' (UC 96/271; cf. also 96/283).

Even granting for the sake of argument the purported merits of the practice, subscription to articles of faith is at best redundant, says Bentham, since there is an inherent defect in the practice itself, a dilemma which the advocates of oaths have 'never yet repelled nor ever will be able'. Either subscriptions serve to preclude a diversity of opinions regarding articles of faith in those who sign them or they do not, 'if they do, they are Tyrannous, if they do not, they are useless' (UC 96/274). Whichever is the case the consequences are surely pernicious: 'On examination it will be found that in the [clerical] *order* this practice implants many vices and not one virtue—in the state many mischiefs and not one advantage' (UC 96/291).

Bentham's message is clear: what 'religious truth' (or rather the truth about religion), like all other truths, needs more than anything else from legislation is 'the liberty of making itself heard' (UC 69/14). England is far from being the home of toleration frequently pictured by foreign observers, and Bentham is certain that they would revise their assessment if they could be made to 'see what labor [*sic*] is spent & to how little purpose to impetrate [?] for it [i.e. England] a blessing which otherwise they might suppose it to have this long time been enjoying' (UC 96/266).

3. A hiatus in the attack

That Bentham had abolition, or at the very least a major reform, of the practice of subscription in mind when he wrote upon the subject in the early 1770s, is implied by his musing that his strictures may be 'out of Season' and might better 'serve for another parliament, or another Age' (UC 96/266). Perhaps the failure of the 'Feathers Tavern Petition', backed as it was by so large a number of Cambridge Divines, had brought home to some the futility of hoping for even a limited reform at that time. Bentham, for one, was certainly not deterred. Yet his material went undeveloped and remained of a fragmentary nature. There are perhaps several reasons for this: his pressing concern with his reply to Blackstone, his lifelong habit of leaving projects incomplete to be returned to on a future occasion, and, more interestingly, his discovery of another publication on the topic of religion which he said left 'nothing for me to add' (UC 96/138). An article by Joseph Addison in volume 5 of *The Spectator*, no. 459 (1712), would appear to be the publication meant by Bentham, his reference appearing amid a list of chapter or topic headings (relating to subscription, oaths, and juries) under the general title 'INTRO Sanction Religious. Abuses debilitative of the Religious Sanction. Catalogue of'.[15]

The theme of Addison's article is the division of Christian duty into 'morality' and 'faith' and the reasons why the first is pre-eminent over

---

[15] The list of chapter or topic headings reads: '1st Subscriptions; 2nd On the Catechism; 3dly Custom-House Oaths; 4 False findings of Juries; 5 Pleasantrys [?] of Judges; 6 Coroners Inquests; 7 Oaths of Observance to University Statutes; 8 Forced unanimity of Juries' (UC 96/138).

the second. Briefly, the argument is that the excellence of faith consists only in the influence it has on morality. Underlying this is the critical stance that the 'pure and uncorrupt' doctrines of Christianity may not be those embraced by the Anglican Church, and that 'Persecuting Men for Conscience Sake' is bad policy:

> besides imbittering [*sic*] their Minds with Hatred, Indignation, and all the Vehemence of Resentment, and insnaring [*sic*] them to profess what they do not believe; we cut them off from the Pleasures and Advantages of Society, afflict their Bodies, distress their Fortunes, hurt their Reputations, ruin their Families, make their Lives painful, or put an End to them.[16]

Bentham's manuscripts on subscription are written in similar utilitarian vein, but that there was nothing left for him to add to Addison's brief four-page attack must be seriously doubted. His own experience at Oxford would have made interesting, even poignant, reading on the subject, as later writings were to show. Moreover, the matter of subscription had recently occasioned a heated public dispute, and, for a young man keen to make his mark in the world, this would appear to have offered an excellent opportunity to unite controversy with the sincere belief that there was a wrong to be righted. Nor, when so much had been said and published by clergymen themselves on the matter, would Bentham have had to fear prosecution by the Attorney-General for the 'blasphemous' nature of his views. Whatever the reason for his restraint he abandoned the subject and returned to his work on jurisprudence and to his critique of Blackstone. Not that the topic was entirely forgotten. Bentham was always adept at combining current interests with his study of the law, and in *A Comment* we find him turning aside from his main subject to score a general hit against 'every-thing-as-it-should-be' Blackstone and against Oxford, where he had heard him lecture. Blackstone, he records, typified those 'nurtured in the Sanctuary of religion where a man steps not across a gutter but to break a Law, nor breaks a Law but he must break an oath' (*Comm.* 80). And again, after applauding the contribution made by Lord Kames's *Historical Law Tracts* (1758) to the development of 'an accurate and instructive branch of moral science' and for giving 'an account of the Principles of Law that could bear the test of criticism', he explained Kames's success with the observation that no 'subscribing University' could have produced such high calibre work (*Comm.* 313–14 n.).

---

[16] J. Addison, *The Spectator*, ed. D. F. Bond, 5 vols. (Oxford, 1965), iv, No. 459 (Sat., 16 Aug. 1712), 120.

During the next forty years Bentham periodically took an interest in the plight of the Dissenters but he wrote little of consequence on the subject.[17] He contemplated writing a reply to a letter published in the *Public Advertiser* of 12 May 1789 on the subject of toleration (UC 169/152), and his interest was aroused again the following year by a pamphlet written by the nonconformist Duke of Grafton, which included criticisms of the Anglican Liturgy and of the practice of subscription.[18] In a letter to Grafton (7 Sept. 1790?) Bentham remarked that his own concern with 'the tyranny exercised by the church over the consciences of men', and 'its pernicious influence over the public morals' is not inferior to the Duke's. His animosity towards the advocates of subscription is manifest:

The Rt. Rev. supporters of this profligate system find no difficulty in disclaiming all regard to liberty of conscience: but they will hardly deem it prudent openly to disclaim all regard/profess an equal disregard to truth/veracity, which they must do ere they can say a syllable in favour of the habitual perjury held up to observation here. (*Corr.* iv. 201)

With this letter to Grafton Bentham included a copy of chapter 5 of his *Draught of a Code for the . . . Judicial Establishment in France* (printed Mar. 1790), which contains a short section on 'Oaths of Office' pointing out the perjury frequently caused by requiring professions of belief on religious matters as a prerequisite to accepting public office (*Works*, iv. 285–304). Grafton replied (9 Sept. 1790) commending Bentham's observations and agreeing that the 'tyrannical System' had to be exposed in order that a general conviction of its absurdity be created preliminary to an organized attack in parliament (*Corr.* iv. 202). The required work of exposé, however, was not forthcoming until twenty years later, when Bentham embarked on a sustained and vigorous consideration of religious issues. None of his views on the pernicious-ness of the practice of subscription had changed in the interim, as the

---

[17] George Wilson kept Bentham informed of events while he was in Russia (Jan. 1786–Nov. 1787). In a letter of 24 Apr. 1787 he wrote: 'The Dissenters have failed to get the Test Act repealed, but the division was respectable, and they are not discouraged. They are very angry with Pitt, whom they will probably no longer support as they did at the general election. Priestley has written him a letter, a printed one, I mean, full of rage against Pitt, the Trinity, and the Church Establishment—clever enough, and very bold, but very indiscreet, and certainly prejudicial to the cause' (*Corr.* iii. 533). The letter by Priestley to which Wilson refers was published as *A Letter to the Right Honourable W. Pitt* (London, 1787).

[18] Duke of Grafton, *Hints, etc. Submitted to the Serious Attention of the Clergy, Nobility and Gentry, Newly Associated, by a Layman* (London, 1787).

section on university oaths in *Swear Not at All* shows (*Works*, v. 209–19), but now they featured as just one element in an all-encompassing offensive mounted by Bentham against Church institutions, practices, ritual, doctrines, and Christian beliefs in general. Qualms about the ecclesiastical mode of administering religion, expressed in the manuscripts on subscription, fostered doubts about the worth of religion as an agency of moral regulation, and these soon begat doubts about the truth of fundamental Christian doctrines and about the existence of God. The process was underscored from first to last by the peculiar principles upon which Bentham's approach to social analysis rested. In the later writings his position on religious matters is unequivocally expressed, but it is abundantly clear that he had begun thinking along these lines over forty years before he brought himself to risk the judgement of public opinion by publishing his blasphemy.

4

Oaths, Irish Catholics, and Blasphemy

THE first of Bentham's writings on religious topics to appear in print was *Swear Not at All* (printed in 1813, published 1817; *Works*, v. 187–229), and it is of particular interest as it provides a link both with his earliest complaints about the Church and with his writings on evidence in the first decade of the new century. Some time between 1809 and 1811 Bentham had occasion to return to the subject of oaths when investigating their use in courts of law (UC 96/138) and *Swear Not at All* was a product of this.[1] The title-page states that it was 'Pre-detached from an Introduction to the "Rationale of Evidence" ', a work printed in 1812 (*Works*, vi. 1–187); it appears that Bentham 'extracted' it from the material for chapter 9 of this work because it broke the thread of his discussion of the use of oaths in courts of law.[2]

Bentham's interest in the subject of oaths may also have been revived by the parliamentary debates on the Toleration Act of 1812.[3] Though he had little to say about the Act, he certainly was not satisfied with the retention of oaths required for the certification of Dissenting Ministers, for in February 1813 he was busy collecting information regarding subscription to articles of faith by the clergy.[4] The passing of the Unitarian Toleration Act in July of that year served to sharpen his interest. The imperfections of this measure, he commented later, were due to the sinister interest of the bishops who 'refuse to relinquish the power they have over people' (*CE*, p. xxxvii). It failed to annul all previous statutes imposing penalties against 'impugners of the Trinity', did not include Ireland within its terms of reference, and did nothing to alter the law regarding blasphemy. The charge of blasphemy was a frequent resort of government at this time, used to suppress literature deemed to be of a seditious or libellous nature as well as tracts aimed

---

[1] See C. K. Ogden, *Jeremy Bentham 1832–2032* (London, 1932), 87.

[2] A précis of the main arguments of *Swear Not at All* appears in the *Introductory View of the Rationale of Evidence*, in *Works*, vi. 28–9.

[3] For a discussion of the particulars of the act see Davis, *Dissent in Politics*, pp. 171–84.

[4] There is a letter from Henry Brougham to JB (9 Feb. 1813) written in response to the latter's enquiries for information regarding clerical subscriptions at UC 9/26–7.

directly at the Church and Christian beliefs. Bentham found this a particularly irksome feature of English Common Law and it was to figure again as a factor influencing his decision to publish *Swear Not at All*. In the Advertisement at the front of the pamphlet Bentham says that he was induced to publish it in 1817 because of,

> the addition so lately made of the scourge of religious persecution to the yoke of despotism:—for a pretence for punishment as for blasphemy . . .; and by men by whom the profession of piety has been converted into an instrument of power, the exertions so lately made, to bolster up by the force of their punishments the imbecility of their arguments. (*Works*, v. 189)

In a letter to the Unitarian MP, William Smith, in February of 1818 Bentham mentions in particular the blasphemy cases of William Hone and George Wright which took place the previous year (*CE*, preface), and these would appear to be the prosecutions he has in mind. Here, then, Bentham took up where he had left off in the 1770s and set out to bring the system of subscription and oath-taking to the ground.

1. The case against oaths

The text for *Swear Not at All* is taken from Matt. 5: 34. Ten years after the work was published Bentham remarked to Bowring, the constant companion of his later life, 'Was ever text more clear than that, "Swear not at all",—but it has been cavilled away by glosses and meanings which in no other case would be listened to for a minute' (*Works*, x. 582). In writing the material finally published as *Swear Not at All* Bentham set out to strike a general blow at the system of oath-taking by stripping the biblical text of all its 'glosses and meanings'. It was a masterful piece of polemic and, as one critic has observed, 'one of those great strokes by which Bentham from time to time struck at abuses'.[5] In seeking to expose the needlessness and mischievous consequences of oaths he employed four distinct lines of argument: (*a*) oaths are ineffectual in achieving their professed aim and frequently detrimental to the moral understanding; (*b*) they involve the unwarranted presumption that God will punish an oath-breaker; (*c*) the divine punishment threatened for the breaking of an oath is of such an uncertain nature that the mere uttering of an oath cannot be relied upon as testimony to the honesty of the swearer; and (*d*) oaths are a bulwark against innovation and a support to misrule.

[5] *DNB* ii. 275.

(*a*) According to Paley the most forceful argument for preserving oaths was the strictly utilitarian consideration that individuals have to trust one another 'and they have nothing better to trust than one another's oath'. Echoing the words of Locke's *Epistola*, he argued that the breaking of oaths, 'in its general consequence, strikes at the security of reputation, property, and even of life itself'.[6] Like Beccaria before him, Bentham sought to disprove the logic of this argument.[7] Oaths, he declared, are either useless or they are pernicious. Any potential security to be gained from the use of oaths in England has been sacrificed by the trivial use to which they have been put. In the essay *Of Indirect Methods of Preventing Crimes* Bentham had commented that, 'Oaths are degraded when they regard trifles, when they are employed upon occasions in which they will be violated by a kind of universal convention; and more especially when they are required in cases in which justice and humanity will make an excuse for, and almost a merit of, their violation' (*Works*, i. 567). A similar argument receives elaboration in the pages of *Swear Not at All*. Oaths binding us to frivolous obligations or unjust laws (as Paley also seems to have acknowledged)[8] are invariably broken upon the belief that God never meant to sanction such absurdities or such tyranny. Moreover, the nature of an oath does not vary with the character of the policy or law to which it is attached. Either an oath is binding or it is not. At Oxford, however, the 'mendacity-restraining' sanctions—the fear of shame or punishment, either at the hands of our fellow-men or at the hands of God—'have notoriously no application'; everyone takes oaths, all violate them, and nobody is ever punished or put to shame (*Works*, v. 196). Oaths to observe the statutes of the universities extracted on admission to Oxford and Cambridge are 'objects of continual, notorious, and open violation' (*Works*, v. 195). 'In both seats of piety', Bentham remarks, 'so perfectly and universally does it appear to be understood, that, applied to the purpose in question at least, an oath is a mere *matter of form*, i.e., that it amounts to nothing, and is of no use,—and that, where it is not punishable, *perjury* is a sort of thing that no man need put himself to the trouble of being ashamed of' (*Works*, v. 215). In fairness, the corrupting influence of university oaths was a feature that had previously occurred to Paley, who observed on one occasion that in some cases such oaths were impracticable, inconvenient,

---

[6] Paley, *Principles*, in *Complete Works*, ii, Bk. III, pt 1, ch. 4, p. 124.
[7] Beccaria, *On Crimes and Punishments*, ch. 11, p. 29.
[8] Paley, *Principles*, in *Complete Works*, ii, Bk. III, pt 1, ch. 16, p. 122.

useless, and had even become unlawful.[9] In *Swear Not at All* Bentham likened university oaths to Custom House oaths—ceremonies largely devoid of use. That most of the ordinances violated are useless and that their violation produces little mischief is beside the point—the oath ceremony includes an assertion and 'by the falsity of that assertion *sincerity* is violated' (*Works*, v. 216). The violation is a form of perjury which once committed is the more easily repeated, such that the habit of perjury is produced by custom (*Works*, v. 217). Bentham was appalled that at Oxford even barbers, cooks, bedmakers, errand boys, and other servants of the university were sworn in English to the observance of a medley of statutes penned in Latin—such oaths, never understood, were never kept.

Bentham did not deny that oaths might prove useful from time to time, but whatever efficacy an oath might have could be traced to its relationship to the moral sanction and not to its religious affiliation. As he put it in *The Rationale of Judicial Evidence* (1827): 'in most points and with most men, a declaration upon oath includes a declaration upon honour: the Laws of honour enjoining as to those points the observance of an oath'. Here deference is paid to the religious ceremony only in appearance; in reality it is paid to the 'moral judgement'. This is especially so in the case of judicial testimony, where the supposed power of the ceremony 'acts in conjunction with two real and efficient ones: the power of the political sanction and the power of the moral or popular sanction' (*Works*, vi. 312). But even where oaths are successful in binding a person to keep their word they are frequently productive of other mischiefs. For instance, in the *Book of Fallacies* Bentham points out that there is no guarantee that oaths will always be used for beneficial purposes. The offence for which God's wrath is meant to be a punishment is not the act which the oath was intended to prevent but 'the profanation of a ceremony' (*Fall*. 68). In other words, it does not matter for what purpose an oath is employed; if it is broken it is this which is to be punished. But, 'No sort of security is given, or can be given that it will be applied to the most beneficial purpose rather than to the most pernicious' (*Fall*. 68). Naturally, Bentham regarded the latter as the most likely on the grounds that if the purpose is beneficial then the act is likely to take place with or without an oath.

Bentham reserved his greatest scorn for the use of oaths in courts of law. Already in manuscripts dating from 1778–80, headed 'On

---

[9] Paley, *Principles*, in *Complete Works*, ii, Bk. II, pt 1, ch. 21. See also Bentham, *The Rational of Reward* (1825), in *Works*, ii. 210 and App. A, pp. 26–62.

Torture', he had likened the jury system to a form of torture. One of the consequences of the stupidity of requiring an unanimous verdict from a jury was to make the oaths of jurors redundant. The way the system works is that, 'A question is proposed to them to which they are required to say Yes or No: and this is always in a man's power. If they will do neither, they are to be shut up without meat, drink, fire or candle: that is they are to be starved: and if this obstinacy continues invincible they are of course to be starved to Death.[10] The threat of starvation completely dissolves any quibbles the jury might have about keeping to their oaths to deliver an honest verdict. Under these circumstances perjury is unavoidable:

There is indeed an impropriety, and a very glaring one in their being obliged all of them to say Yes or all of them to say No, when perhaps a number of them think oppositely. The answer is given upon oath; so that in effect this process is neither more nor less than torture applied to 12 men to force a certain number of them to commit perjury. As it stands, however, nobody even complains of this practice of closeting a jury away until they arrive at an unanimous verdict—it seems that 'there is no kind of perjury which custom will not render innocent in the eyes even of a religious people'.[11]

This attack on judicial oaths represents another facet of the comprehensive offensive mounted by Bentham from the 1770s onwards against England's legal system. In *Swear Not at All* he continued the attack. Here his argument is that the punishment for perjury is confined to that supposedly involved in the ceremony of an oath— Divine retribution—and as such this is an insufficient sanction to prevent the occurrence of mendacity (*Works*, v. 197–8).[12] In addition to this, however, he also claimed that oaths posed an obstacle to justice by excluding the evidence of Quakers and atheists. The case of Quakers he had already addressed some forty years before in the manuscripts for 'Crit[itical] Jur[isprudence] Crim[inal]'. Quakers are prevented by their faith from taking oaths; they understand the maxim 'swear not at all' literally. But to disregard the testimony of such persons on the grounds that they refuse to take an oath is an affront to

---

[10] Bentham on Torture', ed. W. L. Twining and P. E. Twining, in *Bentham on Legal Theory*, ed. M. H. James, *Northern Ireland Legal Quarterly*, 24:3 (1973), 53. The MSS 'On Torture' are at UC 46/63–70. A similar argument appears in the *Rationale of Judicial Evidence*, in *Works*, vi. 273.

[11] 'Bentham on Torture', ed. Twining and Twining, p. 53 n.

[12] Bentham offers more observations on the 'mendacity-licence' given by the judicial process in *An Introductory View of the Rationale of Evidence*, in *Works*, vi. 22–4.

honesty and an incentive to crime. On occasions where the only
evidence is that provided by a witness 'forbidden by a precept
sanctioned by the Religious Sanction from taking the Oath', the
consequence is that the criminal is set free 'and he and other criminals
derive from this impunity an . . . encouragement to fresh crimes'. In
case we should doubt that this could possibly happen in an English
court, Bentham notes that an 'Incendiarist' escaped by just such a
means, and refers us to the 'Gazeteer for April 19th 1776 or some day
in that week' (UC 69/20). The argument is repeated almost verbatim
in *Swear Not at All* (*Works*, v. 201).

Bentham's protest against the exclusion of atheists as witnesses and
jurors followed similar lines. Any 'presumption of improbity' which
can be afforded by atheism is very slight, and the cause of justice is
perverted by the exclusion of atheists from giving testimony on the
grounds that they refuse to take an oath. He found it especially galling
that an atheist could be excluded from giving evidence, since it could
only be known that he was an atheist by his own veracity, hence it was
his own honesty that provided the grounds for exclusion (*Works*, vi.
106).[13]

(*b*) The argument that oaths involve an unwarranted presumption
that God will punish an oath-breaker is to be distinguished from the
more tenuous claim that oaths are in their nature unchristian or
antichristian (the Quaker position that the precept 'swear not at all' is
to be taken literally). To the precept 'swear not at all' Bentham allows
of no exceptions, arguing that neither God nor any of Christ's apostles
specified any grounds for an exception to this maxim. The Mosaic Law
only condemns those that swear by the Lord's name 'falsely' (Lev. 19:
12), but Christ's law is more precise in declaring that 'Ye shall not
swear *at all*' (*Works*, v. 219). Bentham knew his Bible well and rarely
missed an opportunity to quote from it whenever it might embarrass
the Church or contradict its teaching. 'But above all things', he quotes
the apostle James (5: 12), 'swear not: neither by heaven, neither by

---

[13] Forty years later J. S. Mill was to argue along similar lines in the essay *On Liberty*
(1859), in *Collected Works*, xviii. 239–40. Though Mill, like Bentham, slightly misstated
the legal issue—it depended upon the fear of Divine retribution, not belief in a future
life—they offered arguments which increasingly gained acceptance in England. In the
wake of the case of Charles Bradlaugh later in the century (in 1885 Bradlaugh refused to
take the oath required of MPs), an act was passed in 1888 allowing the oaths of
unbelievers and at the same time giving them the right to affirm rather than swear an
oath (see the *DNB* article on Bradlaugh and J. E. Courtney, *Free Thinkers of the
Nineteenth Century* (London, 1920), ch. 3.

earth, neither by any other oath: but let your yea be yea, and your nay, nay, lest you fall into condemnation' (*Works*, v. 220). It was the Church of England that sanctioned the use of oaths and not the teachings of Christ.[14]

Bentham's argument of 'unwarranted presumption', however, is of a different order to this interpretive account of what Christ meant by the precept 'swear not at all'. This second argument is based upon a logical flaw in the practice of oath-taking. The binding force of the obligation imposed or undertaken by an oath is derived from the religious sanction, and it is the purpose of the ceremony to impress upon the swearer's mind the force of this sanction. But it is presumptuous of man, claims Bentham, so to invoke the might of God; it is to pretend to exercise power over the Almighty, and this is an absurdity— 'man the legislator and judge;—man the despot, God his slave' (*Works*, v. 192). The supposition involved here is that God will punish persons who break their oaths, but whether he punishes the breaking of an oath or not we cannot say, since 'the scene of its influence is placed in a state of things of which no human being is in this life supposed to be or about to be witness' (*Works*, v. 192). What right then, asks the sanctimonious Bentham, have we to call upon God in this manner? Is God in any way bound to do what is expected of him? The questions are, of course, rhetorical. If God is not bound then the obligation and the sanction upon which it is founded are vacuous. If he is bound then to whom is he bound? If it is to the person who imposes or administers the oath then there is no one who cannot be master of God. All who administer oaths can, to this extent at least, control the actions of the Almighty: 'Of all the worms that crawl about the earth in the shape of men there is not one who may not thus impose conditions on the supreme ruler of the universe' (*Fall.* 68)

(*c*) For Bentham the limits of toleration are the limits of human credulity; what is not credible (that is, conformable to the known physical world) cannot be entertained. In his early works on ethics and legislation, he mounted a forceful case to prove the uncertain nature of the belief in a future state of rewards and punishments. In his later writing on oaths the case is presented no less forcefully. The

---

[14] The last of the Thirty-nine Articles, entitled 'Of a Christian man's oath', states that Christ only forbade 'vain and rash Swearing' and asserts that 'we judge, that Christian Religion doth not prohibit, but that a man may swear when the Magistrate requireth, in a cause of faith and charity, so it be done according to the Prophet's teaching, in justice, judgement, and truth' (Bicknell, *A Theological Introduction to the Thirty-Nine Articles*, p. 445).

experiential and linguistic considerations which characterized the earlier analysis produced similar results in *Swear Not at All.*

In many cases, Church doctrines chief among them, Bentham found principles tending to the deliberate commission of falsehood, or as John Hill Burton phrased it in his introduction to the *Works*, 'to the designed obliteration of the distinction between truth and a lie' (*Works*, i. 38). The practice of administering oaths constituted just such an example for Bentham of the deliberate commission of falsehood. The supposition upon which the efficacy of oaths depended was the certainty of punishment for disobedience. The exaction of this penalty, however, is never witnessed by anyone, and if it ever were suspected that the 'almighty executioner' had failed to perform his duty in *any* particular instance then the effect of the ceremony of oath-taking would come to nought. No one can say with certainty that there ever has been an instance when God has punished a person for breaking an oath; there are no empirical grounds upon which to base the belief that God will punish or ever has punished an oath-breaker. What 'knowledge' we have of God's wrath is necessarily of an uncertain nature, hence the supposition of certainty by the Church is clearly a 'mere fiction', and in proportion as this is admitted, says Bentham, so is the ceremony of oath-taking divested of its binding force, and of any useful influence ascribed to or expected of it (*Works*, v. 192).[15]

Bentham thought this a damning criticism to mount against oaths, but it is to be doubted whether it really is as telling as he seemed to think. As on many other occasions when he attacked fundamental articles of Christianity he allowed no consideration of that part of human nature upon which beliefs, like that in a punishing or rewarding God, depend. Paley touched the heart of the matter as it regards oaths when he commented, 'oaths are nugatory, that is, they carry with them no proper force or obligation, unless we believe that God will punish false swearing with more severity than a simple lie, or breach of promise'.[16] For the faithful the supposed uncertainty of God's punishment is not a consideration. Their belief in the probability of punishment is not founded on any experience of the afterlife, yet it is on this belief, and not on certainty, that the ceremony of oath-taking

---

[15] Citing Bentham on oaths, J. S. Mill expanded the argument regarding the uncertainty of the supposed punishment to include 2 further considerations: (*a*) the remoteness at which the supposed punishment is to be administered; and (*b*) the manner in which punishment is expected to be administered (*Utility of Religion*, in *Collected Works*, x. 413).

[16] Paley, *Principles*, in *Complete Works*, ii, Bk. III, pt 1, ch. 16, p. 124.

depends. It draws its power and efficacy, in other words, from faith and not from anything material to the sanction itself. Bentham sought to undermine this belief by exposing the uncertain nature of Divine punishment, but that it is unknowable in any absolute, scientific, or certain sense alters not a whit the opinion among the faithful that it exists.

(*d*) The ultimate objective in Bentham's analysis of oaths was to expose their political exploitation by ecclesiastical and secular government, for whom they constitute a sophisticated method of popular domination (*Works*, v. 194). This final offensive against oaths is founded upon Bentham's profound dissatisfaction with the curtailment of religious liberty by government and related to his long-standing distaste for the 'alliance' of Church and State which oaths, along with other methods of exclusion, served to maintain. To understand why these practices are kept up, says Bentham, we need only consider 'the particular interests of those by whom they are set on foot', and in so far as these interests are 'repugnant to the general interest' the institutions and practices they employ to further them are pernicious (*Works*, v. 221). Take for example the imposition of oaths at the universities: to what is the continuance of this practice indebted? 'Answer—Not so much its *absolute* and intrinsic, as to its *relative* importance; relation being had to the grand object of objects—*jargonice, the peace of the church*: in plain language, the preserving from disturbance the ease of so many high-seated persons, spiritual and temporal, sacred and profane' (*Works*, v. 217). University oaths, then, are not pernicious solely because of the habit of perjury they nourish, but also because of the political purpose they serve. In the eyes of the Church innovation is a sin worse than perjury; attempts at reform are attempts to remove the Church from its happy position as the chief ally of secular government, from which it derives its privileges and prestige. Hence, the Church will always resist moves to alter the practice of imposing oaths at the universities in order to prevent unruly elements from entering its ranks. For 'profit is derived from it by *the ruling few*', and this, remarks Bentham in an apparent allusion to Warburton, is 'a fundamental . . . article, in the only "alliance" ever spoken of that was not purely imaginary, "*between Church and State*" ' (*Works*, v. 227).

In some cases an oath prevented individuals from doing what they knew to be right; at other times an oath afforded them a ready excuse for the commission of some wrong. The political consequences could be disastrous. For instance, George III laid on his Coronation Oath the responsibility for both the war with the American colonies and his resistance to the demands of the Catholics. He had sworn to maintain his dominions entire and to preserve the Church of England. The Coronation Oath (1689), therefore, is 'an oath applied to the practice of misrule'. By it the monarch is bound in perpetuity to 'maintain the law of God, the true profession of the Gospel, and the Protestant reformed religion established by law' (*Works*, v. 208; cf. also *Fall.* 69). The consequence is that the monarch is bound to maintain discriminatory policies against the majority Catholic community in Ireland and to deny all Dissenters in the realm relief from the abuses of the Established Church. 'A more ingenious or successful operation of ecclesiastical polity', remarks Bentham, 'never was performed.' He suggests the following piece of irony as a suitable amendment to the Coronation Oath: 'And will you, to the utmost of your power, resist all innovations in religion and government, or in church and state? King. "All this I promise to do . . . so help me God" ' (*Works*, v. 208). On this account the Coronation Oath is 'an engine serving with equal effect for defending *Protestantism* against *Catholicism*, and *Church-of-Englandism* from reform and improvement, in every imaginable shape'. Moreover, it provides an efficient means for preserving all and any abuses presently found to be profitable to government and gives legitimacy to all abuses that might subsequently be introduced (*Works*, v. 208).

As if to prove that Bentham was not far off the mark, on 27 April 1825 the Duke of York, heir apparent to his brother George IV, delivered a House of Lords' speech repeating the stock arguments against Catholic Emancipation, and ended by declaring that whatever position he might one day occupy, he would always consider the English monarch bound by the oath to defend the Established Church.[17] It is to the particular plight of the Irish Catholics that we must now turn.

2. The plight of the Irish Catholics

One of the principal aims of *Church-of-Englandism* as it was planned by Bentham in 1812 was to aid the cause of Catholic Emancipation (UC

---

[17] E. Halévy, *A History of the English People in the Nineteenth Century*, trans. E. I. Walker and D. A. Barker, 6 vols. (London, 1949–52), ii. *The Liberal Awakening 1815–1830*, 224.

6/1).[18] The situation of the Catholics in Ireland was very different from that of other nonconformist religions in Britain. Though in later life Bentham sought to bring Catholics and Dissenters together in a unified front against intolerance, he always knew that the political discrimination suffered by the former was immeasurably worse and required special legislation. Other oppressed believers, such as the Jews, also required relief, but their plight was commonly the consequence of ordinary prejudices harboured by the English people rather than the effect of official measures.[19] According to Bentham the Jews were persecuted on account of their reputation for the 'odious' practice of money-lending. Naturally, prejudice is not considered a legitimate reason for oppression, and the Jews, as with all religious minorities, should be tolerated in their religious practices. Moreover, offences against the Jews, like all offences against religious sects or groups, should be considered offences against the State and be punishable by law.[20] This is consistent with Bentham's demand for the equality of all religions—all Churches, including a disestablished Anglican Church, were to be supported directly by money collected from their congregations, not by public funds.[21] His appeals for relief were always meant to encompass all religions, as when he pleaded in 1773: 'Is the contempt for the rights of conscience to last for ever?' (UC 96/325). Where liberties were withheld on account of religion of whatever kind he spoke out. Accordingly, in *A View of the Hard Labour Bill* (1778) he argued that provision should be made for religious services in the 'labour-houses' for nonconformist believers as well as the adherents of the Established Church. Catholics, 'with their numerous sacraments', were to be given a special dispensation allowing them to receive their own priests. For the Jews Bentham saw no other solution than a separate 'labour-house' in which they would have their own

---

[18] The material on the plight of the Catholics in the 'Church' MSS (UC Boxes 5–7) still awaits a comprehensive examination; in this sec. I offer only a summary of the particulars of Bentham's position.

[19] One commentator has suggested, however, that Bentham's views on the Jews can be taken to be representative of his attitude towards all sects and groups discriminated against on the grounds of religious beliefs, including such disparate elements as Unitarians, heretics, and Catholics. This being the case, nothing need be said about any of the other categories of oppressed religious minorities; what Bentham writes of the Jews can be taken to stand for them all; *see* L. C. Boralevi, *Bentham and the Oppressed* (New York, 1984), ch. 4, an earlier version of which, entitled 'Jeremy Bentham and the Jews', appeared in *European Judaism*, 13 (1979), 22–8.

[20] Boralevi, *Bentham and the Oppressed*, pp. 83–4; see also *IPML* 201–2.

[21] Bentham, *The Theory of Legislation*, p. 134.

rabbis, cooks, and butchers, the cost of which would be paid by the whole community of Jews in England (*Works*, iv. 24).

None the less, we would be mistaken if we thought that Bentham's attitude towards those discriminated against on religious grounds was always and everywhere the same. As a philosophical atheist, for instance, it is not surprising that Bentham's attitude towards atheism and atheists would involve features not to be found in his concern for religious minorities. It is also the case that his attitude towards the Irish Catholics—though he never distinguished the cause of the Catholic religion in formal terms from that of other nonconforming religions— was largely shaped by political factors which are hardly relevant to his concerns for other religious minorities.

The Catholics, although they formed the vast majority of the Irish population (over 80 per cent at this time), were cruelly oppressed by the ruling Protestants. Political inequality, based on religious and racial differences, was always worse in Ireland than in England. A special 'penal code' was used to exclude Catholics from property, public service, and the professions, reduce them to the state of second class citizens in their own country, extirpate the Catholic religion, and destroy the sense, and very existence, of Irish nationality. The Protestant Ascendancy, made up of the rich, episcopalian, and Anglo-Irish land-lords, denied any significant political influence to the Dissenters, chiefly of Scottish descent, who lived mainly in Ulster, and opposed any kind of political representation for the Catholic native Irish. Thus in Ireland, as in England, the demand for greater political liberty was bound up with the desire for greater religious freedom, but the barriers to change were very much higher.

Few aside from Edmund Burke were prepared to champion the cause of Catholic Emancipation in the English parliament in the last quarter of the eighteenth century. Burke, who opposed both separation and union in favour of a paternal colonialism, advised an unknown Irish correspondent in 1797 that 'if nothing can be done on your side of the Water, I promise nothing will be done here . . . You will be left to yourselves by the ruling power here'.[22] A year later when the expected rebellion broke out it was largely a popular rising of desperate Catholics in the southeast of the country, determined to protect themselves from the violence of the Orange Order. The rebellion was crushed long before French assistance arrived, but it was a definite

---

[22] Quoted by J. Conniff, 'Edmund Burke's Reflections on the Coming Revolution in Ireland', *Journal of the History of Ideas*, 47:1 (1986), 42.

signal to parliament that something should be done about the condition of the Catholics in Ireland. For a while nothing was done; quiet indifference prevailed, facilitating the maintenance of the Protestant Ascendancy. It was not until 1800 that the Act of Union was passed and even then the hoped for integration (the course taken by Scotland after 1707) did not occur. A few minor pacifying concessions were made to Catholics, but their real grievances went unaddressed as English policy returned to one of inattention.

Bentham was one among few Englishmen to take an active interest in Ireland's majority Catholic community. Initially, he saw their plight as akin to that of any oppressed religious minority and offered toleration as the solution to the problem, but as his eye trained itself on democratic reforms in the second decade of the nineteenth century his view of Ireland took on a more radical character. He saw that the political and the religious were not so easily separated when addressing the Irish Question; the core issue was the exclusion of Catholics from the Irish political community. In later life Bentham became convinced that only independence and democratic institutions could produce the greatest happiness in Ireland. At the same time, he never forgot that he was dealing with a peculiar kind of religion, one which differed from other religions in several fundamental respects and which he himself found particularly abhorrent. Putting his aversions to Catholicism to one side, however, he frequently voiced the view that the subjects of the Vatican should not be singled out for harsh treatment. Conceding his prejudices in an unpublished manuscript of 1775 he wrote:

If there is one set of notions to which my own opinions are averse more than another, it is Popery: this being the case, no Papist so bigoted, I could declare myself more cordially disposed to him, more of his way of thinking, let him agree with me in the single article of toleration, than with him whose sentiments and affections discordant with them in that were in all other respects in unison with my own. (UC 27/9)

Bentham was to express similar sentiments forty-five years later in a letter to his friend Richard Carlile (10 Apr. 1820), at the time imprisoned for his publication of the 'blasphemous' works of Thomas Paine: 'I am not a Catholic: at the same time were it my misfortune to see a Catholic incurr [?] for his opinions the sort of treatment which you have incurred [?] for yours, my sympathy for his suffering, my antipathy . . . towards the authors of them as such, would not be less intense in that case than in yours' (UC 10/19). In the case of the

Catholics (as in that of the Jews)[23] Bentham presents personally the example of a tolerant attitude, overcoming his own antipathetic feelings.

The same statutes, at least in theory, excluded both Dissenters and Catholics from national and local public offices and, as the debates of the early part of the nineteenth century were to prove, the question of exclusion inextricably linked their interests and fates. The increasingly powerful Unitarian Association was especially loud in its condemnation of the opposition of other religious sects to the repeal of intolerant laws. As its spokesman, John Bowring, undoubtedly with the blessing of Bentham, demanded that the campaign for relief be waged on basic principles. The claims of the Dissenters should be 'urged only on the broad ground of denying the right or policy of the magistrate's making religious opinion or profession the ground of pretence of civil preference or exclusion'.[24] Subsequently, many in the ranks of the Whigs and Radicals came to believe that once relief had been won for the Dissenters the emancipation of the Catholics would be politically expedient, if not unavoidable. In February of 1828, on the eve of emancipation, Bentham drew up an 'Address Proposing a plan for uniting the Catholics and Dissenters for the furtherance of religious Liberty', in which he advocated (*a*) the repeal of every statute which put anyone at a disadvantage on account of religious opinions, and (*b*) the prevention of judges from resorting to Common Law in order to avoid any such legislation. Bentham's main concern, however, was that English Catholics should join with all dissenting sects in order to form a council to mediate in the Irish situation (*Works*, x. 593–4). Religious toleration, in other words, was not enough as a solution to the plight of the Irish Catholics.

It was no coincidence that Bentham's greatest interest in Ireland occurred at a time when political questions headed the agenda in his radical campaign to restructure English institutions. For the Irish Catholics the political and the religious were two sides of the same coin, and for Bentham the growing movement for nonconformist relief

---

[23] Noting the disparity between Bentham's official writings, especially *The Defence of Usury* (1787), and his personal attitude towards the Jews revealed in his correspondence while in Europe (1785–8), Boralevi comments that 'we should look with greater admiration upon his defence of the oppressed Jews, precisely because he showed himself able to overcome his personal prejudices' (*Bentham and the Oppressed*, p. 91).

[24] John Bowring in the *Monthly Repository*, NS 1 (1827), 377–8, quoted by Davis, *Dissent in Politics*, p. 237. For a discussion of the role played by Dissenters in the campaign for Catholic Emancipation see ch. 12 of *Dissent in Politics*.

in England was an important ally in the cause of political reform, both in England and in Ireland. It is against this background that we must view his efforts on behalf of the oppressed Irish Catholics.

Bentham's particular interest in the social and political situation in Ireland seems to have begun in the early 1790s. In 1790 he had ideas for an Irish Panopticon and attempted to initiate a prison reform movement in Ireland,[25] and in January 1793 Romilly wrote to him to ask for a loan of 'the proceedings of the Irish Catholics' which Bentham, evidently, had been reading (*Corr.* iv. 415). Nine months earlier Thomas Law (the brother of Paley's friend John Law, Bishop of Clonfert) informed Bentham: 'The Protestants in Ireland are most enraged at this Government for making them be just to the Roman Catholics. I am preparing a speech for wednesday—this is the beginning. If you tell me it is nonsense I will burn it. We feel philanthropy but have many obstacles to oppose' (*Corr.* iv. 423). There are also some manuscripts dating from *c.*1800 concerning a scheme for Irish education (UC 106/ 76–80), one aim of which was to diminish the proselytizing zeal of the Catholic clergy by making the political establishment more acceptable to them and to their flock.[26] The Unitarian Toleration Act of 1813, which omitted the Irish from its terms of reference, caused Bentham to cast a closer eye on the situation and, as we have already noted, led him to print, though not to publish, his tract on oaths. Five years later, in a letter to William Smith (Feb. 1818), Bentham was happy to record that the Irish Catholics had obtained some measure of relief from the penalties imposed for blasphemy: 'While the ink is yet wet, comes from my bookseller my copy of the statutes of last session, and in it the statute of the 7th July 1817, 57th George II. cap. 70, which then, for the first time extends to that island the relief which, such as it is, had four years before been vouchsafed to ours' (*CE*, p. xxxi). Such as it was, however, the concession was a minor one, and in 'Radicalism Not Dangerous' (1819–20) Bentham returned to the offensive. This pamphlet is marked by a particular sensitivity to the situation of the unrepresented Catholics in Ireland. Bentham saw in this political

---

[25] See for instance *Corr.* iv. 137–45, 171–9, 185–99; and Ogden, *Jeremy Bentham*, App. 11.

[26] On 29 Sept. 1818 Bentham drew up a 'Proposal for the Instruction and Improvement of the Moral Character of the Irish Labourers in New York', addressed to the Honourable De Witt Clinton, Governor of the state of New York. This proposal was based on the ideas of an Irishman, Thaddeus Cornellan, and had already been tried elsewhere; see *Works*, x. 500–3; and B. Taylor, 'Jeremy Bentham and the Education of the Irish People', *The Irish Journal of Education*, 14:1 (1980), 25–8.

exclusion a deliberate policy of government to use the religious division as an excuse for discrimination (cf. *Works*, iii. 613–20). In 'Extracts of a Letter from Bentham to the Greeks' (24 Nov. 1823) the same theme is adumbrated: 'Of all other governments, the least bad is that of England. Yet, under England, six millions and a half Irishmen groan in irremediable distress, under unrelenting tyranny. They are kept hungry and naked by priests, and other creatures of monarchy, who fatten on their spoils' (*Works*, x. 539). A year later words were no longer enough for Bentham and he sent a letter (9 Dec. 1824) and a donation of £5 to Daniel O'Connell's Catholic Association,

in the humble and cordial hope, that his oppressed brethren of the Catholic persuasion, not attempt redress by insurrection; but unite with the liberal among the Protestants for the attainment of security for all, against depredation and oppression in every shape, by the only practicable means—Parliamentary Reform, in the radical and solely efficient mode. (*Works*, x. 544)

Bentham's frustrations are revealed in an apparently unsent portion of this letter, suppressed at Bowring's bidding (though later published by him) where he states that if it came to 'extermination' then his sympathies would be with the Catholics, since it is they who are oppressed, and not with the Protestants, who were the oppressors. Having vented his spleen, however, Bentham quickly cautioned O'Connell that 'extermination could not have place without being mutual', and that for the good of everyone reform must be 'accomplished without blood' (*Works*, x. 544).[27]

Daniel O'Connell's efforts in bringing emancipation about can hardly be exaggerated.[28] His relationship with Bentham was a close if occasionally volatile one. 'O'Connell', wrote the ageing Bentham, 'I love you with a father's love!' O'Connell in return, in one of his famous impassioned speeches (July 1828), avowed himself 'an humble disciple of

----

[27] Writing to the radical MP for Westminster, John Cam Hobhouse (1786–1869; from 1851 Baron Broughton de Gyfford), of an unidentified supporter of Catholic Emancipation, Bentham noted: 'The conversion of Catholics into Radicals is what he has taken for the corner-stone of his influence, and thereby of his interest: he is, accordingly, as I am against Catholic Emancipation by any other instrument than radicalism, or at any other time than at or after the triumph of radicalism' (*Works*, x. 524). The MSS for this letter are at UC 13/143–6, dated '1820 Dec. 12', but it appears that the letter was actually sent on 31 June 1821. The name of the person to whom Bentham is referring, omitted from the printed text, is unreadable in the manuscripts, but it may have been O'Connell.

[28] For O'Connell's role in Catholic Emancipation see Halévy, *The Liberal Awakening*, pp. 266–72.

the immortal Bentham'.[29] In an anonymous letter to Henry Hunt (*c.*1828) Bentham speaks of O'Connell as 'the only man perhaps in the world, by whom, for many years to come, Radical Reform, or any approach to it can be brought upon the carpet, with any the smallest chance of success' (*Works*, x. 5). The following year O'Connell, like Bentham a lawyer by training, offered his services to the old sage in the business of law reform (*Works*, x. 20), and the latter, in turn, thought of founding a Law Reform Association to do for the law what O'Connell's Catholic Association had done for his fellow Catholics (*Works*, xi. 21–8; cf. also x. 594–605, xi. 20–30, 63–5). Nevertheless, from time to time Bentham had occasion to remonstrate with his brilliant but impatient disciple. He begged the Irishman to refrain from his angry tirades against the moderate reformers among the Whigs: 'Do not run amuck (malay like) against all your friends, except a comparatively small number of zealous Catholics.' He cautioned him to be tolerant of other men's opinions and to put aside 'the advocates gown' when debating issues in the Commons. 'Dan, Dear Child', he wrote on another occasion, 'whom, in imagination, I have [*sic*], at this moment, pressing to my bosom—put off, if it be possible, your intolerance' (*Works*, xi. 26; cf. also xi. 25–9).

It may well have been O'Connell's example that inspired Bentham to publish his only sustained commentary on the Irish Question in the *Book of Fallacies*, which appeared in 1824. Here the political firmly clasped hands with the religious as he wrote sympathetically of the situation of the Catholics in Ireland and critically of the consolidation of Protestant power following the Act of Union. His theme was 'exclusion' and the religious fallacies which underlay this policy, but his primary concern was for the political consequences of the maintenance of Protestant rule in a land where Protestants constitute the minority. In the chapter on the 'Fallacies of Danger', under the section headed 'Imputation Founded on Identity of Name', he criticized those who enlist history in their efforts to justify the present situation and resist reform. The kind of argument he has in mind begins by pointing out the pernicious designs and measures of Roman Catholics in the past, and then uses this as an excuse to persecute Catholics in the present (*Fall.* 90–1). To impute intentions to individuals on the basis of their faith, however, is to commit what Bentham calls a 'fallacy of confusion'— in this case one that is designed to tar with the same brush all those

---

[29] Quoted by Atkinson, *Jeremy Bentham*, p. 199.

persons 'ranked in the same class by being designated by the same name' (*Fall.* 174).[30] This was the aim of a particularly mischievous tract singled out by Bentham for special consideration, entitled *The Cruelties of Catholics*,[31] the aim of which was to persuade the reader of the evil consequences to be expected from giving relief to Catholics. But the barbarities of the Catholics of former times have their limits, says Bentham; the real barbarism is now perpetrated by those who, like the author of this malicious tract, prolong religious and political discord (*Fall.* 175–6). Much worse is the fact that this attitude is reflected in the administration of Ireland itself, where the exploitation of religious differences is the mark of government. Nor should this surprise us, says Bentham, since it is obviously in the interest of those sinecurists and placemen, who are the representatives of the Crown, 'to treat the majority of the people of Ireland on the double footing of enemies and subjects; and such is the treatment which is in store for them to the extent of their endurance'. In other words, the interest of the Catholic many 'is avowedly, and so long as the government lasts, intended to be kept in a state of perpetual sacrifice . . . to that of the few' (*Fall.* 91). Protestant clergymen are of little use to Catholics who refuse their ministrations and revile them as plunderers. Ironically, it is the lack of duties attending Irish preferment that increases its attractiveness, not to mention its profit, for English clergymen. 'Is not this estimate', asks Bentham 'the root of these scruples, by which oaths imposed to protect Protestantism from being oppressed are employed to secure it the pleasure of oppressing?' (*Fall.* 173).

The repeal of the Test and Corporation Acts (1828) and the passing of Catholic Emancipation (1829) did much to relieve political tensions, but for those whose ultimate aim was the secularization and democratization of English government, these were only preliminary phases of a broader political programme. As Bentham's disciple and sometime editor, Thomas Perronet Thompson, commented in the emancipation debate: 'The struggle for fairness of representation in Ireland, is only the cause of the people of England tried under Irish names; and they are waiting for the decision of this question, before they proceed

[30] This is a 'fallacy' previously considered by Bentham in a sheet of MS headed 'Intolerance': 'Obj[ection] 3. Catholics in former times were bloody and mischievous Ec. Answ[er] 1. A. was formerly guilty and dangerous. Therefore B. ought to be held in chains & punished. This is the old story of the Wolf and the Lamb' (UC 5/48). This sheet of MS (probably dating from 1812–13) also contains the outline of a discussion of the plight of the 'papists', but it went no further at this time.
[31] I have been unable to locate bibliographic details for this tract.

to their own.'[32] That some measure of reform had been achieved at all, however, was occasion for rejoicing among the radicals. When Wellington fought a duel with Lord Winchelsea prior to the passing of the Emancipation Act Bentham, fearing for the cause of reform, sent a remarkable letter of remonstrance to the Duke castigating him for his irresponsible action: 'Here am I, leader of the Radicals, more solicitous for the life of the leader of the Absolutists than he himself is!'[33] But any comfort Bentham may have felt on the passing of the Act was only a momentary affair. The political dimension of the Irish Question had still to be addressed. In 1831, in an unsent letter signed 'Pacifus', he was still criticizing the government for its 'determination to coerce, and risk a civil war, rather than to consent to the Repeal of the Union'. Repeal, naturally, would have meant disestablishment of the Anglican Church in Ireland, and this was an aim dear to Bentham's heart, but it was the stupidity and cynicism evident in the policy of coercion that he found so insufferable:

the M.P.'s to the amount of a few hundreds, are determined to go forth, to gird on their armour, and with fire and sword to lay Ireland waste, subdue the insolent Irish, and by God's help, which it will cost them no more than one day's fasting to secure, to establish an aristocratical tyranny of the inhabitants of the one island over those of the other; laying it waste, in the meantime, with fire and sword for the godly purpose.[34]

Given the official opposition to the repeal of the Act of Union, Bentham can be forgiven for thinking that the Irish could expect little by way of concessions in the foreseeable future. In the end his only suggestion for producing greater harmony and unity of feeling between Great Britain and Ireland was to rename the United Kingdom 'Brithibernia' (*Works*, x. 467). But he well knew that such linguistic surgery was only cosmetic and, while impositions were still used by an alien ruling élite for the oppression of an indigent native people, could never solve the problems of the Irish Catholics.

---

[32] 'The Catholic Question', *The Westminster Review* (1829), quoted by Clark, *English Society*, p. 358.

[33] JB to the Duke of Wellington (22 Mar. 1829), quoted by Halévy, *The Liberal Awakening*, p. 278. Wellington was the Tory Prime Minister responsible, against stiff opposition from within the ranks of his own party, for introducing the bill for emancipation (13 Apr. 1829). The duel came about as a consequence of Lord Winchelsea's severe censure of the bill which Wellington took as a personal insult (ibid. 274). In 1982, on the 150th anniversary of Bentham's death, the Duke of Wellington public house, situated in the vicinity of UCL, was renamed, ironically, the Jeremy Bentham.

[34] From a letter signed 'Pacifus' preserved among Bentham's correspondence for 1831, quoted Ogden, *Jeremy Bentham*, p. 86.

It is, then, the political dimension of the plight of the Irish Catholics which makes it a very different and much more problematic case for Bentham than that of other religious minorities. It is true that in terms of religion he consistently argued for universal toleration as the principal remedy to the problems facing nonconforming religions, but when it came to Ireland religious toleration without independence and democratic institutions could achieve very little.

3. A case of blasphemy

Though several of his works, particularly the writings on religion, could be described, as John Colls described the volumes on religion, as 'volumes of blasphemy and slander . . . against the Author of Christianity and His people',[35] Bentham was never prosecuted for sedition, blasphemy, or libel. In other parts of the world his work was sometimes seen as dangerous enough to require suppression,[36] and Romilly was to the forefront of those in England who repeatedly cautioned against the publication of certain of his more threatening anti-establishment writings, but his luck, for one reason or another, always held. Even so, his own good fortune in avoiding prosecution did not make Bentham any the less antagonistic to the efforts of government to curtail freedom of expression in England.

A crucial area in which the State interfered with religious beliefs was in their written expression. Bentham found it odious that there should be punishment for the supposed crime of blasphemy. What constituted blasphemy under the Common Law was vague and fluctuating. This was a prime example of the uncertainty and unpredictability of the Common Law which Bentham had long since vowed to extinguish. The employment of such methods to quell the expression of dissenting opinions was one of the most disgusting of affronts to his tolerant sensibilities. It was, he thought, a pretence for closing off legitimate

[35] J. F. Colls, *Utilitarianism Unmasked: A Letter to the Rev. M. A. Gathercole . . . on the Life, Death, and Philosophy of Jeremy Bentham* (London, 1844), 10.

[36] For e.g.s see J. R. Dinwiddy, 'Early Nineteenth-Century Reactions to Benthamism', *Transactions of the Royal Historical Association*, 5th ser., 34 (1984), 51. Surprisingly, none of Bentham's works (including those on religion) was indexed by the Vatican, presumably because they did not reach a large enough audience to trouble the Church of Rome. This mark of influence was to fall to J. S. Mill, whose *Principles of Political Economy with Some of their Applications to Social Philosophy* (London, 1848) was added to the Index in 1856.

enquiry and, less obviously but just as blameworthy, a fraud by which organized religion protected its privileged position as the official interpreter and conveyor of the word of God. The Anglican clergy take it for granted in any contest of opinions that theirs is the authentic voice of God but, Bentham points out, in so doing they take for granted exactly that which is in dispute. The upshot is that those who contest the teachings of the Church, who argue with its priests, are guilty of disrespect and not merely of disrespect towards the clergy but towards God, and are therefore guilty of blasphemy. It would be a great service, Bentham reflected, if the term 'blasphemy' were banished altogether from the English language (*CE* 227–9 n.). By its use liberties supposed to be held sacred by all Englishmen—the freedom to hold and express beliefs and opinions of whatever religious hue—are constantly infringed.

The issue became pressing in the years following the Napoleonic Wars, when prosecutions for sedition, blasphemy, and libel were used extensively by the government in its attempt to stem the tide of opposition and the spread of heretical literature. In law 'seditious libel' was loosely defined as any written censure upon 'public men' for their conduct, or upon the laws or institutions of the country. But as James Fitzjames Stephen remarked, if literally applied as defined it was a law 'wholly inconsistent with any serious discussion of political affairs', and 'so long as it was recognised as the law of the land all such discussion existed only on sufferance'.[37] It was plainly the view of the judges of the day, encouraged by the government, that any attempt to put 'subversive' notions before the lower orders was sedition or blasphemy, or both, and punishable under the Common Law even when it did not offend against any specific statute.[38] Bentham would not have forgotten the seditious libel case brought against John Wilkes in 1769,[39] but not since the days of the French Revolution had social unrest forced the hand of the government into actions of so oppressive a nature. Matters came to a head in early 1817 when, in the light of the recent disturbances stirred up by the efforts of 'Orator' Hunt and others to petition parliament for democratic reform, the cabinet

---

[37] J. F. Stephen, *A History of the Criminal Law in England*, 3 vols. (London, 1883), ii. 348.
[38] G. D. H. Cole, *Richard Carlile 1790–1843* (London, 1943), 8.
[39] Bentham cut his political teeth on a Wilkesite issue in 1770 when he published a letter signed 'Irenius' in *The Gazeteer and New Daily Advertiser* (3 Dec. 1770), in which he argued, contrary to Wilkes and others, that impressment was a useful practice. For a brief discussion see Long, *Bentham on Liberty*, pp. 50–1.

became alarmed and rushed through the House of Commons bills suspending Habeas Corpus (24 Feb. 1817), and enforcing a few other laws which had been allowed to lapse concerning the incitement of troops to mutiny, restrictions on public meetings, and (following an assassination attempt on the Prince Regent on 28 January of that year) concerning the personal safety of the king. On 25 March the Lords passed the last of the bills, the Seditious Meetings Act. Two days later Lord Sidmouth, the Home Secretary, asked the Lord-Lieutenants to instruct the Justices of the Peace that in future every magistrate was empowered to order the arrest of any person believed to be responsible for the public sale of blasphemous or seditious literature. This constituted an unprecedented extension of the jurisdiction of the magistrates. Ill-defined as this jurisdiction was, Sidmouth's instructions were conveniently employed by one magistrate as reason enough to refuse to sanction a mineralogical society on the pretext that the study of mineralogy led to atheism.[40] Nor were the absurdities confined to this extreme example. Attacks on the Established Church, exposure of abuses in the armed services and corruption in government, revelations concerning the 'packing' of juries, all were to be met with the same weapon—prosecution for blasphemy or seditious libel. It hardly seemed to matter which charge was laid, the consequences were generally the same: heavy fines and prison terms varying from one to six years. On this state of affairs Bentham was moved to comment in the *Plan of Parliamentary Reform* (1817), wryly no doubt but also with a sense of urgency:

The plains, or heights, or whatsoever they are, of Waterloo, will one day be pointed to by the historian as the grave not only of French but of English liberties. Not of France alone, but of Britain with her, was the conquest consummated in the Nederlands. Whatsoever has been done and is doing in France will soon be done in Britain. Reader would you wish to know the lot designed for you? Look to France, there you may behold it. (*Works*, iii, p. iv)

Two years later the passing of the Six Acts seemed to confirm Bentham's worst forebodings. A comprehensive code of legal restrictions was introduced for the first time in England with the declared intention of restricting the right of public assembly. With certain exemptions it was henceforth illegal for anyone to attend a public meeting outside closed doors with over fifty persons in attendance, and all meetings held with the object of discussing any grievance of a public character or any

---

[40] Halévy, *The Liberal Awakening*, pp. 23–5.

question concerning Church or State. Several bills were introduced to restrict the freedom of the press, one of which was an Act for the more effectual Prevention and Punishment of Blasphemous and Seditious Libels. This coupling of sedition and blasphemy in the same category of offence was a shrewd tactical move by Sidmouth, for there were many attracted to the democratic politics of the radicals but who were shocked by the antichristian character with which the movement's leaders had imbued its pamphlets.[41] Henceforth, any remotely irreligious comments in a tract or journal could be used as an excuse for the suppression of literature suggestive of dissatisfaction with government.

It was against this background that Bentham defiantly chose to publish *Swear Not at All* in 1817, and explained in the Advertisement that the reason for his publishing a tract which had lain upon the shelf for over four years, was 'the addition so lately made of the scourge of religious persecution to the yoke of despotism'. He could not but be aware of the risks he ran in publishing the pamphlet, and even if he were oblivious to the dangers at that time, a year later the difficulties he experienced in finding a publisher for *Church-of-Englandism* (and the warnings of the ever cautious Romilly), would surely have made him cognizant of the grave situation in which he was placing himself by publishing literature openly critical of established institutions. Anonymity was out of the question since no publisher would now countenance publishing an anonymous work so obviously of a radical nature. To do so would mean certain prosecution and imprisonment. Bentham hit on the device of including his exchange of letters with the Unitarian MP William Smith in the belief that this would lessen the risk of prosecution, but that little notice was taken of the work and that it came from the hand of a respected, if radical, old gentleman may also have been factors persuading the Attorney-General to stay his hand. The correspondence with Smith is important for another reason: it contains Bentham's most precise statements of the failings of statute and Common Law regarding the offence of blasphemy.

In reply to an enquiry from Bentham, Smith (16 Feb. 1818) explained that though the Unitarian Toleration Act of 1813 was intended to repeal the penal statutes against 'Impugners of the Trinity', he was persuaded by Manners Sutton, the Archbishop of Canterbury, whose support he was keen to enlist, to exempt the statutes regarding the

---

[41] Ibid. 71. For details of the Six Acts see pp. 70–2.

crime of blasphemy, a crime which he thought 'should still be left open to the animadversion of the Common Law'. That they shared the same view as to what constituted the crime of blasphemy apparently was sufficient grounds for Smith to agree to the archbishop's request. 'I have no doubt', Smith wrote to Bentham,

His Grace also, understanding by the term 'Blasphemy', of course, not that constructive and inferential Imputation of the Crime which might be fastened on every Doctrine relative to the Divine Nature differing in any respect or degree from that of the established Church, (an Interpretation wholly subversive of the very Liberty and Relief intended to be granted,) but that which is its common and, I imagine also, its legal Import;—The Use of Language and Epithets in themselves reproachful, reviling and abusive, levelled immediately at the Majesty and Character of the Supreme Being. (*CE*, pp. xx–xxi)

Bentham takes up the point in his reply (Feb. 1818): Smith's tranquility is misplaced, turning as it does on a definition of the word 'blasphemy' which he would gladly share if only the law did not have the habit of saying it meant something else. The Common Law, as Bentham never tired of reminding anyone who cared to listen, is 'the expression of the will and pleasure of one or more set of men, whose interest is, on this ground, in a state of diametrical opposition to the universal interest', and it is this law under which prosecutions for blasphemy are usually brought (*CE*, p. xxxix). What constitutes 'blasphemy' according to the Common Law is far different from the definition agreed between Smith and the archbishop, as recent trials have shown. 'Sir', enquires Bentham, 'have you not heard of Mr. *Hone* and *his* blasphemy? Sir, have you not heard of Mr. *Wright* of Liverpool, and *his* blasphemy? Mr. *Wright*—a divine, whose blasphemy is, if I mistake not, pretty exactly of the same stamp with your own piety and that of Dr. Belsham?' (*CE*, p. xl). Smith, Wright, and Belsham were all Unitarians and as such still subject to certain restrictions as a result of the imposition of oaths. This is what Bentham referred to when he remarked that under the Common Law even the liturgy of the Established Church is 'put upon a level with God', and under the name of 'blasphemers' it can 'grind to powder' all Christians who express a religion different from that of the Church. 'Know you not', Bentham asks his correspondent,

that, according to the tenor of this maxim, '*Christianity is part and parcel of the law of England*' that any thing and every thing, which it shall please the piety of this or that bench to call *christianity* will thereby be so? that every thing that it shall please the same piety to call an *offence* against the said *christianity* will thereby be so, and the offender liable to be *visited*, as the phrase is, with any and all such instruments of destruction as the hand of *precedent* has now presented to the piety of that same pre-eminently learned bench? (*CE*, p. cli)

What constitutes blasphemy is deliberately left vague, says Bentham, and as such this notion is a precious instrument of oppression in the hands of authority. It can be used to oppress persons of any religious persuasion whom the Church or its secular protector hold to be a threat to the stability and order of the State. Of the vagueness of the term Bentham remarked: 'Of him to whom it is . . . applied the word blasphemy conveys not any the faintest conception [of meaning]: but a most correct concept does it convey to the Mind of him by whom it is thus applied' (UC 7/102). Such is the pliability of the Common Law, for which reason Bentham remained its inveterate critic.

Bentham was particularly chagrined at the authorities' treatment of the publisher Richard Carlile (1790–1843). Carlile had a history of promoting radical works, including several of his own ventures in free-thinking, and had been imprisoned in 1817 for his part in the Hone affair. William Hone (1780–1842) was a popular political satirist of the period and an associate of Paine, who dared to publish a collection of parodies on the Lord's Prayer and other sacred writings in 1817, but withdrew them from circulation under threat of prosecution. Without Hone's knowledge Carlile made it his business to reissue the parodies and both men were subsequently arrested on the charge, indicative of the deliberate policy of confusing legal terms, of 'blasphemous libel'. Hone was eventually acquitted after three trials by London juries who, so it is said, 'laughed immoderately at his wit and were unmoved by the shocked admonitions of judge and counsel'.[42] John Taylor, one of Bentham's many correspondents at the time, wrote to him commenting on the Attorney-General's conduct in the trials:

Whatever respect you may entertain for the legal knowledge of our Attorney General, I am persuaded that you will join with me in despising his attainments as a Theologian, when he asserts (and he did so in Hone's trial) that *the Creed* (Bp Pearson's Creed) is of equal authority with the Bible. What is this but another attempt to degrade the religion of Jesus, by putting it upon the same level [as] anonymous (for who were these Apostles?) and consequently unauthorised publications![43]

[42] Cole, *Richard Carlile*, p. 7.
[43] John Taylor to JB (16 Nov. 1818), MS inserted at p. 32 in the BL copy of J. Bowring, *Memoirs of Jeremy Bentham* (London, 1838), shelf-mark C.61.c.15.

If he did not share Taylor's outrage over the apparent 'blasphemy' of
the Attorney-General, Bentham would still have sympathized with the
utterance of the complaint.

For his part in the affair Carlile was detained for eighteen weeks
(Aug. to Dec. 1817) before being released following Hone's acquittal.
But in the December of the following year he was prosecuted again,
this time for publishing a collection of the works of Thomas Paine, and
was indicted six times (1818–19) before eventually being sentenced in
November of 1819 to six years in Dorchester Prison and fined £1,500.
At the same time nine of Carlile's shop assistants were also arrested
and served sentences ranging from six months to three years. This
series of prosecutions provided J. S. Mill with the impetus to write a
series of five letters under the signature of 'Wickliffe' (after the
fourteenth-century reformer John Wycliffe), 'going over the whole
length and breadth of the question of the free publication of
all opinions on religion'.[44] Carlile remained within the walls of
Dorchester until 1826, returned in 1830 for a further three years and,
finally, served another ten weeks in 1834–5, on this latter occasion for
the non-payment of Church rates.[45]

Carlile's indictment of 1818 was based on the charge that he was an
atheist, but Bentham cared little whether the bookseller was an atheist
or not. In a letter of encouragement and support (10 Apr. 1820) he
wrote:

> You are if I mistake not a theist and it is for this that you are imprisoned [?].
> Were it for being . . . an Atheist, a Quaker, a Methodist among Church of
> Englandists or other Protestant among Catholics, or a Catholic among Church
> of Englandists that you were a sufferer my sympathy with your sufferings, my
> antipathy towards the authors of your sufferings would still be the same. (UC
> 10/17)[46]

[44] Three of these letters were published in the *Morning Chronicle* (Jan.–Feb. 1823)
under the title 'Free Discussion'. J. S. Mill, *Autobiography* (1873), ed. J. Stillinger, in
Collected Works, i. 89. Mill also published an article on the Carlile prosecutions in the
Edinburgh Review (July 1824), in which he argued that only the intolerant are not to be
tolerated; see A. Bain, *John Stuart Mill: A Criticism with Personal Recollections* (1882; repr.
New York, 1969), 33.

[45] While in Dorchester Carlile managed to publish *An.* and *Mother Church Relieved by
Bleeding* (in 1822 and 1823, respectively), free from the danger of further punishment. It
was Place's idea that Carlile should publish *An.*, for the very reason that he had less
to fear from prosecution than any other London bookseller; see A. Bain, *The Minor
Works of George Grote* (London, 1873), 18 n.

[46] The version of this letter which appears at *Works*, x. 527–8, has been edited
(presumably by Bowring), but for the sake of convenience I quote from the published
text wherever possible. Bentham understood that Carlile had declared himself a theist

The issue was one of principle and measured against this the prosecution was an 'odious' one. 'Your cause', he wrote to Carlile, 'is, in my eyes, the cause of all dissenters of every denomination, from the corruptive demoralising, and stupefying tyranny of every established and persecuting Church' (*Works*, x. 527). The absolute freedom to express one's opinions should be a right secured to everyone; to prosecute a person for the expression of an opinion, religious or political, is not only an act of immorality, but an act of unmitigated tyranny. 'No man', he continues, 'is so lost to shame, as to maintain, that, in any other part of the field of thought and action, it can be subservient to justice, it can be otherwise than subversive of justice, to suppress any relevant argument on either side, while those on the other side are free' (*Works*, x. 528).

Bentham always held up the United States as his ideal in arguments of this nature, and in June of 1817 he gave a list of questions to John Quincy Adams enquiring how atheists and blasphemers fared on the other side of the Atlantic, convinced that they could do no worse than in Britain (UC 12/10).[47] Adams replied that there had been no prosecutions for blasphemy since independence was declared in 1776 (UC 21/84). This reinforced Bentham's belief that those fashioning constitutions or codifying laws should emulate the United States and omit religion from their terms of reference: 'In Republican America there is no punishment for free enquiry, or pretence of punishing seditious meetings and blasphemy; there is therefore no sedition there' (*Works*, iii. 562). In the seventh of his 'Letters to Count Toreno' (1822) Bentham took his own advice and recommended that the proposed Spanish penal code be amended to omit punishment for blasphemy. The Spanish people should have 'the complete liberty of publishing whatsoever they please on the subject of religion, without

but at this time he was more truly a deist in the manner of Thomas Paine. While in prison, however, he was converted to a thoroughgoing atheism based on a Holbachian materialistic view of the universe. 'I advocate the abolition of all religions without setting up anything new of the kind', he wrote in 1821 (quoted by Cole, *Richard Carlile*, p. 6). Carlile's irreligion is best seen in his *Address to the Men of Science* (London, 1821), but for his later conversion to the 'scientific–allegorical' interpretation of Christianity see Cole, *Richard Carlile*, pp. 22–3. In 1836 Carlile took out a licence to preach this religion and styled himself 'Reverend'. The substance of his later religious views can be gleaned from his *Church Reform* (London, 1834).

[47] Adams recorded in his diary under the same date the following: 'He gave me a paper of written questions, which he desired me to answer related to the state of religious opinions in the United States, and particularly to the effects which an avowal of infidelity may have upon a person's reputation or his condition in life', *Memoirs of John Quincy Adams*, ed. C. F. Adams, 12 vols. (1874–7; repr. New York, 1970), iii. 551.

exposure to punishment in any shape, or impediment to the circulation of such their discourses' (*Works*, iii. 547). This, then, is Bentham's ideal arrangement, one which he encouraged governments around the world to adopt. The prescription is a simple one: where religious liberty reigns there is no blasphemy. The times, however, were as yet unpropitious for such a radical formula to be easily accommodated in England.

4. Freedom from religion in a Utilitarian society

That Bentham had a personal interest from time to time in the lifting of the restrictions on freedom of expression is unquestionable, but his agitation for a more tolerant attitude by government towards dissenting religious opinions was far more than intermittent or episodic. It spanned almost his entire adult life, from his first jottings on subscription to the interest he took in later life in the cause of the Catholics and in the offences of blasphemy. No one work contains a distillation of his arguments for religious liberty, and in the past two chapters we have had to review an array of published and unpublished literature in order to piece his views together. However, there is little doubt that this literature yields the substance of a consistent and coherent stand by Bentham on the issue.[48] While detailing the secular character of his utopian Utilitarian society in the *Constitutional Code* he pointed to the irreligious and inhuman aspects of intolerance against which he had waged a lifelong struggle:

Direct profession of atheism is profession of atheism, and nothing worse. Endeavour to crush a man for the profession of atheism, is virtual confession of atheism, coupled with the practice of insincerity and intolerance. In proportion to every man's love of humankind, and of those virtues on which its felicity

---

[48] In private life Bentham may not have been so tolerant of the opinions and beliefs of others. John Colls, his one-time amanuensis, relates that on discovering a private chapel at Ford Abbey, Bentham's country retreat, he enquired of his master whether it might be reopened for the use of household servants. 'The only answer vouchsafed to my proposal', he writes, 'was a look of surprise, with which a feeling of suspicion was evidently struggling, that I was either beside myself, or that I knew not what I asked: he then contemptuously turned upon his heel, and left me: and, from that day forth, I had to content myself with "communing with my heart" in secret.' For Colls, 'the precise amount of intellectual freedom' he enjoyed in Bentham's retinue was 'the liberty *of agreeing with him* in all he said and wrote; not of differing from him on any, [even] the minutest point!' (*Utilitarianism Umasked*, pp. 22, 25).

depends, insincerity and intolerance of difference in opinions, whatever be the subject, will ever be odious. (*Works*, ix. 453)

Freedom of expression is a fundamental instrument by which the people can protect themselves against misrule; it is a means by which the private citizen can preserve or claim for himself whatever securities he deems necessary to his existence and well-being. As such, freedom of expression is a check on the activities of government and is, therefore, an essential part of the utilitarian remedy for oppression.

Having said this, it would be a mistake to construe Bentham as a libertarian in the modern sense. To do so would be to ignore the exhaustive and pervasive role he envisaged for the legislator in the Utilitarian society. It is true that as a general rule of jurisprudence Bentham believed that the legislator should leave individuals free to think and do what pleases them, in so far as they do not produce harm to others. But he also devised elaborate arrangements whereby the legislator might persuade or influence the citizen to maximize his happiness in an officially sanctioned manner.[49] Though he argued for complete freedom of discussion, he also indicated that the cultivation of certain attitudes or beliefs (for example, belief in the natural order as an independently existing phenomenon, as distinct from a divinely constructed and controlled universe) was within the jurisdiction of the legislator. The manipulation of the moral sanction through 'indirect' legislation (principally education, but more generally social conditioning) was the means to foster correct thinking towards the end of maximizing happiness. Indeed, Bentham's commitment to the techniques of natural science and the utopian passion that informed his analysis of society made it unlikely, even impossible, that he could stop at an orthodox libertarian stand on toleration. The tensions in his thought between, on the one hand, pleas for freedom of expression and, on the other, plans to fashion a society in which, regardless of individual quirks and characteristics, each person would pursue the greatest happiness under the watchful eye of the legislator, are not always apparent in his writings concerning religious liberty. Nevertheless, it is clear that religious liberty was never meant to be merely a reformulation of a traditional plea for toleration. As an essential ingredient of his argument Bentham also included the notion of freedom *from* religion, and this takes us *ipso facto* into a secular world in

---

[49] It is perhaps more accurate to say that Bentham thought an individual to be 'a better judge than anyone else' regarding his interests, but not the only judge. See Steintrager, 'Language and Politics', p. 11.

which the legislator has a free hand in creating the conditions in which religion and religious institutions will disappear or 'wither away'. Bentham was convinced that the freedom to question religious doctrines and practices and to state the grounds of one's own atheism were essential to the destruction of the ascendancy of any particular religion over any other. Ultimately, he believed, such liberty would lead to the destruction of all religion. It is in this respect that the political and the philosophical are so closely related in his thoughts on religion. For his advocacy of religious liberty is entailed by the theoretical principles enunciated in his writings on metaphysics and logic. It is the lack of an empirical foundation for religious beliefs which makes the claims made on behalf of the utility of the religious sanction so preposterous. The existence of an all-powerful God ever ready to expend his wrath on an oath-breaker, for instance, is not a truth that can be scientifically grounded. In short, both the idea of God and those of his various attributes are fictions without empirical foundation. The uncertain nature of the religious premisses upon which the ceremonies of oath-taking and subscription to articles of faith are founded serves to undermine the efficacy of these practices, such that oaths and subscriptions frequently come to be viewed as empty pronouncements. This, of course, is exactly what they are for Bentham. But the hypocrisy engendered by oaths and subscriptions means that they serve to foster habits of mendacity and perjury. The consequences are that injustices are perpetrated in courts of law and the political establishment finds a ready means to strengthen its corrupt rule. Penal laws against Catholics and other Dissenters and prosecutions for blasphemy are additional methods of oppression employed by government to preserve intact the political and religious regimes of England, and which pose obstacles to the maximization of happiness. Relaxation of the terms of exclusion, such as that advocated by Paley and others, barely touched the heart of the matter of this corruption and misrule. For Bentham complete liberty and nothing less would do.

The Alliance of Church and State

For the application of a radical remedy to this radical evil, the times, even by the confession, or rather proclamation, of those by whom it is most cherished, seem ripening apace.

CE, Plan of the Work, p. liv.

THAT Bentham was hostile to the episcopacy and to its association with secular government has never been in doubt. What I trust I have already given sufficient grounds to verify is that his opinions on questions of ecclesiology, as with all other compartments of his social science, follow logically (if not chronologically) from his analysis of the illusory nature of beliefs in an immaterial reality and the harmful psychological and social effects of propagating such beliefs. However, it is evident in the early fragments on subscription of the 1770s that Bentham had not yet thought beyond the conventional explications of the relationship between Church and State, which had their source in the classical defence of the 'alliance' mounted by William Warburton earlier in the century.

What were commonly thought to be the ends that the union of Church and State served? First, to guarantee that Christianity was taught and dispensed to the people. Secondly, to ensure that the English nation observed Christian principles in its laws and government policies. Thirdly, to maximize the support which each institution afforded the other—just as religious sanctions are useful to secure civil government, government is useful in the maintenance of religion.[1] It was generally argued by its supporters that an Established Church was a necessary component of any civilized community. In a sermon of 1747 Bishop Butler typically announced that 'A constitution of civil government without any religious establishment is a chimerical project of which there is no example.'[2] Warburton described in elaborate detail the nature of this contract in *The Alliance between Church and State* (1736). In *The Divine Legation of Moses* (1738) he summarized his position thus: the reasonableness of the union between the

[1] See G. K. Clark, *Churchmen and the Condition of England 1832–1885* (London, 1973), 27–8.
[2] J. Butler, sermon given at Westminster Abbey (1747), *The Works of Joseph Butler*, ed. W. E. Gladstone, 2 vols. (Oxford, 1893), ii. 366.

Church and State is firmly grounded on its utility, for whoever would secure civil government must support it by propagating the belief in God and in rewards and punishments in a future state, and whoever would establish such a religion needs the protection of the civil magistrate.[3]

Ignoring Warburton's more fanciful discussions of the supposed 'compact' between Church and State, Church apologists later in the century tended to employ the same language when describing the union. John Brown and William Paley justified it on strictly utilitarian grounds: the Church must be protected because it is the means to inculcating religious truth and, therefore, necessary to the salvation of souls. The abstract theory of a hypothetical alliance had no role in this justification. Church and State were simply aspects of the same society. The moral role of the State was defined by the fact of its Christianity, and the sanctions behind its claim to obedience were rooted in Scripture and in the doctrines of the Established Church. In other words, the limits to the claims of the State were prescribed by the law of God as interpreted by the national Church. And what was meant by 'national' demanded not only official recognition by secular government of the status of the Church, but also its active support in maintaining both the position and privileges which the Church and its ministers enjoyed. In this respect, says the Church historian Elliott-Binns, even so-called liberal churchmen, like Paley and Bentham's friend Samuel Parr (1747–1825), 'regarded the Church itself as a kind of government department; and organized religion as chiefly useful for preserving morals and supporting venerable institutions, as in fact the cement of the whole social structure'.[4]

Bentham, who had read Warburton with some interest in the 1770s,[5] was certainly aware of the nature of the alliance defended by eighteenth-century Churchmen. But he had not yet articulated the view that through its alliance with government the Church promoted its own interests at the cost of those of society, and was, thus, a principal source of misrule. *Church-of-Englandism and its Catechism Examined*, published in 1818, was to perform this task.

In 1809 or 1810, when engaged on what was eventually to appear as

---

[3] Warburton, *The Divine Legation of Moses*, in *Works*, ii, Bk. II, sec. 5, *passim*.

[4] L. E. Elliott-Binns, *Religion in the Victorian Era* (London, 1946), 47.

[5] Bentham showed a familiarity with Warburton's work when writing of the religious sanction in 'Crit[ical] Jur[isprudence] Crim[inal]' in the mid-1770s (UC 69 and 140, *passim*).

the *Plan of Parliamentary Reform* (1817), Bentham thought of producing a fifteen-chapter companion piece on organized religion under the working title 'Church. Abuse of Influence' (UC 28/32). However, aside from a brief listing of 'Propositions on parish priests, how to improve their education and make them useful', dated 20 August 1810 (UC 21/75), the work did not proceed as planned.[6] Instead, in 1812 Bentham drew up another much more extensive outline (UC 6/1–148) and began work in earnest on several of its chapters. According to a note dated July 1818, this work was 'written before Church of Englandism' but was 'not published or finished' (UC 6/27). What remains of this first attempt are sections of text under the titles 'Doctrine', 'Service', and 'Discipline' (UC 5/94–316; 6/149–209), dated 1812–13 with a few additions in 1814. Some of this material made its way into *Church-of-Englandism*, but the vast majority of the manuscripts are concerned with the topic of subscriptions to articles of faith—a matter subsequently relegated to a second-order consideration in the published volume of 1818—and, as the outline confirms, the original work was planned as a much grander enterprise than Bentham managed to produce in draft. For example, according to the outline he had intended to include sections on the history of Christianity, on the utility of religion, on doubts about the divine mission of St Paul, and on the religious-based antipathy towards homosexuality (cf. UC 6/31–71, *passim*). That these are among the themes later developed by Bentham in other volumes on religion is revealing of the unity of his ecclesiological work as a whole during this period.

---

[6] This is probably not the earliest occasion on which Bentham considered writing a work on the Church. There is a single sheet of jottings at UC 108/108, probably written between 1790–8, on Church establishments with reference to Edmund Burke. The MSS in UC 5/33–93 are harder to pin down; amongst a variety of topics related to organized religion, they contain fragments on the causes and forms of intolerance, 'Church Service', 'Church Power', 'Subscriptions Paley', 'Church Reform', and the 'Science of Divinity'. At UC 5/36–7 there is a 38 section outline of a proposed work on the Church, dealing with the gradual phasing out of Church institutions, and similar suggestions are to be found in *CE*, App. IV. This makes 1809–13 the likely period in which these fragments were written, but it is difficult to be precise. Though it was Bentham's practice from 1800 onwards to date his work, these MSS are undated. At UC 5/36 he mentions a pamphlet by the Duke of Grafton as the subject-matter for a section of a work on the Church with the title 'Principles of Ecclesiastical Polity' (UC 5/33). The tract in question is almost certainly Grafton's *Hints, etc. Submitted to the Serious Attention of the Clergy, Nobility and Gentry*, published in 1789. Since Bentham wrote to Grafton commending this work on 7 Sept. 1790 (*Corr.* iv. 201), it is safe to assume that the MSS at UC 5/33–93 were written no earlier than this.

It was the Church's involvement in education, however, which persuaded Bentham to alter the focus of his work on organized religion. In 1813 he had made a start on an outline for a new school curriculum, strong in natural science and devoid of religion. This was the work eventually published as the *Chrestomathia*. It was a logical and timely extension of his social science, an application of the principles of his legislative-cum-educational theorizing designed to produce a society in which the greatest happiness would have full sway in both public and private affairs. Now, convinced that the Church had only founded the National Society for Promoting the Education of the Poor in the Principles of the Established Church (in 1811) in order to thwart the efforts of the Dissenter Joseph Lancaster (1778–1838) and others to establish nonsectarian schools for educating the poor, Bentham embarked on an expansive critique of the pernicious role of the Church in education and coupled this with his more general criticisms of the Anglican Establishment. The result was *Church-of-Englandism*, a more scathing and far-reaching analysis of official religion than was initially planned, but a work none the less rooted in the manuscripts of 1812–13.

That the published volume is a synthesis of two distinct bodies of work is to some extent revealed by its chaotic format. In its nearly 800 pages there are two prefaces, a detailed plan of the work, and three separate parts to the main text: (*a*) an introduction in five parts on the 'exclusionary system' operated by the National Society; (*b*) 'The Church of England Catechism Examined'; and (*c*) five appendices on various aspects of 'Church-of-Englandism', including suggestions for the reform of the Church. There are four different series of pagination, footnotes which occasionally run on for several pages, and not infrequently one encounters footnotes to footnotes. It is to be regretted that Bentham did not employ an editor to relieve him of the tedium of arranging his material (as George Grote did for *An.*). Samuel Romilly was approached but his reluctance even to proof-read the text, 'to note as he read such passages as to him should present themselves as dangerous' and to suggest amendments 'as he thought might ensure safety', is perhaps understandable given the length and confusion of the manuscripts. Bentham, however, did not think so. To his secretary John Herbert Koe he confided that Romilly 'has broken his promise to me'. It was Bentham's view, a harsh one, that Romilly had balked at the section on sinecures and the overpayment of offices which, as a Whig expectant of position, 'he toils to have his share in the disposal of ', and then foreseeing the direction of the work read no more.[7]

Though a friend and an admirer for many years, Romilly had a history of caution where Bentham's more radical and potentially offensive works were concerned. In 1793 he advised Bentham not to publish *Truth versus Ashurst* because it contained praise of the French, and the work did not appear until 1823 (*Works*, x. 288). In 1802, after reading Bentham's strictures on the role of the Duke of Portland's ministry in the Panopticon affair, Romilly warned him that to publish was to risk a charge of libel (*Works*, x. 399–400). Again, it was Romilly who persuaded him not to publish *The Elements of the Art of Packing* in 1810 for fear of prosecution by the Attorney-General, and Bentham agreed to delay publication until a more tranquil day should present itself (*Works*, x. 450)—it eventually appeared in 1821. Already regretting the publication of the radical *Plan of Parliamentary Reform* in 1817, and believing that *Church-of-Englandism* could 'not fail to shock all persons who have any sense of religion', Romilly was quick to advise that it be suppressed. Bentham ignored this and also refused to listen to later requests that the printed volume should not be distributed.[8]

Francis Place showed none of Romilly's reticence where radical politics or the propagation of unbelief were concerned, and he readily busied himself looking for a publisher for *Church-of-Englandism*.[9] This proved to be no easy task at a time when booksellers and publishers of anonymous tracts deemed to be blasphemous or libellous by the magistrates were liable to prosecution under English Common Law. This may well have forced Bentham to abandon his plan to publish the book as the work of 'An Oxford Graduate'. In an attempt to lessen the risks of prosecution for the bookseller Bentham hastily inserted at the front of the book (*CE*, pp. xiv–xliii) printed versions of his correspondence with the respected Unitarian MP William Smith, on the subject of the Unitarian Toleration Act of 1813. But in the end only the author's name on the title-page would do.[10]

---

[7] JB to John Herbert Koe (7 and 14 Jan. 1818), Koe MSS, from transcriptions at the Bentham Project, UCL. This contradicts the view of Alexander Bain that Romilly 'agreed with every tittle' of *CE*; see *James Mill: A Biography* (1882; New York, 1967), 452.

[8] *Memoirs of the Life of Sir Samuel Romilly*, 2 vols. (3rd edn. London, 1841), ii. 489–90.

[9] See JB to Francis Place (14 Jan. and 6 Feb. 1818), MSS inserted in the BL copy of *CE*, shelf-mark 4106.bb.6.

[10] JB to Francis Place (6 Feb. 1818), ibid.

The completed work has many dimensions. In the preface Bentham states that it had its genesis in his experiences with the discipline and doctrines of the Church while at Oxford (*CE*, pp. xiii–xv). The implication is that the book has been a long time in the making. That it was published primarily as an attack on the National Society and in particular on the use of the Catechism in the schools they controlled is not in doubt. But the work, as we have seen, was never meant to be merely this. Begun in 1812, after a false start in 1809 or 1810, and aborted in 1813 only to be taken up again in the following year, it was intended to be an all-embracing critique of the entire Church Establishment, including a comparison between the Churches of England and Scotland, a review of recent legislation touching on religious affairs, and an examination of Anglican ceremonies, rituals, and sacraments. To this Bentham added in 1814–16 a preface in which he described his introduction to clerical intolerance at Oxford and provided a preamble to his strictures against the National Society.

The main theme of the work is the general attempt to measure the value of the Established Church and its doctrines against the standard of utility, and in the process to provide an analysis of Church influence intended to expose the reciprocal corrupt services that the Church and State perform for each other. It occurred to Bentham in the first place that 'the main root of all abuse in the field of religion and Government [is] an Established Church' (UC 158/157, a marginal for *CE*, Plan of the Work). In other words, the very fact that it was an establishment made it fertile soil for political patronage. Now this legally privileged institution also sought a leading role in the education of the nation's young, an education which was to consist principally in the inculcation of the tenets of the Church Catechism. The effect on the minds and morals of the nation's young Bentham believed would be disastrous. The purpose of his critique of the Catechism was to show the errors and deceptions inherent in the Church doctrines that it was meant to instil in the young. A 'mixture of error and insincerity', he argued, they cannot command rational assent (*CE*, App. IV, 369–70), and in the absence of such assent either these doctrines are forced on unwilling persons or in their confusion people are persuaded to accept them on the basis of authority. In either case what may have been only a 'momentary mendacity' frequently leads to 'perpetual insincerity', and these are the circumstances in which a habitual dependence on authority serves the sinister interests of the Church.

5

The Lancasterian Controversy and Religious Education

THE role of religion in education was a contentious topic of discussion during the early decades of the nineteenth century. In 1797 Dr Andrew Bell (1753–1832), an Anglican clergyman who had spent some time in India experimenting with educational methods, published his account of the 'Madras System' (first adopted in the Charity School of St Botolph's, Aldgate), *An Experiment in Education*. A year later the Quaker, Joseph Lancaster, opened the non-sectarian Borough Road School in Southwark, in which the teaching was conducted, very much as Bell recommended, according to a monitorial plan, subsequently known as the Lancasterian System. Lancaster acknowledged his debt to Bell when he came to descibe his own educational scheme in his *Improvements in Education* (1803). At a time of serious religious rivalry, however, the successes of the one camp quickly upset the other. Bell's religious lessons were carried out strictly in line with Church principles; Lancaster would have nothing but the Bible. The Dissenters saw in the Lancasterian System a means of promoting education among the poor which was both effective and cheap. The debate came to a head in 1805 when George III subscribed to the schools being established by Lancaster, declaring his wish that every child in his dominions should be taught to read the Bible. Few could have foreseen the trouble this would cause. The king's expression of goodwill for the Lancasterian schools soon raised the question whether it was safe to teach the Bible without the safeguard of an authorized interpretation. Mrs Trimmer, a noted advocate of the Sunday School movement, was among the first to express such doubts. It was she who claimed that as a schismatic Lancaster was weakening the Established Church, and stigmatized his 'schools for all' as training schools for the coming revolution.[1] In a public lecture, it is said, Coleridge read a passage from the book in which Lancaster explained

---

[1] 'Mrs Trimmer on Lancaster's Plan of Education', *Edinburgh Review*, 17 (1806), 177–84. See also Stephen, *The English Utilitarians*, ii. 18.

his methods, which he then roundly denounced, comparing the Lancaster schools to prisons, 'and flung the book to the ground with a theatrical gesture of disgust'.[2]

The real question, then, was between the Established Church and Dissenters as to whether the Church Catechism or the Bible alone was to be the means of instruction. The controversy aroused great bitterness between the contending factions and a scurry of activity. In 1809 the Dissenters formed the Royal Lancasterian Institution (from 1814 the British and Foreign School Society) with the patronage of the Prince Regent, and with the Duke of Bedford and Lord Somerville as its presidents. It was the alarming progress made by the Dissenters in establishing schools that made the Church turn to Bell as the convenient instrument of their rival organization, and in 1810 the Church resolved to establish its own school system. The following year was founded the National Society for Promoting the Education of the Poor in the Principles of the Established Church.[3]

1. *The genesis of Bentham's critique*

Bentham entered the fray wholly disaffected with the entire ecclesiastical system, but it would be wrong to think that his own ideas for a secular system of education were already formed at this time. The first manuscript pages of the *Chrestomathia* date from 1813 (UC 149/192–201), and one is hard put to find anything on education before this. It is true that on several previous occasions he had considered developing embryonic thoughts on the proper mode of education to be employed in England. In 1783, for instance, he wrote a letter on the subject to Dugald Stewart—a letter described by Bowring as an inquiry into 'The effects of Scottish education upon the public morals' (*Works*, x.

[2] Halévy, *The Liberal Awakening*, p. 531. See also 'Bell and Lancaster's Systems of Education', *Quarterly Review*, 6 (1811), 264–304.

[3] The founding meeting of the National Society took place on 16 Oct. 1811 with Charles Manners-Sutton, Archbishop of Canterbury, as chairman. It defined the purpose of the society thus: 'That the National Religion should be made the foundation of National Education and should be the first and chief thing taught to the Poor, according to the excellent Liturgy and Catechism provided by our Church', Minute Book of General Committee, i. 1–2, cited by H. J. Burgess, *Enterprise in Education: The Story of the Work of the Established Church in the Education of the People prior to 1870* (London, 1958), 23; for a discussion of the foundation of the society see ch. 2 of this work. Coincidentally, Bentham's half-brother Charles Abbott, the Speaker of the House of Commons, was involved in the establishment of the National Society.

129).[4] There is also a fragment on education dated 1795 with the heading 'Educational Encyclopedia' (UC 107/37). The only other occasions on which Bentham had cause to comment on education were associated with his memories of Westminster and Oxford, a concise summary of which can be read in a letter to Toribio Nunez (UC 13/132, 21 Apr. 1821). Moreover, even when he began to advocate a system of education free from the interference or influence of religion in the second decade of the nineteenth century, it is also true that he did not see fit to oppose those schools established by Joseph Lancaster. So long as the religion taught was free from all interpretations of Scripture associated with specific sects or Churches, he saw no reason to criticize them (at least in public), and indeed took their part against the National Society in the ensuing debate. There was, naturally, a tactical dimension to Bentham's support and he could not be counted upon to continue it once organized religion had bowed out of the fray.

What all this reveals, however, is that Bentham's ideas on systematic education did not precede the 'schools for all' controversy, but rather developed as a consequence of his interest in this issue. Far from being in the vanguard of the struggle for a national system of education, Bentham came to focus on the matter at a time when it was already a hotly disputed question. Like James Mill, he was convinced that the Church had only established the National Society in order to thwart the efforts of Lancaster and others to establish nonsectarian schools.[5]

---

[4] More precisely Bentham's concern in this letter was with the question whether and to what extent 'the influence of religious instruction is beneficial, upon the whole, to the temporal interests of society, and [whether] the labours of the clergy . . . contribute towards turning this influence to account'. Bentham also asked for figures regarding the incidence of crime in Scotland. He was apt to think, he explained (though his logic is baffling) that Scotland paid its clergy less than in England and would, therefore, be found to have less crime! If this were so, his conclusion would be that 'in Scotland, the clerical work is not only done for less money than in England, but better done' (*Works*, x. 130). The reduction of clerical work merely to the fight against crime must have struck Stewart as taking the secularization of the functions of religion too far. To Bentham, however, it was entirely consistent with his treatment of the religious sanction as merely another social sanction and of the Anglican clergy as merely a branch of the political establishment. For drawing my attention to the letter from JB to Stewart I am indebted to Douglas G. Long, ' "A Host of Scotch Sophists": Jeremy Bentham and the Scottish Enlightenment' (unpublished), a paper presented to a conference on The Political Thought of the Scottish Enlightenment in its European Context, at the University of Edinburgh (28 Aug. 1986).

[5] In 1811–12 Mill became involved in the Bell–Lancaster dispute and in 1813 was instrumental in the founding of the West London Lancasterian Association at Westminster, the object of which was to extend the benefits of the Lancasterian System to the middle classes. Bentham offered part of his garden behind the Recruit House in

To Bentham this was just another attempt to keep the people in subservience, blind to the corruption so rife within a society dominated by the 'alliance' (*Fall.* 23–4).[6] His sarcasm could hardly be contained. It is argued, he remarked, that if Lancaster's schools spread 'the Bible might prevail over the Catechism, and the Church of England might then be brought to an end' (*CE* 54–5). In other words, the justification for introducing the Madras System is the preservation of Church and State for, if the Catechism is not substituted for the Bible the Church will fall, 'and from thence the inference is—that the *State*, i.e. the *Constitution* of the State, will fall along with it' (*CE* 90 n.). Bishop Howley, in his *Charge to the Clergy of London* (1815), gave voice to this version of Church policy when he acknowledged the intimate connection between, on the one hand, the Church's involvement in education and, on the other, 'national welfare and the stability of our establishments, political, civil, and religious'.[7] None of this, however, is to the point, says Bentham. The real truth is that the clergy have for long neglected their duty as instructors of the people and are now induced to fill the role for an entirely selfish reason. After being neglected for the past thirteen or fourteen years Bell's system had belatedly been summoned forth to combat the Lancasterian schools; it was now thought to be the indispensable instrument for the preservation of the national religion. But what this means, argues Bentham, is the

Birdcage Walk, St James's Park, as a site for the proposed school, and this inspired him to complete his programme of utilitarian studies, subsequently published as *Chrestomathia* (1816–17). The school was never built. Apparently 'Bentham imposed so many restrictions, and made so many difficulties, that his garden was presently abandoned' (Bain, *James Mill*, p. 87). Later in the decade Mill assisted Bentham in his proposals for the Chrestomathic School, and his concerns for the practical side of the dispute with the Church is illustrated by his pamphlet *Schools for All, in Preference to Schools for Churchmen Only* (London, 1812), reprinted in part in *James Mill on Education*, ed. W. H. Burston (Cambridge, 1969), 120–83. For a discussion of Mill's suggestions for educational reform see R. A. Fenn, *James Mill's Political Thought* (New York, 1987), ch. 3. The early socialist, William Thompson (1775–1833), was also an admirer of Bentham's proposed educational reforms. He attempted to set up a school along chrestomathic lines at Cork shortly after the Napoleonic Wars. Failing in this, he moved to London and lived at Bentham's house for some 15 months in 1822–3; see G. Claeys, *Machinery, Money and the Millenium: From Moral Economy to Socialism, 1815–1860* (Princeton, 1987), 90.

[6] For a similar view see J. Mill, 'A Review of the Arguments of Dr Herbert Marsh and others, in Opposition to the Lancasterian Plans for Educating the Poor', *The Philanthropist*, 2 (1812), 57–108. It seems likely that Bentham had discussed his views on Church involvement in education with Mill, so reminiscent are some of Mill's arguments in this essay of those of Bentham in *CE*.

[7] W. Howley, Bp. of London, *A Charge to the Clergy of London at the Primary Visitation of that Diocese in the Year 1814* (London, 1815), 31.

preservation of 'their own worldly and anti-Christian power, their own factitious dignities, their own overpaid places, their own useless places, and their own sinecures' (*CE* 94 n.). Moreover, funds levied by 'forced contributions' from all Englishmen regardless of religious persuasion, and which might have found their way into the nonsectarian Lancasterian schools, were now employed to support a system that excluded a large number of the nation's children from receiving education (*CE* 94 n., 92 n.). What this high level of capital investment in the National Society's school system proved, according to Bentham, was its moral bankruptcy, since it was apparent that 'no man would ever embrace it *gratis*, and upon conviction, . . . if he were not either paid for so doing, or living under the expectation of being paid for it' (*CE* 95 n.).

The lack of religious motivation in the affair seems genuinely to have shocked Bentham. Such is the degree to which 'worldly anxiety' is ascendant over 'decency', he declared, that the character of Christianity is hardly professed to be regarded in any other capacity than that of 'a state engine': 'an engine, employed in the manufactory of the matter of corruption, for a cement in the *Warburton Alliance* between *Church* and *State*, a cement for the wall of defence built up for the protection of the whole stock of overpaid places, needless places, mischievous places, and sinecure places, sacred and profane' (*CE* 99). On these terms religion is merely a tool of control to serve sinister interests retaining no spiritual value whatever.

2. 'Figurantes *on the politico-religious theatre*'

The role of the bishops, with their guaranteed seats in the Lords, had long been singled out by Bentham as an obstacle to reform. In the battle against Lancaster they were once again to the forefront. The actions of Manners-Sutton, the Archbishop of Canterbury (1805–28), in particular, were closely scrutinized by Bentham.[8] To Francis Place he announced his intention to enquire of William Smith 'for some

[8] This is not the same Archbishop of Canterbury whom Bentham slighted in a letter to Reginald Pole Carew (20 July 1791) on the occasion of the 'Church and King' riots in Birmingham: 'Is it true that the Archbishop of Canterbury was seen to "Ride in the whirlwind and direct the storm" at Birmingham sitting astride a broomstick in his best bib and tucker, with his Privy-Councillor the Devil at his elbow?' (*Corr.* iv. 321). Milne remarks in a footnote to this letter that 'Bentham's reference to the Archbishop is a misconceived joke: John Moore (1730–1805), who was Archbishop of Canterbury, 1783–1805, was a philanthropist and moderate reformer.'

good behaviour' of the archbishop 'to set off against his misdeeds in the business of the National Society'.[9] In *Church-of-Englandism* Manners-Sutton is the villain of the piece, the 'false Christ', with whom Bentham is obsessed and whom he is determined to expose (*CE*, App. II, 177). The archbishop and the bishops are accused of deliberately introducing exclusionary policies to serve the sinister interests of the Church: '1. Of the institution of this society, the ultimate object has not been the advancement—either of intellectual instruction in general, or of the religion of Jesus. 2. Of this same institution the sole ultimate object has been—the preserving from reformation the abuses with which the Church of England establishment is replete' (*CE* 87). This is the conclusion Bentham draws from a close, and it must be said tedious, study of the first three annual reports of the transactions of the National Society (1812, 1814, 1815). The reports are declared to be 'spurious' and 'purposely deceptious', and the society's General Committee, presided over by the archbishop, condemned as the perpetrator of a 'fraud'.

The substance of Bentham's charge of fraudulence is that the publications of the proceedings of the society reveal that its work is really the product of one or possibly a few of its members, and not of the many notables it lists as having attended and taken part in its deliberations. Those responsible are the archbishop and the secretary of the society, the Revd T. T. Walmsley (*CE*, p. xxxviii). The reports are spurious in so far as they represent decisions as having had the concurrence of the whole body, when in most instances they have been the work of the archbishop acting on his own authority. They are 'purposely deceptious' in so far as there has been a deliberate attempt to persuade the public that they were the result of the deliberations of various committees or of the General Committee, a list of the 250 members of which is published in each report (*CE* 1). Moreover, in the reports there are discrepancies between the lists of contents and the substance of the papers themselves, particularly where the allocation of funds is concerned. What made the fraud a more serious matter in Bentham's eyes, however, was the fact that the archbishop and all the bishops were implicated in the deception. The business of the society, he declared, is 'in altogether unfit hands', the hands of 'impostors' (*CE* 77). In appearance the bishops formed only part of the society; in

---

[9] JB to Francis Place (14 Jan. 1818), MS insert in BL copy of CE, shelf-mark 4106.bb.6. For Manners-Sutton's efforts to reform the Church see Clark, *Churchmen and the Condition of England*, pp. 45–6.

effect they formed the whole. Hiding behind a tissue of lies they approved the activities of the society as a body even though only a few were ever seen actively to promote its interests. In this way 'the intolerant part of the Bishops and their adherents, being but too probably the major part, continue . . . to enjoy the benefit of wickedness, without standing exposed to the disgrace so justly due it' (*CE* 75).

Bentham went to extraordinary depth in his scrutiny of the reports in order to expose the misrepresentations of its committees, their fictional meetings, the fictional persons who attended them, and where and upon what dates the discussions of the society were said to have taken place (cf. *CE* 111–28). The claim of Report III (1815), that many of the first men in the Church and in political life have been consulted about the tasks of the society, is typical, and is denounced as 'mere invention' (*CE* 187 n.). The report also notes that at all the deliberations 'his Grace was constantly presiding' (*CE* 179).[10] But at what deliberations and in what manner presiding?, demands Bentham. All this 'secrecy' surrounding the formation and activities of the society required an explanation, and Bentham finds it in the motives which lay behind the 'mystery':

1. Fear of the odium, so justly attached to the *exclusionary system* . . . 2. Unwillingness to let it be seen, by how *small* a portion, of those to whom the right of co-operating could not but be imparted, . . . 3. Advantage seen, in the great facility afforded by the darkness with which the face of this deep was covered:—the facility of practising upon the country . . . the imposition that consists in causing men to believe that bodies of men . . . have throughout been bearing a part—in a business, which throughout has been in truth the work of one and the same individual . . . 4. Convenience, afforded by the exclusion, applied not only to all witnesses, but even to all discussion itself. (*CE* 185–6).

Here, then is the 'fraud', planned and executed from the beginning by the bishops, those '*Figurantes* on the politico-religious theatre' (*CE*, App. IV, 308). By their conduct they have forfeited whatever claim they might otherwise have had to the trust of the people; they have shown themselves to be morally untrustworthy.

Bentham's suspicion of decisions made by committees or boards of persons is partly responsible for his invective against the bishops. The absolute necessity of individual responsibility was a cardinal principle of Benthamic public administration, according to which 'a Board is a screen' which permits 'transgressions be [they] ever so enormous' to

---

[10] All quotations from the annual reports of the National Society are as per Bentham.

escape 'not only unpunished . . . but unreproached'. Moreover, boards provide a ready-made excuse for the extension of patronage and, hence, of corruption. Where boards exist 'flies in plenty are glad to buzz about the while and make as if they too helped to turn it' (UC 7/132). Nor is the secrecy of the work of committees warranted. As with Panopticon and his recommendations for democratic reform, the remedy Bentham suggests is 'universal and constant inspection', on the grounds that 'nothing is thorough [*sic*] well done, unless in some shape or other Inspection has a hand in it'. For to allow a betrayal of trust to go unpunished 'is to transfer with impunity every public to every private and personal interest' (UC 7/133).

The evidence Bentham offered to substantiate his prosecution of the bishops, it must be said, fell well short of proof. But if he exaggerated the supposed deception perpetrated in the bishops' manipulation of the National Society, he was on firmer ground when he accused them of pursuing a policy of exclusion by only admitting the children of professed Anglicans into the society's schools. It was their proclaimed policy to inculcate into the minds of the youthful poor the 'fixt principles' of the Church. In the name of these principles the National Society had proceeded to exclude one part of the community of the poor from education, while compelling the other part 'to come within the pale of the church dominion' (*CE* 52). Bentham found this notion of 'fixt principles' to be historically absurd. The Church altered its principles when it separated from Rome 'whose principles had been fixt for almost as many centuries as [those of the Anglican Church have] been for dozens of years'. If tradition was to be the arbiter of 'fixt principles', then let the archbishop 'go to Rome—prostrate himself at the feet of the original Holy Father and then, and not till then, let him call upon us to prostrate our understandings and wills before their fixt principles' (UC 7/136). The zeal of the clergy is to be deplored and their methods are to be condemned. The punishment they threaten for the refusal to adhere to the creed of the Church is exclusion from their schools; the reward for compliance is instruction. Where arguments are wanting the recourse will always be to the sanctions of reward and punishment to influence the will, but this is to misapply sanctions because the end in view is that of a particular interest and not that of the well-being of the community at large. Was it not, Bentham asks, God's intention to redeem all humanity by the birth and death of Christ? The bishops, by restricting the benefits of education to a small proportion of those who profess the religion of Christ, act contrary to this fundamental article of belief. It is their intention to instruct no one,

other than those who, in the character of subjects to their governance, are content to be perpetual contributors to those *riches*, in which they put their trust; to that *power* which they abuse; to those *factitious dignities*, with which they deck their names; to that *purple*, and that *fine linen*, in which they strut; to those *pomps and vanities*, which in their babe and suckling state they renounced, and they are seen with so much anxiety mounting guard upon, in their Church regnant and Church militant state. (*CE* 68).

The manner of exclusion is clearly indicated in the society's reports. For example, the report of 1812 announces that the society will only contribute financial support to those schools in which the masters are members of the Anglican Church—a form of bribery, remarks Bentham (*CE* 106). The list of books recommended for use in the schools is meant to ensure that the curriculum of the schools is uniformly determined (cf. *CE* 134–44)—among these were reading books produced for use in the society's Central School, including the *Catechism Broken into Short Questions* and a child's book of Church doctrine with the title *The Chief Truths of the Christian Religion*.[11] In addition the report of 1815 requires that no schoolmasters '*take upon themselves* to originate any variations from the practices of the Central Schools'—a rule, sneers Bentham, which is 'the natural product of that mixture of pride, and jealousy, and fear, and indolence, and imperiousness, which characterises little minds in great places' (*CE* 144 n., 146 n.).

3. The 'prostration of understanding and will'

Bentham took great delight in *Church-of-Englandism* in pointing out the discrepancy that exists between the National Society's policy of exclusion and the Christian religion the Church professed to believe. The essence of the discrepancy consists in the fact that in the National Society's schools the Church Catechism is substituted for the Bible, the vehicle of instruction employed by Lancaster. By making the Catechism the keystone of the curriculum the National Society is guilty of carrying out a deliberate scheme of 'anti-Christian exclusion' (*CE* 175). The scheme is antichristian, Bentham maintains, because

---

[11] Burgess, *Enterprise in Education*, p. 33.

the Catechism is the means by which 'Church-of-Englandism' is substituted for the religion of Jesus—as such it is a 'bad substitute' for the Bible (*CE*, p. xxxv). The Catechism completely eschews scriptural quotations and even references to the Bible, a practice which incurs 'the just suspicion of misrepresentation'. In this respect the Presbyterian Church of Scotland preaches a far purer form of Christianity; it supplies both quotations and references to the Bible in its formulary and this is just as it should be in any summary of Scripture used for instruction (*CE*, 24–5). Having only the Catechism and not the Bible before them children come to revere the first and not the second; it is the Catechism which becomes 'the object of faith' (*CE* 45). But Bentham was not prepared to take this argument further, to show what precisely about Christianity was missing from the Catechism. The comparison with the Scriptures he introduced entirely for tactical reasons. In truth he had no more use for the Bible, save as a fruitful source of useful quotations (the Devil quoting Scripture, one might say)—as in the case of the precept 'swear not at all'—than he had for the Catechism. His case against the use of the latter in schools was built upon the strictly utilitarian ground that the inculcation of its principles was detrimental to both the intellectual and moral facets of a child's nature (*CE*, pp. xxx–xxxii; cf. also pp. xxi–xxii, 21).

Bentham's examination of the use of the Catechism in the schools of the National Society provides us with several of the liveliest parts of *Church-of-Englandism*. Perhaps one reason for this was his long-harboured antipathy towards the Catechism and its doctrines. As a child, he tells us, he suffered greatly as a consequence of the 'inability to beat into my memory the words' of an exposition of the 'formulary'. The exposition, Bentham recalled, was 'by some *Archbishop*: his name began with a W. which is all I now recollect about this nightmare, by which my sleep was so long disturbed' (*CE* 4 n.). Later, in fragmentary reflections on the Catechism, written *c.*1773, he condemned it in no uncertain terms as 'this crude composition of a semi-barbarous priesthood' (UC 96/300). A few years later still, his interest in the sociological consequences of the abuse of language led him to denounce it as 'the obscure comments of [*sic*] an obscure text' (UC 100/34, *c.*1776). Unquestionably these were strong indicators of Bentham's growing disaffection with the doctrinaire and primitive inflexibility of the manner in which the Church imposed its tenets on innocent children, a process which he had personally experienced at Westminster. Now, in *Church-of-Englandism* it was his declared purpose to expose the Catechism's 'poisonous nature' once and for all.

In the light of its manifest defects, Bentham found the assumption of infallibility implicit in the imposition of the Catechism by the Church particularly galling. The argument that the Bible is complex and needs interpretation in order to be understood by a small child was quietly ignored. To Bentham the Catechism was 'spurious matter' which children would not be any the better for having learnt by heart. Central to this argument is Bentham's distinction between the 'understanding' and the 'will'. The former is that to which argument appeals and which can be won over by the persuasion of reason; the latter is the source of the volitions upon which we act and is formed according to the motivation provided by the sanctions of pleasure and pain. The reasonable person will act according to the apparent reasonableness perceived in a proposed action; where reason does not prevail the will can be directed by the inducements of pleasure or the threat of pain, or a combination of the two. At the bottom of Bentham's charge against the National Society's use of the Catechism was the acknowledgement that the episcopacy fully understood the human psyche and was very willing to employ methods calculated to influence, to shape, and control it. The sinister character of this control did not depend on the personality of the person who administered the Catechism, but on the nature of the interaction between the administrator and the persons to whom it was administered. What distinguished sinister from benign influence was the difference between, on the one hand, the action of will on will and, on the other hand, the action of the understanding on understanding. In Bentham's ethics the appeal to rational argument, that is, to consequentialist calculation, was the proper and acceptable mode by which one person may influence the mind and actions of another. By comparison, the overpowering of one will by another—save with the aid of legal sanctions designed to further the public good was an improper and thus a sinister mode of influence.[12] That the Catechism contained matter tending to the 'prostration of understanding and will', Bentham points out, is openly avowed by William Howley, the Bishop of London, who expressly stated it to be the aim of the National Society and the reason for employing the Catechism in its schools (*CE*, p. xliii; cf. also App. I,

---

[12] See Hume, *Bentham and Bureaucracy*, p. 182, where he paraphrases Bentham on this topic from UC 125/47–52. These MSS are headed 'Parliamentary Reform' and dated 1811.

passim). In his *Charge to the Clergy of London* Howley set forth the Church's position thus: those of the nonconforming sects outside the pale of the Anglican Church (the Unitarians were uppermost in his mind) were ' "generally" . . . men of some education, whose thoughts "have been little employed on the subject of religion; or who, *loving rather to question than learn*, have approached *the oracles of divine truth* without that *humble docility*, that *prostration of the understanding* and *will*, which are indispensable to proficiency in Christian instruction" '.[13] It is such remarks as these that lend credence to Bentham's claim that it was not the word of Christ, but the Church's scriptural 'interpretation' before which children were to prostrate themselves in the schools of the National Society. In this regard the bishop stood condemned by his own words, since to interpret the Scriptures, he admonished, was 'arbitrarily imposing a meaning unwarranted by the usages of language'.[14] Yet, is this not exactly what the Catechism represents? It is clearly implied that the 'oracles of divine truth' were to be found here and not in the Bible (*CE* 93). Hence it is not the case that the understanding and will are prostrate before God; they lie prostrate before the Church and its formulary—the prostration is of 'man before man', and a mind which is prostrate is 'a mind in the lowest state of debility' (*CE*, App. I, 89). It is in this manner that the Church employs psychological sources of influence to serve a sinister end, to infuse obsequiousness generally among the people. For the unquestioning subservient child will become the unquestioning subservient adult and the Church will thereby be protected from criticisms while its privileges are made secure.

Another of Bentham's complaints about the use of the Catechism was that like subscriptions to articles of faith it fostered a habit of insincerity in the child. To demand assent from a child too young to understand that to which he was assenting was to 'force him to *tell lies*'; the consequence of this is that the child will 'contract the *habit* of lying' (*CE* 12). For personal reasons as much as any other this was a grievance very close to Bentham's heart. *Church-of-Englandism*, he confessed at one point, was published as a kind of atonement for his 'sin' of perjury at Oxford; it was his 'duty' to provide 'reparation' by 'repentance' (*CE*, pp. xxvi–xxvii). The religious tone of Bentham's language should not distract us from the basic sincerity of his

---

[13] Howley, *A Charge to the Clergy of London*, p. 23, quoted by Bentham, *CE*, App. I, p. 88. Bentham's emphases.

[14] Ibid. 22, quoted by Bentham, *CE*, App. I, p. 92.

confession. What he says here is surely indicative of the long-felt bitterness he experienced over the oath-taking ordeal to which he was subjected as a young scholar at University, and which he found in later life a perpetual cause for complaint. The mode of instruction employed by the National Society was another source, and perhaps the most detrimental source, of the insincerity which the Church had reduced to common practice.

What form did this insincerity take when a child subscribed to Church doctrines via the Catechism? In the first place, the child avowed belief in all the articles of the Christian faith. This was a promise to believe an innumerable host of things hardly any of which were understood (*CE*, Catechism Examined, 13–14). This, claims Bentham, strikes at the root of all religion and all morality: 'forasmuch as, in giving utterance to this mass of absurdity, the child is forced to say that *he believes it*,—while, at his years, at any rate, to believe is not possible,—thus it is that the duty and practice of *lying* forms part of every Church of England child's first lesson' (*CE*, Catechism Examined, 15). Nor is mendacity confined to the instance of avowal. Indeed, it is something which stays with the child for life; it inculcates the habit of lying, of insincerity, the notion that it is acceptable to assent to doctrines which are not understood and hence cannot be believed. That Bentham does not distinguish here between belief in terms of faith and belief in terms of empirically grounded knowledge is, of course, indicative of his entire approach to religion. But his indifference to the distinction does not only reflect the polemical reductionism of some of his arguments; it also serves to detract unnecessarily from the strength of his case in other regards. His discussion of several of the articles of belief contained in the Catechism provides a case in point.

Those articles of belief which Bentham singled out as particularly absurd were the notion of the Devil as God's protagonist, the idea that God was conceived by the Holy Ghost, the claim that Christ was born of a virgin mother and that the son of God died a mortal death, and the doctrines of the Trinity and the Communion of Saints. In treating of these various propositions he turned his irony to good effect, but it is his theory of language which is the foundation of the analysis. As we have seen, Bentham's metaphysics dictates that words must correspond to objects, or they must be capable of reduction by paraphrasis to real entities. If in a given case neither is true or possible then the word in question is a fiction generating confusion and capable of misapplication in unscrupulous hands as a means of deception. Never could there have been a subject so open to an attack founded on the demand for definitions and clear and unambiguous language as the Church Catechism. We need not, however, follow Bentham through his entire critique; its character is readily conveyed by a few brief examples.[15]

The doctrine of the Trinity Bentham declared a glaring example of a proposition lacking any obvious sense, but in which children were expected to avow belief. Such an avowal was to utter 'sounds without sense; mere words without meaning'. If the Holy Ghost is the Holy Spirit of God, why do we need to profess belief in both God and in his spirit? 'Believing in a man, what more do you do, by believing in his spirit likewise?' It is only to 'string words upon words,—and then, for every word, believe, or pretend to believe, that a correspondent really existing object is brought into existence' (*CE*, Catechism Examined, 20, 22). The article of belief in 'the Holy Catholic Church' was similarly dismissed by Bentham. Is it the Church of England that is meant here or is it the Roman Catholic Church—the Church of the Papists, who once persecuted English Protestants? What is it that makes the Church 'holy'? The article is a confused proposition to which no explanation is so much as hazarded. Bentham is sure that if the 'poor child' were to think upon the subject 'how distressing must be the perplexity, into which he here finds himself plunged?' (*CE*, Church Catechism, 23, 24). The Catechism, it seems, is nothing but a mass of confusing propositions to which a child is made to give assent without any understanding of what it is he has assented to. He is made to declare 'that he believes whatever is thus forced into his mouth, without knowing so much as *who* it is that put it where it is, much less *what* it is'. The only thing learnt from this mode of instruction is 'the art of *gratuitous assertion*—the art of speaking and writing without thinking—and the art of making groundless inferences' (*CE*, Catechism Examined, 27, 28). Such are the pernicious consequences of 'catechitical instruction'.

Bentham's analysis is exhaustive and he offers many other criticisms of the doctrines contained in the Catechism. I will mention only two others, regarding the sacraments of baptism and communion. These, according to Bentham's literalist interpretation of the New Testament, are found to have received no sanction from Jesus; they are entirely the

---

[15] For Bentham's critique of the Apostle's Creed see *CE*, Catechism Examined, pp. 17–30.

fabrication of the Church.[16] So far as baptism was concerned, Bentham suggested that Christ's example of washing the feet of his Apostles was a more instructive ceremony for the clergy to follow in regard to their congregations, though he acknowledged that the bishops were hardly likely to stoop so low (*CE*, Catechism Examined, 62–3; App. II, 167–8).[17] For communion Bentham had particularly harsh words. The transubstantiation or metamorphosis of bread and wine into body and blood, he condemned as, 'the *pure* grimgribber of modern *technical* theology'. In Luther's reform of Roman Catholic theology the body and blood of Christ are said to accompany the bread and wine. This theory of consubstantiation Bentham called 'the *adulterated* grimgribber', and found in it a source of even greater confusion than in the theory of transubstantiation: 'on the *con* plan the mess has more matter in it than in the *trans*: and the more the worse.'[18] On either version the idea of communion was little better than 'cannibalism'. The trick in the explanation, noted Bentham, was to refer to the 'spiritual sense' of the proposition—an appeal to a purer sense superior to the carnal or temporal sense. By such means is something false or absurd made true or reasonable. If there is a mind to subdue this is the way to accomplish the task, by introducing 'the *spiritual* sense—alias the *nonsensical* sense' (*CE*, Catechism Examined, 68–72).

According to Bentham, then, the 'avowed object' of the bishops in

---

[16] See *CE*, Introduction, 238–45; Catechism Examined, 2–11, 47–72; App. II, pp. 154–67.

[17] Bentham declined to be godfather to the first-born child of his trusted assistant John Herbert Koe in the following whimsical words: 'A propos of his Bratship, I told you I could not endure to take part in that abominable ceremony [of baptism], but if you have a mind to give my name—my surname—for a Christian name well and good. You will then have a Bentham to tyrannize over, as you yourself have been tyrannized over by one: and, according to Juggical justice you may revenge yourself on the young one for what you have suffered under the old one', JB to Koe (7 Aug. 1816), Koe MSS, from a transcription at the Bentham Project, UCL. Étienne Dumont agreed to stand as godfather in place of Bentham and Koe subsequently christened his son Bentham Dumont Koe.

[18] Art. XXVIII of the Thirty-nine Articles, 'Of the Lord's Supper', distinguishes the Anglican interpretation from the Roman Catholic belief in transubstantiation which, it is said, 'cannot be proved by Holy Writ; but is repugnant to the plain words of scripture, overthroweth the nature of the sacrament, and hath given occasion to many superstitions'. Bentham appears, however, to confuse the Catholic and Anglican versions of the sacrament. On the Anglican view, 'The Body of Christ is given, taken, and eaten, in the Supper, only after an heavenly and spiritual manner. And the means whereby the Body of Christ is received and eaten in the Supper is Faith' (Bicknell, *A Theological Introduction to the Thirty-Nine Articles*, p. 382).

enforcing the use of the Catechism was nothing more nor less than the introduction of a system of intellectual and moral slavery. The schools of the National Society were the instruments of the 'tyrants and sub-tyrants' in the ecclesiastical hierarchy; the result was oppression and persecution. For this reason the clergy's declared object of making good Christians by instructing them in Church tenets was genuine only if by that is understood the subjection of the many to the few.

4. Education without religious instruction

The remedies suggested by Bentham for the evils resulting from Church education were aimed at ameliorating the exclusionary aspects of the system and should by no means be thought to be his last word upon the subject. Though his preference was for secular education he did not declare outright for the abolition of schools operated by the Church, at least not in *Church of Englandism*. His first recommendation was that any texts used in the schools which included matter to which the children of nonconformist parents could not sincerely subscribe must be eliminated from use. All that should remain for the purposes of religious instruction were those discourses of the New Testament ascribed either directly to Jesus or to one of his four 'biographers' (as we shall see in Chapter 8 Bentham had little patience either for the Acts of the Apostles or for Paul's Epistles). Secondly, Bentham argued that the laws restricting teaching licences only to those who subscribe to the doctrines of the Anglican Church must be repealed. Given these changes no child would be forced to profess personal belief in articles of faith contrary to those of its parents, and the children of heretics and unbelievers would not be excluded from instruction. Special provisions might also be made, for example, for the children of Jews. No Jewish children should be made the subject of any attempt to convert them while at school; their religious instruction should be the responsibility of their parents and not the school (*CE*, App. III, 183–5).

Such suggestions for reform, however, only half-heartedly disguised Bentham's preference for secular education. Nor did his reforming zeal stop here. Bentham came to view the Church's involvement in education as a tactical move by the clergy meant to serve their own interests at the cost of the community. Indeed, he thought this plain in the National Society's first annual report of 1812. Here it is declared that there should be a national system of education and that it should be founded on the national religion. The reasoning, per Bentham, was disingenuous. Quoting the report's own words, '*if the great body of the people be educated in other principles than those of the Established* Church, the natural consequence must be to alienate the minds of the people from it, or render them indifferent to it, which may, in succeeding generations, prove *fatal to the Church*, and to the State itself' (*CE* 89 n.). Education was to be employed to assist the Church in its battle for survival: organized on a national basis, purportedly to enhance the education of England's poor, its real purpose was to preserve the privileges of the clergy (*CE* 93–4 n.). The blatant insincerity with which the Church thus imposed its religion—through the use of oaths, subscription, the administration of the sacraments, and the use of the Catechism—was ample proof for Bentham that the school system sponsored by the National Society was nothing more than 'a state engine . . . employed in the manufactory of the matter of corruption, for a cement in the *Warburton Alliance* between *Church* and *State*' (*CE* 99). In this respect the Church had forsaken its spiritual purpose and deprived the moral order of any support it might have expected from this quarter. More than this, however, it had become the fount of every abuse and imperfection not only in religion but in secular government as well. Hence this 'radical evil' cried out for the application of a 'radical remedy' (*CE*, p. liv). The hierarchy was too entrenched to be reformed by piecemeal measures; the 'euthanasia' of the Church and nothing less would do (*CE*, App. IV, 193). The Church must be disestablished, her secular functions taken over by the State and, with fair compensation to the clergy, her property sold off. What interest had perverted Bentham believed interest better instructed could rectify. Utility was no longer to be used as an aid to the philosophical justification of things as they are; it was now the foundation of the demand for the reconstruction of things as they ought to be.

6

Anticlericalism and Disestablishment

WHEN the term 'anticlerical' is employed what is usually meant is that the person expressing such views is an opponent of the clergy of the established religion in a state, a critic of Churchmen who wield the power of their Church as a social sanction, holding out threats or promises of rewards over and above those which pertain to the spiritual nature of their faith as inducements to compliance with doctrines and practices. In so far as any preacher or priest employs such methods the anticleric will condemn him. In these terms Bentham was certainly anticlerical, and was so from a very early stage of his life. In his Commonplace Book of the years 1774–5 he noted: 'In England the clergy are scorpions which sting us. On the continent they are dragons which devour us' (*Works*, x. 74). In the 'Preparatory Principles' manuscripts of *c.*1776 his invective was in the same vein: here he developed a brief history of the priesthood beginning with the role of priests in primitive societies employing the language of 'extraordinary providences' to interpret natural occurrences, and ending with the priests of the modern age who have abandoned their role as enforcers of morality and who seek to maintain their privileged position in society by perpetrating vicious 'nostrums' (UC 69/166–7). On another occasion in the early 1770s, under the title 'Divines', he castigated the clergy as a major impediment in the path of social improvement: they 'fail not to perceive that men cannot grow wiser to the great concerns of Society, but at their expence: hence an instinctive hatred of all such wisdom'. The people must be warned of the interests the clergy pursue and be taught to 'set their shoulders against that influence' (UC 96/318; cf. also 96/315). And again, he remarked in the same set of manuscripts: 'No solid or comprehensive System of reformation even in matters of civil polity is to be looked for, till a clear majority of each House of Legislature be cleansed from the last dregs of superstition' (UC 96/320).[1] What must be expunged were 'those principles of what kind soever they be, which point to any . . . [other] end of human Legisla-

---

[1] UC 97/11–16, under the general heading 'Legislation—raw materials', also contains much fragmentary material on 'Obstacles. Divine' (*c.*1770–4).

tion than the greatest happiness of the greatest number pursued through
. . . obvious and experimented means' (UC 96/320; cf. also 69/166).

Though Bentham did not mean to banish the beliefs of any one
religion as distinct from any other, it is clear in these early jottings that
he had 'Church-of-Englandism' in view. His one-time amanuensis
John Colls, later himself a clergyman, testified to Bentham's partiality
on this point:

> However strong his hatred of Lawyers may have been, he left no doubt in my
> mind, . . . that his antipathy to Clergymen was immeasurably greater—
> Clergymen, I mean, of the Church of England;—not Unitarians, Socinians,
> and similar teachers, whom he presumed to have either no principles at all, or
> to be staunch admirers of his favourite 'voluntary system'! towards *such as these*
> he was more tolerant.[2]

Though he was often an unreliable critic Colls's judgement here is
correct—Bentham thought the dissenting clergy to be largely free of
the vices which infested the Anglican Church. No other clergy, he
would often say, is indifferent to religion, demands a profession of
belief in that which is not believed, extorts money for doing nothing, or
looks upon Church services as hardships which have to be paid for in
order to render them desirable. No other clergy resists the introduction of
practical ameliorative social legislation or receives benefits from the
hands of the Crown.

1. Clerical 'misrule'

When Bentham came to consider religious affairs at length in later life
his anticlericalism, fuelled by the battle with the bishops over
Panopticon and their opposition to other attempts at improvement,
became bitter and more specific in nature.[3] In the 'Church'
manuscripts of 1812–13 he condemned the coercive power of the
clergy outright: 'Give them any such coercive power; you give them a
sinister interest which . . . produces the misrule exemplified in all
Church history.' The clerical order was instituted neither by God
nor by Jesus, nor is it sanctioned by Scripture. But words uttered
two thousand years ago will not prevent archbishops and bishops

---

[2] Colls, *Utilitarianism Unmasked*, p. 35.
[3] For the inauspicious role played in the Panopticon affair by Samuel Horsley (1733–1806), Bp. of Rochester and Dean of Westminster (from 1802 Bp. of St Asaph), see *Corr.* vi, *passim*.

from doing what it is in their interest to do: 'Mans [*sic*] conduct is governed not by the clearest words much less by a part of a discourse interpreted in an infinity of ways; but by his interest—his present interest' (UC 6/33). Nonresidence, sinecurism, plural benefices, preferment hunting, 'pastoral rapacity', the sale of pews, compulsory rates and tithes, the neglect of duties—these are all subjects Bentham intended to address in the aborted early critique of the Church (UC 6/53–65). He asked a selection of questions which sufficiently indicates his train of thought: 'Ought government to interfere in religion?' 'Ought a particular class of men to be set apart by Government for the service of religion?' 'Ought pay for them to be raised by force?' 'These instructors *ought* they as such, to have any share in government?' (UC 6/65).

Bentham's anticlericalism did not cease or change character throughout his long life. In 1828, in a letter to Daniel O'Connell, he was still lashing out at 'priest ridden' England (*Works*, x. 595), and, on the eve of his death, he reiterated his anticlericalism in typically strident terms in the intriguing pamphlet *Auto-Icon: Or Farther Uses of the Dead to the Living* (based on MSS principally dated 1831, printed 1842 but not published). 'From its birth to its death', he wrote,

the priest keeps his fixed predatory eye on the prey he covets, . . . No sooner are you born, than priestcraft lays hold of you, and till you have paid toll to it, keeps shut against you the gate of the road which conducts you to your rights, and in return for the money, perhaps the 'utmost farthing' thus extorted from your friends, tells them that he has *christened* you; and unless this be done to you, and done by him to you, heaven, he informs him [*sic*], has no comforts for you, nor will earth have any of which it is in his power to deprive you. (*AI* 16).

On this view the Church of England is composed of two classes—'the plunderers and the plundered' (*CE* 123). Contrary to the teaching of the Gospel, that no Apostle is greater than any other and that it is not he who possesses the most power but he who renders the most service that is to be venerated (Mat. 18: 3–4), the bishops of the Church 'wallow in a compost made of *riches*, *power*, and *factitious dignity*' and 'call aloud for "*humble docility*" ' (*CE* 104–5). It is this which distinguishes the clergy of the Established Church from that of other religions in England, and it is this which lies at the heart of their efforts to maintain the security of the Church.

If this is so obvious a fact, why is it not detected by the public? The reason is that the people are mystified; the ecclesiastical branch of the

Establishment is held up as an object of reverence because it is 'sanctified'. They 'behold *sanctified*, and by sanctification protected, abuses so much beyond any, of the establishment of which, in their own branch, they durst suffer themselves to entertain so much as a ray of hope' (*CE* 128). On top of this it is claimed that the sacred part of the Establishment (the bishops in the House of Lords) is necessary to the maintenance of the constitution. What this means, however, is merely that the 'holy bench' will do the bidding of its political master, the monarch. The maintenance of the monarchy, the source of ecclesiastical patronage, is the political aim of the clergy, and for this they expect to be duly rewarded. 'Obsequiousness, thus constant and universal, is the fruit and conclusive evidence of equally constant corruption: obsequiousness to corruptive influence on the one part, exertion of it on the other.' Thus understood, corruption can be seen to be vital to the existence of the constitution, condoned in its entirety by the adherents of the Warburtonian 'alliance' (*CE* 129).

Bentham's attack on the 'alliance' was all encompassing, penetrating (as he thought) to the very heart of the problems it posed for social improvement. In the *Plan of Parliamentary Reform* he had given a sketch of the 'temporal' nature of the constitution and expounded the democratic causes of annual parliaments, secret, and universal suffrage. In *Church-of-Englandism* he promised to tackle the 'spiritual' nature of the constitution (*CE*, p. xi). In the event he went to extraordinary lengths to address a host of absurdities he believed inherent in both the institutions and doctrines of the Church, the pernicious objectives of which, he claimed, were diametrically opposed to the interests of the people. The analysis followed similar lines to Bentham's critique of the political establishment.

Fear of executive power and government corruption greatly influenced the reformers of the early nineteenth century, but the intellectual influence of Bentham's utilitarianism was also a factor. Though he rejected the doctrine of natural rights—the standard ground upon which to base a claim for parliamentary reform—as fictitious nonsense, Bentham still concluded that parliamentary reform was essential. It was the most effective means of mitigating misrule and enhancing the prospects for the maximization of general happiness. According to the tenets of his utilitarianism each person prefers his or her own interest to that of others and each person is usually the best (though not the only) judge of his or her own interests. If this is so, then all individuals together must be regarded as the best judges of the public interest, of which the interest of each constitutes a part. By the same measure, however, governments will be more interested in serving the interests of the governors than those of the governed. Bentham's solution to this problem is continual inspection; to prevent the abuse of power governors need to be continually watched and various structures must be developed to ensure that they pursue the well-being of society. The most effective way to ensure that governors promote the greatest happiness of the greatest number, he concluded, is to allow everyone an equal right to judge and control the actions of the governors. Only if parliament were elected by virtually all the people could representatives be made to serve the proper end of government and thus secure their own re-election. The hidden agenda here, of course, is suggested by the fact that the proper end of government is best pursued by adopting the kind of beneficial penal, judicial, educational, and social reforms that Bentham had advocated for much of his life. In short, parliamentary reform was the essential key to progress towards the creation of a thoroughly Utilitarian society. Bentham's utilitarian principles led him to the conclusion that representative democracy was the most effective system both for restricting the self-interest of the governors and for promoting the welfare of the governed. Parliamentary reform was justified, therefore, on expedient and utilitarian grounds.

Though the analysis was similar, the case of the Church differed in so far as its democratization was a practical impossibility. Nevertheless, as in the political world so in the ecclesiastical it was in the interest of the ruling few that the subject many remain in a state of dependence, deprived of a political will of their own: 'Such being their interest, acting in obedience to a general/universal and inviolable law of nature/sanction, they act in the direction . . . in which they are directed to by that interest/sanction.'[4]

The psychological mechanisms of clerical oppression were given particular attention by Bentham. The special position of the Church supplied the means to the institutionalization of intolerance, but this is only a symptom, though admittedly a most mischievous one, of what Bentham perceived as a far more pervasive fault in the political and

---

[4] Bentham MSS in the 'Commonplace Books of James Mill', 5 vols., London Library (unpublished, *c.*1800–35), ii. 64. These MSS are in the hand of Bentham, numbered 61–7, and dated 1813. Almost certainly they belong with the MSS at UC 5/94–316. I am indebted to Professor R. A. Fenn of the University of Toronto for drawing my attention to these MSS and for providing me with transcriptions.

social structure of the English State. In an early manuscript (*c.*1773) headed 'Subscript. Alliance' his comprehension of the nature of the alliance still lacked a full understanding of the sinister interests which maintained it, but the direction of his later train of thought was sufficiently indicated:

The alliance with the Church is beneficial to the State—be it so—But by what means? By the inculcating of the belief of a future State—but not merely of a future State, but of a future State of Rewards and Punishments—but not merely of Rewards and Punishments, but of Rewards and Punishments bestowed on men according to the influence of their actions on the happiness of society. (UC 96/288).

Here Bentham anticipated the argument against religious asceticism found in the *Introduction*, but consumed as he was by his legal studies the sinister dimensions of the relationship between Church and State lay undeveloped in his thought for some time.

2. The 'sinister' interests of the clergy

Consistent with the reasoning of the *Introduction* (*IPML*, ch. 10), in the 'Preface on Publication' to *Church-of-Englandism* Bentham eschewed the imputation of 'bad motives' to explain the conduct of the bishops: '*Bad motives*? No, Sir; there is no such thing as a *bad motive*' (*CE*, p. xxxiv). However, when considering the activities of the clergy he was often prone to contradict this injunction regarding the neutrality of motives: 'Changing the word *interest* to the word [*sic*] motives and intentions—the objects they pursue are bad objects—the intentions with which they act are *bad intentions*—the motives by which they are actuated and their conduct determined are *bad motives*.'[5] Despite the transparent inconsistency, this is the reasoning upon which Bentham's notion of 'sinister' interest rests. Any interest is sinister to the degree that it tends to operate in a sinister direction, that is, in any direction other than that prescribed by utility (*Deon.* 110). Accordingly, a sinister interest is described as, 'Any the effect or tendency of which is to serve a *less* at the expense of a *more* extensive interest; or in the case of an individual, an interest of *less*, at the expense of one of greater, *value*' (*Deon.* 18). In the case of the clergy, Bentham sought not only to expose this interest but to clear away the fictions behind which it was

---

[5] Ibid.

promoted. When he announced in *A Fragment* that 'the season of *Fiction* is now over' he meant only to signal that the battle had commenced (*FG* 441). Forty years later the battle continued in the pages of the *Book of Fallacies* (1824). Here he consistently connected interests and fictions as partners in the cause of misrule: fictions are of the utmost importance to those who have a sinister interest 'to keep the human mind in such a state of imbecility that shall render it incapable of distinguishing truth from error' (*Fall.* 231). In *Church-of-Englandism* Bentham turned his attentions to the specific interests of the Anglican clergy and the fictions they employed in order to promote them. He concluded that the alliance between Church and State was promoted from no other motive than the self-interest, which is as much as to say the 'sinister' interest, of the clergy.

Just as linguistic analysis had revealed to Bentham the ambiguities of legal terminology so it also exposed the fictions and fallacies associated with organized religion, ambiguities which conveniently cloaked the malpractice of the clergy. The Anglican Church, a palpable illustration of an institution based on sinister interests, was all the more to be closely scrutinized because of the traditions upon which it was founded and the supposed sanctity it infused into its ritual. As we saw in Chapter 1, he thought the term 'Church' to be well suited for creating a respect for the clergy which they little deserved. The advantage to the clergy of the continued use of this ambiguous notion was a share in the coercive power of government and the protection of all the abuses and imperfections which attached to this part of the official establishment (*Fall.* 172). According to Bentham's nominalist metaphysics the whole could never be greater than the sum of its parts. Hence, he concludes, it is the vagueness of language that lies behind the creation of a Church that is to be obeyed, is capable of being disobeyed, and therefore of being violated or threatened (*Works*, viii. 250–1). The need for secular protection is thus made apparent and supplies a convenient defence of the union of Church and State. As Bentham put it in an unpublished manuscript for the aborted work on the 'Church': 'the whole constitution is held up to view in the lump: its excellence is pronounced: and the whole being thus excellent, such it is asserted without ceremony, [must be] each and everyone of them—this among the rest—one of its parts. Such then is the mode—the only mode in which any thing by way of defence is attempted' (UC 6/63). The defence is, however, an appropriate one, since 'whoever is engaged by interest in the support of any one government abuse, is engaged in the support of all, each giving to the others his support in exchange' (*Fall.* 42).

In the manuscript pages of the original Appendix III to *Church-of-Englandism* (omitted at publication for reasons of space), Bentham outlined a recent occasion when the influence at work in the union between Church and State was crudely employed in the cause of corruption (UC 7/8–80). A Justice of the Peace and brewer of ale in Canterbury, named Abbot, was charged with using 'adulterating ingredients in his beer, whereby . . . not merely the revenue is defrauded but the health of His Majestys [*sic*] subjects highly endangered' (UC 7/17). To assist his defence Abbot was able to obtain memorials from several notables including Dean Andrews, at the time the Dean of Canterbury and Rector of St James, which were presented to Chancellor of the Exchequer Nicholas Vansittart.[6] The dean claimed to be protecting Abbot from a miscarriage of justice, but in actuality, says Bentham, he was exercising his influence with government to prevent justice from taking its proper course. The conspiracy was unashamedly performed; all that was required was a letter from a high-ranking Churchman to one of His Majesty's chief ministers. There was no mystery involved in the transaction: 'the possessor of the overpaid place and the sinecure—the place for which little is done and that little useless—and the possessor for which nothing at all is done, or so much as undertaken to be done—these two, are as is the custom, one' (UC 7/18). The outcome of the dean's petition was that the prosecution against Abbot was dropped by order of the House of Lords (UC 7/29–30; 23 Nov. 1814). What this revealed to Bentham was the extent of the network of relations between Church and State, the corruptness of the bond between them, and its capacity to reach to all levels of society and political life.

Not surprisingly, efforts to mitigate the corruption met with stern opposition from the clerical ranks. Elliott-Binns has remarked with some justification that the Churchmen of the early nineteenth century were so frightened by the spirit of reform that they 'lost all belief in themselves and in their Church'.[7] Even the smallest encroachment upon their power and influence sent them into outrageous moods of defiance. 'The Church is in danger!' was a cry heard by Bentham on

---

[6] Bentham had unsatisfactory dealings with Vansittart concerning schemes to introduce a forgery-proof currency and annuity notes, as well as over the Panopticon (see *Corr.* vi, *passim*).

[7] Elliott-Binns, *Religion in the Victorian Era*, p. 38.

too many occasions when reform was under discussion. In the *Book of Fallacies* he offered a caricature of a clergyman who on hearing the demand for 'No sinecures!' did not fail 'to join in the shout of "No innovation! Down with the innovators!" in the hope of drowning out, by these defensive sounds, the offensive ones' (*Fall.* 99). The protection of abuses was the sole object in view and the tactics used in defence were predictable: 'To each and every question having in view some reform or improvement in the official establishment, the answer is one and the same: "You are an enemy to the Church, monster, anarchist, Jacobin, leveller, and so on" ' (*Fall.* 172). Even to set out to examine the official religion of England was to some a sign of hostility (UC 6/30). An incipient paranoia manifested itself to the point where the ecclesiastical establishment felt itself under continual siege. Perceiving themselves threatened at every turn, the clergy looked to policies of exclusion to safeguard their position. In large part it is this which explains why the 'schools for all' controversy broke upon English society in the early decades of the nineteenth century. Under the pretext that the Church's role as the watchman of the nation's morals was endangered by the efforts of the non-established religions to organize a national schools system, the bishops sought to assert a monopoly over education.

3. Vices and remedies: the 'euthanasia' of the Church

The abuses of the clergy were tackled by Bentham in the lengthy Appendix IV of *Church-of-Englandism* under four headings: vices of doctrine, vices relating to service, vices relating to pay, and vices of discipline. As we have already spent enough time on vices of doctrine they need not detain us. They can be reduced to two: (*a*) the claim to infallibility presumed by the clergy stood on 'no other ground than that of the temporal power possessed by them'; and (*b*) the forced subscriptions to articles of faith in the Catechism and Church ritual, not only led individuals into error, but also bred a tendency to insincerity that restricted the free exercise of their judgement (*CE*, App. IV, 369–70).

Vices relating to service were usually the consequence of the manifest unfitness of most clergymen for their profession. Non-residence and pluralism accounted for the fact that the instruction of parishioners was a duty rarely performed. In addition, there were parishes without churches and where churches did exist they were often inadequate for the numbers they must accommodate. It was not uncommon also to find churches situated in remote parts of a parish making it inconvenient for a large proportion of its inhabitants to attend the services and receive religious instruction. Finally, though we must assume with tongue firmly in cheek, Bentham was appalled that pews were reserved for the rich of the parish at the expense of the 'unopulent many' (*CE*, App. IV, 370–2).

The vices relating to pay turned mainly upon complaints, often heard in this period, about tithes and Church rates. All households in the parish were required to pay tithes and rates regardless of religious affiliation or financial standing. Tithes were a levy raised by the Church in country parishes from all occupants of property, save those who could establish their impoverishment. The proceeds were ostensibly used for the upkeep of the church, to provide materials for services, and to pay the salaries of the pastor and his clerk. 'In a widespread and mundane fashion', writes one commentator, 'the matter [of tithes] symbolized the whole question of maintaining a Church establishment and its privileges.'[8] Church rates, which applied to both town and country parishes alike, proved to be even more provocative in embittering relations between the Church and the various nonconforming sects, who viewed it as an unjustified imposition.[9] There was also the church-building tax to consider. As Bentham was to complain to O'Connell (15 July 1828) 'not only non-Church-of-Englandists, but Church-of-Englandists *themselves* object to be taxed for addition to be continually made to the existing number of rests of reverend sinecurists'. The mischief it creates, he explained, is 'the taking the money by force out of the pockets of the proprietor, and adding it to the mass of the matter of corruption by which, with such unhappy success, men are urged to profess to believe that which they disbelieve' (*Works*, x. 595–6). Where tithes and rates are high they are oppressive and where payment is excessive it seduces the minister away from his duties to pursue other pleasures (*CE*, App. IV, 372–4). Here again the Scottish Church compares favourably with the Anglican. In Scotland tithes are not raised from all and sundry at a set rate, but are a rent charged on estates, which the exertions of the priest cannot increase (UC 6/57).

[8] G. I. T. Machin, *Politics and the Churches in Great Britain 1832 to 1868* (Oxford, 1977), 18.
[9] See O. Chadwick, *The Victorian Church*, 2 vols. (Oxford, 1966, 1970), i. 81–4.

Finally, Bentham considered vices relating to discipline. The Church hierarchy, he claimed, has so many levels that it produces a confusion in the ordinary mind. But, as we might expect, his real target is the authority of the bishops. Their position in the Lords 'fills them with pride and ambition: and sets them to exercise temporal dominion over their fellow priests'. For their power they are responsible to no one; they exercise it on their own authority away from the gaze of the public. This power is augmented by the ecclesiastical courts whose law and judicature is both complicated and corrupt, swelling the patronage available to the bishops (*CE*, App. IV, 375–6). As the judges are the appointees of the bishops, nepotism is rife, and, as in the profane judicatories, the sole object of technical procedure is 'maximization of delay, vexation, and expense' (*CE*, App. IV, 300–2).

Bentham's suggested remedies for these vices should not be taken too seriously. After all, the real end in view was not a reformed Church, which he did not think possible, but disestablishment. He stipulated two objectives: the positive objective was to make religious instruction and worship 'beneficial to the joint interests of piety, morality, and economy'; the negative objective was to introduce reforms in such a way as 'to produce as little disturbance as possible to established habits, expectations, and prepossessions' (*CE*, App. IV, 385). In general Bentham's proposals followed principles laid down elsewhere in his writings, most notably the *Constitutional Code*, for the institution of sound administration. Pay should be equated with service and all excesses turned over to the government; changes should be so ordered that no one would suffer unduly in regard to powers, dignities, or pecuniary interests; and the system of Church discipline should contract 'as the existing functionaries drop off' to be replaced gradually by a system characterized by 'efficiency, simplicity, and frugality' (*CE*, App. IV, 386). All remedies proposed according to these guidelines, however, are intended as just so many steps in the secularization and gradual disestablishment of the Church of England.

Regarding vices of service, in the 'Church' manuscripts Bentham suggested that just as in any other sphere of public administration 'the mode of appointment should be that which affords the best promises of relative aptitude' (UC 6/66). In an interesting parallel with the democratic flavour of his politics during this period, Bentham considered the election of pastors by their congregations to be the best method of achieving this aim, on the grounds that since it is they who will pay his salary they are the most likely to make a well considered choice. It is absurd, he writes, 'if he is chosen by less than the majority of his flock, still more, if chosen by one of his flock only', but it is even more so 'if chosen by person or persons not of his flock' (UC 6/67).[10] Bentham's aim was to weaken the Church hierarchy, just as he would the secular aristocracy, by having the local clergy, as in some Nonconformist religions, chosen by and responsible to the local congregations. This preference for congregational control was founded on criteria of sound management, in which respect the Anglican was surpassed by the Scottish Church, and these two by the Nonconformist Churches: 'In the English Established Church may be seen the forms of discipline without the substance: in the Scottish *form* and *substance* both: in the Non-Established Churches, no form, but nevertheless the substance, and this but the better for being *without* the forms' (*CE*, App. IV, 289; cf. also 386–92). Bentham was certainly aware of the consequences of ecclesiastical democratization: to apply the principle of popular election to the Church hierarchy would be to make religious doctrine itself subject to popular determination. By implication it would ultimately make religion a private, voluntary, non-political affair—the alliance between Church and State would be broken.

Bentham's disestablishmentarianism did not stop here, however, but descended into the minutiae of clerical administration. He proposed that the duties of reading the liturgy and sermons in services be taken over by competent members of the congregation or appointed clerks. The sermons should be chosen from a collection compiled and authorized by the Church. Ignoring his own earlier pronouncements against doctrinaire preaching, Bentham believed that this would reduce the financial burden of paying a minister and at the same time exclude 'the two great bugbears, *heresy* and *schism*' from being preached from the pulpit (*CE*, App. IV, 214; cf. also pp. 206–8). The work of the minister was to be reduced to that of performing acts of beneficence about the parish. In a manner symptomatic of Bentham's thirst for statistics, he argued that in order to perform these duties the better the minister should acquire knowledge of the science of 'Pastoral Statistics'. He should have at his disposal data regarding the population of the parish, the material circumstances of his parishioners, and the nature of their dwellings. Since it was impossible for ministers

---

[10] Bentham found biblical support for this in the election of Mathias by the Apostles: 'They showed . . . that in the Christian world, if government in any shape has divine right for its support, it is in the shape of democracy;—representative democracy—operating by universal suffrage' (*NP* 217).

not resident in their parishes to acquire this knowledge, non-residence should be abolished (*CE*, App. IV, 216–19).

The remedies regarding pay had their source in Bentham's opposition to the financing of the Church by involuntary taxation. When coupled with sinecurism, non-residence, and pluralism—all resulting in the non-performance of duties—clerical salaries were '*obtained on false pretences*, . . . by that species of immorality' commonly known as 'swindling'. Clergymen, on Bentham's reckoning, should only receive payment for services performed in point of quality and quantity, and not as attached to the office or particular living possessed. At present, he claimed, clerical salaries were paid in inverse proportion to the duties performed: the more a minister is paid 'the more powerfully is he drawn from, and set above, the habit of holding, and disposition to hold, intercourse with those persons, by whom . . . his services are most needed' (*CE*, App. IV, 244, 236–8). As to the calculation of pay, Bentham recommended that on the death or removal of an incumbent minister his duties should be taken up by a parish clerk who was to be paid only half as much again as he presently received, the salary to be paid from the Poor Rates. The parishioners were to have the power to appoint any one they pleased to perform the parish duties but on no account for a higher wage than that which would be paid to the clerk. All other payments were to be made on a voluntary basis. On the death or removal of a bishop or archbishop, the lands and houses attached to the see were to be sold by auction and the proceeds given to a Church Reform Fund—a fund established to facilitate the changes Bentham advocated. The same was to apply to the holdings of deans, canons, prebendaries, and all other sinecurists. Scholars in expectation of scholarships or fellowships at the universities were to be adequately compensated if their expectations were thwarted by the sale of such lands and possessions. All 'tithes in kind' were to cease upon the death of an incumbent, to be replaced by a strictly regulated land tax. Where the patronage of the parish was in individual hands a proportion of the money received from the sale was to be given to the patron, and in the case of the suspension of tithes in kind he should receive a government annuity equal in value to his share of the sale. Extra compensation was to be paid if a patron had a son of not less than fourteen years who was being groomed for the Church. Where the patron was the Crown no such allowances were to be paid. By this method Bentham supposed 'that vast mass of the matter of wealth, operating in the hands of the Chancellor, in the shape of the matter of corruption, would be sunk, and the Constitution relieved from the pressure of it'. Finally, in a sly hit at the universities, Bentham proposed that the places left vacant by the death of college Fellows be filled by retired army or navy officers. The purpose of this, he explained, was to 'save the University Colleges from dilapidation and the University Towns from desolation' (*CE*, App. IV, 391–2; cf. also 387–90).

Concerning remedies related to discipline Bentham's suggestions were focused almost entirely on policies to undermine the prestige and power of the bishops. Archbishops and bishops were to be appointed as before by the Crown, but new holders of office were not to be given a seat in the Lords—the elimination of the bishops' legislative power was the end in view. Instead, bishops were to perform only those Church functions directly related to their office, and they were to be paid a salary from the Church Reform Fund commensurate with their service without regard to dignity (*CE*, App. IV, 388).

Naturally, Bentham was aware that he was only scoring political points with these proposals for reform, and he was merely being his usual disingenuous self when he announced that the only real sufferers (if the reforms were implemented) would be those clergymen who had hopes for preferment. He well knew, also, that his remedies would serve to accomplish much more than merely to redistribute clerical wealth: 'true it is', he acknowledged, 'that of this precluding plan, death of Excellent Church has from the very first been the acknowledged object' (*CE*, App. IV, 396). The aim all along had been the confiscation of the benefices and livings of the Church, and thereby the extinction of established religion. This is the 'radical solution' to the defects of the Church which he had announced near the beginning of *Church-of-Englandism* (*CE*, p. liv). Dissolution, whether forced or voluntary, was the only remedy: '*Cacothanasia*, bad death,—or *Euthanasia*, good death . . .—under one or the other of these names will the end of the system, whenever it takes place, be found characterizable' (*CE*, App. IV, 197).

Before we leave this subject it is worth reflecting for a moment on the consistency between the principles of Bentham's utilitarianism and his proposals for dispossessing the Church of its property. In all his writing on property he does not appear to have considered Church property, and he certainly never spoke of it as a special case. For instance, in an early jotting of *c.*1774 he treated theft from a Church like theft from any other 'public fund'; the only difference he allowed was in the application of the epithet 'sacrilege' to distinguish it from similar crimes (UC 69/7). Moreover, though Bentham sympathized with the French Revolution (if not with the methods or rhetoric employed by the revolutionaries), he denounced the confiscation of Church property and the policy of restoring property to the descendants of Protestants persecuted under Louis XIV as an attack on security (*Works*, iv. 338). The idea of a revolutionary change in the distribution of property was anathema to Bentham who, it has been said, 'virtually identified property with human feelings—pleasure, security, expectation'.[11] Later on, with the turmoil experienced by France in mind, he wrote in typically strident terms:

A revolution in property! It is an idea big with horror which cannot be felt in a stronger degree by any man than it is by me . . . it involves the idea of possessions distributed, or expectations thwarted: of estates forcibly ravished from the living owners, or opulence reduced to beggary, of the fruits of industry made the prey of rapacity and dissipation—of the levelling of all distinctions, of the confusion of all order and destruction of all security.[12]

Bentham, then, was certainly no leveller. Though he recognized that the laws creating property have created riches this was only in relation to poverty, and poverty was not the work of the laws but 'the primitive condition of the human race'. The principal aim of the laws was security, for this was essential to the happiness of society, and in so far as the legislator disturbed security he produced a proportionate sum of evil.[13] His first duty was to maintain the distribution as it was actually established, for no one can be despoiled without the security of all being thereby imperilled. Security was 'the foundation of life; subsistence, abundance, happiness, everything depends on it'.[14]

How can Bentham's plans for the dispossession of the Church be made compatible with his general views on the security of property? The problem disappears when it is noted that he made a distinction between the ideal of security and what is practicable in actuality. The first demands that nothing should ever be taken from any one; the second is satisfied if nothing beyond what is necessary for the preservation of the rest is taken. The confiscation of Church property can be justified, therefore, in terms of the 'sacrifice of security to security'.

[11] D. G. Long, 'Bentham on Property', in T. M. Flanagan and A. Parel (eds.), *Theories of Property: Aristotle to the Present* (Toronto, 1978), 226.
[12] Bentham, *Supply without Burden: Or Escheat Vice Taxation* (1795), in *Jeremy Bentham's Economic Writings*, ed. W. Stark, i. 304–5.
[13] Bentham, *Theory of Legislation*, ch. 9, p. 113.
[14] Ibid., ch. 11, pp. 119–20.

The security of the possessions of the people at large, the many, has precedence over that of the clergy, who are the predatory few. Bentham's equation is simple but a little misleading, since it depends on the further distinction between what might be interpreted as an 'attack' on property and what he refers to as a 'defalcation'. He explains the distinction thus:

An attack is an unexpected shock, an evil which cannot be calculated, an irregularity which has no fixed principle. It seems to put all the rest in peril; it produces general alarm. But a defalcation is a fixed, regular, and necessary deduction which is expected; which produces only an evil of the first order; but no danger, no alarm, no discouragement to industry.[15]

The case for confiscating the property of the Church, therefore, rested on the violation of security caused by its collection of taxes, to which it allowed no exceptions either on grounds of religious profession or material wealth. Ireland provided the extreme example, where a people forbidden the public exercise of their religion were forced through tithes to maintain a religion they regarded as hostile to their own. On Bentham's terms this amounted to a double violation of security, productive of political as well as civil unrest.[16] Hence he argued that the Church in Ireland must be immediately disestablished. The violation of the security of non-Church of Englandists in England, Bentham claimed, was only a degree less severe, and equally justified disestablishment.

Bentham's call for disestablishment, needless to say, fell on deaf ears. Nevertheless, his ideas had a modicum of influence on those about him, most notably James Mill, who wrote several tracts on Church reform, and the radical Joseph Hume, who in 1823 was busy introducing motions in the House of Commons designed to abolish sinecures and other corrupt practices. In a letter to Samuel Parr (23 Feb. 1832) Bentham referred to Hume as 'the only real representative the Commons of England have in the House', and cheekily requested of Parr information regarding his prebendial sinecure that might be of assistance to Hume. What this letter also reveals, however, is Bentham's resolve to speed the 'euthanasia' of the Church. 'On the 4th next month', he writes,

Joseph Hume makes his motion on the subject of Irish Tithes. Excellent Church, with all her paraphernalia, must on that occasion of necessity be

---

[15] Ibid., ch. 13, p. 124.
[16] Ibid. 134.

brought on the carpet. Some suggestions over and above what there is in
'Church of Englandism,' the political part of which he is getting by heart, are
furnishing [*sic*] to him just now by myself and others: inter alia, that in all times
churchmen, who if any proposal is made to apply to church property to any of
the uses to which it is pretended to be destined, cry out 'sacrilege!' have at all
times been the plunderers of it to the utmost of their power; for the benefit of
themselves and those who are nearest and dearest to them, just as any other
men would have been in their places.[17]

Hume, it appears, remained a zealous disestablishmentarian for the
rest of his days. *The Christian Rememberancer* of 1841 dryly records that
Hume had taken it upon himself to warn young men considering
ordination that they should not expect to receive compensation after
the Church is disestablished. They enter it, Hume warned, with their
eyes open 'when its charter is on the eve of being cancelled by the
authority which gave it, when it is admitted on all hands to be not
useless only, but actually detrimental'.[18] The foreboding, it must be
said, was a trifle premature.

4. The resilience of the Church of England

It has been no part of my intention to defend the Church of England
against Bentham's polemic.[19] It should be said, however, that even
after Catholic Emancipation 1829, the Great Reform Act 1832, the
Oxford Movement, and the disestablishment of the Church in Ireland
in 1871 the Anglican Establishment remained in being. It found some
eloquent defenders ready to gather about its standard, among them
Coleridge, who argued that the constitution of the United Kingdom
included the idea of the national Church as well as the idea of the
constitution of the State. He described them as 'two poles of the same
magnet; the magnet itself, which is constituted by them, is the
CONSTITUTION of the nation', and lamented that the toleration of other
religions had led to the Church's demise from its former position of

---

[17] *The Works of Samuel Parr*, ed. J. J. Stone, 8 vols. (London, 1828), viii. 10–12. The
'political part' of *CE* referred to by Bentham is that contained in *Mother Church Relieved
by Bleeding.*
[18] Quoted by Elliott-Binns, *Religion in the Victorian Era*, p. 41.
[19] For a more balanced view of the ecclesiastical establishment in Bentham's lifetime
the following works should be consulted: Clark, *Churchmen and the Condition of England*,
chs. 1–2; Elliott-Binns, *Religion in the Victorian Era*, chs. 1–2; Machin, *Politics and the
Churches*, ch. 1.

being a truly national Church.[20] It is worth quoting an extract from his address to 'the Liberalists and Utilitarians' at length, for it is fairly representative of the conservative plea in the early nineteenth century, that the movement towards the secularization of the State be halted before it is too late:

I hold it the disgrace and calamity of a professed statesman not to know and acknowledge, that a permanent, nationalized, learned order, a national clerisy or church, is an essential element of a rightly constituted nation, without which it wants the best security alike for its permanence and progression; and for which neither tract societies nor conventicles, nor Lancasterian schools, nor mechanics' institutes, nor all of these collectively, can be a substitute. For they are all marked with the same asterisk of spuriousness, shew the same distemper spot on the front, that they are empirical specifics for morbid *symptoms* that help to feed and continue the disease.[21]

Eloquence of this kind was not designed to move the radicals from their cause but to rally the Church's defenders. The elder Thomas Arnold was one who recognized his duty, and in the *Principles of Church Reform* (1833) he appealed to disaffected Protestants (those not yet beyond the pale of orthodoxy) to return to the Anglican fold. Gladstone was another who rallied to the Church's standard. In *The State and its Relations with the Church* (1834) he argued that the State is obliged to profess the religious truth which it sees, to provide for the public worship of God, and to encourage this truth and form of worship by political coercion. Later in life, however, he reconsidered his position and admitted that the book was probably obsolete when it appeared. He thought himself the last man on a sinking ship.[22]

Yet the Church survived. A liking for old things and the inability to fill the gap should the Church be abolished, were the reasons cited by the younger Mill for its continuance.[23] Perhaps part of the reason also lay in the nature of the critique mounted against it. There are certainly grounds for supposing that Bentham and James Mill were correct in their view that the Church only took an interest in the systematic education of the children of the poor after the Lancaster schools had shown how much could be done. It is also true that much needed funding for the schools of Dissenters was subsequently redirected to

[20] S. T. Coleridge, *On the Constitution of the Church and State According to the Idea of Each*, ed. J. Barrell (1830; London, 1972), 22, 49.

[21] Ibid. 153.

[22] J. Morley, *The Life of William Ewart Gladstone*, 3 vols. (London, 1903), i. 179.

[23] J. S. Mill, 'Coleridge' (1840), in *Collected Works*, x. 142.

the National Society, and that only the children of Anglicans were instructed in the schools it established. All these are good reasons for criticism, but at the same time Bentham frequently sacrificed the persuasive force of his critique by burying it beneath the tedious and frustratingly rhetorical analysis of the National Society's tepid reports. The exhausting repetitiveness of his accusation that the bishops were engaged in fraudulent activities is particularly trivial. We are left aghast that he could have expended so much time on such matters. But this is simply typical of Bentham's incessant attempt to be thorough and of his proneness to harbour a grievance much longer than would seem reasonable. The language of his attack was shamefully vitriolic and in this respect we can say of *Church-of-Englandism* what Mary Mack wrote of the *Book of Fallacies*, that it is to be regretted that 'Bentham fought his enemies with their own weapons', that he employed 'emotive meanings and propaganda'. Frustrated that his 'quiet analyses went unheard . . . he raised his voice'.[24] References to the Church as 'the Whore of Babylon', to the clergy as 'plunderers' and 'oppressive tyrants', to the Catechism as 'a state poison', and the like, are common throughout the text. The only contemporary reviewer of *Church-of-Englandism* was moved to comment upon Bentham's style:

in the language of vulgar scurrility, his vocabulary is copious and original, and all the terms of abuse that he can find or invent are profusely distributed on whatever is within his reach. In his indiscriminate railing, it is impossible to recognize any marks of the conviction of a liberal philosophy, or the warmth of a generous enthusiasm for theoretical perfection.[25]

Denunciations of the motives of the bishops, usually unsubstantiated, are also frequent, even though Bentham had already supplied a lengthy discussion in the *Introduction* concerning the neutrality of motives and ruled out all judgements based upon them (*IPML*, ch. 10; *CE*, App. IV, 221). There is a hollow ring to the repeated charges against the clergy for there was no one more fully aware that motivation is an extremely complex phenomenon which defies simple definition. Moreover, the invective against the bishops was surely libellous, and it was not very wise of Bentham to pursue it so far; it is difficult to imagine a magistrate in the troubled days of 1818 having too much difficulty in bringing a charge of blasphemy against the old sage, as Romilly

---

[24] Mack, *Jeremy Bentham*, p. 168.
[25] [W. Gifford], 'Jeremy Bentham's *Church-of-Englandism*', *Quarterly Review*, 21 (1819), 176.

certainly thought would happen. Here Bentham's ponderous style may well have protected him, since it is probable that few ever managed to muddle their way through the almost 800 pages of exhaustive detail that constitute *Church-of-Englandism*.

We might also question the cogency of some of the arguments Bentham employed. As a piece of abstract criticism *Church-of-Englandism* is an impressive exposure of the Church's dogmatic teaching, but by utilitarian standards the use of such a critique is suspect. If we accept the greatest happiness as our standard, the question, as R. A. Benn has said, is not what is ideally true or right, but what, in a given age and society, is possible and expedient.[26] The Catechism might not be as good as *Chrestomathia*, but it had been employed and accepted for several centuries as a useful guide for what children should be taught to believe. When the choice lay between the use of the Catechism in schools and the withdrawal of support for schools by a large section of the community, the utilitarian's decision should not have been in doubt. But Bentham frequently vacillated between the possible and ideal in the application of his utilitarianism; the more practicable economic and jurisprudential writings, for example, will always contrast starkly with the idealism of such writings as the *Constitutional Code*. In *Church-of-Englandism* he let himself be carried forward by his denunciatory invective against the clergy to visualize a world without a clerical establishment, and what there is of practical value in the work is almost entirely obscured by his urge to define exhaustively this feature of a society based on utilitarian principles.

[26] A. W. Benn, *The History of English Rationalism in the Nineteenth Century*, 2 vols. (New York, 1962), i. 301.

PART III

Natural and Revealed
Religion

BENTHAM'S criticisms of natural and revealed religion received their most comprehensive treatment in the *Analysis of the Influence of Natural Religion on the Temporal Happiness of Mankind* (1822) and *Not Paul, but Jesus* (1823). In these works religion in general and Christianity in particular are by turns ridiculed, denounced as anti-intellectual, and condemned as socially pernicious. Bentham would have been well pleased that from a reading of the *Analysis* Sir Leslie Stephen concluded that utilitarianism 'logically implied the rejection of all theology'.[1] This was precisely Bentham's intention. At the same time, however, there is a tactical dimension to his choice of arguments in these books which must be noted. When Bentham had the doctrines of St Paul or those taught by the Anglican clergy in mind, the contrast he made is with the pure or true doctrines of Christianity. But when his analysis focused on the latter they were found deficient strictly in terms of utility. Nevertheless, the aim of these volumes is transparent: it is the elimination of religion, not only as a source of influence or social control in the hands of an unscrupulous clergy, but from the mind altogether. This was part and parcel of Bentham's developing view of the secular society. Aware that to remove institutions was only to touch the surface of the obstructions to progress posed by religion, he focused his sights on the beliefs which lay at the roots of organized religion. It is in this respect that the *Analysis* and *Not Paul, but Jesus* can be said to represent Bentham's final assault in the campaign against religion, and thus constitute a logical step beyond the political critique mounted in *Church-of-Englandism*.

[1] Stephen, *The English Utilitarians*, ii. 40.

7

Natural Religion

What steps do you take to prove a man has committed murder? You produce a witness who saw him level his pistol at the head of the deceased, heard the report, and beheld the man drop. But this testimony derives all its persuasive force from the warrant and counter sign of experience. Without this it is perfectly useless.

An. 99

To avoid running the risk of prosecution for blasphemy the *Analysis* was given to the world under the pseudonym 'Philip Beauchamp'. Why this particular name was chosen remains a mystery. The work was begun in 1815 (*CE* had been largely completed by then), but there is an outline dating from 1811 establishing that the overall plan had been clear in Bentham's mind at the outset of that decade in which the Church and its doctrines occupied most of his time.[1] As we have seen, however, the subject-matter—the disutility of the religious sanc-tion—was not new to Bentham even then. Whenever he wrote of law and the role of sanctions from the early 1770s onwards he added to the stockpile of his displeasure the mischief perpetrated by the religious sanction, and looked to the day when the legislator would no longer have to take the religious sensibilities of the people into account. Seen from this point of view, the *Analysis* represents the systematic gathering together of all Bentham's previously stated grievances over the influence of the religious sanction in the temporal concerns of society.

The utilitarian argument of the book, as pedantic as it may appear to be in places, was by no means irrelevant at a time when Paley and others had sought, successfully in the eyes of many, to harness utility to Christian theology. J. S. Mill saw the worth of directing arguments against this policy of convenience: the supposed usefulness of religion was an important question at a time when religious faith was weak and the belief in its social and moral value standard. Mill greatly approved

[1] This outline is at BL Add. MSS 29807/2.

of the general tendency of the *Analysis* and employed some of its arguments in his essay on the *Utility of Religion* (1874).[2]

1. 'Natural Jug'—'alledged Revealed Jug'[3]

There has been some debate concerning the authorship of the Analysis. That the book is based on Bentham's manuscripts is not in doubt. The British Library has four volumes of manuscripts which were sent by Bentham to George Grote, who was to edit the work, in the winter of 1821.[4] Grote had made the acquaintance of Bentham through James Mill, to whom he had been introduced by David Ricardo in 1819.[5] In the main the manuscripts are in the hand of John Colls, Bentham's amanuensis of the time, or in the hand of Bentham himself. The article on Grote in the *Dictionary of National Biography* records that a comparison between the finished work and these manuscripts 'shows the enormous amount of labour required to bring them into form', and comments that 'Grote had practically to write the essay leaving aside the greater part of the materials before him and giving to the remnant a shape that was his rather than Bentham's'.[6] Leslie Stephen concurs with this view.[7] On the other hand, M. L. Clarke argues 'that Grote conscientiously reproduced Bentham's arguments, and that there is nothing of his own in the substance of the

---

[2] Mill refers to the 'searching character' of *An.*, which he says 'produced the greatest effect upon me' and 'contributed materially to my development' (*Autobiography*, in *Collected Works*, i. 73). In an earlier draft of the *Autobiography* Mill mentions that 'the volume bearing the name of Philip Beauchamp, which was shown to my father in manuscript and by him given to me to read and make a marginal analysis of, as I had done of the *Elements of Political Economy*, made a great impression on me' (ibid. 72). It has been suggested to me by Professor R. A. Fenn of the University of Toronto that the 'marginal analysis' to which Mill refers may have been copied or employed in some fashion in the notes made on *An.* by his father. These notes are to be found in the 'Commonplace Books of James Mill', ii. 77–8, 74–5, 73, in that order.

[3] For the meaning of 'Jug' and its associated terms see above Introduction, n. 5.

[4] BL Add. MSS 29806–9.

[5] H. Grote, *The Personal Life of George Grote, Compiled from Family Documents, Private Memoranda, and Original Letters to and from Various Friends* (London, 1873), 21–2. Mrs Grote says nothing here of her husband's hand in *An.* It is interesting to note, however, that Grote had already written an 'Essay on Magic', dealing with the belief in the agency of invisible beings and described by his biographer as 'a reasoned attack on the idea of supernatural intervention'; see M. L. Clarke, *George Grote: A Biography* (London, 1962), 29. The essay survives in manuscript (BL Add. MSS 29531). For Grote's involvement in *An.* see ibid. 21, 182.

[6] *DNB* viii. 728–9.

[7] Stephen, *The English Utilitarians*, i. 316.

book'.[8] In some measure both views are correct: Grote did have to put a large number of the manuscripts aside and it is his style rather than Bentham's in which the work is penned, but it is from Bentham's manuscripts that the substance of the work is drawn and it is according to his plan that the arguments were arranged. In a letter to Grote of 9 December 1821 Bentham introduces the manuscripts for Grote's 'tactical powers' to 'make good use of', and refers to them as 'a garden of good fruits'. The remainder of the letter then proceeds to give a general outline as to how Grote might set about his task: 'This volume might come out first: reserving for one or two ulterior ones, the proofs from the text of the Jug.'[9] In a second letter Bentham offered to look the manuscripts over and see whether it might be possible to 'do any thing more towards rendering the work more methodical, correct, clear, concise and comprehensive'. 'Should it be found necessary', he adds, 'grudge not the trouble of recomposing . . . [and] if any considerable additions be found requisite, nobody can be better qualified for making them than yourself.'[10] It was in this manner that Bentham authorized the young and eager Grote to rewrite and, if necessary, to make additions to his original material. In the event Bentham's directions of 9 December were closely followed. However important Grote's editorial duties, therefore, and these should not be underestimated given the great bulk of manuscripts he was asked to deal with (intended, as we shall see, for a much larger study than the published work represents), we can be sure that the Analysis truly reflects Bentham's opinions on the topic of the influence of the religious sanction on temporal happiness.

The book was eventually published in 1822 by Richard Carlile, who (as we have noted) was already serving a harsh six year sentence in Dorchester Prison for publishing blasphemous literature and, hence, unlikely to be prosecuted further for this, his latest affront to the religious sensibilities of the English establishment. Though Bentham's authorship was not long a secret, Grote's hand in the work was not revealed until after his death. His wife Harriet made no mention of the book in her life of her husband, but one of the reviewers of this biography let the secret out in the *Edinburgh Review*. Confirmation eventually came by way of the 1875 edition of the *Analysis* and the

---

[8] Clarke, *George Grote*, pp. 30–1.
[9] JB to George Grote (9 Dec. 1821), BL Add. MSS 29806/1, from a transcription at the Bentham Project, UCL.
[10] BL Add. MSS 29807/12–13, from a transcription at the Bentham Project, UCL.

French translation of that year, both of which make clear Grote's involvement, the latter describing it as 'd'après les papiers de Jer. B., par G. Grote'.[11]

Bentham's intentions regarding the *Analysis* were first set out in a detailed Plan of the Work that he sent with the other manuscripts to Grote under the general title 'The Usefulness of Religion in the Present Life Examined'. It appears that he projected not one but two or possibly three volumes or parts. The first book was to deal with the usefulness of natural religion and the remainder with revealed religion, particularly the doctrines of England's official religion.[12] This general approach was reiterated in the letter accompanying the manuscripts sent to Grote:

As it strikes me at the present the best way would be to stop in the first instance at the subject of the Natural Jug, showing its inefficiency to useful purposes, and then its efficiency to mischievous purposes bringing in the question of verity considered in respect of its inefficiency to useful purposes for want of *sufficiently apparent verity*. On this occasion will be shown its incapacity of affording a directive rule, and in comparison of the human sanction the inefficiency of that superhuman sanction as a remedy against temptations. In speaking of its efficiency to mischievous purposes, here might be an occasion if advisable to bring in all the several mischiefs produced by alledged revealed Jug, in the first place independently of Establishments, in the next place by means of Establishments. Having been the actual, they might be mentioned as the *natural*, results of Natural Jug: and in that character they might be mentioned without reference to the particular alledged revealed Jug of which they have been the fruits. In many, perhaps in most instances, the mischievousness of them will be manifest, upon the face of their several denominations or descriptions.[13]

To translate this verbiage: the first volume was to have been an examination of the truth and utility of the 'Natural Jug' (i.e. natural religion), which was to be supplemented 'if advisable' by an extension of the analysis to include the truth and utility of the 'alledged revealed Jug'. The lines of demarcation between the two, however, were deliberately blurred by Bentham, the aim being to attribute to natural religion that which was usually thought to be the product of revelation—thus yet another tactical ploy. As he says: 'Having been

---

[11] *La Religion naturelle, son influence sur le bonheur du genre humain, d'après les papiers de J. Bentham par George Grote* (Paris, 1875).

[12] The Plan of the Work for *An.* is at BL Add. MSS 29807/157–62.

[13] JB to George Grote (9 Dec. 1821), BL Add. MSS 29806/1, from a transcription at the Bentham Project, UCL.

the actual, they might be mentioned as the *natural*, results of Natural Jug: and . . . might be mentioned without reference to the particular alledged Revealed Jug of which they have been the fruits.' The language appears confusing: it is said that the 'fruits' of revealed religion are actually the 'results' of natural religion. But the confusion is only apparent. At the beginning of the *Analysis* Bentham defines natural religion as 'all religious belief not specially determined and settled by some revelation (or reputed revelation) from the Being to whom the belief relates' (*An.*, p. iv). In the letter to Grote, however, it is clear that Bentham trusted the *Analysis* to suggest that so much of religion could be attributed to the natural workings of the mind that doubt would be cast upon that portion supposedly the result of revelation. Psychological confusions caused by the inability or incapacity to comprehend objective reality, therefore, are the source of the readiness of the mind to court religious beliefs. Bentham's tactic of equating the beliefs of revealed religion with those of natural religion becomes transparent when, having cautioned the reader that by the term religion he is to be understood to mean '*mere Natural Religion*', he adds that by '*sacerdotal class* . . . it is only the ministers of Natural religion who are designated' (*An.*, p. vi). But who among the clergy are not to be considered ministers of natural religion? This tactic became still more apparent when Bentham turned to discuss the deficiencies of the moral code enjoined by revelation (*An.* 58–64)—a discussion, one can be forgiven for assuming, that would be out of place in a work genuinely devoted to an examination of the tenets of natural religion. Finally, Bentham reduced the idea of natural religion to the belief in the existence of 'an almighty Being, by whom pains and pleasures will be dispensed to mankind, during an infinite and future state of existence' (*An.* 3). But, as we have seen elsewhere, this is precisely how he understood all religion: that is, in terms of a social sanction. The critique of religion in the *Analysis*, therefore, cannot be taken to be directed solely at natural religion, but must be seen as an attack on religion in general and specifically on the belief in futurity which, for Bentham, is the product of the prevalent ignorance of the real workings of the world. Annoyed by the pious conclusions about the benevolence of God and the happy state of the world deduced by Paley and other Christian apologists, he set out to subject this belief to what he regarded as the true utilitarian test: of what misery and of what happiness in this life is religion the source?

The theme of the *Analysis*, therefore, is a broader one than the limitations of Bentham's title might suggest; not only is it not merely concerned with natural religion, but its general objective is to show that conflict between legitimate attempts at political reform, on the one hand, and arbitrary power, on the other, can only be resolved with the destruction of all beliefs of a religious or other-worldly nature. Religion, Bentham notes, (probably with Paley's religious version of the doctrine of utility in mind),

has been affirmed to be the leading bond of union between the different members of a society—to be the most powerful curb on the immoral and unsocial passions of individuals—to form the consolation and support of misfortunes and declining life—in short it has been described as the most efficient prop both of inward happiness and of virtuous practice in this world. (*An.* 1)

The truth of these assertions forms the subject-matter of Bentham's inquiry. He finds that the inducements of Heaven and Hell provide no rule of guidance whatever for the pursuit of earthly happiness. On the contrary, they frequently suggest rules of action unconducive to the attainment of happiness. Moreover, such is human nature that fears of future punishment outweigh the hopes of future reward, and this produces an overall loss of happiness due to the disquietude that is occasioned by contemplating the prospect of death. Finally, the threat of God's wrath in the hereafter affects the conduct of individuals in this life by preventing them from learning and obeying the rules which experience alone can teach them. In this respect religion introduces perplexity and confusion into the science of morality.

There is no other piece of sustained writing in Bentham's voluminous opus, published or unpublished, in which he is more emphatic that individuals and communities in general would be happier if they could find a way of living without religion. The pernicious consequences of religion for human happiness had for long been a stock-in-trade of his social science. What set the *Analysis* apart from the earlier researches was the exhaustive manner in which Bentham tested the belief in the afterlife against a conception of the world based on the methodological premisses, as he understood them, of natural science.

2. *The argument from design*

In applying the methods of natural science to theological questions Bentham felt that he stood on firm ground and, despite the fact that the two men shared similar assumptions about human nature, beheld a recognizable enemy in the shape of William Paley. It was in the work of Paley that he encountered the classic statement of the argument from design, the principal prop of orthodox natural theology in the eighteenth century. The a priori argument for the existence of God based on intuition, effective where it fell in with commonly held beliefs, was unconvincing to the person who simply denied the existence of the intuition. In contrast, the argument from final causes purported to rest on common ground with the philosophy which demanded empirical proof. The existence of the Deity, it was thought, could be inferred from the ordered workings of nature, in just the same manner that the existence of a watchmaker could be inferred from the existence of a watch. Accordingly, this was Paley's argument in the *Natural Theology* (1802). His aim was to construct an empirical theology; its logical base was natural theology which is presented as a branch of science and therefore amenable to the usual scientific tests. By this means it was hoped that the existence of an agent essential to the working of the machinery of the world could be established beyond reasonable doubt.[14]

The essence of Paley's argument is conveyed by an analogy between a watch and the mechanism of the world. While we can attribute the existence of a rock in a desert to chance, to the effects of wind, rain, heat, frost, or volcanic action, an explanation in terms of the natural elements would not be appropriate if it were a watch that were discovered in a similar location. The complex arrangement of wheels, cogs, springs, and balances, all operate in harmony to produce the regular measurement of time. It would be simply implausible to attribute the construction of the several parts of the watch to the chance operation of the natural elements; rather we are persuaded that an intelligent mind is responsible for its form and presence. To this, Paley adds certain comments which enhance the analogy between the watch and the world. First, it would not shake our inference of a designing intelligence if we had never seen a watch before and were not aware from direct observation that watches are products of human intelligence: we have never seen a world before the one we now inhabit. Secondly, it would not invalidate our inference from the watch to the watchmaker if it turned out that the watch's mechanism was

---

[14] The following is a paraphrasing of Paley's argument in the *Natural Theology: Or Evidences of the Existence and Attributes of the Deity Collected from the Appearances of Nature* (1802), in *Complete Works*, iii. 2–7.

unreliable: the mechanism of the world, subject as it is to occasional natural disasters, appears to be less than perfect. Finally, our inference is not undermined if we are not able to discover or comprehend all the functions of the watch: the same can be said of the mechanism of the world.

According to Paley's analogy, then, the world is as complex a construction as any watch: the rotation of the planets, the regular procession of the seasons, the mutual adaptation of the parts of living organisms, all suggest design not chance. Now it is true that the classic critique of the argument from design is to be found in Hume's *Dialogues concerning Natural Religion*, published in 1779, a full generation before Paley's *Natural Theology* appeared. But the theologian took no account of the criticisms of the philosopher, thereby enabling his own version of the argument to stand in pristine state. Hence the need for Bentham to tackle the matter once again. As it turned out he, in turn, omitted to acknowledge Paley's contribution to the debate. Nevertheless, it is clear that it is the watch/world analogy that lies behind his critique of the argument from design, and what he has to say of it serves to highlight the general character of his scientific approach to religion.

Like Hume, Bentham met the argument on its own ground, that is to say, the world of experience. He found it to be 'completely extra-experiential'—it described the transition from confusion to order but no one has ever had experience of this 'preliminary chaos'. Nor was the original creative power of God certified by experience. Hence to introduce the notion of an 'omnipotent will' in order to explain the facts was really no explanation at all, but rather a collection of meaningless words. The interests of the present life require that we should never deviate from experience, and 'also require that we should not attempt to account for the original commencement of things—because it is obvious that experience must be entirely silent upon the subject' (*An.* 97, 98). The argument from design sounded plausible because it applied reasoning which is undeniably valid when appropriately employed: the inference from a watch to a watchmaker sounds persuasive because we know what is meant by a watchmaker and sufficient of what is involved in making a watch. However, when the inference is that the world was created by an intelligent being we infer the action of an unknown being performing an inconceivable operation upon inconceivable materials. As such the inference is really illusory or else results in the assertion that the phenomenon is inexplicable. It was on these grounds that the argument from design is unscientific despite its claim to be based on scientific premises.

The disjunction between the belief that the world was created by an intelligent agent and an individual's experience of the world itself required no further elaboration for Bentham. However, as Hume had shown, this was not a conclusive argument against the belief in design, since a distinction could be made between beliefs which are reasonable and those which are irrational.[15] Reasonable beliefs for Hume are those which are influenced by thought and judgement, and these correspond to beliefs the truth of which is sufficiently indicated by the available evidence. These are to be distinguished from 'non-rational' beliefs which Hume further separated into (*a*) beliefs which are held despite the existence of evidence that makes it more reasonable that we adopt an alternative set of beliefs, and (*b*) 'natural beliefs' of naïve common sense to do with the nature of the world which are universal and a necessary precondition for action. The first class of non-rational beliefs it would clearly be irrational for a person to hold, but the second class (though non-rational) are yet reasonable beliefs for us to have about the world. The belief in God, according to Hume, belongs to this second category of beliefs, that is, to the class of natural beliefs. In the *Dialogues* he argued that there is no evidence either a priori or a posteriori to justify belief in God, but that it is common sense that we should assume his existence in accordance with the belief that the world is the product of a designing agent. There is no evidence that makes it more reasonable for us *not* to believe that the world is the result of design.[16] Later in the *Dialogues* Philo makes it clear just how little is involved in this natural belief which is impressed upon individuals by their assumption of an ultimate principle of order in the universe: like the belief in causation, it is a necessary prerequisite of action. Nobody, Hume points out, behaves as if the world is a chaos.[17] Moreover, we might take the liberty to append to Hume's argument the consideration that those who possess such a belief seldom permit

---

[15] For the following summary of Hume's position I am indebted to J. C. A. Gaskin, *Hume's Philosophy of Religion* (London, 1978), 130–9.

[16] D. Hume, *Dialogues concerning Natural Religion*, ed. N. K. Smith (1779; London, 1947), 88.

[17] Ibid. 98. But Gaskin points out that the belief in design, even in this limited and insignificant sense (insignificant in terms of religion), is unlike the belief in causation: neither is it universal nor does it necessarily influence our actions in any particular way (*Hume's Philosophy of Religion*, p. 139). Even so Hume's argument—that there exists no evidence to make it more reasonable for us *not* to believe that the world is the product of design—remains valid.

metaphysical considerations to wrest it from them. We might also observe that the contrary is also true: those who lack this belief are seldom persuaded to adopt it because of metaphysical considerations. Even so there have been profound thinkers who have sought to discover some metaphysical basis by which to transform this 'non-rational' into a rational belief. Henry More, Ralph Cudworth, John Ray, William Derham, Sir Richard Blackmore, William Whiston, Samuel Clarke, David Hartley, and especially Robert Boyle and Isaac Newton,[18] to name only a few, took up the scientific cudgel in the defence of religion, primarily by providing arguments for the existence of God on the basis of the principle of design in both the physical universe and the human body. This should not surprise us. Even though religion may properly be a matter of faith rather than reason, still a philosophical person can hardly help wondering whether it might, at least in part, be also a matter of reason and whether, in particular, the existence of God might be something that can be not merely believed but shown or proven. In contrast to this, we have Hume's position: there might not be sufficient evidence to prove the existence of God, but this does not mean that it is insane for us to believe that the world is the product of design. Experience cannot decide the matter either way.

This subtlety of reasoning—the product of a sceptical mind—was not shared by Bentham. For Bentham either there was undeniable evidence to support a proposition or there was not; if there was not, then it was a belief which had nothing to do with the world of experience and as such was irrelevant to any discussion of the relationship between individuals and their world. It must be said on Bentham's behalf, however, that he was not so much concerned with the truth of the proposition that 'God created the world' as with the problem of what kind of world exists. Hence his discussion focused in large measure upon the supposed attributes of God.

[18] H. More, *Divine Dialogues* (1668); R. Cudworth, *The True Intellectual System of the Universe* (1678); J. Ray, *The Wisdom of God Manifested in the Works of Creation* (1691); W. Derham, *Physico-Theology: A Demonstration of the Being and Attributes of God from his Works of Creation* (1713), and *Astro-Theology: A Demonstration of the Being and Attributes of God from a Survey of the Heavens* (1715); Sir R. Blackmore, *The Creation* (1712); W. Whiston, *New Theory of the Earth* (1696), and *Primitive Christianity Revived* (1711–12); S. Clarke, *A Discourse Concerning the Being and Attributes of God* (1704–5); D. Hartley, *Observations on Man* (1749); R. Boyle, *The Origin of Forms and Qualities according to the Corpuscular Philosophy* (1666), and *A Disquisition about the Final Causes of Natural Things* (1688). Newton summarized his view in the 'General Scholium', added to Bk. III of the *Principia Mathematica* (1687) in 1713, and rev. in 1726.

Even if we grant, which Bentham does not, that the world was created by a designing intelligence we are still not justified on his account of the matter in ascribing any intentions to its creator other than what are actually realized in the visible constitution of things. In so far as nature and history testified to a certain degree of justice and beneficence in the distribution of pleasure and pain, the author of nature could be credited with justice and benevolence; but if on examination we perceive inequalities of fortune in the world irreconcilable with our notions of morality, we have no grounds for inferring that God's intentions have been thwarted in the execution (*An.* 19–20). Here Bentham joined hands with Voltaire, whose attack on optimism and on the nature of divine providence in the aftermath of the Lisbon earthquake of 1755 had so shaken the intellectual comfort of the Christian world. In Voltaire's case the assault launched in the *Poème sur le désastre de Lisbonne* was directed at the philosophical optimism proclaimed by Pope in his *Essay on Man* (1733–4). Voltaire rebelled against the fatalistic assumption that things must be the way they are. How can natural disasters and human wars be reconciled with belief in a benevolent God? Either we are guilty and he must punish us, or he is totally indifferent to our lot. In either case his ways are inexplicable to us, and the philosophers can offer us no more useful advice than teaching us to doubt. Moreover, the fatalistic quality of optimism is cruel, for it invites us to acquiesce and to give up all striving for improvement. Though Bentham could not bring himself to share this dark mood of pessimism, what Voltaire had to say of the nature of God found an echo in the thought of the philosopher of Queen's Square Place.

Not surprisingly, Bentham attempted to demonstrate the impossibility of individuals forming any other idea of God's attributes than a damning one. The less people know of something the more they feel threatened by it. In this case it is ignorance of the afterlife which leads a person to fill the void by imagining its terrors, for fear, points out Bentham, is 'the never-failing companion and offspring of ignorance' (*An.* 5). Only knowledge can protect us from these superstitious fancies, and 'wherever our knowledge fails us and we are reduced to a state of unprotected helplessness, all our sense of security, all anticipations of future ease, must vanish along with it'. An unknown future necessarily comes fraught with misery and torment (*An.* 6). Added to this, because pain, measure for measure, is a stronger sensation than pleasure (Bentham ignores the difficulties this presents for calculation) so the idea of a posthumous existence is more likely to be conceived as a state of suffering rather than of enjoyment. To the extent that individuals use nature and experience as a guide in their speculations the Supreme Being will be seen as more likely to impose pain than to grant pleasure. This is the case because to those struggling to satisfy their needs 'pain alone, and want or uneasiness, which is a species of pain, are the standing provisions of nature'. Pleasure, on the other hand, is 'artificial and invented' (*An.* 7).

It is our uncertainty about what is in store for us after death, then, that leads us to fear the worst. But even where the rewards of the afterlife most readily come to mind it is, claims Bentham, 'impossible to conceive an expectation more deplorably uncertain' (*An.* 47). His point is that though such expectations can be intense and durable to the utmost extent, this is the work of the imagination and not the result of experience. Naturally, given specific circumstances, one may imagine the consequences of a potential act and this could provide a legitimate motive to perform it.[19] But to visualize futurity is 'to exalt the conceptions of fancy to a level with real and actual experience, so that the former shall effect the mind as vividly as the latter', which, Bentham adds wryly, 'is the sole characteristic of insanity, and the single warrant for depriving the unhappy madman of his liberty' (*An.* 49).

Experience was the touchstone of this account and on these terms it was inconceivable to Bentham why religion should exercise the least influence upon human conduct. By contrast the pleasures and pains of this life unavoidably affected our conduct—experience teaches us the actions to which they are attached. Such knowledge was simply not available to us in respect of a posthumous existence. Any conceptions we hold of the character of this future world could only be based upon the perceptions we have formed of the character of the Deity, and such perceptions are too often distinguished by their failure to account for all the evidence. So far as Bentham was concerned the predictable result of the 'fundamental data' should be no more nor less than the conception of a capricious and tyrannical Being productive of 'extreme and unmixed fear' (*An.* 16). The temper of mind which fear supposes in such an agent is the disposition to do harm, and experience should convey to us the idea of an agency which we are unable to comprehend or frustrate, hence the idea of tyranny (*An.* 17). To assume, as the

---

[19] See the distinction between pleasures and pains 'in prospect' and pleasures and pains 'in esse' at *IPML* 98.

religious exponents of utility do, that the Deity treats us with favour and kindness is a presumption entirely inconsistent with reality, and even if it were consistent it is part of the essence of caprice that present behaviour provides no security for future behaviour. The actual conception of the Deity according to Bentham should really be a mixed one, perceived as fluctuating between good and evil 'but infinitely more as an object of terror than of hope' (*An.* 20).

Bentham's explanation of why men and women continue to revere the Deity was typically shallow and depended on a psychological assumption which was necessarily speculative. For he posited it as a general characteristic of human nature that it is towards those who have 'the largest power of inflicting evil upon us, and who confers on us the most insignificant favours, that our encomiums are the warmest, our censure the most gentle and sparing' (*An.* 25). From this Bentham inferred that we generally conceive of God as differing only in degree from earthly possessors of power; the only substantial difference in perception is that the Deity is thought to have an added advantage over the earthly despot because it is supposed that he is 'the unseen witness of every thing which passes our lips—indeed even of our thoughts' (*An.* 27). Given that such is the character of the Deity based on the evidence of experience, what defence do we have? On the premiss that the tyrant is only angered by the happiness of those beneath him, while acts of benevolence to those weaker than himself give him cause to exult in his own power, the best defence is to refrain from actions that give pleasure.[20] Asceticism is the inescapable consequence of despotic rule:

He who is thus absorbed in love of dominion, cannot avoid loving the correlative and inseparable event—the debasement of those over whom he rules; in order that his own supremacy may become more pointed and prominent . . . Besides, his leading aim is to diffuse among his subjects the keenest impressions of his own power. This is, in other words, to plant in their bosoms an incessant feeling of helplessness, insecurity and fear; and were this aim realized, everything which deserves the name of happiness must, throughout their lives, be altogether overshadowed and stifled. (*An.* 29)

According to Bentham, this analogy provided the only clue for us as to what actions the incomprehensible and all powerful Deity will find

---

[20] In his study of the nature of despotism Robert Browning was to arrive at a similar conclusion: 'the best way to escape His ire/Is not to seem too happy.' For a discussion of the points of correspondence between *An.* and Browning's *Caliban* see W. V. Harris, 'Browning's Caliban, Plato's Cosmogany, and Bentham on Natural Religion', *Studies in Browning and his Circle*, 3: 2 (1975), 95–103.

agreeable or disagreeable. From our experience of 'terrestial potentates' we draw 'the directive rule to which the inducements of natural religion affix themselves'. In the total absence of experience the only resource that we have at our disposal is by way of this analogy (*An.* 28).

For Bentham, then, the utility of beliefs consisted in their conformity with the perceptible physical world (*An.* 93–4). For this reason he could not accept the 'noble lie' or 'double truth' view of the social utility of religion advocated by Voltaire and others. All human errors, he insisted, were just so many consequences of 'unsanctioned belief', that is, belief in 'uncertified experience'. Beliefs in anything other than objective verifiable reality only serve to derange the mental system and to prepare the intellect to receive unspecified quantities of other useless and uncertified beliefs. The disjunction between, on the one hand, apparently useful beliefs not based on experience and, on the other hand, what we know of the actual workings of the world, impaired our capacity to make sound judgements regarding our welfare (*An.* 94–6). In other words, experience was absolutely necessary to wellbeing. As it turned out Bentham concluded that not even the first principle of religion—the persuasion of the existence of God—could be founded on experience, since we could not have experience of something that was not all in one place but everywhere and at all times present. The attempt to invent words to explain this absurdity is unavailing. The terms 'invisible', 'omnipresent', 'infinite', 'eternal', and their like are abstractions irreducible to real entities. By the terms of this metaphysic, such terminology was the consequence of the imagination not of experience.

The assumption upon which Bentham's position rested was that the course of nature had always been constant and would remain so. The inviolability of its laws, he allowed, was a 'gratuitous assumption', but he argued that it was an essential assumption to our notion of truth—it is 'the root from which all incompatibility between any two assertions, and therefore all proof of the falsehood of either, is derived' (*An.* 101). It does not seem to have occurred to Bentham that such an approach severely curtailed the kinds of truth available to us. Assertions, for example, dealing with mathematical formulae and even those integral to his own social science (regarding human psychology) do not fall within its rubric. Evidently, Bentham was more interested in the polemical point than in the internal logic of his argument, for he followed the above statement with the remark that if we did not assume the uniformity of nature we would never have 'the power of distinguishing the true methods of procuring enjoyment or avoiding pain, from the false ones; . . . qualifying us indeed for the kingdom of heaven, but leaving us wholly defenceless against the wants and sufferings of earth' (*An.* 101). Bentham could not accept that a pious believer in God's omnipotence might also be thoroughly content in this life. The preference for reason and science over divinity was the only rational choice to be made. The whole fabric of human happiness depended on the conformity of belief with experience, and in posing a threat to this conformity the extra-experimental beliefs of religion diminished human happiness.

3. The 'distorting influence' of religious beliefs

According to Bentham, a fundamental source of the disjunction between beliefs and experience, causing weaknesses and even insanity in the mind, was religion itself. The religious sanction, he argued, was frequently used to elicit unwarranted beliefs. The 'distorting influence' of religious exercises placed belief in the catalogue of duties and merits, while unbelief is placed under the head of crimes and offences. The consequence is that whenever the religious sanction is effective it apparently induces a man to believe 'that which he would not naturally have believed, and disbelieve that which he would not naturally have disbelieved' (*An.* 110). But in the natural course of things it is upon the basis of evidence that an individual makes a decision; rewards and punishments, therefore, are 'a lateral and extraneous' force inducing apparent belief irrespective of proof. While a book is in a person's hand no one will say it is not, but in matters where truth is not immediately ascertained but depends on the comprehension of 'various and widespread fragments of evidence', there is no restriction on the selection and emphasis of certain kinds of evidence. It is in cases like this, says Bentham, that hope and reward can provide a motive for setting some preferences above others; the 'mind gravitates almost unconsciously towards the gainful side, as it shrinks from the terrors of the opposite prospect' (*An.* 111). An odd paradox of psychology is often discernible on these occasions: the weaker the evidence the greater the merit in believing. Bentham's reasoning is instructive here:

if it is necessary to encourage belief by an artificial bounty, it would be useless to apply this stimulus to any doctrine which would of itself command the assent of mankind. The bounty must go where it is most needed; that is to the support of doctrines which have little or no support of their own—and the largest slice of it to those which require the greatest encouragement, and would stand the least chance of being credited without it. (*An.* 112).

The religious sanction induces belief not according to reason—the 'only safe director' where the pleasures of this life are concerned—but according to a calculation of illusory profit or loss (*An.* 112). The inducements of religion produce a 'habit of credulity' tending to blind and confuse, 'rendering a man an easy prey to deceit and error, and thereby exposing him to incessant disappointment and loss' (*An.* 113).

Drawing upon arguments previously voiced in the early writings on legislation (cf. esp. *LG* 196), Bentham admitted that there were a few cases when the religious sanction actually served a useful purpose: where crimes were difficult to detect the threat of human penalties was often ineffective, and religion might then act as a restraint on action. But such exceptional cases were few and undetected crimes Bentham thought (optimistically one feels), would decrease in frequency as legal systems moved in step with the progress of philosophy and were better constructed. By a typically paradoxical turn of logic, he then argued that the present general inefficiency of the religious sanction in preventing crimes was really a good thing: such are the fanciful thoughts regarding the torments of Hell that the deficiency of the punishments of damnation in terms of propinquity and certainty 'practically annuls the most dreadful of all expectations'. To put it another way, the mind draws comfort from the uncertainty and remoteness of the consequences that constitute the penalties threatened by the religious sanction (*An.* 50).

That Bentham did not give due consideration here to the religious mind is evident. He writes of the temptation to commit a crime as absorbing 'the whole soul' such that it is difficult in many cases to counteract it even by the most immediate and unequivocal prospects of punishment, and that this is only exacerbated by the remote and uncertain nature of the punishment threatened by the religious sanction (*An.* 52). The argument, however, is unconvincing. For it could plausibly be replied that it is not on the occasion of temptation that religion works most efficaciously. The religious conscience is not summoned up on the occasion of temptation; rather it is in constant attendance. The truly pious person is usually disposed to habits of behaviour such as rarely lead to the temptation to commit crime. Like the utilitarian, in fact, they hardly need to reflect or calculate on every particular occasion on which they are tempted, but knowing that something is wrong they automatically dismiss the temptation as unconformable to the prescriptions of their faith. Bentham simply ignores considerations of this kind, convinced that the mind into which posthumous apprehensions find an easy admittance is generally in 'a state of timidity and depression', susceptible to such 'horrors and wretchedness' (*An.* 52). That this is little more than a caricature of the religious mind there can be no doubt, and it is made even more outrageous when Bentham claims that such a nervous disposition borders on insanity and 'frequently terminates in it' (*An.* 53).

What efficacy the religious sanction does have, Bentham believed, could be traced to the popular or moral sanction, particularly to the care individuals take over the kind of figure they cut in the world. Naturally, he explained, it is in a man's interest to keep his concern for reputation from view 'pretending to be influenced only by genuine veneration for the being whom he worships'; however, there can be no doubt that it is the popular sanction which not only 'enforces the delivery of the homage', but 'also compels the deliverer to carry all the marks of being influenced solely by religious inducements' (*An.* 56). By a piece of grand self-delusion the individual endeavours to convince himself that he is genuinely motivated by devotion to God; his account of his conduct, originally insincere, he will eventually be able to convert into an 'unconscious and unintentional error'. In such a manner, argued Bentham, do religious inducements enlist in their service the arm of public opinion. It being in our interest that our neighbours should be virtuous, we thus know that if we act in a virtuous manner public opinion will approve of our conduct. The consequence is that individuals apply the same encouragements and prohibitions, though from different motives, to pious and impious behaviour as they apply to genuine virtue and vice (*An.* 57). Persons, then, who are scrupulous renderers of religious services find it in their interest 'to swell the merit of performing them, and the criminality of neglect, to the highest possible pitch, in order to create a proportionate distribution of their esteem'. The more deeply we impress this conviction upon those with whom we associate, the greater will be the veneration afforded to us (*An.* 58). Thus what we take to be the consequence of religion is more properly the result of a sensitivity to public opinion.

Several examples are brought to light in order to substantiate this argument, each one of which is meant to reveal the inefficacy of the religious sanction when public opinion either opposes or does not support it.[21] None of the examples is convincing. First, faced with the possibility of a duel the religionist accepts. No one will give him credit for his attachment to the Deity, says Bentham, simply because he declines a duel; they will merely think him a coward. Secondly, public opinion does not forbid fornication, but 'leaves the divine admonition to operate unsupported', and 'the state of all great cities notoriously attests' to the extent to which this is successful. Thirdly, 'simony' (the selling of ecclesiastical offices) is also forbidden by the religious code with equal strictness, but is practised with equal frequency. Fourthly, in taking an oath a person calls upon God's vengeance should he break it, but the expectation of divine punishment 'has not, when stript of the consentient impulse of public opinion, the slenderest hold upon his actions' (*An.* 60–1). Perusing these examples one has the impression that for Bentham every crime committed would stand as a testimony to the inefficacy of religious beliefs. In fact the attempt to prove the irrelevance of individuals' beliefs to their commission of a crime can at best establish that in this or that particular instance the dictates of religion have been subordinated to other considerations.

More interesting is Bentham's argument that religion perverts the popular sanction. No temporal advantage, he argued, is gained by the enlisting of public opinion by religion; it merely 'draws off a portion of the popular favour, from its legitimate task of encouraging acts conducive to human felicity'. It 'cheats the public into the offer of a reward for conduct always useless, sometimes injurious—and embezzles part of the fund consecrated to the national service, for bribery on the personal behalf of the monarch'. Thus distorted, the popular sanction becomes 'the unconscious instrument of evil', since now the terms of moral approbation and disapprobation are transferred to actions with no legitimate connection to public happiness. The deceit is doubly to be deplored because it casts the science of morality 'into utter darkness and embarrassment' (*An.* 86–7). Reverting to the analysis of the *Introduction* (cf. esp. *IPML* 21–9), Bentham argued that moral actions are then subject to relativist considerations and the moralist, unable to range actions under a common rule, is forced to set them down 'in a catalogue one after another, as distinct and heterogeneous dictates of a certain blind and unaccountable impulse, which he terms a *moral instinct* or *conscience*'. In other cases, where individuals all agree, the moralist 'appeals to this universal consent as an invisible testimony to

---

[21] J. S. Mill argued similarly in his essay on the *Utility of Religion* (1874) and in the process cited Bentham's examples referred to here (*Collected Works*, x. 413–17).

the justice of the feeling, and extols the uniformity of nature's voice'. Where individuals happen to differ, the moralist 'compliments the particular sect or public, for whom he writes, as having singly adhered to the path of right and the dictates of nature, and bastardizes the rest of mankind as an outcast and misguided race' (*An.* 88). Religion, by its misapplication of praise and blame, is the main cause of this reduction of the science of morality to a 'stagnant and useless condition'. It has introduced fictitious intuitions into that science (*An.* 89).

Bentham's conclusions are that the religious sanction is not merely impotent but pernicious, and that its consequences are only beneficial to the community in so far as public opinion comes to its aid, or in so far as it produces casual and peculiar associations in the minds of some few believers who form an exception to the larger body. However, to build a general doctrine on the evidence of these few believers is a perilous way of proceeding in the science of morals. This science, therefore, is to be contrasted with the supposed science of the clergy, which is founded not on concrete experience but on extra-experiential principles. In Bentham's words (apparently alluding to Paul's Epistle to the Hebrews, 11: 1), it is the science 'of those things which we neither see, nor feel, nor hear, nor taste, nor smell; but which nevertheless, we are supposed to know without any experience at all'. Yet this false science, he laments, has gained for itself a distinct and privileged position and 'reflects on its practitioners and professors all that credit which is annexed to superiority in any other department' (*An.* 136). It subsidizes a standing army of 'wonder-workers',[22] who deprave the intellect, cherish superstition, and form an unholy alliance with 'the sinister interests of the earth' (*An.* 121, 140). In this sense the science of morals, the science of politics, and science *per se*, ultimately depend for their advancement on the elimination of this alliance and of the false science upon which it is based.

4. The spiritual value of religion

For Bentham, therefore, a world without religion would be no loss but really a positive good. He believed that the ethical imperative to

---

[22] The phrase (used repeatedly by Bentham in *An.* and *NP*) is borrowed from C. Middleton, *A Free Enquiry into the Miraculous Powers* (London, 1748), where it is frequently used to refer to those fathers of the 'primitive' or early Church said to have possessed supernatural powers. Bentham did not always use it to descry the Anglican clergy; e.g. in *NP* he employed it to describe Ananias (the instrument by which Paul's vision was returned to him by Jesus) as Paul's 'wonder-working surgeon' (*NP* 33).

contribute to the general happiness could only be advanced once religion was no longer a factor confusing the minds of the people. When religion is eliminated it leaves behind motives provided by the moral and political sanctions sufficient for the maintenance of useful conduct and ample to deter individuals from conduct injurious to it. Nor will the benefits to society of pious persons be lost since the motive to benevolence, properly understood, does not change on the supposition that the end of life comes with the termination of earthly existence. The truly benevolent will remain benevolent regardless of whether the supposed rewards of the afterlife really exist or not. Practices beneficial to human happiness are the same the world over although enacted with varying degrees of strictness from one culture to another. It cannot be the case, therefore, that the qualities which confer temporal benefit are peculiar to Christianity, since these are capable of universal growth in every climate (*An.* 37–8).

Bentham, of course, was willing to admit that the dictates of Christianity sometimes coincide with those of utility, but his response to this was that on these occasions Christianity is superficial. Furthermore, such occasions of coincidence are infrequent: the mandates of religion diverge so strikingly from the decrees of legislators that it is altogether impossible for them to be directed to the promotion of temporal happiness (*An.* 39–40). Leaving aside the fact that what ought to be (laws founded on utility) is here confused with what is, by arguing in this fashion Bentham does little justice to the inspirational and spiritual value of Christianity which it is impossible to reduce to a set of rules to be compared with human laws. The underlying problem with Bentham's argument (here and throughout *An.* generally) is the failure to adhere to the distinction between revealed and natural religion. Christianity is the product of revelation and cannot be reduced to (even if it finds support from) natural religion in the manner chosen by Bentham. It is something more than merely the belief in a future day of reckoning and this 'something more', defined in terms of faith and love, is what Bentham never could translate into terms acceptable to his social science. Consequently, he ignored it, preferring to concentrate on the fruitless (from the point of view of the believer) exposing of the extra-experiential character of religious beliefs.

8

Revealed Religion

... it rests with every professor of the religion of Jesus to settle
with himself, to which of the two religions, that of Jesus or that of
Paul, he will adhere: and, accordingly, either to say, *Not Jesus but
Paul*—or, in the words of the title to this work, *Not Paul but Jesus*.

NP, p. xvi

EDITORIAL questions similar to those which surround the publication of the *Analysis* hang over the production of *Not Paul, but Jesus*. The
book appeared in 1823 under the pseudonym 'Gamaliel Smith', but
Bentham's authorship was not long a secret. At least one critic knew
that it came from the hand of 'a celebrated writer on legislation'.[1]
However, according to a note by Francis Place in his personal copy of
the work 'the matter of this book was put together by me at Mr.
Bentham's request in the months of August and September 1817—
during my residence with him at Ford Abbey, Devonshire'.[2] The
meaning of 'put together' here is the source of whatever doubts exist
about Bentham's authorship. Graham Wallas asserts that the manuscripts for *Not Paul, but Jesus* were 'rearranged, condensed and "pulled
together" in making the book'.[3] It may be that Place had some
hand in this, but it is difficult to substantiate what actually occurred.

[1] 'Ben David' [pseudonym of the Unitarian minister John Jones], *A Reply to Two
Deistical Works, entitled 'The New Trial of the Witnesses', Ec. and Gamaliel Smith's 'Not Paul,
but Jesus'* (London, 1824), 1. So sure was 'Ben David' that Bentham was the author that
he later referred to him by name (ibid. 173 n.).
[2] This copy, inscribed 'From Mr. Bentham Sep. 29, 1823, FP', is in the Library at
UCL. Alexander Bain records that Edwin Chadwick, a close companion of Bentham in
his later years, once told him that Bentham began the book in 1815 as a result of the
deterioration in his sight: 'He was living at Ford Abbey; and the only book he could read
was a large type Bible belonging to the house. He then fell upon what he conceived the
discrepancies between the Gospels and the Acts of the Apostles' (Bain, *James Mill*,
p. 151). But this is a fanciful claim disproved by a letter from JB to John Herbert Koe
(29 Oct. 1817; Koe MSS, transcription at the Bentham Project, UCL), in which it is
revealed that the deterioration of Bentham's sight occurred as a consequence of
consulting a small type Bible as part of the research for *NP*.
[3] See the note attached by Wallas to Place's personal copy of *NP* at UCL (see n. 2
above).

Unfortunately, Place's letters and diaries make no mention of the matter.[4] What we do know is that some of the manuscripts for *Not Paul, but Jesus* were not written until 1819, 1821, and even 1823.[5] Only a small portion of the manuscripts upon which the published work is based are extant, most of the remaining manuscripts that go by the title 'Not Paul' being material suppressed by Bentham or which he hoped would appear at some future date. This material includes a 'Church History from Jesus' Ascension to Paul's Conversion' (UC 139/445–571, dated 1817, 1819, and 1823); an unpublished appendix with the title 'Paul's Inducements' (UC 139/332–444, dated 1816–18 and 1823); suppressed material on the doctrinal differences between Paul and Jesus (UC 161a/141–214, dated 1816–18); the intended second volume or part to *Not Paul, but Jesus*, entitled 'Sextus', which is a discussion of asceticism (UC 74a/35–222, dated 1814 and 1816) and harks back to the earlier fragments on 'Sexual Nonconformity' of *c.*1774 and 1785 (UC 73/90–100 and 74a/1–26; UC 72/187–205 and 74a/27–34); and, finally, the planned third part of *Not Paul, but Jesus* (a continuation of part 2) with the title 'Asceticism: Its repugnancy to the religion of Jesus' (UC 161b/215–523, dated 1816–18).[6] What remains of the material upon which the published work is based accounts for only a few of its many sections (UC 139/212–331, dated 1813, 1815, 1817, and 1821). Consequently, it is difficult to say with precision just how much of a hand Place had in the book.[7]

Having said this, Place's involvement in the production of the book at some level cannot be doubted. Entries in the diary of John Colls reveal that the manuscripts were passed to Place via Bowring in January 1821, and the *Summary View of a Work, intitled Not Paul, but Jesus*, published later that same year, announced that the work would be speedily published. Yet on 25 January 1823 Bentham was still

---

[4] At the same time, we should note Wallas's remark in *The Life of Francis Place*, p. 84 n.: 'the whole Utilitarian circle for obvious reasons kept that side of their work rather quiet'.

[5] In the note attached to Place's personal copy of *NP* Wallas points out that while the manuscripts are mostly dated 1817 in Place's hand, there are some dated 1818. To this the *DNB* adds that during Place's stay at Ford Abbey in the late summer of 1817 he was hard at work learning Latin, such that it does not appear likely that he could have completed the task as he reports (*DNB* xv. 1277).

[6] BL Add. MSS 29806–9 contains material used by Grote for *An.* and MSS intended for subsequent parts of this work (dates vary between 1811–21, but mainly 1811, 1815, 1819, and 1821), of which there are sections related to the material intended for *NP* (specific references contained in notes to this ch.).

[7] The above dates are those given in Milne, *Catalogue of the Manuscripts of Jeremy Bentham*.

enquiring of Place how the work was progressing (UC 173/92). In his *Autobiography* Place explicitly attributes the work to Bentham and even allowing for modesty there is no reason to doubt this.[8] As a confessed atheist Place welcomed the publication of anti-religious literature and would eagerly have assisted in any such enterprise.[9] But he was no Greek scholar (Bentham worked from a Greek Bible) and the levity with which the subject of revelation is approached is quite beyond anything Place is reputed to have been able to manage.[10] There seems little doubt that he played only a minor role, and that purely as an editor of sorts, in the publication of what the mysterious Martha Colls described in a letter to Étienne Dumont as 'the comical book'.[11] Amusingly enough, the relevant part of this letter ends with the report that some people are saying that a new sect will be established based on the teaching of 'Gamaliel Smith'. But perhaps a sect of anti-religious utilitarians was not so far-fetched an idea.[12]

1. The secular Christ

When finally published *Not Paul, but Jesus* drew several sharp attacks.[13] The Revd T. S. Hughes flatly accused 'Gamaliel Smith' of

---

[8] *The Autobiography of Francis Place (1771–1854)*, ed. M. Thrale (Cambridge, 1972), 8.

[9] For evidence of Place's atheism see ibid., pp. xxiii, 45–6, 121, 197–8 n.

[10] That Place's own writing is uniformly dull and humourless is testified on all hands (see the article on Place in the *DNB*; Thrale's introduction to Place's *Autobiography*; Wallas's *Life of Francis Place*, p. 39).

[11] Martha Colls to Dumont (29 Nov. 1823), Dumont MSS 33, iii, fo. 382, Bibliothèque Publique Universitaire, Geneva, from a transcription at the Bentham Project, UCL. There appears to be another version of this letter at UC 10/132–5. The identity of Martha Colls remains a mystery—could it have been Bentham playing a practical joke on Dumont? That *NP* was considered humorous by the Bentham circle is also testified by a letter from Thomas Wright Hill to JB (UC 10/146, 8 Mar. 1824).

[12] As I shall discuss below in the Conclusion, Bentham had a 'dream' (in or around the year 1780) in which he envisaged himself as 'a founder of a sect, of course a personage of great sanctity and importance. It was called the sect of the *utilitarians*' (UC 169/79). The text of this alleged 'dream' is given in full with notes in App. *B*.

[13] Revd T. S. Hughes, *A Defence of the Apostle St. Paul against the Accusation of Gamaliel Smith, Esq. in a recent publication, entitled 'Not Paul But Jesus'*, pt. 1 (Cambridge, 1823), and *On the Miracles of St. Paul Being Part II of a Defence of that Apostle against the Accusation of Gamaliel Smith, Esq.* (Cambridge, 1824); D. B. Wells, *St. Paul Vindicated: Being Part I of a Reply to a Late Publication by Gamaliel Smith, Esq.* (Cambridge, 1824); E. W. Grinfield, *The Doctrinal Harmony of the New Testament exemplified; ... To which is added A Letter to the Author of a Book entitled 'Not Paul But Jesus'* (London, 1824); 'Ben David', *A Reply to two Deistical Works* (see n. 1 above).

plagiarism,[14] and it seems probable that Bentham did borrow from a work by the Deist Peter Annet (1693–1769), entitled *The History and Character of St. Paul Examined* (*c.*1750). That Bentham lifted the idea for the 'Conversion Table' (inserted at the front of *Not Paul, but Jesus*) from Annet, at least, is probably true. But *Not Paul, but Jesus* went far beyond Annet's brief work.[15] It expanded on the treatment of certain passages in Paul's Epistles, introduced additional topics, and relied on the interpretation of the original Greek terms in which the Bible was first written. Most notably, as Professor Steintrager has said, 'the idea of distinguishing between Paul and Jesus, though vaguely implicit in Annet, was Bentham's device for trying to appear as a sincere, reforming Christian'.[16] Bentham's critics were certainly not taken in by the ploy. Edward Grinfield charged Bentham with hypocrisy and described him as 'a deist in disguise; an unbeliever, who has not the candour and courage to avow his principles'.[17] The Revd D. B. Wells also noted that *Not Paul, but Jesus* was 'evidently dictated by a spirit of hostility towards Christianity itself'.[18] The Revd T. S. Hughes, the Christian Advocate of Cambridge University (whose official task it was to respond to such literature), was equally convinced of the real intent of the work: 'to support and beautify the Christian edifice, by removing one of its main pillars, and principal ornaments!'[19] If 'Gamaliel Smith' were allowed success in this it would be but a short time before he would target his attack 'not only against St. Peter, but against a much higher character'.[20] 'Ben David' (pseudonym of the Unitarian Minister, John Jones) echoed these sentiments: the tactic of *Not Paul, but Jesus*,

[14] Hughes, *On the Miracles of St. Paul*, p. ii. Hughes also suggested that 'Gamaliel Smith' owed a debt to others among his 'predecessors in the paths of infidelity', and referred to 'arguments drawn from the old stores of Morgan, Chubb, Bolingbroke and Paine' (ibid. 12, 17).

[15] Coincidentally, Annet's book was translated into French by Boulanger (or more likely Holbach using the deceased Boulanger's name as a disguise), and was retranslated into English and published by Richard Carlile in 1823—the same year as *NP* appeared—as *A Critical Examination of the Life of St. Paul. Translated from the French of Boulanger*. Boulanger's (i.e. Holbach's) *Examen critique de la vie et des ouvrages de Saint Paul* first appeared in Amsterdam in 1770.

[16] Steintrager, 'Report on the Problems of Editing Bentham's Writings on Religion', p. 6.

[17] Grinfield, *The Doctrinal Harmony of the New Testament*, p. 110.

[18] Wells, *St. Paul Vindicated*, p. i.

[19] Hughes, *A Defence of the Apostle St. Paul*, p. 11.

[20] Ibid. 21. Hughes was no less perceptive when he associated Bentham's animosity towards St Paul with an extreme political stance, designed to encourage discontent with the civil and ecclesiastical establishments, the monarchy, the laws, and the constitution (ibid. 8).

he announced, was merely a 'snare' to entrap the reader, and he was sure that 'if this publication succeeded, it might soon be followed by another from the same pen, entitled "Neither Paul nor Jesus"'. *Not Paul, but Jesus*, he complained was a work of such a frivolous nature that it shocked even 'free thinking Christians'.[21]

Whatever the shock occasioned by the appearance of *Not Paul, but Jesus*, it would undoubtedly have been all the greater had some of the suppressed material been published as Bentham intended. (I leave a discussion of Bentham's case against homophobic prejudice to the next chapter.) In particular, the manuscripts reveal Bentham's true sentiments regarding the historic Jesus and the political motives that inspired his actions.[22] According to Bentham, Christ's real mission was not to establish a religion or to advance a specific morality, but to acquire sovereign power over the Jewish nation. It was only when his movement began to fail that he developed the notion of a spiritual kingdom as a cover or refuge to prevent the detection of his revolutionary plot before it was sufficiently advanced.[23] When pressed, he claimed that he was only an orator or a moralist, a social reformer therefore, and not a revolutionary.

That a moral teaching emerged from the words and deeds of Christ does not seem to have made any difference to Bentham. He not only rejected belief in the divinity of Jesus, but thought that the moral doctrine of the Gospels was in no way useful or edifying. Its defects, he claimed, were that it was not stated in clear and concise language; that it took no account of the peculiarities of time and place in which it was composed; and that it did not provide specific quantities of punishment

---

[21] 'Ben David', *A Reply to two Deistical Works*, pp. 172, 191. Bentham's irreverence, always apparent in the text of *NP*, became scurrilous in a letter to John Herbert Koe (29 Oct. 1817) regarding the work. Upon being informed by Koe of the praise of an unnamed French admirer he replied: 'Suppose not that I am "puffed up". I have learnt of Saint Paul, to boast of not boasting: as to the glory I give it to God, who gives it back to me again with the additional glory of piety and humility for the use of it. In the French man I behold Saint Peter: that Peter who to save his bacon denied Christ. Well—we have all of us our weaknesses (No. 1 always excepted) And so the snivelling [?] dog would not give up his place! Whom shall I have with me in paradise? As for Saint Paul amongst other discoveries, I have discovered his identity with Cobbet [*sic*]: Cobbet is as surely he as Pythagoras was Panthoides Euphoribus: at the time of the Trojan war if you happen to remember it.' And again in the same letter he writes: 'I have found that Locke was no more the author of Acts than you were. You don't remember writing any such thing do you? I think you must have been very young when you wrote such stuff if you did' (Koe MSS, from a transcription at the Bentham Project, UCL).

[22] Professor Steintrager spent considerable time reviewing this material and it is his account I follow here. See 'Language and Politics', pp. 4–20.

[23] BL Add. MSS 29806/332, cited Steintrager, 'Language and Politics', pp. 4–5.

for the infringement of its rules even when these rules were known. At any rate, Christ's moral teaching was only a pretext. In the Sermon on the Mount, he preached the social class of virtues solely for the purpose of uniting his followers behind his revolutionary aims. General benevolence was not the direct object of his efforts, but only a means to a very different political end.[24]

Now, on Bentham's behalf it should be said that his view of Christ's mission is not so far wide of the mark that it can be dismissed as trivial or frivolous.[25] Running throughout the New Testament there is a detectable dual epistemological pattern—that is, events can be construed religiously or naturalistically—which leaves room for the kind of interpretation that Bentham provides. In the study of a man, Jesus of Nazareth, and a movement which arose in connection with him, there exists much data of an ambiguous nature. It is possible to see him as the Messiah, the one in whom the world was to witness the divine Son of God living a human life and suffering for the good of humanity, and to view Christ in this way is to share the faith of the New Testament writers. But it is also possible to see Jesus simply as a self appointed prophet who got mixed up in politics, clashed with the Jerusalem rabbis, and, therefore, had to be eliminated. To view him in this light is to see him as Bentham did. Later in the century the French historian and critic Ernest Renan (1823–92) was to write of the doings of Christ and Paul in the same secular tradition as Bentham. The Scriptures were to be treated as works of history, by the same criteria as profane historical works, and the key to critical analysis was the 'incontestable data' the Scriptures contained.[26] Renan, like Bentham, disdained to indulge in the language of mysticism to describe Paul's experiences. The Christ who revealed himself to Paul on the road to Damascus, for example, was not a revelation in the sense the Christian

[24] BL Add. MSS 29806/332; 29807/44–54, 97; and 29806/207–8 (see Steintrager, 'Language and Politics', pp. 5–7).

[25] Similar claims about Christ's mortality and about the political character of his teaching can be found in H. Maccoby, *Revolution in Judea: Jesus and the Jewish Resistance* (London, 1973), esp. ch. 9.

[26] This approach is amply portrayed in Renan's introduction to *Saint Paul*, in *The History of the Origins of Christianity* [*Histoire des origines du christianisme*, 8 vols., 1863–83], 5 vols. (1888–90; repr. London, n.d.), iii, pp.i–xxxi. Renan's text ends with Paul still 3 years from martyrdom. The reason given for closing the study so abruptly is that after Paul's arrival in Rome (where he is confined and eventually tried and executed) 'we cease to tread on the ground of incontestable data; we begin to grope in the obscurity of legends and of apocryphal documents' (ibid., p. xxx). The 'apocryphal documents' are the 2 letters to Timothy and the letter to Titus, which are said to be unreliable because of the 'insoluble contradictions' they contain (see ibid., pp. xiii–xxiii).

world came to understand it, but rather Paul's 'own ghost'; hence 'he listens to *himself*, thinking that he hears Jesus'.[27]

Nevertheless, if Bentham's approach to the Scriptures can be defended on such grounds as these, we might yet pause to consider that his argument, so far as it touches on the moral worth of Christ's teachings, is not really to the point in terms of the utilitarian calculus. For is it not consequences rather than motives that have to be considered when estimating the morality of an action? Bentham seems to have recognized the possibility that such an objection might be made. His point, as Professor Steintrager explained, was rather that Christ's seizure of power could only be achieved by 'bloody, violent, and destructive means', and such methods are incompatible 'with the exercise of any considerable influence on the part of the social class of motives'.[28] But the more serious criticism made by Bentham is that the salutary effects of Christ's teaching are only apparent. He taught what was 'necessary at the moment to the formation of that particular community' which he was seeking to establish, but this is 'incompatible with the continuance either of every other society, or even of that very society in and to the formation of which they had served'.[29] The practice of absolute benevolence, the denigration of self-regarding affections, and the praise of meekness, when enjoined without any qualifications, would together conspire to destroy society. No society could have the stability and security it needs to flourish by adopting such a moral code:

By the utmost prevalence of the self-regarding and dissocial affections they could not be made to suffer for so much as they would by the pursuit of the dictates of the social to the degree here recommended, coupled with the debilitation or extinction of the self-regarding and dissocial:—the self-regarding suffice for preventing the dissocial from presenting any such fatal effects.[30]

As usual Bentham read the New Testament in a literal fashion and interpreted the words of Christ strictly. A Mandevillian interpretation is the result: if all of us seek to do good to others whenever and wherever we can then we would destroy ourselves; by neglecting our

[27] Ibid. 298, emphasis added.
[28] BL Add. MSS 29807/97, quoted by Steintrager, 'Language and Politics', p. 7.
[29] BL Add. MSS 29806/471, quoted by Steintrager, 'Languages and Politics', p. 7.
[30] BL Add. MSS 29808/79, quoted by Steintrager, 'Language and Politics', p. 7. For other MSS on the same theme see 29806/492; 29807/225; 29808/62–4, 66–8, 70–4, 76–86.

labours to serve others we would give up all security and the requirements for our own preservation. Such an attack on the founder of Christianity, if it had been published, would no doubt have been thought outrageous, yet it was clearly Bentham's intention to see it in print at some time.[31]

2. *The fraudulent Paul*

In *Not Paul, but Jesus* Bentham's critique of religion is carried on at a more leisurely pace and at a different level than in the more rigorously argued and concisely written *Analysis*, but he had the same end in view—the undermining of basic Christian beliefs. Not all the arguments of this protracted examination of the conduct and doctrinal teachings of St Paul need detain us. In the first two chapters Bentham tackled in exegetical, not to say intemperate, fashion the five scriptural accounts of Paul's 'inward conversion' and dwelled upon the detrimental consequences for the Christian Church of his 'outward conversion'. Why was questioning Paul's conversion so important to Bentham? It is true that the discrepancies between the accounts of the conversion may not deserve much attention, but Bentham was acutely aware that Paul had radically altered the direction of Christianity, and that this process began with his claim to have been converted by Christ in a vision on the road to Damascus. Had it not been for this, for his Epistles, and missionary work it is doubtful if Christianity would have conquered the Western world. More likely, as with other Jewish heresies before it, it would have been stamped out or absorbed into the mainstream of Jewish faith. It was this fact which made Paul's conversion pivotal in the development of Christianity and, therefore, which required that Bentham focus part of his critique upon it. Hence, chapters 3–10 of *Not Paul, but Jesus* are taken up with the endeavour to disprove the notion that Paul was given a supernatural commission and to establish that this was seriously doubted by the other Apostles and disciples contemporary with Paul at Jerusalem. In proof of Paul's insincerity Bentham brings two supposedly false assertions to view in

---

[31] Believing this design to be unmistakeable and that Bentham's intention to publish all the work was unequivocal, Steintrager planned to do exactly that in his proposed edn. of *NP* for *CW* and to supplement this with the manuscripts on 'sexual nonconformity'. I deal with these latter MSS below in ch. 9.

chapters 11–12: the one, Paul's false account of the number of witnesses to Christ's resurrection (1 Cor. 15: 6); the other, his prediction of the immanent end of the world (1 Thess. 4: 15–17). In chapter 13 the supposed miracles of St Paul, as attested in Acts of the Apostles, are examined and shown to be natural events upon which 'a sort of supernatural colouring has been superinduced' (*NP*, p. xi). In support of the case against Paul's miracles in chapter 14 Bentham questioned the authenticity of Acts. Additional doubts are cast upon Paul's character in chapter 15 when Bentham considers the reports of his five trials (as recorded in Acts), and the main body of the text is completed by a final chapter containing a general comparison between the teachings of Paul and Jesus's chosen Apostles. Finally, Bentham includes an appendix in which he gives the headings of material suppressed from the book and provides some additional evidence regarding the nature of the worldly inducements and fanatical ambitions that supposedly motivated Paul (*NP* 375–403),[32] a view which was later to find an echo in Renan.[33]

The polemical nature of the work is evident throughout. By exposing St Paul as a fraud and by contrasting his ascetic teaching with that of Christ, Bentham's plan was to strike at the historical foundations of Christianity. What emerged, however, is but a thinly disguised attack on the religion of Christ itself. As early as 1812 Bentham had planned to strike a blow at Christianity by exposing St Paul and his teachings. In the outline for the abandoned work on the Church he advanced the view that 'disbelief in the divine mission of Paul, is not inconsistent with belief in that of Christ' (UC 6/63). In 1815 he returned to this subject and made it the ostensible theme for what was largely finished in 1818 and eventually published as *Not Paul, but Jesus* in 1823. The standard version of St Paul's life and teachings at this time was given by Paley in his *Horae Paulinae* (1790) and Bentham read this in preparation for the writing of *Not Paul, but*

---

[32] Bentham originally intended to include 'a short but critical sketch' of the early history of the Church; see *Summary View of a Work, intitled Not Paul, but Jesus* (London, 1821), 6. But in the Plan of the Work at the front of *NP* he tells us that this was set aside 'for another time, or another hand'. Considerations of space coupled with '*vis inertiae*' are the excuses offered for omitting this history, and also for omitting the full appendix exposing the material inducements which set Paul upon his ambitious plan to become master of the youthful Christian Church (*NP*, pp. xiv–xv).

[33] 'When Paul was with his flock, he existed alone, all others were crushed or seen only through him' (Renan, *Saint Paul*, p. 299; for the 'proud, unbending, unsociable' Paul see ibid. 301).

Jesus.[34] At the conclusion of *Horae Paulinae* Paley summed up the character and accomplishments of the saint as follows:

Here then we have a man of liberal attachments, and in other points of sound judgement, who had addicted his life to the service of the gospel. We see him, in the prosecution of his purpose, travelling from country to country, enduring every species of hardship, encountering every extremity of danger, assaulted by the populace, punished by the magistrates, scourged, beat, stoned, left for dead; expecting wherever he came, a renewal of the same treatment, and the same dangers, yet, when driven from the city, preaching in the next; spending his whole time in the employment, sacrificing to it his pleasures, his ease, his safety; persisting in this course to old age, unaltered by the experience of perverseness, ingratitude, prejudice, desertion; unsubdued by anxiety, want, labour, persecutions; unwearied by long confinement, undismayed by the prospect of death. Such was St. Paul.[35]

This is the eulogistic version of St Paul with which Bentham took issue.

Repetitious, long-winded, painstakingly detailed, making much use of ridicule as a test of truth, *Not Paul, but Jesus* is an odd work, pretending to treat of doctrine but actually containing few discussions of a doctrinal nature. Only on the question of the resurrection of the dead is Paul seriously brought to task for doctrinal irregularity: 'Paul preached the resurrection of the dead. Agreed. But *that* resurrection of the dead which he preached, was it not a resurrection, that was to take place in the life-time of himself and other persons then living? And— any such resurrection, did it accordingly take place?' (*NP* 373). Bentham, however, found it useful from time to time to use the doctrines taught by Jesus to bolster the principle of utility against the principle of asceticism which he attributed to the teaching of Paul. It is to this principle, he claimed, that the mischiefs of contemporary Christianity can be traced. Preaching 'in declared opposition' to the eleven Apostles of Jesus, Paul espoused doctrines which are responsible for many of the antagonisms occasioned by Christianity down through the centuries, despite its otherwise benevolent system of morals. Paul's words are an

[34] This is evident from 2 letters Bentham wrote to John Koe (10 and 29 Oct. 1817; Koe MSS, transcriptions at the Bentham Project, UCL), and from MSS fragments containing extracts from the comments on *Horae Paulinae* at UC 139/1–2, 82, 223–6. The critics of *NP*, almost without exception, relied upon Paley's version (see esp. Wells, *St. Paul Vindicated*; Hughes, *A Defence of the Apostle St. Paul*, and *On the Miracles of St. Paul*).

[35] W. Paley, *Horae Paulinae: Or, the Truth of the Scripture History of Paul Evinced* (1790), in *Complete Works*, iii. 533–4.

encumbrance from which it can only be beneficial for Christianity to dissociate itself (*NP*, p. vi).[36] To contrast Paul with Jesus was, therefore, a handy polemical device well suited to Bentham's purpose.

According to Bentham, the most notorious and malicious legacy bequeathed by Paul to the Church was the notion of the 'Antichrist', a 'fabulous' invention 'created by Paul, and nursed by the Church of England, translators of the Bible' (*NP*, p. xii). As used in the New Testament (1 John 2: 18, 22; 4: 3; and 2 John 7, *passim*) the term 'Antichrist' refers to persons who deny Christ. However, in the hands of Paul (2 Thess. 2: 3–4), followed by the early fathers of the Church (cf. esp. Rev. 13: 18) the term came to signify a great force filling the world with evil, and whose defeat would lead to the Second Coming. In this extended sense the Antichrist has been taken to be, at different times, the office of Roman Emperor, specific emperors (first, and most notably, Nero), Mohammed, and (by Wycliffe, Luther, and Revd Ian Paisley, and others) the Vatican Popes. Bentham described this invention in a range of detrimental terms, such as a 'spiritual monster', a 'hobgoblin', the 'child of the self-appointed Apostle's brain' (*NP* 295 n.), and saw in it the source of manifold human misery. Could the notion be extinguished from the Christian mind, he believed that it would calm 'a mass of disquietude, which how completely soever groundless, is not the less afflicting, to the minds into which it has found entrance' (*NP* 277). The real Antichrist, according to Bentham, is Paul himself—'an Antichrist of flesh and blood' (*NP* 372).

In *Not Paul, but Jesus*, then, we have what purports to be a comparative view of the two entirely different religions embodied respectively in Paul's Epistles (particularly Romans) and in Jesus's Sermon on the Mount. In actual fact what we are given is a historical investigation of the relations between Paul and the original Apostles intended to discredit the motives and actions of the former. Paul is portrayed as the converted persecutor of the Church, ambitious, worldly, an intriguer, ready to manipulate the community of Christians in order to attain his own selfish ends. The core of Bentham's argument for this interpretation turns on the fact that the 'temporal enjoyments' Paul obtained from his work were of such a magnitude that he needed no other reason for pursuing the course of action that he did (*NP*, p. xiv). The motive of

---

[36] That the modern character of Christianity can be traced to the teachings of St Paul Bentham believed was amply supported by Francis Gastrell (1662–1725), Bp. of Chester, *Christian Institutes: Or the Sincere Word of God* (1707), a work almost entirely based on the maxims of faith and morality found in Paul's Epistles (*NP*, p. xiv n.).

his faked conversion on the road to Damascus was nothing more than 'temporal advantage'.[37] As a consequence of his career as a persecutor of the Christians, Paul was well aware of the pecuniary rewards to be gained by the leader of this sect. He 'could not . . . have failed to obtain a considerable insight into the state of their worldly affairs', and would also have been aware of the offer of the sorcerer Simon of Samaria to purchase at great cost from the Apostles a share in the government of the Church. The refusal of the sorcerer's offer would surely have served to publicize the commercial possibilities of the Church, and to Paul's 'alert and busy mind' the Church would have appeared as 'an inviting field of enterprize' (*NP* 70)—the Protestant ethic in primitive action, one might say. Employing the expertness he had acquired in the Greek language, Paul set out to establish 'an empire over the minds of his converts' and, by that means, to acquire that power and opulence which he so desired (*NP* 73). The agreement that he reached with Peter and the other Apostles, to work only among the Gentiles, made admirable sense for a former prosecutor of the Christian Jews. Furthermore, for his scheme to work Paul needed the charismatic name of Jesus and this meant the sanction of his chosen Apostles (cf. *NP* 73, 124, 369). The principal objective of this ambitious plan was to become the 'President of the Christian Commonwealth' (*NP* 156).

Bentham's interpretation of Paul's conduct has been assailed by more than one critic. A. W. Benn, for example, argues that *Not Paul, but Jesus* was entirely out of step with the age in which Bentham wrote: 'Appearing in 1822 [*sic*], it only becomes intelligible when read in the light of his personal circumstances, his absolute isolation from the intellectual currents of the age, his entire ignorance of history, and the low vein of human nature generated by the habit of relying on motives of pecuniary interest.'[38] We might demur from one or two of the charges contained in this attack, but the theory of imposture, it is true, had been completely discredited by the time Bentham wrote. Few dissented from Paley's opinion in *A View of the Evidences of Christianity* (1794), that the Apostles were credible witnesses because they were willing to stake their lives on the reality of the events they professed to have seen. The device of concentrating on motives was a variation on

---

[37] Bentham compares the 3 accounts of the conversion contained in Acts 9: 1–18 (the 'Historical Account'), 22: 3–16 (Paul's 'First or Unstudied Account'), and 26: 9–20 (Paul's 'Oratorical or Studied Account'; see also Paul's allusions to this at 1 Cor. 15: 8, and Gal. 1: 11–17). The discrepancies he finds amount to 5 omissions and 5 direct contradictons (see *NP* 11–20 and the 'Conversion Table' at the front of *NP*).

[38] Benn, *The History of English Rationalism*, i. 302.

the old theme of imposture. Another commentator has described the effort as 'bizarre beyond all description'.[39] To be sure, Bentham was no biblical critic and was ill-equipped to be sensitive to the symbolism and figurative language of the Scriptures. If the several accounts of Paul's conversion given in Acts differ one from another then the differences he believed could be used to show the impossibility of the conversion ever having taken place. The conversion, therefore, was an imposture. But Bentham had an overriding purpose in his polemic, and it was not to understand Christianity but to argue it out of existence. Whatever resources came most readily to hand he employed. That the distortion of history and holy texts mattered little to him he willingly confessed. 'An error', he writes, 'if such it be, which . . . has now for upwards of seventeen centuries past, maintained its ground throughout the Christian world, cannot, without the utmost reluctance, be parted with: for dissolving the association so unhappily formed, scarcely, therefore, can any argument which reason offers be deemed superfluous' (*NP* 367). If in noting every occasion on which Paul speaks of money, collected ostensibly for the benefit of his congregations, it could be insinuated that he used it for himself, then Bentham was ready to employ such a means. Nor was the connection with the sinister interests of the modern Church and its corrupt clergy to be missed. Part of the appendix to *Not Paul, but Jesus*, which reproduces the titles of the chapters and section heads of the discarded material on the history of the early Church, was utilized as a vehicle for attacking 'Church-of-Englandism'. So long as the religion of Jesus continued in its pristine condition 'all was good government, all was equality, all was harmony', but gradually 'despotism took possession of it, and made an instrument of it' (*NP* 391–2). We are left in no doubt that the condition of the Church, in both its Catholic and Anglican forms, has altered little since: 'Becoming established, it became noxious, preponderately [*sic*] noxious. For where established is the adjunct to it, what does religion mean? what but depradation, corruption, oppression, hypocrisy? . . . these four: with delusion, in all its forms and trappings, for support' (*NP* 392). Establishment, Bentham argues here, was not enjoined by Jesus but by Paul, this constituting another divergence between their respective teachings.

Renan, whose interpretation of early Church history had so much in common with Bentham's, also showed himself to be acutely aware of

---

[39] D. Baumgardt, *Bentham and the Ethics of Today* (New York, 1966), 488.

the contrast between Jesus and Paul and of the legacy the latter bestowed upon the Church. His pronouncement upon the matter would have impressed Bentham:

True Christianity which will last eternally comes from the Gospels, not from the Epistles of Paul. The writings of Paul have been a danger and a stumbling-block, the cause of the chief faults of Christian theology. Paul is the father of the subtle Augustine, of the arid Thomas Aquinas, of the sombre Calvinist, of the bitter Jansenist, of the ferocious theology which condemns and predestinates to damnation.[40]

More recently, the theologian A. K. Jung has rendered a similar judgement, remarking that in his Epistles 'Paul hardly ever allows the real Jesus of Nazareth to get a word in'.[41] Certainly, the injunctions offered by Paul were not entirely extraneous to the teaching of Jesus reported by the Gospels, but these writers are correct in their detection of differences between the two. The details of Jesus's life are sparsely recorded by Paul: he knows that he was born of a woman (Gal. 4: 5), belonged to David's stock (Rom. 1: 3), bore a human likeness, ate the Last Supper, was betrayed, and suffered Crucifixion. However, there is nothing of the miracles and healings that we find in the Gospel story and, more remarkable still, only one specific allusion to a statement made by Jesus—a reference to a minor point: Christ's alleged opposition to divorce (1 Cor. 7: 10). There is no direct mention in the Epistles of the observations made by Jesus, the parables he taught, or the controversies in which he engaged with the Pharisees and scribes. Paul showed an almost complete lack of interest in the words and acts of Jesus. Even so, we might hesitate before we side with Bentham and charge Paul with perpetrating a deception. Michael Grant, one of Paul's modern biographers, suggests two other possible explanations, both plausible, for the apparent discrepancy; either Paul (who did not know Jesus personally) did not know the facts ascribed to Jesus's career by the Gospels (which were written after Paul's death) or, if he was aware of them, did not feel the need to reiterate what everyone already knew. Grant, wisely, concludes that both explanations contain an element of the truth: on the one hand, Paul probably was not aware of the facts subsequently related in the Gospels, and, equally probably, on the other hand, what he did know did not seem to him necessary to record because his Christian readers presumably already had the

[40] Renan, *Saint Paul*, p. 302.
[41] Quoted M. Grant, *Saint Paul* (London, 1976), 58.

essentials of the relevant account.[42] But this is not to say that the discrepancies between what Paul and Jesus taught are inconsequential. The most important difference between the two turns about the emphasis Paul placed on 'faith'. Faith in what? The faith which Paul came to hold, and desired others to hold with him, was faith in Christ's Crucifixion and in his Resurrection and its redemptive consequences for the human race. I shall return to consider Bentham's views on the subject of faith later on, but for the present it should be said that if it is correct to say that this is the most important feature of Paul's religion, then it was naturally of a kind very different from that of Christ. For this and other reasons ethical comparisons between the two can only be of limited significance.[43]

3. The incredibility of miracles

Of particular interest in *Not Paul, but Jesus* is the discussion of Paul's miracles, including his conversion, since here again Bentham employs the presuppositions of his social science, though the whole discussion is carried on in a language more appropriate to a courtroom than to a philosophical or theological controversy.

Bentham begins *Not Paul, but Jesus* by proposing that the reader should think of him as continuing the critical work begun by Conyers Middleton (1683–1750) in his celebrated *Free Enquiry into the Miraculous Powers*, which first appeared in 1748 (*NP*, p. iii). Indeed, Bentham's praise is ostensibly unrestrained: 'Illustrious in general, and in the Church of England in particular, is the name of CONYERS MIDDLETON. Signal was, and is, the service rendered by him to the religion of Jesus. By that bold, though reverend, hand it now stands cleared of many a heap of pernicious rubbish, with which it had been incumbered and defiled.'[44] We may be forgiven for doubting Bentham's sincerity. Nevertheless, Middleton's achievement warrants consideration.

---

[42] Ibid. 58–9.

[43] As Grant points out: 'in the first place, it is not always easy to say what portions of the Gospels accurately reflect the actual words of Jesus himself. Secondly, Christianity's code of behaviour is not, for the most part, very original, being generally a reproduction of Jewish moral precepts. Thirdly, the whole field of ethics was only of subsidiary significance to Paul, being subordinated in his mind to the pre-eminence of faith' (ibid. 194).

[44] Bentham, *Summary View*, p. 2.

Middleton professed to hold the same opinion concerning the miracles of the early Church as John Locke, whom he quotes from the *Third Letter on Toleration* thus:

he, who will build his faith or reasoning upon miracles delivered by Church-Historians, will *find cause to go no farther than the Apostle's time, or else, not to stop at* Constantine's: since the writers after that period, whose word we take, as unquestionable in other things, speak of miracles in their time with no less assurance, than the Fathers before the fourth century: and a great part of the miracles of the second and third centuries stand upon the credit of the writers of the fourth.[45]

Middleton believed he was following Locke by mounting a similar defence of Protestantism, to secure it 'from being gradually undermined, and finally subverted, by the efforts of *Rome*'.[46] The tactic is to cast suspicion on the motives and credibility of the early Church leaders as a way of questioning the grounds upon which the Vatican Papacy stakes its claim to authority. Middleton's arguments can be briefly stated. First, there is insufficient evidence to believe in miracles performed by 'the Primitive Fathers' who succeeded Christ's Apostles as the leaders of the Church. Secondly, Christ gave 'extraordinary gifts' to the Apostles in order to assist them to overcome the prejudices of Jews and Gentiles and to support them against popular outrage and persecution. But when the work of establishing churches in all the chief cities of the Roman Empire was completed and a regular ministry made ready to succeed them, their need of miraculous powers declined and ultimately these were 'withdrawn', leaving the Gospel to make its way by its own inner strength.[47] In this manner Middleton sought to sweep the ground away from under the Vatican with its pretensions to a divinely sanctioned authority over all the Christian Churches.

We should perhaps note at this point that Hume's first *Enquiry*, containing the section 'Of Miracles', was published in the same year as Middleton's *Free Enquiry*. Many years later Hume confessed his chagrin in his autobiographical 'My Own Life' (1777): 'On my return from Italy, I had the mortification to find all England in a ferment on account of Dr. Middleton's *Free Enquiry*, while my performance was

---

[45] Quoted by Middleton, *A Free Inquiry into the Miraculous Powers*, p. iv, Middleton's emphasis. The reference to Locke is given as '3d on Tolerat. c. x. p. 269'.
[46] Ibid., p. iii.
[47] Ibid., pp. xxvii–xxviii.

entirely overlooked and neglected.'[48] There was every reason to compare the two books. Both tended to undermine the belief in miracles, but whereas Hume was raising methodological difficulties about the possibility of providing adequate historical proof of such occurrences, especially in a religious context, Middleton concentrated principally on the kind of historical evidence actually available. In the first place, he addressed his argument to those Protestants who believed in the occurrence of miracles, but who also held that the age of miracles was now past. This was a precarious position to take, he argued, since it was not readily apparent exactly where the dividing line was to be drawn. Middleton set his sights on this weakness, but in doing so, inadvertently perhaps, he could not help but cast doubt upon the credibility of the miracles of the New Testament. Although he never ventured to question the miracles performed by the Apostles, he attacked the credibility of similar accounts in the early Christian Church. In a series of highly damaging quotations, he exposed the credulity of 'the primitive Fathers', including such a respected figure as St Augustine, and went so far as to cite passages in which others appeared to be deliberately approving pious frauds. Not surprisingly, it was this aspect of Middleton's work that Bentham applauded. Even so, Middleton's critique did not go far enough. Bentham explained that one further step was still wanting:

One thorn still remained to be plucked out of the side of this so much injured religion, and that was, the addition made to it by *Saul of Tarsus*: by that *Saul*, who, under the name of *Paul*, has—(as will be seen) without warrant from, and even in the teeth of, the history of Jesus, as delivered by his companions and biographers the four evangelists,—been dignified with the title of *his* apostle. (*NP* 2)

It would be naïve to think that this was really the extent of Bentham's purpose, for the kind of arguments he brings against Paul's miracles could just as easily be employed against those of Jesus and his Apostles.

Bentham's position on miracles is most succinctly put in the *Table of the Springs of Action*: 'That which is most conformable to the experienced course of nature, say, to experience, is in every instance most probable. Error and mendacity are more conformable to experience than miracles are' (*Deon.* 27). In this respect Bentham had more in common with Hobbes and Hume than with Middleton. Though concerned to maintain

---

[48] Hume, 'My Own Life', in *Inquiry Concerning Human Understanding*, pp. 5–6.

the institutions of the Church under the political will of the sovereign, Hobbes was convinced that its revelatory foundations were less than secure. In *Leviathan* (pt. 3, ch. 37) he argued that it is the ignorance of natural causes which inclines persons to believe in supernatural events and, additionally, that those who lack experience of human tricks are the most easily deceived. Hume, too, in *The Natural History of Religion* (1757) ascribed the origin of religious beliefs to the ignorance of natural causes, adding that such beliefs were assisted by the incessant hopes and fears that actuate the human mind.[49] And in concluding the chapter of the *Enquiry* in which he had cast doubt on the belief in miracles he asserted that:

> the *Christian Religion* not only was at first attended with miracles, but even to this day cannot be believed by any reasonable person without one. Mere reason is insufficient to convince us of its veracity: and whoever is moved by *Faith* to assent to it, is conscious of a continued miracle in his own person, which subverts all the principles of his understanding and gives him a determination to believe what is most contrary to custom and experience.[50]

Bentham, as we shall see, followed closely Hume's analysis, but with one important exception: he was less interested in the pretension to truth of religious beliefs—which he denied—than in their disutility.

As with Hume, there is much common ground also between Bentham's attack on the belief in supernatural events and that provided by the Deists in the early part of the eighteenth century. Matthew Tindal (1655–1733) and John Toland (1670–1722), for instance, questioned the reality of revelation and denied the sufficiency of the proofs advanced on its behalf. Prophecies and miracles, they argued, do not convince that any communication had ever taken place between God and the inhabitants of this world.[51] Their aim, however, was to establish the sufficiency of natural religion as the basis for faith in a divinely created order. In contrast, Bentham believed that he had conclusively shown in the *Analysis* that there were no empirical grounds for the belief in natural religion. Now by attacking revelation, his intent was to complete his critique of the foundations of religious beliefs. What is thus revealed is his entirely secular view of the history of Christianity.

---

[49] Hume, *The Natural History of Religion*, in *Essays Literary, Moral, and Political*, pp. 516–17.

[50] Hume, *An Enquiry Concerning Human Understanding*, in *Enquiries*, sec. 10, pt. 2, p. 131.

[51] M. Tindal, *Christianity as Old as Creation* (1730); J. Toland, *Christianity not Mysterious* (1696), and *Pantheisticon* (1720).

According to Bentham the Bible has special problems which make it an unreliable source from which to draw rules of conduct. Early in his career (*c*.1774) he argued that we must be sure of four things before any credence can be given to Scripture: '1st. The general inspiration of the writer. 2ndly. The particular inspiration of the writer of that passage of his writing. 3rdly. The authenticity of the text: 4thly. The propriety of the interpretation put upon it: in a case where according to that interpretation the doctrine of it would appear to mitigate against a conclusion of utility' (UC 69/19).[52] Naturally, Bentham saw that the demands placed upon a reader of the Bible by these criteria would prevent the easy acceptance of the veracity of the stories it contained. More especially, however, his point was that non-utilitarian interpretations of Scripture were always suspect. Bentham made little of the latter when considering Paul's miracles, but questions regarding 'inspiration' and 'authenticity' were frequently raised in his discussion. In the main it is the disjunction between Paul's claims to be working directly under the command of God on the one hand and the knowledge we have of the Apostle's life and of the actual workings of the world on the other hand, which led Bentham to deny the sincerity of these claims.

Miracles, Bentham had written in the *Analysis*, are founded upon the extra-experiential belief that God interferes in earthly affairs, or more precisely, miracles are 'fictions by which the human intellect has . . . been cheated and overrun' (*An.* 103). Paul's revelation was a fraud of this nature, and Bentham believed that this could be established by reading Paul's own version of the events by which he came to the Christian faith. In the Epistle to the Galatians, for instance, Paul omits to explain the circumstances of his revelation and this draws the retort:

Revelation? revelation from Jesus? from the Lord, speaking from heaven? from the Almighty? On what occasion, in what place, at what time, in what company (if in any,) was it thus received? To no one of these questions does he venture

---

[52] Bentham's attitude fits well Duncan Howlett's characterization of the critical mind in theology, according to which faith in God based upon the Scriptures makes certain demands: first, belief in the validity of the human experiences of the divine which the Scriptures report; secondly, it demands belief in the veracity of those who have claimed to have had such experiences: thirdly, one has to believe in the trustworthiness of the scribe who wrote the story down; and, finally, that the transcript that has come down to our time is a full and accurate copy of the ancient original (Howlett, *The Critical Way in Religion*, p. 190).

to furnish an answer—or so much as an allusion to an answer. Why?—even because he had none to give. (*NP* 66)

The reason for Paul's omission, Bentham explains in his role of prosecutor, is because in attendance when this epistle was delivered were the Apostles and men acquainted with the Apostles, that is, 'men who would surely have denied what he said' (*NP* 68). In the eyes of the Apostles Paul's revelation was a fabrication and it is strange that modern Christians 'who . . . know nothing about it, take it for granted that it was all true' (*NP* 230). A man's will cloaked in revelation is apparently transformed into the will of God and it is claimed that it is the duty of everyone to obey this will. Accordingly, that man's will is obeyed and few bother to consider the grounds of the miraculous transformation.

Reviewing the scriptural testimony commonly cited to support Paul's miracles,[53] Bentham's analysis proceeds in typically peremptory and disdainful fashion. The blinding of Elymas the sorcerer (Acts 13: 6–12) is explained in terms of an agreement between Paul and Elymas to their mutual benefit. The healing of the crippled Lystra (Acts 14: 8–11) is accounted for by portraying Lystra as a vagrant hired 'for a few pence' to act a part designed by Paul. The exorcism of the Devil from Lydia (Acts 16: 16–18) cannot be substantiated since nobody saw the Devil, not even the historian who recorded the deed. The earthquake at Philippi which created the opportunity for Paul and Silas to escape from prison (Acts 16: 25–40) was brought about 'by means altogether natural'. Paul's vision at Corinth (Acts 18: 7–11) cannot be verified since only he was a witness to it. The exorcisms at Ephesus (Acts 19: 1–20) have no evidence of persons, times, or places to support them. The raising of Entychus from the dead (Acts 20: 7–12) is confuted by Paul's own account of the matter. The comforting of Paul by an angel (Acts 27: 20–5) is a lie formulated by Paul himself. His survival of a snake-bite (Acts 28: 1–6) is explained by the fact that the snake, at that moment, 'happened . . . not to be provided with a competent stock of venom' having 'already expended it upon some other object'. Finally, the curing of the father of Publius (Acts 28: 7–10) was not brought about by Paul's intervention but by the fever ceasing of its own accord; to which Bentham adds that, expecting the abatement of the fever, Paul timed his intervention well.

Reading Bentham's description of these miracles it is evident that a

---

[53] These miracles are discussed at length at *NP*, ch. 13, secs. 2–3, pp. 282–334.

person with implicit faith in the never changing laws of nature will always endeavour and be able to provide a naturalistic account for what others consider supernatural events. In fact, however, the effort occasionally borders on the realm of fiction itself. Quite simply, we do not have rational explanations for absolutely everything that occurs in the world, and from time to time the attempt to conjure up a plausible account of an unexpected happening places its own demands on the intellect. The recent phenomenon of the 'moving statue' of the Virgin Mary in Ballinspittle in Ireland, an occurrence witnessed by close to a hundred people on several different occasions, is a case in point. This posed something of a challenge to the sceptics, but a Department of Applied Psychology team from University College, Cork, came up with the explanation without too much trouble. People standing still for a lengthy period of time, they point out, tend to sway and what they are looking at appears to move. To this they add, unnecessarily one feels, that while in daylight the movement is checked against other objects, in darkness (when the Ballinspittle statue had been observed to move) this is not so. The effect, apparently, is exaggerated by the glare from the lights around the head of the Madonna. Explanations of this type put almost as much strain on the mind as the phenomenon from which they are meant to strip the mystery. Bentham, naturally, would have been well satisfied with an account of this order. The problem is that such explanations are never persuasive to a believer. Even if believers grant the natural character of all wordly causes, it is still open to them to say with the German theologian Friedrich Schleimacher (1768–1834) that a miracle occurs when God calls forth the sequence of natural causes leading to the miraculous result;[54] or with Thomas Malthus (1766–1834) that the same power which framed and executes the laws of nature, may change them all 'in a moment, in the twinkling of an eye'.[55] Nor does this contradict Humean scepticism concerning the nature and status of the laws of nature as dependent on, but not bound by, the empirical evidence of our senses. Ultimately, it depends upon what kind of answer is given to the question 'Does God exist?' As Paley says, 'In a word, once believe that there is a God, and miracles are not incredible.'[56]

---

[54] F. Schleimacher, *The Christain Faith* [*Der christliche Glaube nach den Grundsatzen der evangelischen Kirche*, 2 vols., Berlin, 1821–2], trans. H. R. Mackintosh and J. S. Stewart (Edinburgh, 1928). See W. L. Reese, *Dictionary of Philosophy and Religion: Eastern and Western Thought* (New Jersey, 1980), 513.

[55] T. Malthus, *An Essay on the Principles of Population* (London, 1798), 160.

[56] Paley, *A View of the Evidences of Christianity*, in *Complete Works*, i. 64.

To return to Bentham, his treatment of Paul's miracles was strictly in accord with his view that the Scriptures should be read as any other texts of history, that is, according to methods applied to all other areas and periods of human history. If miracles, being events which transcend or violate the laws of nature, do occur then we cannot draw a line, as Middleton and others do, and admit the truth only of a special class of reports of miracles, denying on general historical grounds that any other reports down through the ages could possibly be true. If we do this we give up the possibility of writing history altogether. On the other hand, if we accept the presupposition of a connection between natural causes and natural events then we must deal not with miracles but with stories of miracles. This was clearly Bentham's position and, as we have seen, he found no difficulty in supplying an account of such 'stories'. Some are explained in terms of natural events, some are dismissed because of the lack of corroborative evidence, while others are simply frauds perpetrated by Paul and explained in terms of subterfuge. Bentham's strong case against the belief in miracles, however, is much like that given by Hume in the essay 'Of Miracles': the ultimate standard is always derived from experience and observation and the wise will always proportion their belief to the evidence.[57] The business of miracles, writes Hume, is to tell us something about the supernatural world that we did not know before and could not have known without their aid. All our experience of this world, however, acquaints us with general laws of nature to which the miraculous must be an exception. The case for miracles is entirely founded upon human testimony, but experience has shown that the testimony of witnesses supporting the occurrence of supernatural events is notoriously unreliable.[58] Experience also shows that the common judgement of people down through the ages deprecate testimonies to the miraculous; to dismiss such reports as incredible is the usual response. Added to this, is the fact that different religions have different canons of miracles and all treat with scepticism the miracles of other religions.[59] From this Hume concluded that the majority of people supported him in the refusal to believe in miracles on any evidence that may be produced on their behalf. No amount of testimony in favour of belief in a miracle, he claimed, could conceivably balance, let alone outweigh, the

[57] Hume, *An Inquiry Concerning Human Understanding*, in *Enquiries*, sec. 10, pt. 1, pp. 114, 110.
[58] Ibid. 115–16.
[59] Ibid., pt. 2, pp. 119, 121–2.

evidence against it, or, what comes to the same thing, in favour of the law or laws of nature it allegedly violates.[60]

Though it is not known whether Bentham had read Hume's essay, the principles which inform his analysis of miracles clearly identify him as a critic from the same school of thought.[61] In a manuscript of *c.*1780, he explained 'the dirth of miracles' in the Holy Land at the time of the Crusades in terms of the unlikelihood of violations of the laws of nature (UC 169/78). It was 'ignorance of the powers of nature, of the extent of them, and of their limits', he recorded in his Commonplace Book of 1781–5, that caused the credulity of people regarding miracles (*Works*, x. 146). In *Not Paul, but Jesus* he defined a miracle as 'a special act of Almighty power, an effect produced by means disconformable to the uniform course of nature' (*NP* 326). Miracles, if they exist, must involve 'the suspension of the laws of nature' (*NP* 303). It is worth noting, however, that in condemning miracles in this fashion Bentham appeared to accept the existence of something he had previously denied. In the *Introduction* the 'law of nature' is described as something 'imaginary' and 'pretended', and denounced as 'a vague expression . . . productive of a multitude of inconveniences' (*IPML* 297–8 n., 276 n.). Yet, in *Not Paul, but Jesus*, Bentham does not hesitate to enlist the concept in his efforts to discredit the belief in miracles. None the less, this inexplicable inconsistency, as reprehensible as it may be, should not obscure the central thrust of Bentham's argument, which is that supposed miraculous occurrences are frequently amenable to very ordinary explanations. To persons whose judgement on the subject of miracles has for its ground 'the nature of the human mind as manifested by experience', miraculous appearances are to be accounted for on other grounds than God's interference in the affairs of the world (*NP* 303). Thus if a miracle were reported today, writes Bentham, we should not be surprised if persons who heard of it were sceptical. Who can doubt that if Paul's exorcism of Lydia were 'spoken of in some newspaper, as having happened in the present year' that it would, 'by its disconformity to the manifest state of things, and the whole course of nature, be regarded as too absurd and flagrantly incredible to deserve to be entitled to a moment's notice' (*NP* 308). Moreover, what is believed to have happened at so many centuries distance is accepted

---

[60] For a discussion of the background to the 18th-cent. controversy over miracles and Hume's role in it see Gaskin, *Hume's Philosophy of Religion*, ch. 7.

[61] For a comparison see the sections on Hume and Bentham in Benn, *The History of English Rationalism*, i, chs. 4, 7.

on the authority of the testimony of witnesses, but for the most part such evidence is at best of a circumstantial kind. Bentham's legal training is evident; Paul's revelation is based on flimsy and often conflicting evidence. 'On such evidence', he asks, 'would any judge fine a man a shilling?' And in an extraordinary outburst Bentham censures Locke and Newton, those heroes of the intellectual world, for believing Paul's revelation when the evidence was so slight: 'O Locke! O Newton! where was your discernment!' (*NP* 50). In the case of Paul's conversion, the evidence (or lack of it) he thought especially damning. Paul was supposed to have been accompanied on his journey to Damascus but his is the only testimony to his conversion—there is no 'collateral evidence' from any independent witnesses (*NP* 79, 89).

4. *The nature of evidence*

The legalistic turn of Bentham's analysis is in fact manifest throughout *Not Paul, but Jesus*. It appears that Bentham was so convinced that the lack of corroborating evidence was proof positive against Paul's miracles, that at one point he even thought it necessary to include in the work a section on 'the general foundations of the law of evidence', but subsequently discarded it presumably on account of the lack of space (*NP* 339). Bentham may even have been persuaded to adopt this kind of approach after reading Paley' *Horae Paulinae* which also paid close attention to the status and kinds of evidence that was available in support of the belief in miracles. Archbishop Whately, in a lecture of 1859, went so far as to praise Paley's text as 'an admirable exercise in the art of sifting evidence'.[62] Bentham's own weighing of the evidence in *Not Paul, but Jesus* seems to have been less judicious than the Reverend's, and decidedly less than he would have expected at the hands of Lord Mansfield or any of the other judges of his day. His approach can be faulted on several counts. First, the attempt to reveal the fraud supposedly perpetrated by Paul depends for much of its force on the contradictions and omissions Bentham finds in the competing accounts of his revelation. This notion of conflicting reports of an incident, however, is rarely accepted as conclusive proof that such and

---

[62] Quoted by E. Barker, 'Paley and his Political Philosophy', in *Traditions of Civility* (Cambridge, 1948), 199. After reading *NP* Thomas Wright Hill remarked in a letter to Bentham: 'I never before saw half so far into the nature and value of internal evidence' (UC 10/146, 8 Mar. 1824).

such an event did not take place, even in a court of law. For example, the conflicting newspaper reports of a natural disaster, such as a flood or an earthquake, do not make liars of the journalists who filed the reports. There might exist uncertainty as to the timing of an earthquake and the manner of its occurrence, but this would not lead the reader to doubt whether it had actually occurred. Even should the evidence of other witnesses subsequently make the occurrence of the event in question improbable, the natural reaction is not to move to disbelief of the original reports but to suspend judgement until some future occasion. Bentham's approach is more rigid: he declares that what seems 'improbable cannot be taken for truth' (*NP* 339), yet in every case where events seem improbable he moves directly to disbelief.

Secondly, the evidence brought to support Paul's revelation and his miracles is necessarily of a circumstantial kind, and by Bentham's strict legalistic standards inadmissable or, when faced with the conflicting experience of the laws of nature, insufficient proof of their actual occurrence.[63] But at one point Bentham himself admits that the evidence for Paul's guilt contained in Acts is itself of a circumstantial kind (*NP* 255).[64] For example, the evidence upon which he bases his claim that Paul was ambitious for power and wealth is entirely of a circumstantial kind: Paul was a persecutor of the Christians, he was aware of the power the Apostles wielded in that community and of the wealth to which they had access as leaders of the faithful, *ergo* Paul preached Christianity in order to gain a position of power among the Christians which would give him access to their wealth.

Thirdly, Bentham's employment of a legalistic notion of evidence cut across the grain of his natural science account in the *Analysis*, in which he claimed that all facts are established by experience and observation. In the earlier work his hostility was ably disguised by Grote, who gave the work the appearance of cool scientific detachment. This mask is absent from *Not Paul, but Jesus*. Bentham claimed that the truth of Paul's revelation could be accepted if reliable witnesses could

[63] In a courtroom 'no . . . circumstantial evidence should possess any such legitimately probative force as to warrant its addition, much less its substitution in place of that sort of information which belongs to direct evidence' (*Fall.* 27).

[64] Bentham goes on to claim that the evidence of Paul's Epistles is of a 'direct' kind, but for over 200 pages of text he has built a case against Paul almost entirely on the evidence he finds in Acts. For example, the arguments against Paul's miracles are entirely founded upon Bentham's reading of Acts with no reference to any other part of the New Testament.

be brought forward to testify to it (*NP* 89). But where witnesses to miraculous events—persons who have experienced or observed them—are brought to light their testimony is rejected: it is contradicted by other reports, there are motives which suggest that a fraud has been perpetrated, or we already have a reasonable explanation for the event in question in terms of the laws of nature.

The Unitarian minister John Jones was quick to note Bentham's hostility and the legal bent of his critique:

he displays the spirit, the artifices, and the hostility of an attorney-general; eager to criminate his victim, advancing positions without any regard to truth or consistence [*sic*], without any knowledge of the circumstances of the accused, and without any attention to the laws of the human mind. The volume throughout is penned in the exact style of an indictment or some legal instrument, loaded with useless peculiarities, intersected by parentheses, rendered voluminous and circuitous by continued repetitions.[65]

The assessment can hardly be faulted. Bentham's analysis of Scripture is an inappropriate one, applying as it does the tactics of the courtroom to the mysteries of religion. Paley's position strikes us as the more reasonable of the two: if no single piece of evidence could be said to prove the foundations of the Christian religion, neither could individual data disprove it.[66] When Bentham enlisted the methodology of natural science in his cause, he left little room for half-measures. If the mysteries of religion cannot be established on firm, indisputable empirical grounds then they cannot be reasonably believed; if they can be established on empirical grounds then they must be natural phenomena and can thus be explained according to the laws governing all natural phenomena. The argument is manifestly tautological but, as we have seen, Bentham was very willing on occasion to sacrifice logic for polemic where the claims of religion were concerned. Ultimately, his attack was bound to prove ineffective against both those religionists whose enthusiasm could not be breached by a critique purporting to stand on reason and empirical fact, and those who insisted that the age of miracles was not past. Bentham displayed the faults characteristic of the critical mind in this age, especially the naïve view that stories (of miracles) must be either wholly and straightforwardly true or simply lies perpetrated for reasons of self-interest. But it all served his purpose—to force individuals to question the foundations of their faith

---

[65] 'Ben David', *A Reply to two Deistical Works*, p. 2.
[66] See LeMahieu, *The Mind of William Paley*, p. 93.

and their supposed need for religious institutions. The foundations of religion, he claimed, are illusory, serving only to distract men and women from the pursuit of temporal happiness; religion must be abandoned and society refashioned strictly according to the dictates of utility free from all other-worldly considerations.

9

Christian Asceticism and Sexual Nonconformity

When a man attempts to search [?] this subject [he] may indulge his spleen without controul. Cruelty and intolerance, the most odious and most mischievous passions in human nature, screen themselves behind a mask of virtue.

UC 72/188

On the whole field in which Moses legislates with such peremptory asperity, Jesus is altogether silent. Jesus, from whose lips not a syllable favourable to ascetic self-denial is by any one of his biographers represented as ever having issued—Jesus, who, among his disciples, had one to whom he gave his confidence, and another in whose breast his head reclined and for whom he manifested his love—Jesus, who in the stripling clad in loose attire found a still faithful adherent after the rest of them had fled—Jesus, in whom the woman taken in adultery found a successful advocate: Jesus has in the field of sexual irregularity preserved an uninterrupted silence. Jesus was one person, Paul was another. The religion of Jesus was one thing, the religion of Paul another; where Jesus had been silent, Paul was vehement.

Bentham, The Theory of Legislation, App., 'Bentham on Sex',
p. 497

THOUGH laced with a liberal amount of Benthamic irony and dog-matically argued throughout, the *Analysis* and *Not Paul, but Jesus* are undeserving of the neglect which has traditionally been their due. Not only are they representative of Bentham's desire to expose exhaustively the rotten foundations upon which the English political establishment rested, they also reflect the comprehensive scope of the intellectual constructs of his social science and, therefore, the uncompromisingly secular view he took of the world. However, one aspect of his critique of religion in these books and their related manuscripts should be singled out for special attention: the attack on Christian asceticism and its attitude towards sexual pleasures. As we have seen, when assessed in terms of utility Bentham found Christianity defective as a moral guide. But in its antipathy to physical pleasures, and homosexuality in particular, he found an additional reason to characterize it as the enemy of human happiness under the utilitarian calculus. Two facts make it appropriate that this aspect of Bentham's work on religion should be considered at this point: first, he traced Christian asceticism to the teachings of St Paul; secondly, a large number of the manuscripts dealing with homosexuality were originally intended for a much extended version of *Not Paul, but Jesus*.

The manuscripts at University College London include thirty-six folios of notes in English and French on 'Sexual Nonconformity' (UC 74a/1–26; 73/90–100) probably dating from 1774, that is, around the time Bentham was busy with his assault on Blackstone's *Commentaries*; an essay on 'Paederasty' with related notes, almost certainly from 1785 (UC 72/187–205); 188 folios of notes dated 1814 and 1816 (UC 74a/35–222); and the planned third part of *Not Paul, but Jesus* (a continuation of part 2) with the title 'Asceticism: its repugnancy to the religion of Jesus' (UC 161b/215–523, dated 1816–18). The 1785 material has recently seen the light of day, edited by Louis Crompton.[1] From the 1814 and 1816–18 material C. K. Ogden has published an essay—with the slightly misleading title 'Bentham on Sex'—as an appendix to his edition of Bentham's *Theory of Legislation* (1931), and also several brief selections under the title 'Offences against Taste' as an appendix to his valedictory *Jeremy Bentham 1832–2032* (1932).[2] The manuscripts used by Ogden provide us with a continuation of the argument against Christian asceticism which was a feature of Bentham's line of attack in the *Analysis* and, even more so, in *Not Paul, but Jesus*.

The connection between the views on sex and the critique of religion in *Not Paul, but Jesus* is confirmed by two folios subheaded 'Not Paul but Jesus' (UC 74a/164–71) which are located among the manuscripts entitled 'Sex', and there is a divider at UC 74a/160, dated

---

[1] 'Jeremy Bentham's Essay on "Paederasty"', in 2 parts, ed. L. Crompton, *Journal of Homosexuality*, 3:4 (1978), 383–405, and 4:1 (1978), 91–107. Crompton has also published a comprehensive account of the chronology and content of the other MSS on homosexuality, though one which relegates the religious dimension behind legal and moral considerations (L. Crompton, *Byron and Greek Love: Homophobia in 19th Century England* (Berkeley, Calif., 1985), esp. pp. 38–62 and ch. 7).

[2] The MSS at UC 74a/35–222 are generally headed 'Sex', standing for 'Sextus' and quite possibly an allusion to Sextus Empiricus, the codifier of Greek scepticism of the 2nd and 3rd cents. AD, who (it is claimed by Voltaire) would have us believe that homosexual practices were 'recommended' by law in ancient Persia (see Crompton's introduction, 'Jeremy Bentham's Essay on "Paederasty"', pt. 1, p. 396).

April 1814, which has a note added from April 1816 indicating that the material was to be used in the second part of *Not Paul, but Jesus*. That this was clearly Bentham's intention is reinforced by a twenty-two page prospectus (UC 161a/14–19), prepared in late 1817 for William Beckford (1759–1844), the friend of Byron and author of *The History of the Caliph Vathec* (1784), whom he wanted to prepare the material for publication.[3] The proposed title for the work is characteristically Benthamic:

General idea for a work, having for one of its objects the Defense of the principle of *Utility*, so far as it concerns the liberty of Taste, against the conjoint hostility of the principle of asceticism and the principle of antipathy; and for its proposed title, proposed on the ground of expected popularity or at least protection against popular rage, Not Paul but Jesus. (UC 161a/1)

In the course of explaining the various strategies that might be employed in elucidating this vast and hazardous theme, Bentham suggests that several chapters be devoted to literary and historical topics, including an analysis of the treatment of homosexuals in the fiction of Smollett, Fielding, Wieland, Cumberland, and 'Madam Graffigny'.[4] Much mischief is caused, it seems, from the works of such authors: 'viz. by inflaming the antisocial antipathy'. By drawing attention to 'these instances of groundless censure' Bentham was optimistic that 'the violence of it may, perhaps, be more or less abated' (UC 161a/18).

In Bentham's proposed title for the generality of writings on homosexuality we see his tactic of placing the blame for the Christian attitude towards sexual matters at the feet of Paul in the hope of avoiding condemnation from an outraged public. And, true to his tactic of opposing Jesus to Paul, Bentham points out that one of the main sources of the prejudice against homosexuality are the teachings of Paul (UC 161a/14). The contrast between the anti-asceticism of Christ and the doctrinaire moralism of Paul is elaborated at great length in the later manuscripts. But, as Michael Grant has shown, many of Paul's precepts regarding women, marriage, and sex were not unusually severe given the historical context of his teachings.[5] They are about as illiberal as the general Jewish views of his day, and in some respects

---

[3] Crompton implies that there may have been other grounds for the attraction between Bentham and Beckford, whose homosexuality seems to have been beyond doubt (*Byron and Greek Love*, pp. 119, 269–71).

[4] Crompton informs us that 'Madam Graffigny' is a mistake for Thomas Gueulette (ibid. 273 n; see also p. 95 n.).

[5] Grant, *Saint Paul*, pp. 24–5.

perhaps less so. Women, Paul wrote, must obey their husbands, husbands must repay obedience with love, and neither must abuse, by fornication or perversion, the bodies that have been given them by God (Eph. 5: 25; Col. 3: 19; 1 Cor. 6: 18–19; 1 Thess. 4: 3–8; Eph. 5: 32). These are commonplace injunctions to be found in earlier and contemporary Jewish writings. What has to be said, however, is that Paul did state a decided preference for celibacy over the married state (1 Cor. 7: 1–2, 8–9), and this was in contrast to the general opinion of Judaism which emphasized the duty of procreation. According to Paul, it is better to concentrate on pleasing God, to which the unmarried man is better able to devote his time, than on pleasing one's wife. Nevertheless, Paul's attitude cannot be entirely attributed to his belief in the Second Coming and the importance of saving one's soul. His judgements on sexual offenders are too harsh for that (cf. 1 Cor. 5: 5; 15: 15 ff.). Indeed, as Grant says, Paul's general contempt for the flesh and its pleasures 'has made him one of the principal ancestors and models of all the monastic, puritanical, self-mortifications which flourished and proliferated during the subsequent centuries of antiquity and through the middle ages'.[6] It is this feature of Paul's legacy which invited Bentham's attack.

At the same time, we should also remember that when Bentham singled out Paul for blame for the corruption of Christianity it was a tactical device: his real target was Christianity itself (not exempting the teachings of Christ). When he criticized the religious exponents of utility in the *Deontology* (cf. esp. *Deon.* 166–71), for example, Bentham turned to the Scriptures for evidence of the ascetic attitude which characterized modern Christianity, but it was not Paul's Epistles that he referred to on this occasion, but 'the language therein ascribed to Jesus and his followers' (*Deon.* 168).

It was, of course, not only as a supplement to a critique of religion that the topic of homosexuality was of interest to Bentham. As the dates of the other manuscripts on the subject indicate, it was a subject with which he concerned himself at several stages in his life. Yet religion invariably constituted at least a part of his discussion whenever he felt compelled to consider it. An example of this marriage of issues can be seen in a fragment from 1831, under the heading 'J. B.'s Instruction for Living Happily or Not At All'. Here Bentham coupled

---

[6] Ibid. 25. Though Paul attacked asceticism in Col. 2: 20–3, he was widely read as an ascetic (for relevant passages see J. Passmore, *The Perfectibility of Man* (London, 1972), 85 n.).

together his last thoughts on the topics of suicide and sex, in the process combining two of his lifelong concerns—the critique of the religious sanction and the fight for toleration of those acts not harmful to others:

> To be happy or not to be happy at all: such is the option which Nature has given to every human being: . . .
>
> But to the taking the benefit of the option . . . two conditions . . . are necessary. 1. That . . . he should be exempt from those horrors—from those pains of mind . . . infused . . . by the opium of the existence of man in a life to come. 2. that in regard to pleasures, he should not . . . be delivered from . . . reaping . . . any pleasure which he exercises without producing thereby pain to a preponderant amount . . . either in his own person or the person of another . . .
>
> A notion still extensively prevalent . . . in England is that by which man . . . stands disbarred from . . . reaping, otherwise than in a particular manner, the pleasure of the sexual appetite. Full of inconsistency is this notion. It begins with an all-comprehensive interdiction of pleasure from this source. But supposing that interdiction universally . . . [adhered] to, there would be . . . an end of the human race.[7]

That religion is the 'opium' of the people was, of course, a thought that occurred to another notable atheist later in the century, but Bentham's disgust had its source in the nature of his utilitarian system. He was a staunch opponent of all so-called 'worldly activity' that did not have for its object the greatest happiness, and he particularly reviled that asceticism which isolated individuals and motivated them to take their pleasure in a perverse manner—a happiness based on self-deprivation.

Taking the manuscripts on homosexuality as a whole, then, we can say that Bentham's primary purpose was to advocate decriminalization of an activity which at the time was punishable by death. He argued that homosexual acts did not 'weaken' men, threaten the population, or threaten the institution of marriage, and he documented their public acceptance in ancient Greece and Rome. He opposed punishment on utilitarian grounds and venomously attacked ascetic sexual morality. It is this latter feature of the analysis which interests me here.[8]

---

[7] BL Add. MSS 33551/327–8, quoted by Mack, *Jeremy Bentham*, p. 213.

[8] For a fuller discussion of Bentham on homosexuality, but without any special emphasis on its connection to his views on religion, see Boralevi, *Bentham and the Oppressed*, ch. 3, and the already mentioned work by Crompton (above n. 1).

1. The ascetic attitude

To Bentham, the application of capital punishment for what he regarded as a socially harmless and pleasurable activity stood as a manifest perversion of the true purpose of legislation. Hence he sought to develop a theory to account for the existence of the virulent homophobia in the England of his day. He speculated on its causes and alleged that the reason why homosexuality was so severely punished was the existence of an irrational antipathy to pleasure generally and to sexual pleasure in particular. The chief cause could be traced to the fears and prejudices fostered by that Christian asceticism which had for its source the teachings of St Paul—sentiments which, through the agency of perverted legislation, had been encouraged among the general public.

Arguments against Christian asceticism were frequently voiced in enlightened French circles of the day,[9] but in England, where religion purported to ally itself with utility, hardly an angry word was spoken. As we have seen, it was Bentham's argument in the *Introduction* that the religious person, if he is true to his faith, will almost inevitably forgo certain pleasures which are harmless and thus effectively diminish the greatest happiness of the community. This was a persistent theme in Bentham's ethics. As early as *c.*1774 he was complaining that the Church's attitude to divorce and to fornication was irrational. 'The popular notion among religionists', he writes, 'is that men ought to . . . derive as little pleasure . . . as from every source so in particular from this chief source of pleasure as may be' (UC 69/26). And again, where the pleasures and pains of the future life are great those of the present life diminish proportionately:

If the former exceed the latter to a certain degree, . . . there can be no act of those that tends to accelerate the period at which the former will begin to be experienced but what it is a man's interest to do so soon as it is in his power, whatever may be the pains it may subject him to of the latter kind. Hence it is that a lively faith in the joys of a future life when anything near adequate to what is represented as the intensity of these . . . joys . . . is superior to all human and especially to all mortal punishment. (UC 140/2)

Asceticism mistakenly envisions the possibility of a radical break between the present and the future, allowing individuals to risk and

---

[9] See Gay, *The Enlightenment*, ii. 194–5.

even to court death. To the fanatic, says Bentham in the *Principles of the Civil Code*, the present is 'but a point', and he looks to the future not for its own sake only or even for that of his family, friends and neighbours, but on behalf of the whole species (*Works*, i. 360). The ascetic attitude has its source in the longing for uniformity, the desire to see one's own sentiments universally enforced. This is ultimately self-defeating, argues Bentham, because death marks the end of the life within which we desire. The threat of divine punishment prevents religious ascetics from participating in the engagements that occupy the rest of humankind. They view the prevailing relation between effort and reward as wholly unworthy and look only to the rewards of the afterlife, rewards entirely unlike those of the present life. Asceticism may not appear to be the adversary of utility, but in practice it is so, for to acquire its rewards individuals, at least to some degree, must free themselves from the sort of labour required by utility in this life.[10]

Bentham continued this attack on religious asceticism in the *Analysis*. Here the rule of God is shown to be highly defective so far as human happiness is concerned. People are duped by religionists into the belief that their suffering in this life is only a transient phase, and that any expenditure of suffering will be proportionately rewarded in the next life (*An.* 33). The notion that we have a duty to God is a convenient means to the perpetration of this fraud. Left alone individuals will naturally select that path which is most conducive to their temporal felicity, but thrust any other course upon them and a sacrifice of earthly happiness is the necessary consequence (*An.* 41). To convince those about you of your attachment to the Deity it seemed that only pain would do. In the past tortures such as flagellation and the wearing of sackcloth and ashes were expected, and today the Church still enforced 'useless acts of self-denial', like fasting, celibacy, abstinence from personal and innocent comforts, the gratuitous surrender of property and labour, and the surrender of dignity and honours (*An.* 68–70). Added to this, innocuous pleasures proscribed by the dictates of religion are not fully enjoyed; doubts and opposing motives combine to temper their enjoyment, and afterwards shame and regret frequently follow. What pleasure is enjoyed is purchased by antecedent and subsequent unhappiness (*An.* 75). Those who do not believe in a rewarding and punishing God are an obvious target for the

[10] In the foregoing discussion of asceticism I have benefited greatly from Rosenblum, *Bentham's Theory of the Modern State*, esp. pp. 60 ff.

antipathy of the religious fanatic. Where unbelievers exist the religionist's influence is questioned and undermined. Hence he persecutes the unbeliever, who in turn looks on the believer with contempt; the consequence is 'an immense extension of the principle of antipathy' (*An.* 76). Even against those who are merely negligent in the observance of religious duties the religious fanatic is unremitting in his bitterness. He has a vested interest in the maintenance of religious practices: 'Ascetics reposing their title to the esteem of mankind on a voluntary abnegation of particular enjoyments, naturally endeavour to fasten obloquy on all who indulge in them. Of course the ascetics hate him whom their interest leads them thus to injure' (*An.* 79). The nagging suspicion that they may be wrong plagues religious fanatics, but this secret apprehension only quickens the resolve to bring about a conformity of opinion on the subject. Doubts are 'evinced by their reluctance to allow to the sinner the unmolested profit or loss of his own temerity'. The compulsion to establish conformity increases in intensity in proportion as religious practices diverge, and is characterized by the 'dogmatical assumption' of the validity of one's own tenets and to 'the bitterest invective against all who question them' (*An.* 80). To attest to the rectitude of his own choice of Deity the religionist, wherever he is able, 'musters under the divine banners all the temporal force which he himself can command for the purpose of crushing the rival worshippers, and terminating the influence of the unseen being on whom they rely' (*An.* 82). Finally, the introduction of antipathies into the moral code by religion has aroused an 'aversion towards improvement' among the propagators of Christianity: 'fresh facts', it is claimed, disrupt *the course of nature*, supposed to be established by the Deity' and 'break in upon the laws of nature'. New knowledge, therefore, is seen as an obstacle to God's will, an attempt to alter the laws of nature which God has designed for the universe. In opposing the application of new discoveries, however, the religious fanatic opposes the augmentation of human comfort. It is true, Bentham concedes, that the diffusion of knowledge has weakened the prohibitive tendencies of religion, but the spirit which silenced the discoveries of Galileo lives on and is still a powerful source of human misery (*An.* 90–2). For these reasons religion itself is responsible for a great portion of the unhappiness in the world. Its propagators direct the hatred of people to actions not really harmful to them, and thus religion is seduced from its only legitimate function—that of deterring injurious conduct (*An.* 85).

2. *'Paulism' and decriminalization*

One of the chief pleasures of which religious asceticism was the implacable enemy, according to Bentham, was the pleasure of sexual intercourse. This matter was first taken up by him as part of the study of the penal code he began in the 1770s; it was given a special twist by focusing on the problems posed by homosexuality and 'paederasty'. In doing so Bentham was unique in an age which delighted in the eroticisms of Casanova, but shied away from public debate over the secrets of the bedroom. Bentham's defence of homosexuality was strikingly at odds with contemporary standards of allowable promiscuity, and sensitive to this he quietly suppressed the material lest it jeopardize the success of his other work. That he originally intended to publish, however, there is no question. In an unpublished 'advertisement' for this, his first essay on the subject, he writes:

I have trembled at the thoughts of the indignation that must be raised against the Apologists . . . of a Crime that has been looked upon by many and those excellent men as one among the blackest under Heaven—But the Dye is now cast, & having thus far pursued . . . with undeviating fidelity the principles (of general utility) I at first adopted, I will not (It shall not be said) . . . abandon them from considerations of personal danger. (UC 74a/4)

The thrust of Bentham's remarks in these manuscripts is that the penalties for homosexuality stipulated by English law are unjustifiable. Arguments based on natural law—that homosexuality is contrary to nature—and those based on the 'positive' law of God were singled out for special attention and contrasted with those based on the 'greatest happiness of the greatest number'. Taking this line, Bentham directed remarks against several writers, from Puffendorf and Thomasius to Montesquieu and Blackstone, against whom he enlisted the support of 'the illustrious Beccaria' (UC 74a/3–9). Later in these manuscripts, in a section under the intriguing title 'Castrations to Mr B's [?] . . . by the Daemon of Socrates' (UC 74a/15–16),[11] he reflected at length on the great loss to philosophy had Socrates suffered the fate of English law for his 'irregular' behaviour. But Bentham was also concerned in these

---

[11] Burns and Hart render the title as 'Castrations to Mr. Bentham's . . . [etc.]' (*Comm.* p. xxxv), but Boralevi is probably correct that the full title is 'Castrations to Mr Blackstone's *Commentaries* by the Daemon of Socrates', and that the MSS are connected with *Comm.* ch. 1, sec. 3, which is a discussion of Divine Law (Boralevi, *Bentham and the Oppressed*, p. 67).

manuscripts with the fickle attitude towards homosexuality shown by men when forced to offer an opinion on the matter:

> Another spectacle amusing enough is, to observe the distress men are under to keep the peace between two favourite prejudices that are apt cruelly to jar: they are [one] in disfavour of this vice; the other in favour of antiquity, especially ancient Greece . . . Sometimes they will dissemble and shut their eyes against the fact—sometimes they will attempt to question it. (UC 73/94)

Later in life (1824–5) in a manuscript headed 'Sexual Eccentricities', Bentham was not so circumspect in his choice of words: the banning of sexual pleasure was nothing less than an act of tyranny (UC 68/12).[12] At this early stage in his career, however, prudence easily carried the day and Bentham left the subject alone for another ten or so years, whereafter he again briefly considered it, jotting down his thoughts this time in both French and English.

It was in these manuscripts of the mid-1780s that Bentham set out his most persuasive case for reforming those sections of the penal code dealing with homosexuality. Here the plea for toleration of 'unnatural' acts is presented both from a legal perspective and as an argument against the rigid moral code of Christianity. Christianity, it seems, provides the chief support for the policy of outlawing homosexuality. Religious asceticism was clearly the enemy Bentham had in view:

> This act is one amongst others which some men and luckily not we ourselves have a strong propensity to commit. In some persons it produces it seems, for there is no disputing it, a pleasure: there needs no more to prove that it is God's pleasure they should abstain from it. For it is God's pleasure that in the present life we should give up all manner of pleasure, whether it stands in the way of another's happiness or not.[13]

Pleasure, Bentham went on to argue, is never allowed by the religionist for its own sake but only for the sake of something else, which he calls an advantage or a good but which does not present any idea of pleasure. Even the heterosexual appetite, necessary to the end of the preservation of the species, is only tolerated in so far as it serves this end. Otherwise it is not encouraged and is often discouraged by offering great rewards for celibacy.

---

[12] At UC 68/10–18, an appendix to his 'Penal Code', Bentham briefly recapitulates his attack on asceticism and his arguments for a change in the laws. The first 4 pages are dated 20 Dec. 1824, and the remainder 13 Jan. 1825.

[13] 'Jeremy Bentham's Essay on "Paederasty" ', pt. 2, p. 95.

The attitude of religionists to the sexual appetite has an influential bearing on the state of popular opinion on the subject, but their antipathy is 'grounded only in prejudice' and this raises a profound problem for the legislator who is expected to fall in with this prejudice and dissuade persons so inclined from indulging in the practice.[14] The danger Bentham perceives is that where the place of utility, the only sufficient reason for punishment, is usurped by prejudice, interminable punishment is licensed and 'one should never know where to stop'. Yet the moral disapproval produced by the general antipathy to the practice was already a greater punishment than could be justified.[15]

Nor does the idea that God punished homosexuals by putting Sodom and Gomorrah to fire serve as an example to be copied by human legislators, as Blackstone had argued.[16] Leaving aside the fact that it is an assumption that the people of Sodom and Gomorrah were punished for permitting the practice of homosexuality, the only legitimate ground for God's punishment is that the practice was prejudicial to the welfare of society. If the practice is not detrimental to the well-being of the community then, says Bentham, 'there can be no other reason for society to meddle with it'.[17] If, on the other hand, God punished the act in question on grounds other than the fact that it proved to be prejudicial to public interest, then there exists no reason for us to emulate him. Our reason for punishing an action should only be the utilitarian one that it caused unhappiness; God's reason for punishing, if it is not this, cannot be known by us. Hence, it is not a sufficient justification that because God punished such and such a practice it is also our duty to punish it. Bentham's logic is inescapable:

If any man, under the notion of its being agreeable to God, would do any act that is prejudicial to society, he should produce a particular commission from God given him in that individual instance. If a man without a special commission from God is to be justified in doing any violent act that has ever been done by a special commission from God, a man might as well kill his son because God commissioned Abraham to kill Isaac.[18]

Homosexuality, then, was outlawed merely because of a conventional prejudice. In a sardonic passage Bentham pondered what might be the consequence if it were thought sinful to scratch an itch: 'It is

---

[14] 'Jeremy Bentham's Essay on "Paederasty"', pt. 2, p. 97.   [15] Ibid. 98.

[16] Blackstone had argued in the *Commentaries* that the death penalty for 'buggery' was divinely sanctioned by the biblical story of Sodom and Gomorrah (see Crompton's introduction, 'Jeremy Bentham's Essay on "Paederasty"', pt. 1, p. 384).

[17] Ibid., pt. 2, p. 104.'   [18] Ibid. 105.

wonderful that nobody has ever yet fancied it to be sinful to scratch where it itches, and that it has never been determined that the only natural way of scratching is with such and such a finger and that it is unnatural to scratch with any other.'[19]

Having set down these thoughts on homosexuality Bentham again put the subject aside, only to return to it in the years 1814 and 1816–18 when it took on a new significance in conjunction with his writings on religious matters around the same time. The manuscript pages dated 1814 are headed 'Penal Code' and those dated 1816–18 are headed 'Sex' (i.e. Sextus)[20] or 'Not Paul'. This second group of manuscripts establishes the connection between Bentham's discussion of sexual nonconformity and those strictures against asceticism which he intended to publish as a second (and possibly third) part to *Not Paul, but Jesus*. Once again he prefaced his remarks with an acknowledgement of the risks he would be taking when these manuscripts saw the light of day:

In the present has been found one of those unhappy occasions on which, in his endeavours to render service to his fellow-creatures, a man must expose himself to their reproach . . . Never did work appear from which in the way of personal advantage and disadvantage, never one from which in the way of reputation, never one from which at the hands of public opinion a man had so much to fear, so little to hope.[21]

Once again Bentham decided not to go ahead with his plan to publish these manuscripts as an independent treatise, preferring to use them as part of the intended sequel to *Not Paul, but Jesus*. Their connection with the earlier unpublished material on the same theme, however, is readily apparent.

Bentham followed Helvétius, among others, in arguing that Christians had made the mistake of following the teachings of St Paul and had wrapped up sexual matters in a whole series of disapproving tenets which detracted from the general happiness of the community.[22] Asceticism, Bentham never tired of saying, is not Christianity but

[19] Ibid. 107. Curiously enough Bowring records that Bentham 'suffered much from a cutaneous complaint, the itching of which caused a perpetual irritation'. On one occasion while suffering from this complaint Bentham informed his literary executor that he often dreamed 'of a city, the whole of whose inhabitants have no other enjoyment than seeking to free themselves from the suffering which itching occasions' (*Works*, x. 566).

[20] See above n. 2.

[21] Bentham, *The Theory of Legislation*, App., 'Bentham on Sex', p. 474.

[22] See Smith, *Helvétius*, p. 135.

'Paulism'. The distinction between the teachings of Christ and those of Paul he rehearsed again in these manuscripts on sexual non-conformity (though here he added an irreverent suggestion or two regarding the disposition of Christ himself). He contrasted Jesus with a true ascetic like John the Baptist, pointing to Jesus's rejection of fasting, his liking for wine and enjoyment of feasts, his Sabbath-breaking, and his defence of adulterous women. The crucial message then follows: nowhere did Christ condemn relations between men.[23] Christ's frequent references to the fate of Sodom and Gomorrah are dismissed as irrelevant: he makes not 'the slightest allusion . . . to the propensity in question [as] the sin by which the calamity is produced' (UC 161b/421).[24] And for all their attachment to the story of the destruction of the two cities, nor do the prophets Isaiah, Jeremiah, Ezekiel, Amos, or Zephaniah connect the fate of Sodom with homosexual relations between its inhabitants (UC 161b/464–74).[25]

Bentham's next step, as Louis Crompton has said, was far more daring,[26] and he showed good sense in holding it back from publication during his lifetime. From a close examination of the Gospel of St John, in which the 'beloved disciple' speaks of the particular affection Jesus felt for him, he implied that John and Jesus may have been lovers. It was, he allowed, a topic of 'extreme delicacy' from which 'good taste and self-regarding prudence would require us to turn aside'. On the other hand, human happiness, truth, and 'sound principles of penal justice' demanded that it be discussed (UC 161b/475).[27] What evidence is there to substantiate the implied homosexual relation between Christ and his disciple John, 'in whose breast his head reclined and for whom he manifested his love'?[28] It is necessarily of a circumstantial kind:

If the love which in these passages Jesus was intended to be represented as bearing towards this John was not the same sort of love as that which appears to have had place between David and Jonathan, the son of Saul, it seems not easy to conceive what can have been the object in bringing it to view in so pointed a manner accompanied with such circumstances of fondness. (UC 161b/476)[29]

[23] Bentham, *The Theory of Legislation*, App., 'Bentham on Sex', p. 497.
[24] Quoted Crompton, *Byron and Greek Love*, p. 275.
[25] Ibid. 278.
[26] Ibid.
[27] Ibid.
[28] Bentham, *The Theory of Legislation*, App., 'Bentham on Sex', p. 497.
[29] Quoted Crompton, *Byron and Greek Love*, p. 278.

The conclusion Bentham draws is that the kind of love between Christ and John was different to the fondness he had for the other Apostles: 'For of this sort of love, whatever sort it was, he and he alone is in these so frequently recurring terms maintained as being the object.' Nor could it be said that Christ's affection for John was due to 'any superiority of value' in his preaching: for example, 'nothing is to be found in Saint John by which he can stand in comparison with Saint Peter, and on no occasion is the rough fisherman to be seen "leaning in the bosom of Jesus" or "lying on his breast"' (UC 161b/476–7).[30]

On Bentham's interpretation, then, Jesus saw little harm in anything that gave pleasure: he knew that happiness is composed of pleasures or it is empty, and that each person is the best judge of what gives him or her pleasure (*NP* 394).[31] What Paul and the modern adherents of his teaching find pleasurable is their own affair, but they should not be suffered to impose their prejudices on others.

It would be misleading to argue that Bentham's case against the imposition of legal penalties for 'sexual irregularities' is reducible solely to his antagonism towards religious asceticism. Such hostility clearly formed a significant part of it, but he also argued that homosexuality was not the 'unnatural' act that conventional wisdom supposed.[32] There was no more reason for punishing heresy in sexual preference than heresy in religion; the one like the other must be decided on the grounds of general utility.[33] Utility is the test of whether the legislator should interfere in social affairs, hence it must be decided whether the practice of homosexuality is 'preponderately [*sic*] noxious' to the general happiness or not. Bentham's conclusion quickly follows: it is entirely the affair of the individual if he thinks it worth risking his reputation for the gratification of this pleasure; the legislator has no business in the matter.[34]

---

[30] Ibid. 279. There is another incident in the Gospels employed by Bentham to impute homosexual tendencies to Christ: this is the story mentioned by Mark (14: 50–2) of the boy Bentham called the 'stripling clad in loose attire' (see the quotation at the head of this chapter) who was in attendance at the crucifixion. In a column headed 'The Portfolio of a Man of Letters' (161b/489) Bentham recalled a cryptic reference to Mark's Gospel in the *Monthly Magazine* of 1811 to 'the episode of the cinaedus' (i.e. boy prostitute), and suggested a romance of sorts between Jesus and the anonymous youth. At the very least, the presumption is that Jesus did not find the boy's homosexuality offensive. This is discussed by Crompton, *Byron and Greek Love*, pp. 280–3.

[31] See also the long quotation from UC 161b/497, ibid. 282–3.

[32] Bentham, *The Theory of Legislation*, App., 'Bentham on Sex', pp. 479–80.

[33] Ibid. 492.

[34] Ibid. 477–8.

In fact, Bentham held the language of the penal code partially responsible for the arousal of public disapproval of the practice. Imagination and not reason, he claimed, has been responsible for assigning the terms 'natural' and 'unnatural', 'purity' and 'impurity' when referring to sexual affairs, and it is by the power of these signs that imagination has been guided. But these terms are fictions, psychological ideas productive of confusion. The notion of an impure or filthy body is only clear if what is meant is that it has dirt attached to its surface, but the idea of an impure mind is altogether a different proposition which cannot be reduced to a real entity. Moreover, there is no necessary connection between the idea of an impure body and the idea of an impure mind. Yet this is precisely what is suggested by the legislation governing this matter: 'when from impurity in the body the mind is deemed impure, and upon the fundamental error correspondent practical errors are deduced, then comes the practical error and the practical misery its results [*sic*].'[35] This is 'false logic', the consequence of 'the wandering of the imagination', which is only compounded by the belief that the mind can be rendered pure again by persecution. Bentham explains the process thus:

In so far as the body is covered with filth, the soul . . . is rendered impure; by being exposed to the fire some bodies that had been covered with filth are purified; . . . in so far as the soul is defiled, it is desirable that it be purified; by being exposed to the fire some bodies that have been defiled are purified; therefore from the impurity in question by the exposure of the whole body in question to the fire, the soul that belongs to it will be purified.

Upon the strength of this logic, undefinable is the multitude of innoxious individuals, whose bodies have been consigned to the excruciating and devouring flame.[36]

This false logic Bentham believes can be traced to the language used by the legislator; it creates a confusion which readily aids the antipathetic in their persecution of those who indulge their sexual appetite and this is productive of unnecessary amounts of human misery.

Yet, whatever Bentham can find to criticize in the law for the perpetuation of this undesirable situation, it is still religion which is the chief culprit in the issue. In the law of Moses religion for the first time committed itself to antipathy to homosexuality, and death was the stipulated penalty (Lev. 20: 13). But, 'Under Moses, as under

---

[35] Ibid. 482–3; see also Crompton, *Byron and Greek Love*, pp. 262–3.
[36] Bentham, *The Theory of Legislation*, App., 'Bentham on Sex', p. 483.

Bramah', writes Bentham 'the list of impurities . . . created out of physical impurities or out of nothing was a labyrinth without an end.'[37] Is not the law of Moses repeatedly scorned by Christ? Moreover, a close examination of the Old Testament revealed that in practice the law governing homosexuality was often disregarded (Judg. 19: 21–3; 2 Kings 23: 7; UC 161b/478, 454–5).[38] So why should the laws of England demand death for homosexuals? It is surely a mistaken view to insist that the Mosaic law was meant to give 'direction to practice among nations so far advanced in improvement as even the least advanced of nations of Europe in these our times' (UC 161b/444).[39] The principal cause of proscription is the prejudice derived from religious asceticism, particularly as it comes down to us from Paul. The religious ascetic tolerates heterosexuality because the continuance of the species depends upon it, but homosexuality, lacking the propagation of the species to justify it, is pure pleasure and is therefore condemned:

Notwithstanding the sort of discountenance thrown by St. Paul on the most completely regular mode of gratifying the appetite—a sort of oversight in which the monastic orders had their rise—it seems, according to the reasoning of the religionists, not unreasonable to conclude that the gratification of the appetite in the productive mode, may, notwithstanding any pleasure with which it may happen to be unavoidably attended, be tolerated, but in the case of those modes of gratification of which contribution cannot be the accompaniment, then the cause of tolerance has no place.[40]

Intolerance arises when the religious ascetic, whose overriding aim is to recommend himself to God, treats his own enemies as if they were God's. But the human suffering caused by persecution must be measured against the consideration that homosexuality is a source of pleasure to men and of this enjoyment each must be his own judge.

3. *Religious asceticism* versus *sexual freedom*

The problem posed by homosexuality was somewhat distorted by Bentham when he reduced it to a choice between religion and sexual freedom. In part this is because he believed that the religious ascetic

---

[37] Ibid. 481.
[38] Cited Crompton, *Byron and Greek Love*, pp. 279, 275–6. [39] Ibid. 275.
[40] Bentham, *The Theory of Legislation*, App., 'Bentham on Sex', p. 481.

would inevitably attempt to impose his beliefs on others thereby causing great human suffering. The assumption involved in his argument is that the religious ascetic will always be a fanatic concerned to impress his belief on others. However, there is no necessary connection between religious beliefs and fanaticism, and it is not impossible to conceive of a great number of Christians who would keep their beliefs private and respect the rights of others to do so.

Bentham offered a stronger line of argument in the unpublished manuscripts for *Not Paul, but Jesus*, in which he came very close to arguing that the pleasures of sex *ought* to be preferred to the pleasures of religion, not only because they are less harmful, but because they are greater in intensity and add a greater quantity of pleasure to the general stock of happiness than it is possible for religious pleasures to add.[41] Nevertheless, by arguing in this manner, as Professor Steintrager has said, Bentham seems to have abandoned the axiom that each person is the best judge of his or her own interest. If this is so it is certainly ironic, since his declared purpose in criticizing religion was to emancipate minds from dependence on religion. Bentham certainly did not think that he had abandoned this axiom. Perhaps the correct reading of his position is that the individual must not be taken to be the *only* judge of his own interest.[42] The individual may judge incorrectly,[43] and this leaves room for that form of influence which Bentham thought useful and efficacious—the influence of the understanding on the understanding.

[41] BL Add. MSS 29809/483–91, cited Steintrager, 'Language and Politics', p. 11.

[42] Ibid. We should also note the following remark by Bentham: 'With a benefit of a certain degree of experience it may be delivered in the character of a general proposition [that] every man is a better judge of what is conducive to his own well-being than any other man can be' (*Deon.* 131).

[43] Bentham, *The Theory of Legislation*, App., 'Bentham on Sex', p. 493.

Conclusion

Atheism and the Secular Utilitarian Society

IT is time now to take stock. Though the preliminary work, in several important respects, had been done long before, between 1809 and 1823 Bentham conducted an exhaustive examination of religion with the declared aim of extirpating religious beliefs from the minds of England's citizenry. Applying the utilitarian test at every turn, his critique was squarely focused upon the supposed perniciousness of the reverence for other-worldly beings, for the authority of 'holy books', and the sanctity of churches and their clerical officiates. However, it cannot be said that Bentham's writings on religion profoundly penetrated their subject-matter. Bentham was both a moral atheist, who sought to disprove the utility of the belief in an immortal soul and in an afterlife of rewards and punishments, and an ontological atheist, who denied the existence of God and of a life beyond the world of material reality. His unspirituality, if we can be allowed the term, was a central feature of his system, and this manifested itself in his deliberate avoidance of any genuine attempt to come to terms with the spiritual content of religion and its meaning for the pious believer. How then are we to understand Bentham's critique of religion? The answer is that it only makes sense when viewed against the larger canvas of his aspiration to make his secular social science serve the needs of the Utilitarian society of the future. Taken together, Bentham's views on religion constitute a substantial part of the negative side of his plans for the construction of an entirely secular and rigorously Utilitarian society.

Bentham's battle with religion began in modest fashion with the fragmentary jottings on the practice of imposing subscription to articles of faith, but in its subsequent development, in the writings on ethics and jurisprudence as well as in the later works on the ecclesiastical establishment and on natural and revealed religion, it traversed a whole range of issues. Some of them were of pressing political concern, as when he defended the demands of religious nonconformists for political rights; others were of only incidental interest, as when he took Christianity to task for its intolerant attitude to homosexuality; but always the aim in view was to test the institutions, practices, rituals, doctrines, and beliefs of religion against the standard of utility. The results of this test were invariably negative and stand as a compelling testimony both to Bentham's unmitigated atheism and to his desire to sweep away all religion in order to construct society anew according to the principles of his secular utilitarianism.

The critique of organized religion was always the strong arm of Bentham's offensive. His attacks on the redundancies and pernicious-ness of subscription to articles of faith and of compulsory oaths, on penal laws against religious dissent, and on the Common Law crime of blasphemy, and his defence of the non-sectarian Lancasterian schools were all undertaken against a Church determined to stem progress toward a more tolerant (and, admittedly, secular) society. Even the discussion in *Church-of-Englandism* of the political motives of the bishops in opposing seemingly rational proposals for reform was not entirely misconceived. Were not the bishops the ones who watered down the Unitarian Toleration Bill in 1813, who helped to delay the repeal of the Test and Corporation Acts, and who threw their weight behind the government whenever the tide of seditious, libellous, or blasphemous literature seemed to threaten the traditional order of society?[1] But for all we can say on behalf of Bentham's radical campaign against the Anglican Establishment, the nature of his analysis of reli-gious beliefs is a good deal more problematic. Bentham could not countenance any common ground between the spiritual world of reli-gion and the perceptible world of physical experience; they are, he believed, mutually exclusive worlds. Indeed, in taking his stand on the apparently solid ground of the latter, he confidently declared the non-existence of the former. All his tools of analysis—his commitment to empiricism, nominalism, and descriptive theory of language—served to convince him beyond any shadow of doubt that the life of the spirit is an illusion. Unlike the philosophical sceptic Hume, with whom he had so much else in common, Bentham could not suggest that judgement be suspended when measuring the claims of religion against the standards of empirical science. Rather, like his close friend, the radical Place, he moved quickly and confidently to an outright denial of the truth of

---

[1] See e.g. *Fall.* 215–16, 'Effect Good Government; Obstacle represented as a cause, Station of the Bishops in the House of Lords'.

religion, of the existence of an immortal soul, of a future life, and of the existence of God.[2]

1. Faith and metaphysics

At the heart of the confidence with which Bentham condemned religion lay the scientific framework of his view of the world. From time to time his attacks on religion became a trifle erratic, but he was at least consistent in his naturalism, his insistence that every branch of science be anchored in experience, above all the science of divinity. It is to this source, also, that we can trace Bentham's reluctance to grant any credence to piety as a motivating factor for the truly religious person. More often than not he would dismiss such motivation as either reducible to self-interest or founded in illusion. But was it not the height of injustice for him to suppose that philanthropists inspired by religious beliefs—like the saintly philanthropist John Howard (1726–90), with whom he shared an interest in penal reform,[3] and Bentham's long-time friend William Wilberforce (1759–1853)—tried to do good in the world simply from fear of Hell and hope of Heaven? And to dismiss something as illusory is not to come to terms with the phenomenon itself. Bentham showed little understanding of the distinction between reasoning, which is based on knowledge and experience, and faith, which involves the total personality in submission to the highest ideal. This is not to say that there is no reasoning to be done in religion or theology. As Stephen Toulmin has explained, it is only to mark the differences between the kinds of reasoning that one expects in the realm of science, on the one hand, and in religion, on the other. But what is clear is that the reasons for one's religious beliefs are not and cannot be given in terms of scientific proofs or rational demonstration;

---

[2] Concerning his early doubts about religious beliefs, Place wrote: 'Hume's writings put an end to them for ever, all doubt vanished and I was ever after at ease on this subject' (*Autobiography*, p. 121).

[3] The ideas for the Panopticon scheme had their source in Bentham's association with Howard in the cause of penal reform in the 1770s. It was from 1773 on that Howard devoted himself entirely, for the remaining 17 years of his life, to the idea of prison reform. When William Eden (1744–1814) introduced a bill into the Commons in 1778 demanding the erection of 2 prisons of a new type, Howard was appointed one of 3 'overseers' to implement the terms of the bill and Bentham, inspired by Howard's book on *The State of the Prisons in England and Wales* (1777), responded with a pamphlet entitled *A View of the Hard Labour Bill* (1778; *Works*, iv. 3–35).

ultimately all comes back to faith.[4] When it fulfills its proper role reason plays an important part in religious life. It can, for instance, be employed to criticize theories that are proposed as ruling out a rational belief in the reality of God. On the positive side, it can be used to fill out the implications of what is known by faith—'faith seeking under-standing', according to Anselm—and to systematize what is believed on the basis of faith.[5] But when discussing religious matters we must seek less for rational demonstration than for 'evidences' of their truth. For Bentham reason, or rather science, tells us what is and what is to be expected. Faith, on the other hand, as Paul put it in the Epistle to the Hebrews (11: 1), is concerned with 'the confidence of things which are hoped for, and the certainty of things which are not seen'. In part it was the basic incredibility of the news he had to convey that accounts for Paul's stress on the necessity of faith—faith had to be strong enough to believe in the apparently unbelievable. For instance, Christ's salvation cannot be extended to us unless we believe that 'Christ brings righteousness for everyone who has faith' (Rom. 10: 4). And again: 'The Gospel is the saving power of God for everyone who has faith . . . because here is revealed God's way of righting wrong, a way that starts from faith and ends in faith' (Rom. 1: 16–17). These were utterances by which the Methodist John Wesley (1703–91) 'felt my heart strangely warmed'.[6] Christianity cannot demonstrate its truth in philosophical, much less legalistic, terminology. It would be impossible for Paul to prove that the vision he claimed to have experienced on the road to Damascus had been an objective fact. Christianity must rely upon faith in the irrational (the non-rational, as Hume saw it), that is, upon faith which defies any purely intellectual standard of assessment. Hence, appeals to rationality are wholly beside the point. As Matthew Arnold (1822–88) was wont to say, 'There is truth of science and truth of religion; truth of science does not become truth of religion till it is made religious . . . Let us have all the science there is from the men of science; from the men of religion let us have religion.'[7]

William Paley, who shared Bentham's view of human psychology,

---

[4] S. Toulmin, *An Examination of the Place of Reason in Ethics* (1950; repr. Cambridge, 1970), 216–17.

[5] J. H. Hick, *Philosophy of Religion* (2nd edn. New Jersey, 1973), 66.

[6] Grant, *Saint Paul*, p. 86. Defined by the Vatican Council of 1870, faith is 'a supernatural virtue whereby, inspired and assisted by the grace of God, we believe that the things which he has revealed are true' (quoted by Hick, *Philosophy of Religion*, p. 52).

[7] M. Arnold, *Matthew Arnold's Essays in Criticism, First Series: A Critical Edition*, ed. Sr. T. M. Hoctor (Chicago, 1968), 23 n.

nevertheless knew that the essence of Christianity was internal and mysterious. As he wrote in *A View of the Evidences of Christianity*:

The kingdom of heaven is within us. That which is the substance of religion, its hopes and consolation, its intermixture with the thoughts by day and by night, the devotion of the heart, the control of appetite, the steady direction of the will to the commands of God, is necessarily invisible. Yet upon these depend the virtue and the happiness of millions.[8]

Bentham agreed that evidence was unavailable to support the notion of inner faith, but on his view of things such belief involved a grand act of self-delusion. To the ecclesiastical mind religious knowledge can only be grasped by faith and this is only dispensed by virtue of God's grace. This is not a matter that can be lightly bypassed when considering the foundations of religion. Yet Bentham never discussed the role of faith. In a manuscript of 1773, it is true, he endeavoured to define it, but this is a facile and hopelessly inadequate attempt in which faith is reduced to the 'merit' of believing the incredible: 'The greater the difficulty of doing any thing the greater the merit. The greater the difficulty in believing a thing the greater the merit in believing it.' Such a train of reasoning taken to its limits Bentham thought 'calculated to produce the greatest extravagancies of credulity' (UC 5/15; cf. also 107/259). Faith is here reduced to the outcome of stupidity or ignorance of the 'real' world and this was the conclusion embraced by Bentham. The critical mind which begins by thinking and not believing, and requires that there be empirical evidence that can be tested and verified before anything be accepted as final, is clearly not one that can feel comfortable with the Christian notion of 'faith'. Certainly the critical mind will dissolve any false certainty upon which a person rests his or her religion, but rarely does logic or reason affect the quality or power of religious feelings. In this dilemma lies both the limitations of Bentham's scientific approach, and the failure of his publications on religion to make their mark as serious contributions to the literature on theological matters. Not that he thought of himself as writing theology; he would undoubtedly have been appalled if his books on religion were accepted as religious books—theology to Bentham was merely the ignorance of natural causes reduced to a system. But this cannot excuse the fact that whenever he touched on religion in its more sublime and subtle aspects his criticisms were unsatisfactory. Convinced that scientific knowledge was the one thing needful to maximize

---

[8] Paley, *A View of the Evidences of Christianity*, in *Complete Works*, i. 407–8.

human happiness, he sought to remove religion from its privileged position not only in public life but also in the human heart.

So far as natural religion was concerned, the failure of Bentham's work to have an impact can be traced, at least in part, to the fact that natural theology, in the phrase of D. L. LeMahieu, 'was the spiritual core of the British Enlightenment'.[9] Ever since Newton, theologians had wisely sought to make their methodology and assumptions compatible with the new science. Deep into the nineteenth century this effort, despite the occasional dispute over details, was the centre-piece around which orthodox theologians could rally. Bentham, like Hume before him, challenged this intellectual consensus and sought to shatter the foundations of natural religion. By confronting it on its own terms he believed he could drive this scourge from the human mind. But it cannot be said that Bentham ever understood that the foundations of Christianity were far more than clever manipulations of the argument from design and that, consequently, to expose the logical inadequacies of that argument was to miss the point profoundly. Such an approach could not shake the theological commitment to reconcile the findings of natural science and the dictates of reason with the already existing emotional and spiritual profession of faith in God. Neither Newton nor Paley had faith in God because they believed the argument from design; rather, they accepted the design theory because they had faith in God. By directing their writings to a Christian audience, natural theologians sought to reinforce that faith by the best arguments reason could devise. In the process it was not necessary to reply to the attacks of Hume or Bentham—soothing reassertion became the order of the day.

Part of the problem with Bentham's approach is his formidable attempt to encompass within its reach all forms and aspects of knowledge. In the process a crucial metamorphosis took place in his thinking—crucial, that is, to his critique of religion. In the vocabulary of Bentham's science of society the terms 'method', 'theory', 'logic', and 'classification', are very nearly synonymous. In the 'Essay on Logic' he seemed to recognize as much: 'In the whole field of the art of Logic, so large is the portion occupied by the art of methodization . . . that the task of showing what it . . . can do, is scarcely distinguishable from the task of showing what . . . Logic can . . . do' (*Works*, viii. 261). He also tells us that logic is synonymous with 'a complete Encyclopedia'

---

[9] LeMahieu, *The Mind of William Paley*, p. 31.

encompassing the whole field of thought and action (*Works*, viii. 219), and that to metaphysics falls the lot of clarifying the language of logic and all other branches of art and science (*Works*, viii. 221). In these terms logic and linguistics are barely distinguishable in their relationship to knowledge—each is centrally connected with the enhancement of well-being. More significant still is the fact that for Bentham the theory of language is so closely akin to the theory of knowledge, that the one can easily be substituted for the other with nothing lost in the trade. The critical step in this metamorphosis is not expressly acknowledged by Bentham, but took place very early in his metaphysical speculations. It is the reduction of philosophy to science, and of science to 'metaphysics', defined in terms of a theory of language which insists on the correspondence between reality, words, ideas, and principles. Bentham was not alone in this tendency and Isaiah Berlin is correct to point to the identification of philosophy with science as a 'major fallacy' of eighteenth-century thought.[10] But it is not merely that for Bentham metaphysics meant linguistic analysis; more importantly this step meant that the structure of reality was now seen, could only be seen, in terms of the structure of language. The consequences for religion of this metamorphosis in Bentham's thought were entirely predictable. To borrow an example from Northrop Frye, consider the aphorism 'The kingdom of God is within you' (Luke 17: 21). Now, what Jesus meant by this may not be so easy to say, but we can be confident about what he did not mean. He did not mean that the kingdom of God is 'within' in the sense that vital organs are within our bodies. On questions like this Bentham's descriptive view of language falls down. Indeed, a serious discussion of the passage must begin by rejecting the purely descriptive meaning, and turning rather to the nature of the metaphor signified by the word 'within'.[11] But symbolism and analogical reasoning were no part of the Benthamic empirical–linguistic method.

Those who chose the path of active opposition to this kind of approach to questions of religion, like F. D. Maurice, rejected it on the grounds that it only built a barrier to human communication with God: the idea that there is no knowledge but that which comes through the

[10] I. Berlin (ed.), *The Age of Enlightenment: The Eighteenth Century Philosophers* (New York, 1956), 26.

[11] For a continuation of the discussion see Frye, *The Great Code*, p. 55: 'The sense in Christianity of faith beyond reason, which must continue to affirm even after reason gives up, is closely connected with the linguistic fact that many of the central doctrines of traditional Christianity can be grammatically expressed only in the form of metaphor.'

senses leaves no room for the notion of communion between the
Divine Word, the heart, and the conscience.[12] John Colls, Bentham's
one-time amanuensis, believed that the source of his atheism lay in an
overfondness for 'the intellect' and the refusal to listen to 'the heart'.[13]
The notion that a science of society, including its religious aspects,
could be built upon the same principles employed in natural science
was rejected by Carlyle for essentially this reason. Logic and science,
he claimed, were leading British philosophers into 'the barren wastes
of materialism' and blinding them to the realities of life. The fundamental problem is that the methods of natural science cannot be used
to investigate the invisible world of the human spirit which makes us
what we are.[14] The gap between the two levels of discourse is an un-
bridgeable chasm; empiricism can tell us nothing about that which is
not amenable to empirical analysis and, therefore, it is an inappropriate
method to use in relation to spirituality. It was left to Coleridge to draw
the conclusion that the empirical method leads by strict logical
consequence not to truth but to atheism.[15]

At times Bentham was very ready to relegate 'truth' to a second-
order consideration divorced from its anchor in utility. In an outline
for his work on the 'Church' in 1813 he was quite clear that the
supposed truth of religious beliefs, even if it could be established, was
neither here nor there: 'Utility as to affairs of this life being the sole
object . . . any argument founded on the will of the founder of religion,
or on any other part of Scripture, cannot be in place here' (UC 6/33).
Now, that some useful doctrines are false was a premiss with which the
eighteenth century was well acquainted. We are reminded of Voltaire's
caution to his guests not to talk irreligion in front of the maid lest the
order of society be overthrown, it commonly being assumed that any
collapse of faith would destroy the sanctions of morality. But the
consequences for religion of a theory which regards utility and not
truth as the decisively important characteristic of a belief or doctrine
are disastrous, and Bentham was fully aware of this. He showed a

[12] F. D. Maurice, *The Kingdom of Christ* (1838), 44–5, cited Schneewind, *Sidgwick's
Ethics and Victorian Moral Philosophy*, p. 98.

[13] Colls, *Utilitarianism Unmasked*, p. 3.

[14] T. Carlyle, 'The State of German Literature', *Edinburgh Review*, 46 (1827), 339.

[15] See Mill, 'Coleridge', in *Collected Works*, x. 127. One of the most intriguing items of
Benthamiana is a copy of *NP*, with copious annotations believed to be in the hand of
Coleridge, in the Library at UCL. It is another indication of the lack of interest in
Bentham's writings on religion that these annotations have neither been transcribed nor
analysed.

complete disregard for the status of religious beliefs as early as his earliest scribblings on religious matters (*c.*1773): 'When instead of proving that their tenets are more conducive to peace and utility than their opposites, men betake themselves to declamations on the (beauty and) necessity of Religion in general, I desire them to take notice, that they have abandon'd the cause for which they are contending' (UC 96/ 299). Whether there be three persons in the divine nature or one or more, and whether grace be exalted above free will or vice versa are problems, Bentham claims, unresolvable in theory and whose solution is unimportant in practice (UC 96/292). These questions, like all other questions where the peace and safety of the State are not at risk, are futile (UC 96/296):

it is one thing for a proposition to be true, and another for its being [*sic*] necessary for us to concern ourselves about it—the dwelling upon a mystery tho' true from whence no practical consequences are deducible, may . . . weaken a Religion, and the passing it by unnoticed though true, can be productive of no bad consequences. (UC 96/294)

Bentham, however, was no sceptic—he did not doubt, he denied that which contradicted what he considered sound empirical knowledge. But it never occurred to him that to identify all knowledge as being coexistensive with the knowledge provided by the techniques of science was to circumscribe knowledge unduly, nor that the knowledge so supplied exists itself only by virtue of its connection with knowledge which is extra- or pre-scientific. How can a person know that the methods of natural science are the only ones that lead to truth? This is certainly not a proposition of the kind that can be tested. As one theologian has pointed out, only 'critical common sense' can decide whether all our trustworthy knowledge is scientific knowledge or not, and it is on this that the last word about the truth of the principles presupposed in natural science ultimately rests.[16] The knowledge acquired by the methods of experimental science is not the whole or even the most important part of knowledge, since it presupposes as its basis a wider area of knowledge without which it is itself impossible. The assertion that the techniques of natural science do not provide any grounds for belief in God, even if this were true, would not therefore rule out the possibility that extra-scientific knowledge may provide sufficient justification for theistic belief.[17]

---

[16] A. E. Taylor, *Does God Exist?* (London, 1945), 17.
[17] Ibid. 20.

There are problems, too, with Bentham's critique of revealed religion. With a complete disregard for the status of religious beliefs, he deliberately employed a narrow worldly conception of religion guaranteed to fall under the hammer of his natural science methodology, contrasted the world of experience with the world of the imagination peopled by insane believers in the incredible, and approached the Scriptures more like a prosecutor determined to establish guilt than a philosopher intent on fathoming the nature of his subject. Ridicule, denunciations of motives, and passages of scurrilous irony are all introduced to bolster the indictment. In portraying Christ as a revolutionary bent on overthrowing the authority of Rome in Jerusalem, and in exposing the contradictory statements of the self-seeking ascetic Paul, it mattered little to Bentham whether history was on his side or not. The traditions of Christianity, he argued, are a fraud perpetuated by an unscrupulous sacerdotal class and the detrimental social consequences of their practice is evident to all. The institutions and doctrines they preach must be assailed by whatever tools are to hand. Bentham was fully prepared to mount such an attack in order to impress upon his readers that religion is harmful to them and that its influence on the mind should be entirely eradicated. Even though he explicitly rejected the notion that exaggeration is useful in attempting to persuade individuals to embrace the utilitarian doctrine, to accept utilitarian legislation, and to influence them to perform socially desirable actions, if vitriolic language was called for in order to move the reader to an emotional response on questions of religion he had no qualms about employing it. For all his vaunted reverence for precision in language and for all his warnings about the dangers implicit in its very nature, his critique of religion was frequently carried on in language reminiscent of the rabid anticlerical literature one normally associates with the worst excesses of the French *philosophes.*

Even on purely rational grounds Bentham could not expect to achieve his objectives. He remained convinced throughout his life that to ignore reason and to continue to place trust in the doctrines of religion would, in effect, place unnecessary obstacles in the path of increasing the stock of happiness. But the committed Christian, irrational as it may have seemed to Bentham, is not likely to be moved to disbelief because the ideas of the soul, spirit, or grace are exposed as fictions irreducible to any physical properties or real entities. Indeed, it is just as likely that such an analysis will serve to confirm the faith of the believer by reinforcing the notion that such conceptions must have their source in something that cannot be fully comprehended by mere mortals. This seems to have been very much the argument of Wilberforce in his defence of Christianity in *A Practical View of the Prevailing Religious System of Professed Christians* (1811). Christianity, he argued, cannot be reduced to 'a mere system of ethics', for 'this is to separate the practical precepts from the peculiar doctrines it enjoins'.[18] We must not 'confound the Gospel of Christ with the systems of philosophers', but be 'impressed with the weighty truth, so much forgotten in the present day, that Christianity calls on us, as we value our immortal souls, not merely in *general*, to be *religious* and *moral*, but specially to believe the doctrines, imbibe the principles, and practise the precepts of Christ'.[19] To Bentham, of course, this is an irrational response, but in so far as he relied on plain descriptive language to overcome it he surely underestimated the conviction with which believers hold to their faith, and overestimated the power of his metaphysics to have an impact upon it.

Ultimately, Bentham's utilitarianism, with its materialist and nominalist underpinnings, could not encompass the 'internal' and the 'mysterious' and this impoverished his analysis. At the very point where he touched upon the hidden aspect of human nature in the 'Essay on Logic', for example, he halted the examination. Like Descartes he divided the human frame in the first instance into corporeal and incorporeal substances, but unlike Descartes he denied that the mental was more certain than the corporeal. And whereas Descartes could argue that we can only properly know truths that are self-evident or that can be reached by logical inferences from self-evident premisses, Bentham's materialist metaphysics made such a consideration utterly untenable. Accordingly (the assumption that psychologically the individual is motivated by pleasures and pains, aside), he could only continue the analysis on the physiological side of the division of human nature, and this is a tacit avowal of the limitations of his 'science of man' (*Works*, viii. 253). Whatever cannot be reduced to discrete and concrete entities, he claims, does not exist; but this, in his sense of it, is a tautological statement. Not surprisingly, the belief that human beings do not have a spiritual nature hidden from the human eye fosters a science unable to deal with deep inner

[18] W. Wilberforce, *A Practical View of the Prevailing Religious System of Professed Christians, in the Higher and Middle Classes in this Country, Contrasted with Real Christianity* (London, 1811), 319, 322.

[19] Ibid. 13.

feelings and personality. But it is certainly false logic subsequently to employ this science, as Bentham did, to seek to prove that the belief in a spiritual nature is unfounded or that God does not exist.

2. *The religion of atheism*

Pierre Bayle defined an atheist as one who denied the efficacy of prayer, the existence of a particular providence, and the fear of divine punishment. But Bayle's formulation does not amount to a total rejection of theism, only to a severe limitation on the kind of God that might exist. In contrast, Bentham's Utilitarian society is, and must be, a society of atheists. He was determined to prove that society and politics were possible without religious beliefs of any kind whatever, hence his rejection of religion was total and uncompromising.

Bentham never in so many words avowed his atheism; he was much too cautious to do this.[20] But that he was an atheist in substance there can be no doubt. His destructive criticisms of religious doctrine left no residue that could be of any value. To the utilitarian apostate John Colls, Bentham was that 'hoary headed infidel' who made tasteless jokes at the expense of Abraham and who viewed death merely as the 'altering the modification of matter' (which Colls thought an appropriate notion for an atheist).[21] Edwin Chadwick (1800–90), a close associate in later life, took Bentham's 'infidelity' for granted.[22] Bentham's friend and admirer, the future sixth President of the United States, John Quincy Adams (1767–1848), also had no doubts about the state of his mind on this subject:

The general tenor of his observations . . . was to discredit all religion, and he intimated doubts of the existence of a God. His position was, that all human knowledge was either positive or inferential; that all inferential knowledge was imperfect and uncertain, depending upon a process of the human mind which could not in its nature, be conclusive; that our knowledge of the physical world was positive, while that of a Creator of it was inferential; that God was neither seen nor felt, nor in any manner manifested to our senses, but was the deduction from a syllogism, a mere probability from the combinations of

---

[20] For e.g. see the quotation from JB to Place (24 Apr. 1831) above at Introduction, n. 29.
[21] Colls, *Utilitarianism Unmasked*, pp. 18, 49–50.
[22] See the notes under the heading 'Practical Christianity versus Professing Christianity but practical infidelity', by E[dwin] C[hadwick] at UC 155/9–16 (*c*.1832 [?]).

human reason; that of the present existence of matter we have positive knowledge; that there was a time when it did not exist we assume without proof, for the purpose of assuming equally without proof, an eternal Creator of it.[23]

Making allowance for Adams's cautious phrasing, this is a concise statement of Bentham's secular positivism, but it is also important to note the conviction with which Bentham held his atheism. Duncan Howlett, in his history of the 'critical way' in religion, has drawn our attention to a persistent defect in the religious person's perception of the atheist: he fails 'to see how deeply the so-called unbeliever believes; . . . to recognize that he is an unbeliever because of his *positive* beliefs'. It is on the basis of these positive beliefs that the atheist repudiates the concept of miracles and that he can find no evidence that divine intervention occurs in the world. All the evidence points the other way, to a non-miraculous world.[24] What Adams's statement highlights is the depth of Bentham's conviction, and this helps us to understand better the venom of his attack on religion. He could not remain a passive unbeliever; his profound belief in a material world free from all spiritual content made of him an active, not to say a zealous, atheist, committed to the promulgation of his beliefs, and it gave him comfort when he was in the company of those who shared his opinions.[25] It also gave him cause for much anger when atheists were persecuted and prosecuted for their views. To such intolerance he was always hostile, but even in the ordinary way of things there could be no compromise. The spirit of dogmatic theology poisons everything it touches: by focusing attention and labour on a life to come, religion detracts from the stockpile of happiness in this world and, as such, must be considered one of the principal causes of the world's evils. Simple theism, therefore, without an ecclesiastical establishment or even without Christianity would still be a curse.

Bentham's atheism owes a debt, too, to the French Enlightenment. His vehement and ironic language when disparaging religion frequently reminds us of that used by Voltaire, Helvétius, and Holbach in their condemnations of French clerics and their religious doctrines. Like the *philosophes*, also, Bentham argued that he must destroy in order to

---

[23] *Memoirs of John Quincy Adams*, iii. 564 (diary entry for 8 June 1817).
[24] Howlett, *The Critical Way in Religion*, p. 183.
[25] James Mill provides the testimony for his own unbelief in a letter to Place (6–13 Sept. 1815), BL Add. MSS 35152/163. Sections of 'The Commonplace Books of James Mill' also offer evidence of his unbelief (esp. ii. 82 and iii. 201).

build, and he often followed them in using metaphors of aggression to dramatize his destructive activities.[26] Voltaire used to say, 'I'm tired of being told that twelve men sufficed to establish Christianity, and I'm longing to prove that only one is needed to destroy it.'[27] Bentham thought similarly and in his writings on religion he sought to bring about its destruction. Like Voltaire his hatred of religion increased with the passage of years. He first attacked clericalism and religion as an agency of moral regulation, and he later launched a furious assault upon the Scriptures, Church dogmas, and the person of Christ. The irreligion of both men was militant and aggressive.

Bentham was always loud in his praise of Helvétius's refusal to compromise his scientific principles by making concessions to theology, and his early work on ethics and legislation owed much to the secular positivism of the inspirational *De l'esprit*. But of the influence of Helvétius I have said enough already. Bentham's atheism had much in common, too, with the thought of Baron d'Holbach (1723–89), though it is unclear whether he was familiar with the works in which the baron launched his materialist broadsides. To Holbach 'an atheist is a man who knows nature and its laws, who knows his own nature, and who knows what it imposes upon him'. His principles 'are much less liable to be shaken than those of the enthusiast, who founds his morality upon an imaginary being, of whom the idea so frequently varies, even in his own brain'. But more than this an atheist 'is a man who destroys chimeras prejudicial to the human species, in order to reconduct men back to nature, to experience, and to reason'.[28] Strict empiricists would be forced to suspend judgement, since atheism (like Christianity, they would say) is laying claim to a form of knowledge that essentially lies outside our ken. Bentham, however, preferred to stand with Holbach, condemning religion as a source of human misery and exposing its tenets and doctrines as empty imaginings, the product of intellectual confusion. In this he stood with the French *philosophes*, and his anticlericalism and atheism both come dressed in *philosophe* clothes. Bentham, as many have said before (though not necessarily for

[26] For the relation between destruction and construction in the thought of the *philosophes* and their use of aggressive metaphors see Gay, *The Enlightenment*, ii. 130–2.

[27] Quoted by H. Daniel-Rops [pseud. of Jules Charles Henri Petiot], *The Church in the Eighteenth Century*, trans. J. Warrington (London, 1964), 47.

[28] Baron P. H. T. d'Holbach, *The System of Nature: Or, the Laws of the Moral and Physical World* [*Système de la nature*, 1770], trans. H. D. Robinson (Boston, 1889), 307, 308, 300.

the same reasons), was an English *philosophe*.[29] To this, we might add that he was the last of the English *philosophes*.

In the period following Bentham's death English moralists, and utilitarians among them,[30] resumed the effort to find a place for religion within their thought. Even in France the rigorously critical spirit which accompanied the natural science approach to divinity became blunted by the prophetic fervour and messianic expectation which characterized political thought in the years following the eclipse of Napoleon.[31] During the revolutionary period the French moved decisively away from the atheism of Helvétius and Holbach, with its strict separation of religion and ethics, towards the religious sensibility and civil religion of Rousseau. The desire to build new philosophies to replace the beliefs that had been abandoned served to balance the destructive mood of the Enlightenment. Indeed, the substitution of the Republican Calendar for the Gregorian, the transforming of the parish churches of Paris into Temples of Reason, and the declaration of the Paris Commune that it would henceforth recognize only the religion of Truth and Reason, were fitting preliminaries to Saint-Simon's Temple of Newton and Auguste Comte's Positivist Calendar. The new philosophic systems of Saint-Simon and Comte were in fact new religions. Having rejected Christianity they attempted to retain religious commitment by setting it in a more overtly ethical or political context.[32] Voltaire, too, played a role, though an inadvertent one, in all this. On 11 June 1791 his remains were brought back to Paris to be placed in the Pantheon, the newly created national secular shrine. While alive in the flesh his 'crowning' at the Comédie-Française had unleashed unique demonstrations of fervour; now, the 'saint' who, more than any other thinker of the age, had prepared the way for revolution, returned to take his place as a symbol of the new cult of

[29] Oakeshott goes too far when he asserts that Bentham was a *philosophe* rather than a philosopher, a man with belief in 'encyclopedic knowledge', 'remarkable for his general credulity', who 'begins with a whole miscellany of presuppositions which he has neither the time, the inclination nor the ability to examine'. He has little in common with the philosopher, says Oakeshott: 'For the *philosophe* the world is divided between those who agree with him and "fools"; "science" is contrasted with superstition and superstition is identified with whatever is established, generally believed or merely felt' ('The New Bentham', p. 120).

[30] See esp. Austin, *The Province of Jurisprudence Determined*, and J. S. Mill's essays on religion in *Collected Works*, x.

[31] For a discussion of this period of French thought see D. G. Charlton, *Secular Religions in France 1815–1870* (Oxford, 1963).

[32] Ibid. 4–5.

patriotism that was eventually to reach its most sophisticated form in the hands of Comte.

Though raised as a Catholic Auguste Comte (1798–1857) came to reject all historical religions, including theism. Nevertheless, he refused to accept the epithet 'atheist' as in any way appropriate to describe himself. However, his refusal (in part dictated by the usage and connotation of the term specific to his day) meant only that he had no more interest in atheistic than in theological cosmogonies. Indeed, he looked on atheism, in essence, as itself a kind of theology or metaphysics seeking explanation where there was none to find.[33] His own position, described in *The Catechism of Positive Religion* (1852) and other works, was this: on the basis that the theological foundations of the old organic order had been irrevocably destroyed by the eighteenth-century critique, the problem was to find a positive base for the new emerging order that, because of its perfect rationality, would be resistant to criticism. The positive philosophy (actually a hierarchy of the sciences) was to provide the required base upon which social reconstruction could begin. In the process of developing this scheme Comte ceased to think of himself as simply a philosopher but pictured himself as the founder of a new religion—the Religion of Humanity. He thought of humanity as an organism in a sense higher than the biological; its continuity is that of history and not merely of organic life. In this sense it is a real providence, as distinct from the imaginary supernatural providence of the theologians. Hence it should be the supreme object of devotion. Through an ever ascending hierarchy of love (from family, neighbourhood, city, to country) the Religion of Humanity is destined to become the religion of the human race. And lest we should doubt the systematic shape of the endeavour, Comte sought to organize the 'cult of humanity' in typically Catholic fashion. By investing the new spiritual power with the sacerdotal attributes of the medieval clergy he created a theocracy minus theology. Indeed, if fortunate to live long enough to see its acceptance Comte expected to be saluted as 'the High Priest of Humanity'.[34]

While we may safely assume Bentham's abhorrence for philosophies of this nature, it is noteworthy that he shared with Comte certain peculiarities of character and thought.[35] Both men possessed an

[33] T. Whittaker, *Comte and Mill* (London, 1908), 41.
[34] See A. Comte, *The Catechism of Positive Religion*, trans. R. Congreve (1858; 3rd edn. 1891, New Jersey, 1973), *passim*.
[35] W. Stark compares the psychological peculiarities of Bentham and Comte in

irresistible urge to build a 'system' in which every discipline and science was to find its place and also to account for all aspects of social, political, and intellectual life. The character of their respective utopias was to be dictated by the form of these systems—the one Utilitarian, the other Positivist—and in so far as each prophesied a better world, their prophesy was not for the distant future but for the here and now. Both Bentham and Comte persistently upbraided their contemporaries for delaying the institution of a felicity to which they believed there no longer existed any barriers—historical or scientific—that could not be rationally ignored. Nor can one resist the comparison between Comte's vision of himself as the high priest of Positivism and Bentham's alleged 'dream' (*c.*1781), recounted in language rich in religious allusions, in which he imagined himself as 'a founder of a sect, of course a personage of great sanctity and importance' (UC 169/79). It is clear from this dream that Bentham had an exalted notion of himself as the prospective saviour of England, and very possibly the world. When asked by 'a great man' (probably an early patron, Lord Shelburne) what he should do in order 'to save the nation', Bentham replied, 'take up my book, & follow me'. The book in question was the *Introduction*, and it is certainly implied that as a substitute for Scripture there could be no better blueprint for the salvation of the world. It is, he says, a book with 'the true flavour of the fruit of the tree of knowledge'. Nor was the angel who is supposed to have delivered the book to Bentham one to be fussy about methods; unlike St John, who had to eat his revelation (Rev. 10: 9), Bentham 'had to . . . cram it down the throats of other people' (UC 169/79).[36] The end in view, of course, is the rationally ordered Utilitarian society.

Also like Comte, Bentham frequently employed religious terminology and referred to religious figures when describing his thought and its

'Psychology of Social Messianism', *Social Research*, 28 (1958), 145–57. However, I cannot go as far as Stark to submit that they 'were fundamentally saints', nor reasonably describe them as 'poor maniacs'. Compare Stark's evidence for Bentham's selflessness with G. Himmelfarb's account of the arrogant, conceited, and self-promoting Bentham in her 'Bentham Scholarship and the Bentham Problem', *The Journal of Modern History*, 41:2 (1969), 189–206.

[36] The 'dream' is reproduced in full with notes below in App. *B*. Bentham had another so-called dream in Sept. 1828, the year that UCL opened its doors, which begins: 'Once upon a time, no matter when—it cannot have been long ago—I—no matter who I am—dreamed a dream. Methought I was in the Lecture Room of the London University', UC 31/200; see also J. H. Burns, 'Dreams and Destinations: Jeremy Bentham in 1828', *The Bentham Newsletter*, 1 (1978), 3–20.

importance.[37] In a letter to Dumont (28 June 1802) he rejects the appellation 'Benthamite' to describe his followers and the doctrine they held: 'What sort of animal is that?' Even so, he carries on, 'a new religion would be an odd sort of thing without a name: accordingly there ought to be one for it—at least for the professors of it. Utilitarian (Angl.) Utilitarien (Gall.) would be the more PROPRE' (*Works*, x. 389–90).[38] Not long after, in the *Rationale of Judicial Evidence*, Bentham fancied himself as the 'Luther of Jurisprudence' come to search with 'penetrating eye and dauntless heart' into the cells and conclaves of the law (*Works*, vi. 270 n.).[39]

Others followed Bentham in so picturing the proselytizing character of his utilitarian thought and its disciples. To his American friend, John Neal, Bentham was 'the great high-priest of legislation'.[40] Arnold, who denigrated the total lack of 'edification' in Voltaire's handling of religious ideas (how much less happy he would have been with Bentham's critique is perhaps easy to surmise), also saw fit to allude to the religious character of the utilitarian school. At one place he writes dryly of 'the ardent longing of a faithful Benthamite, traversing an age still dimmed by the last mists of transcendentalism, to be spared long enough to see his religion in the full and final blaze of its triumph'.[41] J. S. Mill provides us with the most famous example of this kind of thing in his *Autobiography*, when he tells us of the effect upon him, in the winter of 1821–2, of his reading of Dumont's edition of Bentham's *Traités de legislation*:

The reading of this book was an epoch in my life; one of the turning points in my mental history . . . The 'principle of utility' understood as Bentham understood it, and applied in the manner in which he applied it . . ., fell exactly into its place as the keystone which held together the detached and

---

[37] For a selection of representative e.g.s see C. F. Bahmueller, *The National Charity Company: Jeremy Bentham's Silent Revolution* (Berkeley, 1981), 66–7, 167.

[38] This is not, as is commonly thought, Bentham's first usage of the term 'utilitarian'; see JB to George Wilson (24 Aug. 1781), *Corr.* iii. 57; and the text of Bentham's 'dream' (*c*.1781) below in App. *B*.

[39] The description of Bentham by Bruce Mazlish as 'a very eccentric version of Jesus Christ' takes such comparisons too far, *James and John Stuart Mill: Father and Son in the Nineteenth Century* (New York, 1975), 132.

[40] *Principles of Legislation from the Manuscripts of Jeremy Bentham*, ed. J. Neal (Boston, 1830), 14.

[41] Arnold continues to relate that 'This respectable man . . . was, perhaps, in real truth, on a pious pilgrimage, to obtain from Mr. Bentham's executors, a sacred bone of his great dissected Master' (*Essays in Criticism*, preface of 1865, 251). Another version of the same appears in the 1875 preface (ibid. 6). For the comment on Voltaire see ibid. 200.

fragmentary component parts of my knowledge and beliefs. It gave unity to my conceptions of things. I now had opinions; a creed, a doctrine, a philosophy; in one among the best senses of the word, a religion; the inculcation and diffusion of which could be made the principal outward purpose of a life.[42]

As it turned out, the 'religion' to which Mill adhered later in life was not the simple utilitarian calculus of Bentham and his father. But I shall come to this presently. For the moment it is sufficient to say that allusions of the kind Mill gives above should not distract us too much. What they suggest is the tendency of the age to liken systems of thought and their propagators to religious and religious figures, and Bentham was no exception to this. That he occasionally went further than this to borrow terms and phrases from religion to describe his thought is also not unusual for the period. Indeed, in the effort to banish traditional religion from the realm of morals and politics Bentham frequently injected his thoughts with something approaching a religious fervour and adopted the language of religion to convey them to his growing congregation. Comte was to do the same, and this is a feature common to their respective systems.

Again like Comte, Bentham occasionally sought to enlist the institutions of conventional religion to serve apparently secular ends. As we know, the main thrust of his later thought on the role of religion went much further than to suggest ways of employing religious institutions for secular purposes—in the ideal secularized world all traces of religious sentiment would be banished; it was to be the first duty of the legislator to do all in his power to eliminate religious beliefs. But Bentham's advice 'To obey punctually; to censure freely'—given in *A Fragment* at the outset of his career (*FG* 399)—was a maxim always to be followed save where sober calculation showed a clear advantage to be had by disobedience. The case of religion he thought to be such an occasion. But to criticize or to destroy with no idea of what was to follow was for Bentham an anarchical approach to political inquiry. Disorder in anything, most of all in political affairs, he always found offensive. Accordingly, he rarely criticized anything without some idea of what was to take its place. The role of the clergy in pauper management—compiling statistics to aid endeavours at poor relief and disseminating information regarding job vacancies—the idea of using churches as banks for the use of the poor after Sunday service (*Works*, viii. 400, 414), and using the clergy as instructors of

---

[42] Mill, *Autobiography*, in *Collected Works*, i. 67, 49.

morality in the poor house Panopticon and in the Panopticon in its originally intended use as a prison (*Works*, viii. 420–1, 427, 431; iv. 47),[43] were all suggestions he made at one time or another for employing the clergy and religious institutions for secular purposes. Bentham seems to have believed that the sentiments attached to these persons and institutions were mistakenly understood to be religious in character and that their transposition to a secular context, therefore, was simply the recovery of their true character and use. A later example of this form of secularization is to be found in Bentham's *Auto-Icon: Or Farther Uses of the Dead to the Living*, in which he recommends that 'phrenologists' replace clergymen in the churches and chapels. The advantage of this is that there would be no 'phrenological sinecures', phrenologists would not cost vast amounts of public money to maintain, and phrenological bishops and archibishops would not be needed. At the same time, the phrenologists would perform all the temporal functions of the clergy—registering births, deaths, and marriages, and conducting the necessary rituals. In addition, the phrenologist would be the instructor and educator of his parishioners (*AI* 7–8). I shall return to this odd pamphlet in a moment.

For the present it should perhaps be said that Bentham was not alone in the utilitarian ranks in making suggestions of this order. James Mill expressed similar ideas for employing religious rites and institutions to serve secular ends. He wrote several articles critical of established religion along the lines taken by Bentham, but his most important contribution was the essay 'The Church, and its Reform' which appeared in the first number of the *London Review* in 1835, the penultimate year of his life.[44] In this radical attack and still more radical series of reform proposals Mill advocated a Church without dogmas or ceremonies, the founding of a 'State religion' in which 'the whole population' might be united.[45] In this religion the clergy were to be employed, like Bentham's phrenologists, to give public instruction in ethics, political economy, and the sciences. The theological content of 'sermons' should be minimal, their aim being to establish in the minds of the congregation 'pure ideas of the moral character of God'.

---

[43] See also Bahmueller, *The National Charity Company*, ch. 7. esp. pp. 197–200.

[44] *CE* is referred to by Mill at several places in the essay and highly recommended. Bain's comment on the article is that 'with all its ingenuity' it 'will have to be remanded to the list of Utopias, among which it will deserve perusal for its constructive suggestions' (*James Mill*, p. 389; for a discussion see Fenn, *James Mill's Political Thought*, pp. 45–50).

[45] J. Mill, 'The Church, and Its Reform', *London Review*, i (1835), 288.

This, of course, is a concession by Mill to public opinion, but behind the conception he wishes to see expounded from the pulpit is surely Bentham's discussion of the supposed attributes of God in the *Analysis*, which we know Mill to have studied in manuscript form.[46] 'It is unavailing', Mill writes, 'to call the Almighty benevolent, when you ascribe to him lines of action which are entirely the reverse. It is vain to call him wise, when you represent him as moved by considerations which have weight only with the weakest of men.' To call the Almighty a loving God while at the same time attributing to him a propensity to punish offenders out of all proportion to the gravity of their offences is clearly a fallacious and pernicious practice.[47] Not that the sermons should be weighed down by discussions of this kind; rather the objective is to enhance social utility. They should be calculated to impart 'as deeply as possible, all the impressions which lead to good conduct', and thereby 'lead us to rejoice in being the instruments of happiness to others'.[48] Apart from sermonizing, the clergy were also to deliver 'useful lectures on various branches of art and science'. In this way craftsmen could be made acquainted with 'the mechanical powers', and the congregation as a whole might be exposed to edifying chemical experiments, acquire 'knowledge of the composition and decomposition of bodies', and receive instruction in the basics of the sciences of botany and astronomy. To these might be added—a modern note here—'lectures on the art of preserving . . . health'.[49] In addition, the congregation should receive instruction in 'political science' and 'political economy', from which they might learn something of 'the laws which determine the rate of wages' and 'laws of nature, by which the annual produce of the labours of the community is distributed'. In this manner—though one assumes that a certain amount of irony is intended—Mill thought the people could be reconciled 'to that inequality of distribution which they see takes place, and which there are people ignorant or wicked enough to tell them, is a violation of their rights'.[50] Finally, 'social amusements', such as music and dancing, were to supplement the educative aspects of Mill's Sunday programme. Churches were to function not only as centres of instruction but also as community centres where meetings, dances, and communal meals could take place.[51]

There is little of consequence in Mill's suggestions for a state religion that one cannot find in Bentham's less fanciful discussions

[46] See above ch. 7 n. 2.   [47] Mill, 'The Church, and Its Reform', p. 267.
[48] Ibid. 269.   [49] Ibid. 290.   [50] Ibid. 291.   [51] Ibid. 293–4.

along the same lines, and they share the same faults. Leslie Stephen's comment on such proposals is apposite: they are illustrative of 'the incapacity of an isolated clique to understand the real tone of public opinion'.[52] The importance of such ideas to us is that, as parts of a general picture of a future Utilitarian society, they assist us to fill out our conception of secular utilitarianism. For what is clear is that the main thrust of Bentham's later thought on the role of religion in society involved far more than an elaborate critique of traditional religious practices and doctrines. He was not content, as it appeared that Mill was, to settle for a reformed Church, even one as edifyingly utilitarian as Mill's state religion. All his proposals for secularizing Church functions and functionaries were just so many steps towards the realization of a society from which all trace of religion had been cleansed.

3. Secularization and 'Farther Uses of the Dead'

In the *Constitutional Code* (parts edited by Richard Doane and published in 1831) Bentham provides us with his most extensive and detailed plans regarding the institutional make-up of the ideal state, his Utilitarian utopia. Here his intentions *vis-à-vis* the secularization of society are more abruptly stated than hitherto. In this vast text (662 double-columned pages in the ill-fashioned version in the Bowring edition of the *Works*) he mentions religion hardly at all, and when he does it is to say why it is to be absent.[53] The opening sentence of Bk. I, ch. 14, 'Established Religion—None', states Bentham's position: 'No power of government ought to be employed in the endeavour to establish any system or article of belief on the subject of religion' (*Works*, ix. 92).[54] The 'truths' of religion must be accepted or rejected free from remuneration promised or penalties threatened by government. The power of the State adds nothing to religious truth, and

---

[52] Stephen, *The English Utilitarians*, ii. 62.

[53] In Rosen and Burns's recent edn. of the first (so far the only) volume of the *Constitutional Code* religion is mentioned on only one occasion and in an inconsequential fashion: there is no obligation for ministers to furnish information regarding their personal opinions on religion; see *Constitutional Code* [*CW*], ed. F. Rosen and J. H. Burns (Oxford, 1983), 292.

[54] That Thomas Peardon in an article-length exposition of the *Constitutional Code* ignores the instructions regarding religion is representative of the usual neglect of the place of Bentham's views on religion within his system; see 'Bentham's Ideal Republic', *Canadian Journal of Economics and Political Science*, 18 (1951), 184–203.

indeed its exercise in this case is liable to be understood as a confession by those who enforce it 'that in their eyes the system thus supported is false'. Added to this is the consideration of the expense of maintaining an established religion, and Bentham delights in pointing out that nowhere in the Scriptures did Christ sanction an order of priests, let alone an Established Church. Nowhere did he say 'give money to those who say they believe in what I have said, or give money to those who teach others to believe what I have said'. Nowhere did he say 'apply punishment to those who will not say they believe what I have said, or to those who say they believe what I have said is false' (*Works*, ix. 93). Finally, in a note to Bk. II, ch. 11, 'on the subject of a Religious Establishment, to be paid for at the public expense', Bentham says all that he has to say in the *Code* on the administration of religious affairs: 'For the business of religion, there is no department: there is no Minister. Of no opinion on the subject of religion, does this Constitution take any cognizance' (*Works*, ix. 452–3).[55]

It is plain that Bentham's attitude to ecclesiastical institutions was much the same as his attitude to political and legal institutions: the Established Church was a public entity which, because of the vested interest of its functionaries in sustaining it in a corrupt condition, was in need of a complete overhaul. The difference, however, was that whereas the reformed political and legal institution would remain an essential feature of the Utilitarian society, Bentham came to believe that even if disestablished, religion would still be an enemy to human happiness, due to the doctrines and beliefs it expounded. To reform the Established Church was not to reform its teachings. It was not sufficient merely to blunt the harmful political effects of religion: as long as religious beliefs constituted an active spring of human action, the rational, that is the temporal, pursuit of self-interest would be thwarted. Irrespective of the additional problems presented by established religion, while individuals are still induced by religious beliefs to forgo the pleasures of this life, political coercion, direct and indirect, will be necessary.

The secularization envisaged by Bentham thus involved more than the disentanglement of the religious and political spheres of social life

---

[55] As usual in this period of his life, the US is Bentham's illustration of a happy state without an official religion: 'Nowhere is anything under the name of religion established in the Anglo-American United States, and where, with such extensively prevalent sincerity, is religion professed, as in those same so happily united States? (*Works*, ix. 453).

(the policy of disestablishment set out in *Church-of-Englandism* was designed to achieve this objective). Ultimately, secularization meant for Bentham the elimination of religious beliefs as influential psychological factors operating on the human mind, and this was to be the task of the legislator. Just as it was to be the first duty of Proudhon's free man to chase the idea of God from his mind, so it is the duty of Bentham's legislator to eliminate religious beliefs from the Utilitarian society, and the most effective way of proceeding along these lines is through education.

Bentham's chief quarrel with the universities was the predominance of religious influences in these places of learning. Educational institutions, he thought, should be free from all taint of ecclesiasticism. His sympathy and support for the project to establish a secular university in London can be traced to this early grievance.[56] The new university, reported *The Times* (6 June 1825), which covered this momentous event closely, was to be established on the principle that there would not be 'any religious tests, or doctrinal forms, which would oppose a barrier to the education of any sect among His Majesty's subjects'.[57] Its main supporters were drawn from the ranks of Dissenters and these, *The Times* reported (9 June 1825), had to be persuaded that it was 'utterly impossible to teach theology in a University intended to comprehend persons of all sects'. Subsequently, *The Times* was able to announce (11 June 1825) that a declaration that 'nothing contrary to revealed religion should be allowed in the instructions in the proposed University' was withdrawn.[58] Maintaining this policy was always likely to present difficulties.[59] Bentham's own

[56] In his eulogy to Bentham Ogden speculates in obscure fashion about the birth of UCL: 'one day it will be realized that this great institution arose directly out of a series of Footnotes, out of the sad case of Mr. Beardmore, and out of "Jug"' (*Jeremy Bentham*, p. 24). The footnotes are those in the *Chrestomathia* and 'Jug' was Bentham's abbreviation for 'Juggernaut', symbolizing (usually, but not always) organized religion. The case of Mr Beardmore is more difficult to identify. An obituary in the *Gentleman's Magazine* (Feb. 1814) reveals the empty life of the rich but not untalented Beardmore, who through lack of intellectual stimulus wasted away his later years in a fashionable and dissolute manner. Ogden comments: 'from his sufferings, or at any rate from this description of them, came the moral impetus for the foundation of London University'. For extracts from Beardmore's obituary see Ogden, *Jeremy Bentham*, pp. 26–8; and for Bentham's involvement in the project to establish UCL see J. H. Burns, *Jeremy Bentham and University College* (London, 1962).

[57] Quoted by H. H. Bellot, *University College London 1826–1926* (London, 1929), 56.
[58] Ibid.
[59] It was to save the Chair of Philosophy from the suspicion of 'theistic teaching' that George Grote opposed the election of James Martineau in 1866 (Benn, *The History of English Rationalism*, i. 305).

exasperation over settling the curriculum of the new University is revealed in a few jottings from *c.*1827, where he offers the query whether it would not be well 'to throw out some of the saints who are doing so much mischief' (UC 107/353).

As one might suppose, Bentham's thoughts on higher education can be traced to the *Chrestomathia*, his experimental tract on utilitarian education. Here religion is banned entirely from the curriculum. There are no concessions to the use of the Bible as in the Lancasterian schools and such as we find Bentham tactically employing in *Church-of-Englandism*. In the *Chrestomathia* he writes:

if instruction in relation to controverted points of *Divinity*, were admitted, whatsoever were the tenets taught, a parent to whose notions those tenets were, to a certain degree repugnant, would not send his child to a school, which numbered among its objects and its promises, the impregnating with those tenets the minds of its scholars. (*Works*, viii. 40)

The Chrestomathic School was not intended to be a boarding school. Hence each pupil was to have ample time at home to receive whatever religious tuition the parents deemed suitable. To those afraid that instruction repugnant to religion would be given at the school Bentham avowed that 'no instruction . . . disrespectful to Religion in general, to the Christian Religion in particular, or to any one form of it, shall ever be administered' (*Works*, viii. 42).[60] One would be right to doubt the veracity of such pronouncements. After all, what *was* to be taught in the Chrestomathic School was a syllabus containing a large dose of the natural sciences, and Bentham was in no doubt as to the consequences for religion of a thoroughgoing education of this kind.

Just how central the abolition of religion was to Bentham's vision of the Utilitarian society can in part be understood by a reading of his 'final' work (printed posthumously 1842), the *Auto-Icon*.[61] Rarely

---

[60] Francis Place, one of the principals in the movement for secular education, reiterated the position of the philosophic radicals on religious instruction in the Chrestomathic School: 'We were not religious ourselves, and therefore had no sectarian notions to teach; we wished the improvement of the people, knew that reading and writing and arithmetic were important steps in the process, . . . As our desire was to teach all, we saw very clearly that the way to teach all was to teach no religious doctrine' (quoted by Bain, *James Mill*, p. 86).

[61] In a note at the head of this pamphlet Bowring (or perhaps John Hill Burton) relates that Bentham spoke of this as his 'last work'. For a discussion of the context in which Bentham wrote this tract, verification of its authenticity and other details concerning its printing, and the execution of Bentham's will as it regards his remains see C. F. A. Marmoy, 'The "Auto-Icon" of Jeremy Bentham at University College, London', *Medical History*, 2 (1958), 77–86.

noticed by scholars in the past, it is an odd utilitarian tract containing several allusions to traditional Christian practices but designed to show, among other things, the irrelevance of religion. Here the immortality promised by Comte's Positivism—the survival in memory, in the thoughts and affections of those whom an individual benefited and loved—finds a parallel in Bentham's suggestions for the creation of 'auto-icons'. For both men, the only real sense in which a person lives on is in posterity (for Diderot, too, this was a more virtuous object than the personal kind of immortality promised by Christianity).[62]

Being an atheist and a rigorous utilitarian, Bentham was almost bound at some point in his life to consider the question, 'Of what use are the dead to the living?' That this question should foster an entire thesis about the usefulness to be derived from corpses, particularly if they are remains of those of achievement and intellect, is also typical of Bentham; but that he should have been thinking along such lines even in his youth is remarkable. Bentham's decision to leave his own body for the purposes of medical research was 'no hasty—no recent determination' but was decided in 1769 (that eventful year in which he read Hume, Helvétius, and Beccaria) on the occasion of his coming of age (*AI* 2). As an indication of the indifference of the twenty-one-years-old Bentham to religious practices his first will is interesting enough, but the request concerning his body, given the age in which he writes, is remarkable:

as to my body my will is that it be buried by the rites of the Church of England, or the rites of any other Church, or no rites at all at the discretion of my Executor [Richard Clark], so that the funeral expenses do not in any wise exceed forty shillings, but it is my Will and special request to my Executor that if I should chance to die of any such disease as that in the judgement of my said Exor the art of Surgery or science of Physic should be likely to be any wise advanced by observations to be made on the opening of my body, that he my said Executor do cause my said body as soon after my decease may be delivered unto George Fordyce now of Henrietta Street Covent Garden Dr. of Physic. (*Corr.* i. 136)[63]

---

[62] For Diderot's view of posterity see J. McManners, *Death and the Enlightenment: Changing Attitudes to Death among the Christians and Unbelievers in Eighteenth-Century France* (Oxford, 1981), ch. 6, sec. 4.

[63] Bentham drew up this will on 24 Aug. 1769, 6 months after his coming of age. Some 2 months before Bentham's death it was sent to Dr Thomas Southwood Smith, the physician who performed the autopsy upon his remains. Smith quoted the final sentence from the will in his *Lecture Delivered over the Remains of Jeremy Bentham, Esq. . . . On the 9 June, 1832* (London, 1832), 4. Bowring wrote of Bentham's final days

In confirming this request in his final will on 30 May 1832 (UC 155/ 23–35), not two months before his death, Bentham showed that he was entirely in agreement with those who argued that people should not be prohibited by law from donating bodies for the purposes of anatomical dissection. The subject of dissection had been a public issue for over a decade before Warburton's Anatomy Act passed into law in 1832.[64] Bentham became actively involved in the campaign in 1826. With the activities of the body-snatchers in mind, in an unsent letter to Robert Peel (24 Apr. 1826) he expressed the fear that murder might occur unless something were done to legalize the donating of bodies for medical research, and went on to propose as a title for a bill: 'A Bill for the more effectual prevention of the violation of Burial Places' (UC 11b/193–5).[65] Several Benthamites (Henry Warburton, John Smith, Joseph Hume, Sir Thomas Baring, Sir James Graham, Spring Rice, Poulett Thompson, and Hyde Villiers, among them) were involved in the 1828 Select Committee on Anatomy, and almost certainly it was Bentham's draft 'Body Providing Bill' (UC 11b/220–4, 6 Nov. 1826) which provided the basis for the first Anatomy Bill of 1829.[66] By donating his own body for medical research it was his intention, first conceived sixty years before, to contribute through example to the lessening of the prejudice which existed against dissection. Today Bentham's auto-icon (or 'self-image') still stands in

thus: 'I have never known a human being to whom the thought of death had so little in it that was disturbing or disagreeable' (*Works*, x. 556). Peter Gay has commented on this characteristic of the atheistic philosophers of the age: 'for men seeking to vindicate the autonomy of philosophy and its superiority to all other guides to life, philosophical bravery in the face of death was simply another argument against the need for religion' (*The Enlightenment*, ii. 88).

[64] The Reform Act received its royal assent the day after Bentham died (6 June 1832), at which point the Anatomy Bill was between its first and second readings in the Lords, passing into law 2 months later. In its final form the Act permitted those having lawful custody of dead bodies to donate them for dissection, thus enabling hospitals and poorhouses to cut expenditure on pauper funerals by donating the bodies of those too poor to provide for their own burial. By creating a cheap, legal, and institutionalized source of bodies, the Act led to the collapse of the body-snatching trade conducted by the likes of the notorious Burke and Hare. For a discussion of the agitation which led to the legalization of the practice of donating corpses for medical purposes see M. J. Durey, 'Body Snatchers and Benthamites: The Implications of the Dead Body Bill for the London Schools of Anatomy, 1820–42', *The London Journal* (1976), 200–25; R. Richardson, *Death, Dissection and the Destitute* (London, 1987), *passim*. And for a discussion of the activities of Burke and Hare, crucial for the history of anatomy in Britain, see ch. 6 of the latter.

[65] Other correspondence between JB and Peel can be found at UC 11b/180–3, 189–92. See also Richardson, *Death, Dissection and the Destitute*, p. 112.

[66] For a discussion of the Benthamite influence see ibid. 108–16.

its box in the corner of the South Cloisters of University College, a reminder of his commitment to this particular utilitarian cause.[67]

In the essay *Auto-Icon*, however, Bentham was to take the idea of the utility of corpses much further. Besides having an anatomical or dissectional purpose, auto-icons were to serve a 'conservative' or 'statuary' function. Of the first Bentham says little. He discusses past methods of preserving bodies and the benefits to be gained from anatomical studies. For the remainder he refers the reader to an essay by Dr Southwood Smith on 'The Uses of the Dead to the Living' (1824),[68] from which his own pamphlet derived its subtitle. Bentham's suggestions under the second head are the more intriguing. He explains the auto-icon (absurdly enough) as a person who is their own image, preserved for the benefit of posterity, and discusses the many uses of embalmed bodies under the following divisions: '1. Moral; including 2. Political; 3 Honorific; 4. Dehonorific; 5. Economical, or Money saving; 6. Lucrative, or Money getting; 7. Commemorational, including 8. Genealogical, 9. Architectural; 10. Theatrical; and 11. Phrenological' (*AI* 3). One of the more curious possibilities Bentham suggests, however, is the use of auto-icons in a religious manner: 'On certain days the Auto-Icons might be exhibited, and their exhibition associated with religious observances. Every sect would choose its own exhibition-day . . . Out of Auto-Icons, a selection might be made for a Temple of Fame—not in miniature—a temple filled with a population of illustrious Auto-Icons' (*AI* 4). Bentham even envisaged 'Temples of Honour and Dishonour', with the transference of auto-icons from one to another depending on the current state of public opinion, and even an 'Auto-Icon purgatory' in which are to stand, with their heads turned away from public view, those auto-icons temporarily out of favour (*AI* 6, 7). Auto-icons, rich, poor, famous, and infamous, are to replace the monuments of conventional religion in the churches, realizing the Christian equality which escapes individuals in life: all are 'on the same level' and 'the beautiful commandment of Jesus would be obeyed; they would indeed "meet together"' (*AI* 3). In addition, 'Dialogues of the Dead' are suggested for their theatrical and educational possibilities.

[67] Bentham's auto-icon has also been the target of several pranks and jibes. It raised this sarcastic remark from Michael Oakeshott: 'What was mortal survived; what was immortal was buried and forgotten' ('The New Bentham', p. 114). See also H. S. Bevington's dreadful poem 'A Bomb for Jeremy Bentham' (1940), in *Nineteen Million Elephants and Other Poems* (Boston, 1950), 33–4.

[68] T. S. Smith, 'The Uses of the Dead to the Living', *Westminster Review*, 12 (1824); later published as a pamphlet, *Use of the Dead to the Living* (Albany, 1827).

Bentham fancies an Elysian Field of the auto-icons of famous philosophers, who, by the aid of actors using mechanical devices, are to converse before a studious audience on the progress of their respective sciences and discuss the ideals for which they laboured while alive in the flesh (*AI* 12–13). Typically enough, he offers snippets of conversations that might take place between himself and Socrates on the subject of happiness and on the philosophical developments of the past two thousand years; with Bacon and d'Alembert on the Encyclopedical Tree'; with Bacon, Dumont, and Montesquieu on the 'Law as it ought to be'; with Locke on the fiction of the original contract; with Porphyry, Locke, and Bishop Sanderson on logic; and with Euclid, Apollonius, Diophantus, Newton, and La Place on mathematics. Finally, pilgrimages to the shrines of dead philosophers are suggested as fitting substitutes for the pilgrimages to the shrines of saints and martyrs (*AI* 14–15).

What are we to make of all this? In the first place, it is obvious that Bentham found it almost impossible to divorce his train of thought from the practices of conventional religion. Yet he insisted on the difference: in his secular observances no spiritual content is to be found. In the secular Utilitarian society there was to be no God, and the absurd idea of an immortal soul was to be banished from discourse. People lived on only through their achievements and their presence as ideas in the minds of those who came after them. There being no supernatural sanction for morality, the reward for contributions to the public good was to be remembered affectionately by one's family and to be commemorated by one's fellow citizens. Religious rewards and punishments in a future life were replaced by the verdict of future generations, a verdict renewed century after century in the case of the truly great.

It is at this point that the affinity between Bentham and his French contemporaries, revolutionary and philosophical, ends. His desire to eliminate the idea of religion, to the end of constructing a new society unhampered by myth, contrasts with the efforts of the French, particularly Comte, to construct a secular equivalent to Christian belief and practice—a secular Religion of Humanity stripped of other-worldly referents. The utilitarian schema is devoid of the dogmas and mysteries which characterize Comte's scheme of social worship. For both Bentham and James Mill the churches are meant to serve first and foremost as centres of instruction, not places in which the faithful are to reaffirm their devotion to humanity. Bentham could not perform the mental gymnastics exercised, for example, by Ludwig Feuerbach (1804–72), the German philosopher and student of Hegel, who, beginning from an ontological base similar to Bentham's was yet able to follow Comte in elevating humanity into the object of a cult.

Like Bentham's, Feuerbach's ontology was grounded in materialism, accompanied by an epistemology viewed in terms of the harmonious working of sensation and reason, with the emphasis on sensation. Immortality he declared an idle dream. The individual is limited and imperfect by nature; but humanity, in its entire stretch from past to future, is not limited, nor is it characterized by the imperfections which obstruct the endeavours of individual human beings. If the essence of religion consists, as Feuerbach maintains, in a projection of human qualities into an object of worship, then the religious projection is best directed towards the human race. In these terms Feuerbach was, like Comte, an anti-theologian who presents us with a philosophically grounded antithesis to all theology while at the same time expounding a Religion of Humanity. He denied the revealed primacy and sovereignty of God, any God, all Gods, in favour of a humanism that finds the essence of religion in the glorification of humanity, and in which all statements about God are translated into statements about 'man'. The concluding paragraph of his *Lectures on the Essence of Religion* (1851), delivered at Heidelberg in 1848, describes Feuerbach's central aim: 'to transform friends of God into friends of man, believers into thinkers, devotees of prayer into devotees of work, candidates for the hereafter into students of this world, Christians who by their own profession and admission, are "*half animal, half angel*", into *men*, into *whole men*'.[69] Feuerbach, like Bentham, denied only in order to affirm, but at the centre of his affirmation is an idealism which is wholly alien to the thought of the latter. 'I deny the fantastic projection of theology and religion', he had written in the *Essence of Christianity* (1841), 'in order to affirm the real essence of man'. To Feuerbach, 'Man is the beginning, the middle, and the end of religion.'[70] He had as little doubt of the illusory nature of the consolations of revealed religion as Bentham,[71] but in deifying 'man' he took up a position closer to that

[69] L. Feuerbach, *Lectures on the Essence of Religion*, trans. R. Manheim (1851; New York, 1967), 285.

[70] Quoted K. Barth in L. Feuerbach, *Essence of Christianity*, trans. of 1841 edn. G. Elliot (1854; New York, 1957), introduction, pp. xiv, xix.

[71] The *Essence of Christianity* caused a tremendous stir in Germany when it appeared in 1841. David Friedrich Strauss (1808–74), who caused a furor with his own radical 'Left-Hegelian' *Life of Jesus Critically Examined* (1835–6), wrote of Feuerbach: 'Today,

taken by Comte. Feuerbach's idealism consists in this: he did not simply accept relations based on reciprocal inclination between human beings (sex, friendship, compassion, self-sacrifice, etc.) as being what they are in themselves, but instead asserted that such relations will come to their full realization only when consecrated and, hence, elevated by the name religion. The point, then, is not that these purely human relations exist (they are fundamental data for Bentham as well), but that they should be conceived of as the new, true religion.[72] By contrast in the Utilitarian society individuals are bound to each other by the ordinary arrangements of the state and by the knowledge that ultimately their own happiness is dependent upon the actions of others. The only notion of common 'faith' they share is trust in utility and in their ability to build a new society free from the superstitions with which the old order was fraught. There is to be no Comtian Positivist priesthood, no modes of public or private worship, no religious signs or symbols, however devoid of mysticism they might appear, no idolization of the feminine virtues, and no 'Great Being' or 'Goddess' for them to contemplate.[73] True, Bentham's Elysian Field was to be occupied by a record of the species' great men (no women are mentioned) similar to those in Comte's Calendar of 'saints' (heroes and benefactors serving as objects of veneration each with its own special day), but it was not humanity that was to be worshipped. For all Bentham's dependence on the theoretical principles of natural science, he could not elevate reason to a position where it became the object of a cult, and neither could he comprehend a Religion of Humanity. The notion of 'humanity' for Bentham could only be an abstraction, a fiction; the presuppositions of his nominalist view of the world dictate that there are only specific individuals in the world, and it was these in their iconized form that he intended to be admired, respected, held in

and perhaps for some time to come, the field belongs to him. His theory is the truth of this age.' Renan, too, though as yet unaware of the scandal his own work would cause, noted the critical importance of Feuerbach in challenging traditional religion: 'if the end of the world were to come in the 19th century, then, of course, he would have to be called the Anti-Christ'; both quotations from E. Kamenka, *The Philosophy of Ludwig Feuerbach* (New York, 1970), 15. Between them, Strauss and Feuerbach provided the seminal works of the Young Hegelian movement: on the grounds that liberation is an act of critical thinking and that conventional religion is the fundamental form of mystification and self-alienation, they held that the criticism of conventional religion was essential for the possibility of all criticism.

[72] Derived from 'religare' the term originally meant 'a bond'; thus for Feuerbach every bond between 2 persons constituted a religion.

[73] See Comte, *The Catechism of Positive Religion*, introduction and pt. 1.

affection, or condemned for misconduct. His aim was not to placate a religious need or simply to redirect religious sentiments to secular objects; he refused to recognize that the human frame was anything more than a complex physiological summation of parts.

The auto-icons, therefore, serve a useful function entirely divorced from spiritual or mystical considerations. They inspire or disgust and are aids to instruction, but no more than this. From the stories of their lives, their failings and achievements, their contributions to the public good, and their crimes against the community we can learn how best to conduct our own lives. But there is no use in our praying at their feet for guidance or forgiveness, for grace or salvation. In this they are impotent. 'Has religion anything to do with the matter?' asks Bentham. 'Nothing at all. Free as air does religion leave the disposal of the dead.' Religon is silent, 'neuter', having nothing to do with the business: 'The religion of Jesus leaves it to rank among things indifferent' (*AI* 16). What separates both Comte and Feuerbach from Bentham is that, far from wanting to abolish religion, they each set out to perfect it.

4. The Utilitarian utopia

As a critic of Bentham J. S. Mill is of special interest. It is well documented that following his mental crisis he embarked upon a reconsideration of the basic values of utilitarianism, out of which he emerged convinced that the human personality is a far richer ensemble than either Bentham or his father had supposed. He did not reject the doctrine of utility, but now he thought that attention should be directed to the 'internal culture of the individual', to the cultivation of feeling, and the development of the aesthetic sensibilities. Utilitarianism, as a science of society, should not be entirely preoccupied with the 'external culture', the purely rational mode of thought and behaviour. What this meant was that the external environment, and by implication the project to fashion the 'correct' conditioning factors originated by Helvétius, did not have the central importance for Mill which it had for Bentham.[74] But there is nothing new in this. More germane to the subject at hand is the fact that it is also true that at various times in his life Mill looked to Comte's Religion of Humanity to provide a focus for the religious and aesthetic sensibilities of a people that had been

[74] G. Himmelfarb, *On Liberty and Liberalism: The Case of John Stuart Mill* (New York, 1974), 7.

brought to understand the illusory nature of conventional religion. There were, of course, important differences between Mill and Comte. No more than Bentham could Mill accept the Roman Catholic character of Comte's new religion,[75] and, as it turned out, Comte's system was never really the purely secular and scientific construction that Mill had at first thought it might be. Later in life he went so far as to denounce it as 'the completest system of spiritual and temporal despotism, which ever yet emanated from a human being, unless possibly that of Ignatius Loyola'.[76] Even so, Mill never let go of the idea of a secular Religion of Humanity and a great part of the posthumously published essay on the *Utility of Religion* (1874) is taken up with discussing it.

Mill's essay opens with a discussion of Bentham's *Analysis*.[77] Mill recognized the worth of Bentham's criticisms of the fundamental beliefs of traditional Christianity and he followed him in emphasizing the danger of associating sound moral precepts with doctrines intellectually unsustainable. What is different, however, is that Mill was not completely negative: he was of the mind that parts of Bentham's argument were pressed too hard, and he allowed some value historically to religion as an aid to ethics.[78] His real contribution in this respect is to present the Religion of Humanity as a suitable replacement for traditional Judaeo-Christian religions, as an equal to them in their best (most positive) manifestations, and as their superior in everything else. Mill did not dispute the value of religion, neither in the past nor in the present, as a source of personal satisfaction and of elevated feelings. But he queried whether to obtain this goal it was necessary 'to travel beyond the boundaries of the world'. His thinking was that 'idealization of our earthly life, the cultivation of a high conception of what it may be made', was capable of supplying 'a religion equally fitted to exact the feelings and (with some aid from education) still better calculated to ennoble the conduct than any belief respecting the unseen powers'. Mill encouraged individuals to identify their feelings with 'the entire life of the human race'.[79] As Rome was to the Roman people and as Jehovah was to the Jews, so the human race— past, present, and future—should be our object of devotion. Mill

[75] J. S. Mill, *Auguste Comte and Positivism* (1865), in *Collected Works*, x. 338, 345–6.
[76] Mill, *Autobiography*, in *Collected Works*, i. 221.
[77] For the influence of *An.* on Mill see ibid. 72–3, and above ch. 7 n. 2.
[78] Mill, *Utility of Religion*, in *Collected Works*, x. 406. On the same page Mill informs us that he intends to make free use of the writings of Comte in this essay.
[79] Ibid. 420.

likened religion to patriotism, not a patriotism stirred by great crises but a continuing (educated and cultivated) patriotic concern to serve the world conceived in its broadest sense. The 'exalted morality', a morality which does not depend upon rewards for action, is in reality a religion (a 'real religion', Mill called it). At the risk of rejecting utilitarianism altogether, he explained that 'outward good works' are only a part of this religion, being 'rather the fruits of the religion than the religion itself'.[80] His final, tantalizing pronouncement upon the matter stands thus:

> The essence of religion is the strong and earnest direction of the emotions and desires toward an ideal object, recognized as one of the highest excellence, and as rightfully paramount over all selfish objects of desire. This condition is fulfilled by the Religion of Humanity in as eminent a degree and in as high a sense as by the supernatural religions even in their best manifestations, and far more so than in any of their others.[81]

The object of this religion and, indeed, the rationale for its very existence, is a sense of unity with humanity and a deep feeling for the general good.

In many ways this conception of religion and its function constitutes a significant ingredient in Mill's later effort to rescue Bentham's vision of the Utilitarian society from its mundane and dependent condition. For Bentham's aim was to build a Utilitarian heaven on earth, but it was to be a heaven without gods, angels, saints, or any other fictional beings or other-worldly entities. The principal agent for constructing this Utilitarian utopia, of course, is the legislator; he it is who, with the aid of education and the sanctions at his disposal must fashion society anew. It is true that Bentham believed that each person is bound to pursue his or her own happiness, and also that each of us ought to promote the greatest happiness of the community. But, as others have pointed out, these are not contradictory statements. Bentham thought that a reasonable person would accept that the greatest happiness principle was the principle on which society in general should be managed, but he did not expect each person to aim at anything other than his own happiness. The best way to maximize the general happiness of the community was for those responsible for the management of society to arrange matters, by employing the necessary

---

[80] Mill, *Utility of Religion*, in *Collected Works*, p. 421–2.
[81] Ibid. 422. See also pp. 422–8, where Mill discusses the points of superiority of the Religion of Humanity over traditional religion.

moral and political sanctions, so that individuals pursued their own happiness in ways conducive to the happiness of others, or at least not detrimental to that happiness. The general importance of this element was plainly stated in Dumont's edition of the *Traités de legislation*, where Bentham wrote that it was the legislator's task to 'determine' the conduct of the citizens, and that ethics is the art of 'directing' people's action in ways designed to maximize the greatest possible happiness.[82] Even earlier, in the manuscripts for the *Essay on the Influence of Time and Place in Matters of Legislation*, a work begun in 1780 and completed *c.*1795, Bentham had suggested something similar while mapping out the general schema of his Utilitarian utopia.[83] Everything turns upon the perfection of the law and its capacity to modify human conduct towards the end of maximizing happiness—what is 'optimized' is 'the condition of mankind' (UC 142/200).

The Utilitarian society, then, is not one in which the State merely stands aside only to act as an arbiter on occasions of dispute. In order to maximize happiness the State has to play a positive role in alleviating the psychological impediments to the pursuit of happiness, whether they be impediments caused by miscalculation or selfishness, or the product of beliefs in an illusory reality. The Utilitarian State must, in a sense, force its citizens to free themselves from these obstacles in the path of general happiness. The secular Utilitarian society is one, therefore, in which the State actively works to stamp out religion. Religion must be entirely absent from this utopia; in its most perfect condition the secular Utilitarian society is peopled by atheists who deny both the existence of a spiritual aspect to their nature and the reality of a world beyond the perceptible universe, and who order their lives in strict accordance with the rational dictates of the principle of utility. In short, a precondition for the maximization of utility is universal atheism. To be sure the inevitable hardships and inequalities of life will not disappear in this Utilitarian utopia:

Fire will burn, frost pinch, thirst parch, hunger grip as heretofore; toil even as now must be the prelude to subsistence: that the few may be wealthy, the many must be poor: all must be tantalized more or less with the prospect of joys,

---

[82] *Traités de législation civile et pénale . . . Publiés en français par Ét. Dumont*, 3 vols. (Paris, 1802), i, pp. xxx, 93, cited Dinwiddy, 'Early Nineteenth-Century Reactions to Bentham', p. 64.

[83] As with so much else, I am indebted to Professor Long for drawing my attention to the rich detail concerning Bentham's vision of the future contained in these manuscripts.

which they are out of hopes of tasting, and how much lighter soever may sit than it does now, coercion must be felt, that all may be secure. (UC 142/200)

Nor could Bentham conceive of the world in any other terms. For all the legislator's ingenuity 'physical sensibility' remained 'the ground of law'. Lacking an understanding of the incorporeal component of human nature, religious or otherwise, and lacking, too, Mill's profound understanding of the capacity of human beings for self-development, Bentham concluded that 'Sense, which is the basis of every idea, is so of every enjoyment; and unless man's whole nature be new modelled, so long as man remains man the stock of sense . . . never can increase' (UC 142/200). In a sombre reflection upon his own vision, Bentham was to remark: 'If this be paradise, paradise is at best what the Asiatics meant by it, a garden: it is still however a very pleasant garden to look to in comparison of the wilderness in which we have as yet been wandering' (UC 142/200). This was the harsh, though improved, reality of Bentham's 'ideal' society. He had no time for the wild utopic fantasies in which others indulged; the basic material of human nature is known and, since this will not change, so the legislator must fashion his policies accordingly, subtly employing educational institutions and the efficacy of the moral sanction in order to direct individuals to pursue the general happiness, and never failing to employ coercive methods when the circumstances dictate. Bentham thought that the Chevalier Chastellux (1734–8) and Joseph Priestley,[84] both to be commended for their contributions to the public weal, went too far when they posited a notion of the species as ever improving towards a 'paradisiacal' future 'to surpass any thing which at present we can conceive' (UC 142/212). To speculate in this fashion is to ignore the basic facts of human nature and the terms of its existence. It is impossible that 'while man is man, the measure of felicity he enjoys [can] attain to any greater bulk/higher standard than that we are and must be perfectly well able to measure and see to the end of even by such lights as . . . we possess at present' (UC 142/213).

In sum, I take Bentham to be saying that the individual, as a 'bundle of sensations', will always remain just that, and this means that in the Utilitarian utopia the onus to achieve reform lies with the legislator, to whose lot it falls to manipulate and coerce individuals into conformity with the dictates of utility. In so far as the legislator succeeds in this

---

[84] Chastellux, *An Essay on Public Happiness*; J. Priestley, *An Essay on the First Principles of Government, and on the Nature of Political, Civil and Religious Liberty* (London, 1768).

task the stock of happiness will be increased, and in so far as he fails it will be diminished. There is nothing inherent in human nature that can save it from this ignoble dependence: pain and suffering are part and parcel of the inhabited world, and all attempts to transcend this reality are chimerical. What progress there is to be had is to be had by altering the social and political arrangements, which must be stripped of all superstitious and mystical elements and all other impediments to the task of maximizing utility. Such a functional utopia is characterized by adequacy and efficiency; however, as Mill and other critics have remarked, Bentham's utopia, spiritually and emotionally impoverished, could never rise to the level of magnificence. Having said that, however, we should not doubt the strength of Bentham's commitment to build this curiously flawed Utilitarian world. His aim was to construct the Utilitarian utopia according to the principles of his exhaustive legislatorial system. Free from all taint of religion, it was towards this end that the sect of the utilitarians, the works of their great founder in hand, were to devote all their efforts.

When Mill praised the work of the religious utilitarian, the Revd John Brown, in his celebrated essay on Bentham,[85] his purpose, not necessarily needless, was to stress that the utilitarian doctrine did not originate with Bentham, but was a feature of the intellectual air of the age before he wrote. However, the real point to be made is that though the doctrine did not originate with Bentham he, more than anyone else, provided it with its secular character, and this was a radical departure from the then prevailing version of the doctrine expounded in England by Brown, Law, Paley, and others. By the time Mill came to reflect on his intellectual inheritance, and as a direct result of the teaching of Bentham and his disciples, the religious aspect was deemed at best to be needless baggage which the doctrine could do without. But when this point has been reached our feet are firmly in the nineteenth century and we have left the eighteenth far behind. It is this shift in ground, from the religious to the secular, precipitated—or at least epitomized—in the main by the teaching of Bentham, that characterizes the difference between eighteenth- and nineteenth-century versions of the doctrine of utility in England.

[85] See above ch. 2 n. 9.

Appendices

A. The Manuscripts on Religion

The current catalogues of Bentham manuscripts, those compiled by A. Taylor Milne and Douglas G. Long, employ two distinct approaches. With few exceptions, Milne catalogued the manuscripts at UCL according to the boxes in which they were to be found. More recently Long, making extensive use of Milne's work, has supplied us with a chronological index of the UCL collection. In their different and complementary ways both these catalogues have been, and will surely continue to be, indispensable guides for scholars interested in Bentham's voluminous stocks of unpublished material. The following list of manuscripts is unlike that of Milne and Long in two ways. First, it is organized primarily according to the thematic relationship that each grouping of manuscripts bears to Bentham's published work on religion—(*a*) organized religion; (*b*) natural and revealed religion—and only secondarily according to boxes and dates. Secondly, I include all the relevant material in the possession of the British Library. This appendix should enable us more easily to appreciate two features of Bentham's critique of religion: the frequency with which he returned to consider several of its important aspects, and how much of his long and full life he devoted to the subject as a whole.

Bentham did not date his manuscripts prior to (and not always after) 1800, hence where I have not been able to view the manuscripts personally I rely upon Milne and Long and occasionally Steintrager. I have received fruitful guidance in compiling this appendix from the latter's unpublished 'Report on the Problems of Editing Bentham's Writings on Religion', Appendix B to the Report by the General Editor [J. H. Burns] of the Collected Works, 12 June 1967.

Organized religion

1.	UC 97/1–116	Legislation—raw materials, containing much fragmentary material on 'Obstacles. Divines' (*c.*1770–4).
2.	5/1–32	Subscriptions (*c.*1773).
3.	96/263–341	Subscriptions: jottings, reflections, etc. mostly titled 'Subscription', but including remarks on penal laws and Dissenters, the Sabbath, trinitarianism, and other topics (*c.*1773).
4.	69/16	Subscriptions (*c.*1774).

5. 73/9–10, 19–24 Penal laws against Papists and Dissenters (*c*.1774).

6. 169/152 On Toleration—to the *Public Advertiser*—Answer by a Church of England man (1789).

7. 108/108 Jottings on Church establishments with reference to Edmund Burke (*c*.1790–8?).

8. 109/40–2 Fragments on Episcopalians, Seceders, Roman Catholics, and Cameronians in relation to Scotch Reform (*c*.1808).

9. 128/32 Marginalia for a work under the title 'Church Abuse of Influence'—an outline of a projected fifteen-chapter work (1809 or 1810).

10. 5/33–93 Causes and forms of intolerance, including fragments on 'Abuses', 'Church Service', 'Church Power', 'Subscriptions Paley', 'Perjury', 'Church Reform', and the 'Science of Divinity' (undated, but probably 1809–13).

11. 21/75 A list of 'Propositions on Parish priests, how to improve their education and make them useful' (20 Aug. 1810).

12. 6/1–209 Outlines, topic suggestions, fragments of text, and chapter and section headings for a work on the practices, doctrines, and institutions of the Church of England (1812–13).

13. 5/94–316 Mainly text for the second part of the intended work on the Church (as indicated above) under the heading 'Doctrine', and principally concerned with the modes of persuasion used to elicit declarations of belief and the evil consequences of such practices (1812–13).

14. BL 'Commonplace Books of James Mill', 5 vols., ii. 61–7: MSS in the hand of Bentham on the Church (1813), almost certainly related to those at UC 5/94–316.

15. UC 158/123–230 Marginalia for *CE*, principally employed in the writing of pt 2 of the Introduction and Appendix IV (1813–15, but mainly 1816).

16. 7/1–160 Material intended for two appendices to *CE* which were omitted by Bentham for want of space—a commentary upon a letter published by Dr Kipling, Dean of Peterborough, on the evils of schism, and a discussion of an abuse of 'influence' involving Dean Andrews and the Chancellor of the Exchequer, Nicholas Vansittart—and other miscellaneous material used in pt. 4 of the Introduction to the published work (1816).

17. 6/210–11 JB to the Unitarian MP William Smith, subsequently published as part of the Preface on Publication at the front of *CE*, pp. xiv–xviii (24 Jan. 1818).

18. BL Add. MSS 33545/258, 262–6: a reply from Smith to JB, also included in the Preface on Publication at the front of *CE*, pp. xviii–xxiv (16 Feb. 1818).

19. UC 13/143–6   A letter from JB to John Cam Hobhouse on the subject of Catholic Emancipation (12 Dec. 1820). See *Works*, x. 523–5.

20. 148/31–9   Outlines for Letter VII to Count Toreno on the subject of religion (see item 21).

21. 148/72–122   Letter VII to Count Toreno on the subject of a Spanish Code—On Religion (1821). See *Works*, viii. 546–51.

22. BL Add. MSS 33551/307–8: draft of a preface intended for a new edition of *CE* (27 Oct. 1822).

23. UC 8/149–73   Fragments for the *Book of Church Reform* (1831).

24. BL Add. MSS 33551/231–8: drafts for the preface to the *Book of Church Reform*.

Natural and revealed religion

25. UC 69/12–20   'Crit[itical] Jur[isprudence] Crim[inal]'—fragments on the religious sanction (*c*.1774).

26. 73/90–100   On sexual nonconformity (*c*.1774).

27. 74a/1–26   Fragments on sexual nonconformity, including an outline marked (at 26) 'Dedicated to J. B.' (*c*.1774).

28. 140/1–2   'Crit[ical] Jur[isprudence] Crim[inal]'—fragments on the religious sanction (1775).

29. 98/53–117   Penal Code—religious sanction (at 53–66), and delits religieux (at 67–117) (*c*.1775–85?).

30. 69/111–12, 175,   'Preparatory Principles'—Divine Law (*c*.1776); prob-
    193, 202   ably used in *Comm.*, ch. 2.

31. 69/132–3, 139   'Preparatory Principles'—'Idea of God—cannot be a foundation of morals'; 'Idea of God useless in Jurisprudence' (*c.*1776).

32. 69/166–7   'Preparatory Principles'—religious sanction (*c.*1776).

33. 87/17–41   Indirect Legislation—the comparative force of the three sanctions, including the religious (*c*.1780).

34. 72/187–205   Paederasty (*c.*1785).

35. 74a/26–34   The beginning of an essay in French on Nonconformité (*c*.1785).

36. 14/19   Deontology private; Catechism or Jug true (*c*.1800).

37. 138/155–60   Mainly jottings on miracles (1811).

38. BL Add. MSS 29806–9: contains the material used by Grote for *An.* and MSS intended for subsequent parts of this work (1811–21, but mainly 1811, 1815, 1819, and 1821).

39. UC 139/1–211   Marginalia, topic headings, extracts from Paul's Letters, for *NP* (1813, 1815, 1817–19).
40. 74a/35–222   Headed 'Code penal—sexual' (1814) and 'Sextus' or 'Not Paul' (1816), the latter intended for the second part or volume of *NP*.
41. 139/212–331   Material employed in *NP* (1815, 1817, 1821).
42. 138/1–154   Outlines and marginalia for the proposed 'True History of Jesus' (mainly 1815, but some dated 1819, 1821, 1822).
43. 161a/141–214   Generally suppressed material on the doctrinal differences between Paul and Jesus, intended as the transition to Sextus, that is, the second part of *NP* (1816–18).
44. 139/332–444   The intended 'Appendix: Paul's Inducements', suppressed from *NP* for want of space (1816–18, 1823).
45. 161b/215–523   'Asceticism: its repugnancy to the religion of Jesus', intended as the third part of *NP* (1816–18).
46. 161a/1–19   A proposal to William Beckford to edit 'Sextus', together with a detailed outline and some fragments for that work (1817).
47. 161a/20–140   Material incorporated into *NP* (1817–18).
48. 139/445–531   The almost completed 'Church History' suppressed from *NP* for want of space (1817, 1819, 1823).
49. 139/523–9   Seven annotated proof sheets of the *Summary View of a Work intitled Not Paul, but Jesus* (1821).
50. 145/1–152   Bible clippings (without annotations) arranged according to topics for *NP* and the proposed 'True History of Jesus' (*c.*1821).
51. 68/10–18   Penal Code—appendix, 'sexual eccentricities' (1824–5).
52. 138/161–9   Drafts on the utility of religion (1825 and 1830).
53. UC 155/9–16   Notes under the heading 'Practical Christianity versus Professing Christianity but practical infidelity', by E[dwin] C[hadwick] (*c.*1832)—a comparison of the professed beliefs and actual deeds of Christians and atheists, including Bentham, described at one point as 'the most eminently practical Christian'.

B. Bentham's 'Dream'

The sheets upon which this transcription is based are not grouped with any other manuscripts, but are in a folder of their own (UC 169/79).[1] A. Taylor Milne gives the date as *c.*1780, but the most probable date is the late summer of 1781, when Bentham was a guest at the Earl of Shelburne's Bowood residence, or shortly thereafter.[2]

My inference is based on two considerations of improbable coincidence. First, Bentham refers in this alleged 'dream' to 'a great man named Ld S', who beseeches him 'what shall I do to be saved? . . . I mean to save the nation?' To which Bentham replies 'take up my book, & follow me'. Earlier in the 'dream' the book is identified as the 'Principles of Legislation', an obvious reference to the *Introduction* (*IPML*). Now, we know that at Bowood in August of 1781 Bentham gave Shelburne a copy of the recently printed *IPML*. As Bentham wrote to his father (31 Aug. 1781), the earl insisted on reading this 'driest of all dry metaphysics' to the company at the house and, as Lord Camden was expected to join the party, he urged Bentham to prolong his stay and submit his proof–sheets to the great lawyer (*Corr.* iii. 69). There can be little doubt that Bentham hoped to have some influence with Shelburne and the company at Bowood and this is clearly implied in the 'dream'.

Secondly, forty years later Bentham recalled a curious scene which occurred within a few days of his arrival at Bowood, and which reinforces the idea that the manuscripts were written in the late summer of 1781. On retiring one evening he unexpectedly came upon his host:

'Mr. Bentham,' said he, candles in hand, 'Mr. Bentham,' in a tone somewhat hurried, as his manner sometimes was, '*what is it you can do for me?*' My surprise could not but be visible. Candle still in hand—'Nothing at

---

[1] Baumgardt printed a version of the 'Dream' (without notes) as an appendix to *Bentham and the Ethics of Today*, pp. 549–50. A comparison with the transcription that follows reveals several omissions and errors in the Baumgardt version.

[2] Bentham's first extant letter to Shelburne, occasioned by his brother Samuel's journey to Russia, for which purpose the earl had provided several letters of introduction, is dated 17 Sept. 1779 (for this and subsequent letters see *Corr.* ii–iii, *passim*). From 18 Nov. 1779 to early June 1780 there does not appear to have been any contact between Bentham and Shelburne. By the end of June Bentham was hoping to have the printing of *IPML* completed (*Corr.* ii. 437). Shelburne's first extant letter to Bentham, inviting him to call at Shelburne House in Berkeley Square, is dated 26 July 1780. Bentham tactfully avoided a meeting at this time (*Corr.* ii. 471), telling Samuel that he felt he should first establish his reputation by bringing out *IPML* (*Corr.* ii. 480, 499, 504). A year later Shelburne called upon Bentham at his chambers in Lincoln's Inn and invited him again to Shelburne House, an invitation which was taken up some time in early July 1781. Soon after Bentham accepted a second invitation, this time to Shelburne's country seat at Bowood in Wiltshire, and here he went in mid–Aug. and stayed until the second week of Oct. (see *Corr.* iii. 24–112).

all, my lord,' said I, 'nothing that I know of; I never said I could. I am like the
Prophet Balaam: the word that God putteth into my mouth, that alone can I
ever speak.' For discernment he was eminent; for quickness of perception
not less so. He took this for what it was meant—a declaration of
independence. He deposited his candles; I went off with mine. If by this
rencontre any expectation of his was disappointed, neither his kindness nor
the marks of his esteem were lessened. (*Works*, i. 249, emphasis added)

The similarity between Shelburne's request here and the request of 'Ld S' in
the 'dream' can hardly be missed.[3]

These references make it highly likely that Bentham wrote these manuscripts
shortly after, or some time during, this initial visit to Bowood. Here it was that
he introduced the company to *IPML* and discussed the prospect of being of
service to Shelburne, and both of these events find impressive echoes in the
'dream'—the text of which follows.

The world is persuaded not without some colour/ground of reason that all
reformers and system–mongers are mad: and not without some colour of
reason. Formerly they had [del: used] to live upon grass-hoppers in deserts:
walk upon/above golden thighs [?] or sit upon three legged stools in temples:
now they live in garrets: from whence in due time they are removed to [del:
Bedlam] Bethlehem.[4] Not of/I don't mean of Judah, but of Moorfields.

My madness has not yet to my own knowledge/consciousness as far as I
can perceive myself, gone beyond a dream. I dreamt t'other night that I was
a founder of a sect; of course a personage of great sanctity and importance.
It was called the sect of the *utilitarians*.[5] [del: There came to me a great man
named Ld S,[6] and he said unto me, what shall I do to save the nation. I said
unto him follow me.]

[3] According to John Bowring, Bentham gave in conversation a different account of
what was apparently the same interview: 'Lord Shelburne asked me what *he* could do for
me. I told him "nothing"; and he found this so different to the universal spirit of those
about him as to endear me to him' (*Works*, x. 116–17).

[4] The priory of the Order of St Mary of Bethlehem had been founded in 1247. It was
first used to house lunatics in 1377 and was controlled by the Crown until 1546, when it
was given to the City of London. From 1557 it was jointly managed with the correction
house at Bridewell by a court of governors. The old premises (on the site of the present
Liverpool Street station) were destroyed by fire, and it was reopened at Moorfields in
1676, increasing its capacity from 50 to over 100 inmates. In the 18th-cent. 'Bedlam', as
it came to be known, was a favourite resort for sightseers.

[5] Possibly Bentham's earliest use of the term 'utilitarian', though it is also used in a
letter of the period he wrote to George Wilson (24 Aug. 1781), where it is used to
describe 'honest Joseph Townshend' (*Corr.* iii. 57). This letter was sent during
Bentham's stay at the Earl of Shelburne's country residence (see n. 2 above) where
Townshend (1739–1816) was also a frequent visitor.

[6] Probably William Petty (1737–1805), 2nd Earl of Shelburne and from 1784 1st
Marquis of Lansdowne, with whom Bentham had a close relationship throughout the
1780s and 1790s. Shelburne had held office in the 1760s, but was in opposition from

As I was musing one night in flew/an angel flew in at my window: I forget his name—but it would be as easy to learn it in heaven where he is [as] well known for the implacable enmity he has to the daemon of chicane as St Michael is by the battles he has had with Satan. He put into my hands a book, which he said he had just been writing with the quill of a phoenix: [del: It had] it was lettered on the back Principles of Legislation:[7] I had no occasion to eat it he said, as St John did his:[8] all I had to do was cram it as well as I could down the throats of other people: they would it had the true flavour of the fruit of the tree of knowledge/good & evil.

One day as I was musing over this book there came unto me a great man named L . . . [?] and he said unto me what shall I do to [del: save the nation?] be saved? I had forgot, continued he I must not talk of my self—I mean to save the nation? I said unto him—take up my book, & follow me.

'We walked about/trudged on a long while in search of adventures without any sort of plan, and without thinking of where we were to go first or when and what we were going about as is the fashion till we spied a man named George[9] who had been afflicted with an incurable blindness and disease [?] for many years.[10] I said unto my apostle give him a page of my book that he may read mark [?] learn [?] and inwardly digest it: [del: He did] The man struggled a good deal at first: and made a good many faces as much as to say this is some of the nastiest stuff I ever tasted in my life:[11] but no sooner was it down than before a man could have said 'ekphatos' [?] up came forth/came out of his bosom seven devils[12] blacker than the blackest of

---

1768 until 1782. He then took office under Rockingham, whom he succeeded as Prime Minister from July 1782 to Feb. 1783. Defeated by the Fox–North coalition, he never returned to power.

[7] *IPML*, largely written 1777–9, printed in 1780, published with corrections and supplementary notes in 1789. For the history of the writing and publication of this work see Burns and Hart's introduction to the *CW* edn.

[8] Throughout the 'dream' Bentham writes in the style and persistently evokes the mysticism of The Revelation of St John the Divine. For this reference see Rev. 10: '1. And I saw another mighty angel come down from heaven, . . . 2. And he had in his hand a little book open: . . . 8. And the voice which I heard from heaven spake unto me again, and said, Go *and* take the little book which is open in the hand of the angel which standeth upon the sea and upon the earth. 9. And I went unto the angel, and said unto him, Give me the little book. And he said unto me, Take it, and eat it up; and it shall make thy belly bitter, but it shall be in thy mouth sweet as honey. 10. And I took the little book out of the angel's hand, and ate it up; and it was in my mouth sweet as honey: and as soon as I had eaten it, my belly was bitter. 11. And he said unto me, Thou must prophesy again before many peoples, and nations, and tongues, and kings.'

[9] Presumably George III (1738–1820; crowned 1760). This and the following references to George are perhaps indicative of Bentham's expectations of enlightened rulers at this time.

[10] Baumgardt reads this as 'an incurable blindness and deafness'.

[11] See above n. 8 (Rev. 10: 10).

[12] The number 7 is consistently invoked throughout Rev.: 7 churches and 7 golden candlesticks (1: 4); 7 seals (5: 1); 7 angels and 7 trumpets (8: 2); a beast with 7 heads (13:

the three crows that were . . . [?] by the man in the Tatler:[13] and the blackest
of all was S—ob [?].[14]

I knew him by the mark of the beast which was so visible in his forehead.[15]
Immediately the man heard every thing that a man should hear and there fell
the [?] scales from his eyes,[16] and not seeing what better he could do with
himself he also followed us. We had not travelled long before we [del: came
to] saw a woman named Britannia lying by the water side all in rags with a
sleeping lion at her feet: she looked very pale, and upon enquiry we found
she had an issue of blood upon her for many years.

She started up fresher faster and more alive than ever: the lion wagged his
tail and fawned upon us like a Spaniel.

---

1); and 7 plagues and 7 vials full of the wrath of God (15: 1, 7). John writes of the 7
churches in Asia and according to some strands of Judaism every entity has its angel. It
was therefore natural that each Church should have its heavenly representative, and that
each should be lit by its own candlestick, that each should have its own star and its own
devil, and so forth.

[13] Baumgardt renders this as 'that were raided by the swan in the Tatler'. *The Tatler*
(1709–11), by Joseph Addison (1672–1719) and Richard Steele (1672–1729); the
reference to the 'three crows' has not been traced.

[14] Unidentified.

[15] Rev. 14: '9. And the third angel followed them, saying with a loud voice, If any man
worship the beast and his image, and receive *his* mark in his forehead, or in his hand, 10.
The same shall drink of the wine of the wrath of God, which is poured out without
mixture into the cup of his indignation; and he shall be tormented with fire and
brimstone in the presence of the holy angels, and in the presence of the Lamb: . . .'

[16] Compare this with Acts 9: '17. And Ananias went his way, and entered into the
house; and putting his hands on him said, Brother Saul, the Lord, *even* Jesus, that
appeared unto thee in the way as thou camest, hath sent me, that thou mightest receive
thy sight, and be filled with the Holy Ghost. 18. And immediately there fell from his eyes
as it had been scales: and he received sight forthwith, and arose, and was baptized.'

One is also reminded of Bentham's reference (in a footnote to the 1823 2nd edn. of
FG) to his discovery of Hume's association of virtue with utility in the *Treatise*: 'For my
own part, I well remember, no sooner had I read that part of the work which touches on
this subject, than I felt as if scales had fallen from my eyes. I then, for the first time,
learnt to call the cause of the people the Cause of Virtue' (*FG* 440 n).

Bibliography

A. Bentham

Manuscripts

British Library Series of Additional Manuscripts.
Bentham Manuscripts at University College London.

Manuscript catalogues

LONG, D. G., *The Manuscripts of Jeremy Bentham: A Chronological Index to the Collection in the Library of University College London*, printed by the Bentham Committee at UCL (1982).
MILNE, A. T., *Catalogue of the Manuscripts of Jeremy Bentham in the Library of University College* (1937; 2nd edn. London, 1962).
WHITTAKER, T., *Report on the Bentham MSS. at University College, London, with Catalogue* (London, 1892).

Collections of works

The Works of Jeremy Bentham, Published under the Superintendence of his Executor, John Bowring, 11 vols. (Edinburgh, 1838–43).
Jeremy Bentham's Economic Writings, ed. W. Stark, 3 vols. (London, 1952–4).
The Collected Works of Jeremy Bentham, ed. J. H. Burns, J. R. Dinwiddy, and F. Rosen (London and Oxford, 1968–), in progress.
—— *A Comment on the Commentaries and A Fragment on Government*, ed. J. H. Burns and H. L. A. Hart (1977).
—— *An Introduction to the Principles of Morals and Legislation*, ed. J. H. Burns and H. L. A. Hart (1970).
—— *Chrestomathia*, ed. M. J. Smith and W. H. Burston (1983).
—— *Constitutional Code*, i, ed. F. Rosen and J. H. Burns (1983).
—— *Deontology together with A Table of the Springs of Action and the Article on Utilitarianism*, ed. A. Goldworth (1983).
—— *First Principles preparatory to Constitutional Code*, ed. T. P. Schofield (1989).
—— *Of Laws in General*, ed. H. L. A. Hart (1970).
—— *The Correspondence of Jeremy Bentham*, i–ii (1752–76; 1777–80), ed. T. L. S. Sprigge (1968); iii (1781–8), ed. I. R. Christie (1971); vols. iv–v (1788–93; 1794–7), ed. A. T. Milne (1981); vi–vii (1798–1801; 1802–8), ed. J. R. Dinwiddy (1984, 1988); viii–ix (1809–16; 1817–20), ed. S. R. Conway (1988, 1989).

Works on Religion

An Analysis of the Influence of Natural Religion on the Temporal Happiness of Mankind, by 'Philip Beauchamp' [ed. G. Grote] (London, 1822; repr. London, 1866; 2nd edn. London, 1875).

La Religion naturelle, son influence sur le bonheur du genre humain, d'après les papiers de J. Bentham par George Grote (Paris, 1875).

Church-of-Englandism and its Catechism Examined (London, 1818).

Mother Church Relieved by Bleeding: Or Vices and Remedies Extracted from Bentham's Church of, Etc., Examined (1823; 2nd edn. London, 1825).

The Church-of-England Catechism Examined (London, 1824; 2nd edn. Ramsgate, 1868).

The Book of Church Reform, Containing the Most Essential Part of Mr. Bentham's Church of Englandism, edited by one of his Disciples (London, 1831).

Not Paul, but Jesus, by 'Gamaliel Smith' (London, 1823).

Summary View of a Work, intitled Not Paul, but Jesus: As Exhibited in Introduction, Plan of the Work and Titles of Chapters and Sections (London, 1821).

Other works by Bentham

A Comment on the Commentaries, ed. C. W. Everett (1928; repr. Darmstadt, 1976).

Auto-Icon: Or Farther Uses of the Dead to the Living, A Fragment (a work based on MSS principally dated 1831, printed 1842 but not published).

Bentham's Handbook of Political Fallacies, ed. H. A. Larrabee (1952; repr. New York, 1971).

'Bentham on Torture', ed. W. L. Twining and P. E. Twining, in *Bentham on Legal Theory*, ed. M. H. James, *Northern Ireland Legal Quarterly*, 24:3 (1973), 39–90.

Bentham's Theory of Fictions, ed. C. K. Ogden (London, 1932).

'Jeremy Bentham's Essay on "Paederasty"', in two parts, ed. L. Crompton, *Journal of Homosexuality*, 3:4 (1978), 383–405, and 4:1 (1978), 91–107.

Plan of Parliamentary Reform, in the Form of a Catechism (London, 1817).

Principles of Legislation from the Manuscripts of Jeremy Bentham, ed. J. Neal (Boston, 1830).

The Limits of Jurisprudence Defined, ed. C. W. Everett (New York, 1945).

The Theory of Legislation, ed. C. K. Ogden (London, 1931).

The White Bull, An Oriental History: From an Ancient Syrian Manuscript Communicated by Voltaire (London, 1774).

Traités de législation civile et pénale . . . Publiés en français par Ét. Dumont, 3 vols. (Paris, 1802).

Extracts

A Bentham Reader, ed. M. Mack (New York, 1969).
Bentham's Political Thought, ed. B. Parekh (New York, 1973).
BURTON, J. H., *Benthamiana: Or Select Extracts from the Works of Jeremy Bentham* (Edinburgh, 1843).
EVERETT, C. W., *Jeremy Bentham*, pt. 2 (London, 1966).

B. Writings of other authors

AARSLEFF, H., *The Study of Language in England 1780–1860* (1967; repr. London, 1983).
ABBEY, C. J., *The English Church and its Bishops 1700–1800*, 2 vols. (London, 1887).
ADAMS, J. Q., *Memoirs of John Quincy Adams*, ed. C. F. Adams, 12 vols. (1874–7; repr. New York, 1970).
ADDISON, J., *The Spectator*, ed. D. F. Bond, 5 vols. (Oxford, 1965).
ALBEE, E., *A History of English Utilitarianism* (London, 1901).
D'ALEMBERT, J., *Preliminary Discourse to the Encyclopedia of Diderot*, trans. R. N. Schwab (1751; Indianapolis, 1963).
ANNET, P., *The History and Character of St. Paul Examined* [n.d., *c.*1750].
ARNOLD, M., *Matthew Arnold's Essays in Criticism, First Series: A Critical Edition*, ed. Sr. T. M. Hoctor (Chicago, 1968).
ARNOLD, T., *Principles of Church Reform*, ed. M. J. Jackson and J. Rogan (1833; London, 1962).
ATKINSON, C. M., *Jeremy Bentham: His Life and Work* (London, 1905).
AUSTIN, J., *The Province of Jurisprudence Determined* (1832; repr. London, 1971).
AYER, A. J., *Language, Truth, and Logic* (1936; 2nd edn. London, 1946).
—— *Hume* (Oxford, 1980).
BACON, F., *The New Organum*, ed. F. H. Anderson (1620; Indianapolis, 1960).
BAHMUELLER, C. F., *The National Charity Company: Jeremy Bentham's Silent Revolution* (Berkeley, 1981).
BAIN, A., *The Minor Works of George Grote* (London, 1873).
—— *James Mill: A Biography* (1882; New York, 1967).
—— *John Stuart Mill: A Criticism with Personal Recollections* (1882; repr. New York, 1969).
BARKER, E., *Traditions of Civility* (Cambridge, 1948).
BARTLE, G. F., 'Jeremy Bentham & John Bowring: A Study of the Relationship between Bentham and the Editor of his *Collected Works*', *Bulletin of the Institute of Historical Research London University*, 36:93 (1963), 27–35.
BAUMGARDT, D., *Bentham and the Ethics of Today* (New York, 1966).

BECCARIA, C., *An Essay on Crimes and Punishments* [*Dei delitti e delle pene*, 1764; first Eng. trans. 1767], trans. H. Paolucci (Indianapolis, 1975).

'Bell and Lancaster's Systems of Education', *Quarterly Review*, 6 (1811), 264–304.

BELLOT, H. H., *University College London 1826–1926* (London, 1929).

BELSHAM, T., *Elements of Philosophy of the Human Mind and of Moral Philosophy* (London, 1801).

'BEN DAVID' [pseudonym of the Unitarian minister John Jones], *A Reply to Two Deistical Works, entitled 'The New Trial of the Witnesses', Ec. and Gamaliel Smith's 'Not Paul, but Jesus'* (London, 1824).

BENN, A. W., *The History of English Rationalism in the Nineteenth Century*, 2 vols. (New York, 1962).

BERKELEY, G., *The Works of George Berkeley Bishop of Cloyne*, ed. A. A. Luce and T. E. Jessop, 9 vols. (London, 1948–57).

BERLIN, I. (ed.), *The Age of Enlightenment: The Eighteenth Century Philosophers* (New York, 1956).

BEVINGTON, H. S., 'A Bomb for Jeremy Bentham' (1940), in *Nineteen Million Elephants and Other Poems* (Boston, 1950), 33–4.

BICKNELL, E. J., *A Theological Introduction to the Thirty-Nine Articles of the Church of England* (1919; 3rd edn. rev. H. J. Carpenter, London, 1955).

BINGHAM, P., 'Bentham's "Swear Not at All"', *Westminster Review*, 5 (1826), 23–58.

BLACKSTONE, W., *Commentaries on the Laws of England*, 4 vols. (1765–9; repr. Chicago, 1979).

BORALEVI, L. C., 'Jeremy Bentham and the Jews', *European Judaism*, 13 (Winter 1979), 22–8.

—— 'Jeremy Bentham's Writings on Sexual Non-Conformity, Utilitarianism, NeoMalthusianism, and Sexual Liberty (including the hitherto unpublished University College Manuscripts)', *Topoi: An International Review of Philosophy*, 2 (1983), 123–48.

—— *Bentham and the Oppressed* (New York, 1984).

BOWRING, J., *Matins and Vespers: With Hymns and Occasional Devotional Pieces* (London, 1825).

—— *Autobiographical Recollections of Sir John Bowring* (London, 1877).

BROGAN, A. P., 'John Locke and Utilitarianism', *Ethics*, 69:2 (1959), 79–93.

BROWN, J., *Essays on the Characteristics of the Earl of Shaftesbury* (1751; 3rd edn. London, 1752).

—— *An Estimate of the Manners and Principles of the Times*, 2 vols. (London, 1757–8).

BUCHDAHL, G., *The Image of Newton and Locke in the Age of Reason* (London, 1961).

BURGESS, H. J., *Enterprise in Education: The Story of the Work of the Established Church in the Education of the People prior to 1870* (London, 1958).

BURKE, E., *The Works of the Right Honourable Edmund Burke*, 12 vols. (London, 1887).

BURNS, J. H., *Jeremy Bentham and University College* (London, 1962).

—— *The Fabric of Felicity: The Legislator and the Human Condition* (London, 1967).

—— 'Dreams and Destinations: Jeremy Bentham in 1828', *The Bentham Newsletter*, 1 (1978), 3–20.

BUTLER, J., *The Works of Joseph Butler*, ed. W. E. Gladstone, 2 vols. (Oxford, 1893).

BUTTERFIELD, H., *The Origins of Modern Science 1300–1800* (Toronto, 1968).

BUTTS, R. E., and DAVIS, J. W. (eds.), *The Methodological Heritage of Newton* (Toronto, 1970).

CARLILE, R., *Address to the Men of Science* (London, 1821).

—— *Church Reform* (London, 1834).

CARLYLE, T., 'The State of German Literature', *Edinburgh Review*, 46 (1827), 304–51.

CHADWICK, O., *The Victorian Church*, 2 vols. (Oxford, 1966, 1970).

—— *The Secularization of the European Mind in the Nineteenth Century* (Cambridge, 1975).

CHAMBER, E., *Cyclopedia: Or, A Universal Dictionary of Arts and Sciences*, 2 vols. (London, 1728).

CHARLTON, D. G., *Secular Religions in France 1815–1870* (Oxford, 1963).

CHASTELLUX [Marquis], J. F., *An Essay on Public Happiness [De la félicité publique, ou considérations sur le sort des hommes dans les différentes époques de l'histoire*, 1772], 2 vols. (London, 1774; repr. New York, 1969).

CLAEYS, G., *Machinery, Money and the Millenium: From Moral Economy to Socialism, 1815–1860* (Princeton, 1987).

CLARK, G. K., *Churchmen and the Condition of England 1832–1885* (London, 1973).

CLARKE, J. C. D., *English Society 1688–1832: Ideology, Social Structure and Political Practice During the Ancien Regime* (Cambridge, 1985).

CLARKE, M. L., *George Grote: A Biography* (London, 1962).

—— *Paley: Evidences for the Man* (Toronto, 1974).

COLE, G. D. H., *Richard Carlile 1790–1843* (London, 1943).

COLERIDGE, S. T., *On the Constitution of the Church and State According to the Idea of Each*, ed. J. Barrell (1830; London, 1972).

—— *The Collected Works of Samuel Taylor Coleridge*, 16 vols. (Princeton, 1971–81).

[COLLS, J. F.], 'Memoir of the Rev. J. F. Colls, B. D.', *The Church Magazine*, 3:36 (1841), 353–60.

—— *Utilitarianism Unmasked: A Letter to the Rev. M. A. Gathercole . . . on the Life, Death, and Philosophy of Jeremy Bentham* (London, 1844).

COMTE, A., *The Catechism of Positive Religion*, trans. R. Congreve (1858; 3rd edn. 1891; New Jersey, 1973).

COMTE, A., *Auguste Comte and Positivism: The Essential Writings*, ed. G. Jenzer (London, 1975).

CONNIFF, J., 'Edmund Burke's Reflections on the Coming Revolution in Ireland', *Journal of the History of Ideas*, 47:1 (1986), 37–60.

COURTNEY, J. E., *Free Thinkers of the Nineteenth Century* (London, 1920).

CRAGG, G. R., *The Church and the Age of Reason* (New York, 1961).

CRIMMINS, J. E., 'John Brown and the Theological Tradition of Utilitarian Ethics', *History of Political Thought*, 4:3 (1983), 523–50.

—— 'Bentham's Religious Writings: A Bibliographic Chronology', *The Bentham Newsletter*, 9 (1985), 21–33.

—— 'Bentham on Religion: Atheism and the Secular Society', *Journal of the History of Ideas*, 47:1 (1986), 95–110.

—— 'Bentham's Unpublished Manuscripts on Subscription to Articles of Faith', *British Journal for Eighteenth-Century Studies*, 9:1 (1986), 33–44.

—— '"The Study of True Politics": John Brown on Manners and Liberty', *Studies on Voltaire and the Eighteenth Century*, 241 (1986), 65–84.

—— 'Bentham's Metaphysics and the Science of Divinity', *Harvard Theological Review*, 79:4 (1986), 387–411.

—— '"A Hatchet for Paley's Net": Bentham on Capital Punishment and Judicial Discretion', *The Canadian Journal of Law and Jurisprudence*, 1:1 (1988), 63–74 (an earlier version appeared in *The Bentham Newsletter*, 11 (1987), 23–34).

—— (ed.), *Religion, Secularization and Political Thought: Thomas Hobbes to J. S. Mill* (London, 1990).

CROMPTON, L., *Byron and Greek Love: Homophobia in 19th Century England* (Berkeley, Calif., 1985).

CUSHING, M. P., *Baron D'Holbach: A Study of Eighteenth Century Radicalism in France* (1914; repr. New York, 1971).

DANIEL-ROPS H. [pseud. of Jules Charles Henri Petiot], *The Church in the Eighteenth Century*, trans. J. Warrington (London, 1964).

DAVIS, R. W., *Dissent in Politics 1780–1830: The Political Life of William Smith, M.P.* (London, 1971).

DICEY, A. V., *Lectures on the Relation between Law and Public Opinion in England during the Nineteenth Century* (1905; 2nd edn. London, 1962).

DINWIDDY, J. R., 'Bentham's Transition to Political Radicalism, 1809–10', *Journal of the History of Ideas*, 36:4 (1975), 683–700.

—— 'Early Nineteenth-Century Reactions to Benthamism', *Transactions of the Royal Historical Association*, 5th ser., 34 (1984), 47–69.

—— *Bentham* (Oxford, 1989).

DUREY, M. J., 'Body Snatchers and Benthamites: The Implications of the Dead Body Bill for the London Schools of Anatomy, 1820–42', *The London Journal* (1976), 200–25.

ELLIOTT-BINNS, L. E., *Religion in the Victorian Era* (London, 1946).

EMPSON, W., [a review of Bowring's edn. of Bentham's *Works*] *Edinburgh Review*, 78 (1843), 460–516.

EVERETT, C. W., *The Education of Jeremy Bentham* (New York, 1931).

FARRINGTON, B., *The Philosophy of Francis Bacon* (Chicago, 1966).

FENN, R. A., *James Mill's Political Thought* (New York, 1987).

FEUERBACH, L., *Essence of Christianity*, trans. of 1841 edn. G. Elliot (1854; New York, 1957).

—— *Lectures on the Essence of Religion*, trans. R. Manheim (1851; New York, 1967).

FRYE, N., *The Great Code: The Bible and Literature* (Toronto, 1982).

GASKIN, J. C. A., *Hume's Philosophy of Religion* (London, 1978).

GAY, J., 'Preliminary Dissertation concerning the Fundamental Principle of Virtue or Morality', prefixed to W. King, *Essay on the Origin of Evil* (London, 1732).

GAY, P., *The Enlightenment: An Interpretation*, 2 vols. (1966; New York, 1977).

[GIFFORD, W.], 'Jeremy Bentham's *Church-of-Englandism*', *Quarterly Review*, 21 (1819), 167–77.

[Duke of GRAFTON], *Hints, etc. Submitted to the Serious Attention of the Clergy, Nobility and Gentry, Newly Associated, by a Layman* (London, 1787).

GRANT, M., *Saint Paul* (London, 1976).

GRINFIELD, E. W., *The Doctrinal Harmony of the New Testament exemplified; . . . To which is added A Letter to the Author of a Book entitled 'Not Paul But Jesus'* (London, 1824).

GROTE, H., *The Personal Life of George Grote, Compiled from Family Documents, Private Memoranda, and Original Letters to and from Various Friends* (London, 1873).

HALÉVY, É., *A History of the English People in the Nineteenth Century*, trans. E. I. Walker and D. A. Barker, 6 vols. (London, 1949–52).

—— *The Growth of Philosophic Radicalism* [*La Formation du radicalisme philosophique*, 1901–4], trans. M. Morris (1928; London, 1972).

HANKINS, T. L., *Jean d'Alembert: Science and the Enlightenment* (Oxford, 1970).

[HARRIS, J.], *Hermes: Or a Philosophical Enquiry concerning Language and Universal Grammar* (1751; repr. Menston, 1968).

HARRIS, W. V., 'Browning's Caliban, Plato's Cosmogany, and Bentham on Natural Religion', *Studies in Browning and his Circle*, 3:2 (1975), 95–103.

HARRISON, R., *Bentham* (London, 1983).

HART, H. L. A., *Essays on Bentham: Studies on Jurisprudence and Political Theory* (Oxford, 1982).

HAZLITT, W., 'The Late Mr. Horne Tooke', in *Spirit of the Age* (London, 1825).

HELVÉTIUS, C. A., *De l'esprit: Or Essays on the Mind and its Several Faculties* (1759; trans. 1810, repr. New York, 1970).

—— *A Treatise on Man: His Intellectual Faculties and his Education* [*De l'homme*, 1777], trans. W. Hooper, 2 vols. (London, 1810).

HICK, J. H., *Philosophy of Religion* (2nd edn. New Jersey, 1973).

HIMMELFARB, G., *Victorian Minds* (New York, 1968).

HIMMELFARB, G., 'Bentham Scholarship and the Bentham Problem', *The Journal of Modern History*, 41:2 (1969), 189–206.

—— *On Liberty and Liberalism: The Case of John Stuart Mill* (New York, 1974).

HOBBES, T., *Leviathan* (1651; repr. Harmondsworth, 1981).

HOLBACH, Baron P. H. T. D', *The System of Nature: Or, the Laws of the Moral and Physical World* [*Système de la nature*, 1770], trans. H. D. Robinson (Boston, 1889).

HOWLETT, D., *The Critical Way in Religion: Testing and Questing* (New York, 1980).

HOWLEY, W., Bp. of London, *A Charge to the Clergy of London at the Primary Visitation of that Diocese in the Year 1814* (London, 1815).

HUGHES, T. S., *A Defence of the Apostle St. Paul against the Accusation of Gamaliel Smith, Esq. in a recent publication, entitled 'Not Paul But Jesus'*, pt. 1 (Cambridge, 1823).

—— *On the Miracles of St. Paul Being Part II of a Defence of that Apostle against the Accusation of Gamaliel Smith, Esq.* (Cambridge, 1824).

HUME, D., *Essays Literary, Moral, and Political* (London, n.d. [1870?]).

—— *The Letters of David Hume*, ed. J. Y. T. Greig, 2 vols. (Oxford, 1932).

—— *Dialogues concerning Natural Religion*, ed. N. K. Smith (1779; London, 1947).

—— 'My Own Life', in *An Inquiry Concerning Human Understanding*, ed. C. W. Hendel (New York, 1955).

—— *A Treatise on Human Nature* (1739; Bk. III 1740), ed. L. A. Selby-Bigge (1888; repr. Oxford, 1975).

—— *Enquiries concerning Human Understanding and concerning the Principles of Morals*, ed. L. A. Selby-Bigge (3rd edn. rev. P. H. Hidditch, 1748, 1751; Oxford, 1975).

HUME, L. J., 'Bentham's Panopticon: An Administrative History', *Historical Studies*, 15:61 (1973), 703–21, and 16:62 (1974), 36–54.

—— 'The Political Functions of Bentham's Theory of Fictions', *The Bentham Newsletter*, 3 (1979), 18–27.

—— *Bentham and Bureaucracy* (Cambridge, 1981).

ITZKIN, E. S., 'Bentham's *Chrestomathia*: Utilitarian Legacy to English Education', *Journal of the History of Ideas*, 39:2 (1978), 303–16.

JAMES, M., 'Public Interest and Majority Rule in Bentham's Democratic Theory', *Political Theory*, 9:1 (1981), 49–64.

JEVONS, W., *Systematic Morality*, 2 vols. (London, 1827).

KAMENKA, E., *The Philosophy of Ludwig Feuerbach* (New York, 1970).

LAW, E., 'On Morality and Religion' and 'The Nature of Obligation of Man, as a sensible and rational Being', prefixed to W. King, *Essay on the Origin of Evil*, trans. E. Law (1732; 5th edn. London, 1781).

LECKY, W. E. H., *History of European Morals from Augustine to Charlemagne*, 2 vols. (London, 1869).

—— *History of England in the Eighteenth Century*, 8 vols. (1878–90; repr. London, 1907).

LeMahieu, D. L., *The Mind of William Paley: A Philosopher and his Age* (London, 1976).

Linder, B., and Smeaton, W. A., 'Schwediauer, Bentham and Beddoes: Translators of Bergman and Scheele', *Annals of Science*, 24:4 (1968), 259–73.

Locke, J., *The Works of John Locke: A New Edition, Corrected*, 10 vols. (London, 1823).

—— *Epistola de Tolerantia: A Letter on Toleration*, ed. R. Klibansky and J. W. Gough (Oxford, 1968).

Long, D. G., 'Physical Sciences and Social Sciences: The Case of Jeremy Bentham' (unpublished), *Proceedings of the Canadian Political Science Association Annual Convention 1975.*

—— *Bentham on Liberty: Jeremy Bentham's Idea of Liberty in Relation to his Utilitarianism* (Toronto, 1977).

—— 'Bentham on Property', in T. M. Flanagan and A. Parel (eds.), *Theories of Property: Aristotle to the Present* (Toronto, 1978), 221–54.

—— '"A Host of Scotch Sophists": Jeremy Bentham and the Scottish Enlightenment' (unpublished), a paper presented to a conference on The Political Thought of the Scottish Enlightenment in its European Context, at the University of Edinburgh (28 Aug. 1986).

—— 'Bentham as a Revolutionary Social Scientist', *Man & Nature/L'Homme et la nature*, 7 (1987), 115–45.

—— 'Censorial Jurisprudence and Political Radicalism: A Reconsideration of the Early Bentham', *The Bentham Newsletter*, 12 (1988), 4–23.

Maccoby, H., *Revolution in Judea: Jesus and the Jewish Resistance* (London, 1973).

Maccoby, S., *English Radicalism 1786–1832* (London, 1935).

McEvoy, J. G., 'Enlightenment and Dissent in Science: Joseph Priestley and the Limits of Theoretical Reasoning', *Enlightenment and Dissent*, 2 (1983), 47–67.

—— and McGuire, J. E., 'God and Nature: Priestley's Way of Rational Dissent', in R. McCormmach (ed.), *Historical Studies in the Physical Sciences*, 6 (Princeton, 1975), 325–404.

Machin, G. I. T., *Politics and the Churches in Great Britain 1832 to 1868* (Oxford, 1977).

Mack, M., *Jeremy Bentham: An Odyssey of Ideas 1748–1799* (London, 1962).

McManners, J., *Death and the Enlightenment: Changing Attitudes to Death among the Christians and Unbelievers in Eighteenth-Century France* (Oxford, 1981).

Malthus, T., *An Essay on the Principles of Population* (London, 1798).

Marmoy, C. F. A., 'The "Auto-Icon" of Jeremy Bentham at University College, London', *Medical History*, 2 (1958), 77–86.

MARTIN, D., *The Religious and the Secular: Studies in Secularization* (London, 1969).

MASON, H., *Voltaire: A Biography* (Baltimore, 1981).

MAZLISH, B., *James and John Stuart Mill: Father and Son in the Nineteenth Century* (New York, 1975).

MIDDLETON, C., *A Free Enquiry into the Miraculous Powers* (1748; Dublin, 1749).

[MILL, J.], 'Commonplace Books of James Mill', 5 vols., London Library (unpublished, *c.* 1800–35).

—— *Schools for All, in Preference to Schools for Churchmen Only* (London, 1812).

—— 'A Review of the Arguments of Dr Herbert Marsh and others, in Opposition to the Lancasterian Plans for Educating the Poor', *The Philanthropist*, 2 (1812), 57–108.

—— 'Southey's Book of the Church', *Westminster Review*, 3 (1825), 167–212.

—— 'Ecclesiastical Establishments', *Westminster Review*, 5 (1826), 504–48.

—— 'The Church, and Its Reform', *London Review*, 1 (1835), 257–95.

—— *Analysis of the Phenomena of the Human Mind*, 2 vols. (1828; repr. New York, 1967).

—— *James Mill on Education*, ed. W. H. Burston (Cambridge, 1969).

MILL, J. S., *The Collected Works of John Stuart Mill*, ed. J. M. Robson et al., (Toronto, 1963–).

MORLEY, J., *The Life of William Ewart Gladstone*, 3 vols. (London, 1903).

MOSSNER, E. C., *The Life of David Hume* (Edinburgh, 1954).

NEWTON, I., *A Treatise of the System of the World* (1728; London 1969).

—— *Isaac Newton's Papers & Letters on Natural Philosophy and Related Documents*, ed. I. B. Cohen (1958; 2nd edn. Cambridge, Mass., 1978).

NORTON, D. F., *David Hume: Common-sense Moralist, Sceptical Metaphysician* (Princeton, 1982).

OAKESHOTT, M., 'The New Bentham', *Scrutiny*, 1 (1932–3), 114–31.

O'CONNELL, D., *The Correspondence of Daniel O'Connell*, ed. M. R. O'Connell, 8 vols. (Shannon, 1972).

OGDEN, C. K., *Jeremy Bentham 1832–2032* (London, 1932).

—— 'Bentham's Theory of Language', *Psyche*, 12:3 (1932), 3–43.

OVERTON, J. H., and RELTON, F., *The English Church from the Accession of George I to the End of the Eighteenth Century* (London, 1906).

PALEY, W., *The Complete Works of William Paley*, 4 vols. (London, 1825).

PAREKH, B. (ed.), *Jeremy Bentham: Ten Critical Essays* (London, 1974).

PARR, S., *The Works of Samuel Parr*, ed. J. J. Stone, 8 vols. (London, 1828).

PASSMORE, J., *The Perfectibility of Man* (London, 1972).

PEARDON, T., 'Bentham's Ideal Republic', *Canadian Journal of Economics and Political Science*, 18 (1951), 184–203.

PLACE, F., *The Autobiography of Francis Place (1771–1854)*, ed. M. Thrale (Cambridge, 1972).

PLAMENATZ, J., *The English Utilitarians* (Oxford, 1958).

POLLOCK, J., *Wilberforce* (London, 1977).

POSTEMA, G. J., 'The Expositor, the Censor, and the Common Law', *Canadian Journal of Philosophy*, 9 (1979), 643–70.

—— *Bentham and the Common Law Tradition* (Oxford, 1986).

PRENTICE, A., *Some Recollections of Jeremy Bentham* (Manchester, 1837).

PRIESTLEY, J., *An Essay on the First Principles of Government, and on the Nature of Political, Civil and Religious Liberty* (London, 1768).

—— *A Letter to the Right Honourable W. Pitt*, (London, 1787).

—— *Disquisitions Relating to Matter and Spirit and The Doctrine of Philosophical Necessity Illustrated* (1777; repr. New York, 1976).

REES, J. C., and LIVELY, J. (eds.), *Utilitarian Logic and Politics* (Oxford, 1978).

RENAN, E., *The History of the Origins of Christianity [Histoire des origines du christianisme*, 8 vols., 1863–83], 5 vols. (1888–90; repr. London, n.d.).

RICHARDSON R., 'Bentham and Bodies for Dissection', *The Bentham Newsletter*, 10 (1986), 22–33.

—— *Death, Dissection and the Destitute* (London, 1987).

—— and HURWITZ, B., 'Jeremy Bentham's Self Image: An Exemplary Bequest for Dissection', *British Medical Journal*, 295 (1987), 195–8.

ROBBINS, C., *The Eighteenth-Century Commonwealthmen* (Cambridge, Mass., 1961).

ROMILLY, S., *Memoirs of the Life of Sir Samuel Romilly*, 2 vols. (3rd edn. London, 1841).

ROSEN, F., *Jeremy Bentham and Representative Democracy: A Study of the Constitutional Code* (Oxford, 1983).

ROSENBLUM, N., *Bentham's Theory of the Modern State* (Cambridge, Mass., 1978).

SCHLEIMACHER, F., *The Christian Faith [Der christliche Glaube nach den Grundsatzen der evangelischen Kirche*, 2 vols., Berlin, 1821–2], trans. H. R. Mackintosh and J. S. Stewart (Edinburgh, 1928).

SCHNEEWIND, J. B., *Sidgwick's Ethics and Victorian Moral Philosophy* (Oxford, 1977).

SCHOFIELD, T. P., 'A Comparison of the Moral Theories of William Paley and Jeremy Bentham', *The Bentham Newsletter*, 11 (1987), 4–22.

SCHWARTZ, R. B., *Samuel Johnson and the New Science* (London, 1971).

SELBY-BIGGE, L. A. (ed.), *British Moralists: Being Selections from Writers Principally of the Eighteenth Century*, 2 vols. (Oxford, 1897).

SHACKLETON, R., 'The Greatest Happiness of the Greatest Number: The History of Bentham's Phrase', *Studies on Voltaire and the Eighteenth Century*, 90 (1972), 1461–82.

SMITH, D. W., *Helvétius: A Study in Persecution* (Oxford, 1965).

SMITH, T. S., *Use of the Dead to the Living* (1824; Albany, 1827).

—— *Lecture Delivered over the Remains of Jeremy Bentham, Esq. . . . On the 9 June, 1832* (London, 1832).

—— 'The Last Act of Jeremy Bentham', *Examiner* (10 June 1832), 378.

STARK, W., 'Psychology of Social Messianism', *Social Research*, 25 (1958), 145–57.

STEINTRAGER, J., 'Report on the Problems of Editing Bentham's Writings on Religion', App. B to Report by the General Editor [J. H. Burns], 12 June 1967 (Bentham Committee at UCL, unpublished).

—— 'Jeremy Bentham's Manuscripts and Writings on the Utility of Religion', *American Philosophical Society: Year Book 1969* (Philadelphia, 1970), 462–4.

—— 'Morality and Belief: The Origins and Purpose of Bentham's Writings on Religion', *The Mill News Letter*, 6:2 (1971), 3–15.

—— *Bentham* (London, 1977).

—— 'Language and Politics: Bentham on Religion', *The Bentham Newsletter*, 4 (1980), 4–20.

STEPHEN, J. F., *A History of the Criminal Law in England*, 3 vols. (London, 1883).

STEPHEN, Sir L., *The English Utilitarians*, 3 vols. (1900; repr. London, 1950).

STRAUSS, D. F., *The Life of Jesus Critically Examined*, trans. of 1835–6 edn. G. Elliot (1848; 5th edn. London, 1906).

—— *The Christ of Faith and the Jesus of History. A Critique of Schleimacher's The Life of Christ*, trans. L. E. Keck (1865; Philadelphia, 1977).

STROMBERG, R. N., *Religious Liberalism in Eighteenth Century England* (Oxford, 1954).

SYKES, N., *Edmund Gibson, Bishop of London, 1669–1748: A Study in Politics and Religion in the Eighteenth Century* (Oxford, 1926).

—— *Church and State in England in the XVIIIth Century* (Connecticut, 1962).

TAYLOR, A. E., *Does God Exist?* (London, 1945).

TAYLOR, B., 'Jeremy Bentham, the Church of England, and the Fraudulent Activities of the National Schools Society', *Paedogica Historica*, 18 (1978), 375–85.

—— 'Jeremy Bentham and Church of England Education', *British Journal of Educational Studies*, 27:2 (1979), 154–7.

—— 'Jeremy Bentham and the Education of the Irish People', *The Irish Journal of Education*, 14:1 (1980), 19–32.

TOOKE, J. H., *The Diversions of Purley*, 2 vols. (1786, 1805; 2nd edn. London, 1798; repr. Menston, 1968).

TOULMIN, S., *An Examination of the Place of Reason in Ethics* (1950; repr. Cambridge, 1970).

[TRIMMER, S. K.], 'Mrs Trimmer on Lancaster's Plan of Education', *Edinburgh Review*, 17 (1806), 177–84.

[TUCKER, A.], *The Light of Nature Pursued* by 'Edward Search', 7 vols. (London, 1768–78).

VERNON, R., 'The Secular Political Culture: Three Views', *The Review of Politics*, 37:4 (1975), 490–512.

VINER, J., *The Role of Providence in the Social Order: An Essay in Intellectual History* (Princeton, 1972).

WALLAS G., *The Life of Francis Place 1771–1854* (1898; 4th edn. London, 1951).

WARBURTON, W., *The Works of the Right Reverend William Warburton*, 12 vols. (London, 1811).

WEBER, M., *The Sociology of Religion*, trans. E. Fischoff (1922; London, 1965).

WELLS, D. B., *St. Paul Vindicated: Being Part I of a Reply to a Late Publication by Gamaliel Smith, Esq.* (Cambridge, 1824).

WHITTAKER, T., *Comte and Mill* (London, 1908).

WILBERFORCE R. I., and WILBERFORCE, S., *The Life of William Wilberforce*, 5 vols. (2nd edn. London, 1839).

WILBERFORCE, W., *A Practical View of the Prevailing Religious System of Professed Christians, in the Higher and Middle Classes in this Country, Contrasted with Real Christianity* (London, 1811).

WILLIAMS, E. N., *The Eighteenth-Century Constitution 1688–1815: Documents and Commentary* (Cambridge, 1970).

WINSTANLEY, D. A., *Unreformed Cambridge: A Study of Certain Aspects of the University in the Eighteenth Century* (Cambridge, 1935).

WISDOM, J., 'Bentham on Division', *Psyche*, 9:3 (1929), 100–3.

—— 'Interpretation and Analysis', *Psyche*, 11:2 (1930), 11–31.

—— *Interpretation and Analysis in Relation to Bentham's Theory of Definition* (London, 1931)

—— and BLACK, M., 'Bentham's Theory of Definition: Critical Discussion', *Psyche*, 11:4 (1931), 79–87.

WOLFF, R. P., et al., *A Critique of Pure Tolerance* (Boston, 1970).

WOLLASTON, W., *The Religion of Nature Delineated* (1722; 5th edn. London, 1731).

Index

Baumgardt, D.: *Bentham and the Ethics of Today* 239 and n.
on JB's dream 313 n., 315 n., 316 n.
Bayle, Pierre, on atheism 282
Beccaria, Cesare: avoidance of religion 81
JB's eulogy to 80–1 and n.
influence on JB 74 and n., 80–1
An Essay on Crimes and Punishment 81 and n., 131 and n.
Dei delitti e delle pene 80 and n.
Beckford, William 256 and n.
proposal from JB to edit 'Sextus' 312
The History of the Caliph Vathec 256
Bell, Dr Andrew 166
An Experiment in Education 165–6
Bellot, H. H.: *University College London* 294 n.
Belsham, T.: *Elements of Philosophy of the . . . Mind . . .* 73 n.
'Ben David': on *Not Paul, but Jesus* 230–1 and n.
A Reply to Two Deistical Works . . . 227 and n., 231 n., 252 and n.
Benn, A. W.: on *Not Paul, but Jesus* 238 and n.
The History of English Rationalism . . . 201 n., 249 n., 294 n.
Bentham, Jeremy: aims in works 271–2
'An Oxford Graduate' 3, 163
bequest to medical science 296 and n.
codewords 3 and n.
and democratic programme 7 and n., 17 n.
dream of 229 and n., 287 and n., 288 n., 313–16; use of The Revelation of St John the Divine 315 and nn., 316 and n.
and experimental science 26
'Gamaliel Smith' 3, 227, 229, 230 and n.
ideal state 292–3
'infidelity', *see* atheism
influences on 7, 17, 28 ff.
emulation of *philosophes* 36–7 and n.; of Gay 71 and n.
and law 43 n.; development of scientific approach to 23, 26
'Luther of Jurisprudence' 228
'Newtonian' system 30
'Pacificus' 147 and n.
'Philip Beauchamp' 3, 207
positivism, Comte 285–7, 296

principles: of knowledge 18, 26, 81; development of 15–16; legal philosophy 25, 41 n.; origin of ethics 9–11; scientific framework of 273 ff.; theme of ethics 259; for the unity of science 34
prison reform scheme, *see* Panopticon
pseudonyms 2–3
psychological peculiarities 286 and n., 287–8
religious radicalism 66–7; nature of analysis of religion 271–2; 'sole object' in 13
shorthand method 27
and society 18
tools of analysis 56, 272
unspirituality 271
use of editors 1, 3; editor-in-chief, *see* Bowring, John
will 296 and n.
see also auto-icon
Bentham, Jeremy: works 2, 4, 148 and n.
'capital work' 41
magnum opus 40–1, 67; scope of 42
phases in development 67–8
as reflection of the age 101
religious 1–6; inclusion in *Collected Works* 6; publication of manuscripts 6, 11–12; reasons for writing 7, 14; as 'second front' 96 and n., 97; self-censorship in 11, 18
viewing in incomplete fashion 57
'Address Proposing a plan for Uniting the Catholics and Dissenters . . .' 142
An Analysis of the Influence of Natural Religion on the Temporal Happiness of Mankind 1, 12, 109 and n., 207 and n., 210–12, 254 ff., 260; authorship of 208–10; intention in writing 12
'Article on Utilitarianism' 29, 75, 78
Auto-Icon: or Farther Use of the Dead to the Living 18, 184, 290, 295 and n., 296 n.; Bowring's note 295 n.
Book of Fallacies 132, 145–6, 190, 200
'Book on Logic' 52–62
Chrestomathia 18, 37, 53, 61, 75, 162, 166, 295; Appendix IV 53 and n.; 'Encyclopedical Table, or Art and Science Table' 45 and n., 46, 53
Church-of-Englandism . . . 1, 5, 6 and n., 56, 101 ff., 160–1, 163, 164, 195,